SIR HENRY LEE (15
ELIZABETHAN CC

CW01558615

For my grandsons, who while growing up always knew far more about tilting and tournaments than was necessary!

Sir Henry Lee (1533–1611): Elizabethan Courtier

SUE SIMPSON

University of Southampton, UK

LONDON AND NEW YORK

First published in paperback 2024

First issued in hardback 2019

First published 2014 by Ashgate Publishing
by Routledge
4 Park Square, Milton Park, Abingdon, Oxon OX14 4RN

and by Routledge
605 Third Avenue, New York, NY 10158

Routledge is an imprint of the Taylor & Francis Group, an informa business

Copyright © 2014, 2019, 2024 Sue Simpson

The right of Sue Simpson to be identified as author of this work has been asserted in accordance with sections 77 and 78 of the Copyright, Designs and Patents Act 1988.

All rights reserved. No part of this book may be reprinted or reproduced or utilised in any form or by any electronic, mechanical, or other means, now known or hereafter invented, including photocopying and recording, or in any information storage or retrieval system, without permission in writing from the publishers.

Trademark notice:
Product or corporate names may be trademarks or registered trademarks, and are used only for identification and explanation without intent to infringe.

Publisher's Note
The publisher has gone to great lengths to ensure the quality of this reprint but points out that some imperfections in the original copies may be apparent.

British Library Cataloguing in Publication Data
A catalogue record for this book is available from the British Library

The Library of Congress has cataloged the printed edition as follows:
Simpson, Sue, 1945–
  Sir Henry Lee (1533–1611) : Elizabethan courtier / by Sue Simpson.
    pages cm
  Includes bibliographical references and index.
  ISBN 978-1-4724-3739-6 (hardcover)
  1. Lee, Henry, 1533–1611. 2. Great Britain – Court and
courtiers – History – 16th century – Biography. 3. Armorers – Great Britain – Biography.
4. Elizabeth I, Queen of England, 1533–1603 – Friends and associates. I. Title.
  DA358.L4S56 2014
  942.05'5092–dc23
  [B]
                                                                    2014013558

ISBN: 978-1-4724-3739-6 (hbk)
ISBN: 978-1-03-292388-8 (pbk)
ISBN: 978-1-315-60920-1 (ebk)

DOI: 10.4324/9781315609201

Contents

List of Illustrations

Acknowledgements

I should like to express my thanks to Viscount de Lisle and Dudley for permission to use the Penshurst Papers, and acknowledge the interest and assistance I have received from the Worshipful Company of Armourers and Brasiers, and the Ditchley Foundation, especially for the use of their illustrations.

My thanks also go to the staff of the many libraries and record offices I have been privileged to use, and especially to Robert Yorke at the College of Arms, London, and to Bridget Clifford at the Royal Armouries Library at the Tower of London. I am particularly grateful to Simon Adams of Strathclyde University for suggesting several sources on Lee which I had not considered. My especial thanks to Paul Everson for allowing me to use his work on Lee's garden at Quarrendon.

Every student needs both encouragement and constructive criticism and these I received in abundance from Alastair Duke and Dilys Hill of Southampton University, and also from Rivkah Zim of King's College, London. My thanks to them for reading some or all of my text, and for listening to my rambling enthusiasms for some of the odder aspects of Sir Henry Lee's life. I enjoyed many interesting discussions with Janet Dickinson and Eleanor Quince at Southampton University, as well as the ever-changing membership of the Tudor and Stuart Seminar at the Institute of Historical Research, London.

Friends among the postgraduate community at Southampton play an important part in any research exercise, and I am grateful for being allowed to try out ideas with this international group. My thanks go especially to fellow-postgraduates Tehmina Goskar and Tobias Metzler for their technical assistance.

Far and away my greatest debt of gratitude is to my supervisor, George Bernard, who patiently read my first stumbling attempts and remained convinced that something readable would eventually emerge. He is a tower of strength for Tudor history and an inspiration to any would-be historian.

Finally, this is for my father, who encouraged me from the beginning, and for John, my husband, who saw it through to the end.

List of Abbreviations

All terms have been given in full at their first appearance in the text.

APC	Acts of the Privy Council
BIHR	*Bulletin of the Institute of Historical Research*
BL	British Library
Bodl.	Bodleian Library
CA	College of Arms
CBS	Centre for Buckinghamshire Studies
Cecil MS	Cecil Manuscripts, Hatfield House, Hertfordshire
CKS	Centre for Kentish Studies
CPR	*Calendar of Patent Rolls*
CSP Border	*Calendar of State Papers Border*
CSP Colonial	*Calendar of State Papers Colonial Series, East Indies, China and Japan, 1513–1616*
CSP Foreign	*Calendar of State Papers Foreign series of the reign of Elizabeth*
CSP Irish	*Calendar of State Papers Irish*
CSP Scotland	*Calendar of State Papers relating to Scotland and Mary, Queen of Scots*
CSP Spanish	*Calendar of letters and State Papers relating to English affairs preserved principally in the archives of Simancas Spanish*
CSP Venetian	*Calendar of State Papers Venetian*
CSPD	*Calendar of State Papers, Domestic Series, preserved in Her Majesty's Public Record Office, Edward IV, Mary I, Elizabeth, James I*
Dasent, *APC*	*Acts of the Privy Council of England*, ed. John Roche Dasent
DHM	Deutsches Historisches Museum, Berlin
EHR	*English Historical Review*
GL	Guildhall Library
HJ	*The Historical Journal*
HMC de Lisle and Dudley	Her Majesty's Commission, Manuscripts of the deLisle and Dudley families

HMC Hastings	Her Majesty's Commission, Manuscripts of the Hastings Family
HMC *Salis.*	*A Calendar of the Manuscripts of the Most Hon. The Marquess of Salisbury, KG. Preserved at Hatfield House, Hertfordshire*
Holinshed, *Chronicles*	*Holinsheds Chronicles of England, Scotland and Ireland* (London, 1577), *RSTC* 1358, all vols
1 Jac I Trinity	*Trinity Term [June–July 1603] in the first year of James 1's Reign* (1603).
LP	*Letters and Papers, Foreign and Domestic of the Reign of Henry VIII*
LPL	Lambeth Palace Library
MMNY	Metropolitan Museum of New York
NLW	National Library of Wales
ORO	Oxfordshire Record Office
PAT	Patent Office
RATL	Royal Armouries, Tower of London
Rot. Pat .	*Rotuloram Patentium*
RSTC	*Revised Short Title Catalogue of Books Printed in England, Scotland and Ireland 1475–1640*
SRO	Staffordshire Record Office
TNA, PRO	The National Archives, Public Record Office.
TRHS	*Transactions of the Royal Historical Society*
V & A	Victoria and Albert Museum
VCH Bucks	*The Victorian County History of Buckinghamshir*
VCH Oxon	*The Victorian County History of Oxfordshire*

Introduction

Autumn was generally regarded as a good time for entertainments in Elizabethan London, both for the Court and the public alike. After the excitement of the annual Lord Mayor's Show on 29 October, the London crowd could look forward to the festivities of All Hallows and the State Opening of Parliament. For the Court, the Queen's return from her summer progress marked the start of a season of entertainments lasting until Shrovetide and Lent. One of the grandest spectacles held in London, and one in which courtiers, ambassadors and Londoners could all participate, was the Accession Day tournament held at Whitehall on 17 November.

The Accession Day tournaments, celebrating the accession of Elizabeth I to the throne on 17 November 1558, were the brainchild of Sir Henry Lee, the self-appointed 'Queen's tournament Champion'.[1] They differed from earlier tournaments in several ways. They started around 1570 and were held on the same date every year, regardless of weather or Sabbath commitments and were only cancelled twice, due to plague in London. Von Wedel, a Swiss traveller, left a graphic eyewitness account of the Accession Day tournament of 1584.[2] He described the tournament ground set up outside the Queen's room in Whitehall Palace, with steps going up to the Queen's windows. Those knights who wished to take part in the tournament entered in pairs, accompanied by their servants and musicians, with some of the servants dressed in ludicrous costumes – as wild men with hair down their backs or as women, depending on the entertainment that was planned for the Queen. As each group approached the staircase leading to the Queen's window, the noble's servants would mount the stairs and read verses or a humorous address to her and then offer a costly gift in their master's name. The three nobles whom von Wedel mentioned by name were the Master of the Queen's Horse, Robert Dudley, Earl of Leicester, the Count of Oxford Edward de Vere and the young Earl of Arundel, Philip Howard. Yet he omitted to name the principal organizer, who was Sir Henry Lee.

---

[1] Lee is often referred to as the 'Queen's Champion'. This was not a title he claimed, nor was it Elizabeth's to give. The hereditary dignity of Champion of England or 'King's Champion' was held by the Dymoke family of Scrivelsby, Lincolnshire. As Robert Dymoke was languishing in jail as a recusant at the time, Lee assumed the *de facto* role of personal champion to the Queen at tournaments.

[2] Lupold von Wedel, 'Journey Made through England and Scotland in the Years 1584 and 1585', *Transactions of the Royal Historical Society* (hereafter *TRHS*), New Series, IX (1895), pp. 258–9, Reproduced in Appendix 3, pp. 209–10.

Sir William Segar claimed that, at Elizabeth's accession on 17 November 1588, Sir Henry Lee had made a solemn vow to 'yearly on that date unless voluntarily vowed (unlesse infirmity, age or other accident did impeach him) during his life, to present himselfe at the Tilt armed, the day aforesayd yeerly, there to performe, in honor of her sacred Majestie the promise he formerly made'.[3] Although we have no contemporary description of Sir Henry Lee in action at the tournaments, what we do have is a 1568 portrait of him by Antonis Mor, which depicts him as a strikingly handsome athletic young courtier (see Ill. 1). Two poetic descriptions also exist. Joshua Sylvester gives the following retrospective description in 1605 of Lee in his prime:

> ... hardy Laelius, that great Garter-Knight,
> Tilting in triumph of Eliza's right
> (Yearly the day that her dear reign began)
> Most bravely mounted on proud Rabican.[4]

George Peele, in *Polyhymnia*, describes Lee as 'Knight of the Crown', and gives a vivid picture of him at the start of his retirement tilt of 1590:

> Mightie in Armes, mounted on a puissant horse,
> Knight of the Crown in rich imbroderie, ...
> Sir Henry Lea, redoubted man at Armes Leades in the troopes.[5]

Who, then, was this Sir Henry Lee who Elizabeth allowed to take the monarch's role of 'leading in the troops in a royal tournament'? If his *memoriam sacrae*,[6] the inscription on his tomb in the now ruined chapel at Quarrendon, near Aylesbury, is to be believed, he was born in 1533 and died 'with a body bent to earth and a mind erect to heaven in 1611'. The seventeenth-century antiquarian and assiduous compiler of gossip and hearsay, Sir John Aubrey,

---

[3]   Sir William Segar, *Honor Military and Civill* (London, 1602), *RSTC* 22164.

[4]   Joshua Sylvester, *Bartas, his Devine Weekes and Workes* (London, 1605). Laelius was the name given to Lee by Sidney in his *New Arcadia*, identified in J. Hanford and S. Watson, 'Personal Allegory in the Arcadia: Philisides and Laelius', *Modern Philology*, XXXII (August 1934), pp. 1–10. Sylvester's use of the name in 1605 would suggest that its association with Lee was recognized by contemporaries. Rabican was the name of Astolpho's horse in *Orlando Furioso*, but its use here is more a literary compliment to Lee than an accurate reflection of the name of Lee's horse.

[5]   George Peele, *Polyhymnia describing the honourable Triumph at Tylt* (London, 1590), *RSTC* 260.

[6]   The full text of this *memoriam sacrae* is to be found in Appendix 7.

claimed he was the natural son of Henry VIII.[7] However, even though Lee's mother, Margaret Wyatt, was lady-in-waiting to Anne Boleyn and, according to family tradition, accompanied her to the block, an affair between Margaret Wyatt and Henry VIII seems highly unlikely. Yet Henry Lee could not have shown greater devotion to Elizabeth I if she had been his sister.

Lee sprang from a well-known Court family. His mother was the daughter of Sir Henry Wyatt, Councillor to both Henry VII and Henry VIII, and he was born in his maternal grandfather's castle at Allington, Kent, in 1533. His uncle was the diplomat and poet Sir Thomas Wyatt, a noted jouster. Lee's paternal grandfather, Sir Robert Lee, having done his service at Court as a young man chose the more prosaic but lucrative path of sheep-breeder in Aylesbury, Buckinghamshire. This gave his grandson Henry the financial freedom of action to serve his Queen as he would choose, As well as acting as Elizabeth's tournament champion, Lee was also lieutenant at the royal palace at Woodstock, where he welcomed the Queen and the Court on four occasions. He was appointed Master of the Armoury at the Tower of London in 1580, and in this role was responsible for the Royal Armoury at Greenwich during the hey-day of its Almain armourers. Unhappily married in 1550 to the daughter of the holder of his wardship, Sir William Paget, Lee became increasingly estranged from his wife, Anne Paget. In the 1590s he met Anne Vavasour a young 'maid of honour' to the Queen. She had been seduced by Edward de Vere, Earl of Oxford, and had suffered the misfortune of giving birth to Oxford's son in the maids' chamber adjacent to the Queen's bedroom. Incensed, the Queen sent Anne and Oxford to the Tower of London. Oxford typically attempted to flee the country and denied paternity, although the child was subsequently raised by his de Vere relatives and became an eminent soldier. Anne remained in the Tower for several years, and eventually became Lee's mistress, living with him, as Sir John Aubrey phrased it, as 'his deerest deere' until his death in 1611.

Regardless of how others described him, Sir Henry Lee only ever described himself as the Queen's Knight. So who exactly was this Tudor courtier gentleman, what sort of life did he lead and how did he make himself indispensable to both Elizabeth I and another frequent visitor to Woodstock, her Stuart successor James I? Surprisingly, the most recent attempt to address these questions is to be found decades ago in the biography of Sir Henry Lee by the theatre historian E. K. Chambers, published in 1936. This drew heavily on previous private research by Viscount, Lord Dillon, the last descendant of Sir Henry Lee to inhabit his home at Ditchley Park, Oxfordshire. Since 1937 new multidisciplinary areas for historical study have opened up. Court Studies has developed as a distinctive area for research, as have Garden and Art History. All of these disciplines offer new

---

[7]   Sir John Aubrey, in *Brief Lives*, ed. Oliver Lawson Dick (London, 1992), p. 350. For a more detailed exploration of both these descriptions see Chapter 2.

and additional insights into the life and times of Sir Henry Lee. Yet perhaps the most succinct description of him came in 1575 from Monsieur de Champenaye, the Ambassador from the Low Counties to England in a conversation with Sir Christopher Hatton. In this he characterised Lee as 'a man Of Arms Richly Armed and Indeed the most accomplished cavaliero I have ever Seen'.[8]

---

[8]   Frederic Perrenot, Sieur de Champagney, Segar *Honor Military and Civill*, Book IV, (RSTC 22164), p. 200.

Chapter 1
The Making of a Courtier Gentleman, 1533–1573

Sir Henry Lee can best be described as a courtier gentleman, belonging to the upper ranks of the gentry class and having the personality and talent to achieve a position at Court. Gentlemen of Lee's standing were not necessarily created; they often came from generations of birth and breeding but were trained from an early age to be conscious of their duties, responsibilities and privileges. Courtiers, on the other hand, could be and were created. To be a successful courtier, one needed contacts at Court, the higher placed the better. If one did not want merely to haunt the corridors of power, importuning for any office that might return a living, one needed to offer a talent acceptable and flattering to the reigning monarch. Above all, one needed the money to sustain the lifestyle, and the ambition, for a career at Court where fortunes could be fickle and could change immediately with the death of a monarch. Sir Henry Lee was thirty-seven by the time he received the first recorded sign of royal favour from Elizabeth I, past the midpoint of man's allotted lifespan and relatively advanced for the life expectancy of the day. His long Court career owed more to his longevity than to an early start. A study of the first half of Lee's life illustrates how he most probably acquired the values that remained with him all his life, how his initially promising Court career was cut short by a change of monarch and how, with discretion, he was able to return to royal favour on his own terms.

Lee's Early Life, 1533–1553

The aspirations and values of a Tudor gentleman in his formative years were influenced by many factors. At this distance in time, it is necessary to rely more on conjecture than evidence when attempting to identify the influences that could have operated upon the young Henry Lee. Certain possibilities can, however, be suggested, such as his own family traditions, his education, the influence of popular conduct books, the society in which he grew up and the circumstances of his wardship.

The traditions within Lee's immediate family clearly contributed to the two guiding principles that remained constant throughout his life – loyalty and service to the monarch and commonweal, and faithful stewardship of his own estates. Born around March 1533, Henry Lee was the first son of Anthony Lee and Margaret Wyatt. Both his mother and father came from families well established at Court, loyal to the Tudors and regarding practical service at Court as the norm rather than the exception. Anthony Lee's father, Sir Robert Lee of Quarrendon, Buckinghamshire, had served at Court in his younger days as Gentleman Usher at the Court of Henry VII, Yeoman Usher to Princess Mary by 1508 and a Gentleman Usher of the Chamber by 1512.[1] Anthony Lee was Gentleman Usher of the Bedchamber to Henry VIII by 1533, while his wife Margaret Wyatt served Anne Boleyn in a similar capacity.

It was probably from the Wyatts that Lee derived his ambition to do something more for his Queen than merely a gentleman's duty to attend Court periodically. The tradition of royal service was paramount in the Wyatt family; Lee's maternal grandfather Sir Henry Wyatt had been loyal to the young Henry Tudor before his victory at Bosworth in 1485 and subsequently had served him in a military capacity in the north of England. He was Master of the King's Jewels from 1488 to 1524, Councillor in 1504 and an executor of Henry VII's will in 1509. Wyatt remained at Court as Councillor to Henry VIII until his retirement in 1533.

Henry Lee was born and spent his early years at Allington Castle in Kent, the home of his grandfather and his uncle, Sir Thomas Wyatt, a loyal servant to Henry VIII as Esquire of the King's Body and as an ambassador (see Appendix 1 for the family tree). Whereas Lee, as a child of three, would have known little of the tension in May 1536 when Sir Thomas was implicated in the fall of Anne Boleyn and thrown into the Tower of London, he might have sensed the family's relief at Sir Thomas's release into his father's supervision in June. The excitement of the King's visit to Allington on 31 July 1536 would have been memorable. Henry Lee was not yet four when his grandfather died on 10 November 1536, and whereas he would have had somewhat limited personal memories of Sir Henry Wyatt, anecdotal stories of this beloved patriarch appear to have been kept evergreen in the family.[2] Sir Henry Wyatt's reputation for integrity and honesty in royal service is recorded in both the letters of his son, Sir Thomas Wyatt, and the testimony of Polydore Vergil, the contemporary chronicler.[3] Together, they create a vivid image of Sir Henry Wyatt, 'welbelouid of many, hatid of none'.

---

[1]   *Letters and Papers, Foreign and Domestic of the Reign of Henry VIII* (hereafter *LP*), ed. J.S. Brewer, R.H. Brodie and J. Gairdner, 23 vols (London, 1864), II, i, p. 872.

[2]   British Library (hereafter BL), Add. MS, 62135 ff. 332–3. *The Commonplace Book of George Wyatt* contains a series of anecdotes collected in the late 1590s from Jane Hawte, wife of Sir Thomas Wyatt the younger, by her youngest son.

[3]   T. Wyatt, *Life and Letters of Sir Thomas Wyatt*, ed. K. Muir (Liverpool, 1953), pp. 38–9; Polydore Vergil, *Anglica Historia of Polydore Vergil*, ed. and trans. D. Hay, Camden Series LXXIV (London, 1950), pp. 6, 95, 149.

In November 1536 Allington Castle and the guardianship of the Lee children passed officially to Sir Thomas Wyatt, although most of his time was spent travelling as ambassador to the court of Emperor Charles V. Lee's own parents were still at Court, and at some point young Henry Lee would have known of the brief confinement of his father, Anthony Lee, on 2 October 1537 for 'consenting to the steling of certain the King's hawkes'.[4] Thanks to Henry Lee's mother, Margaret, 'suying for his deliverance' with the King at Windsor on 10 October 1537, Anthony Lee was released. Their relief must have been tangible, as Thomas Cromwell, the King's secretary and chief minister, remarked that 'they be both merry and the King's Highness is now again good lorde unto him'.[5] The Lees showed their gratitude to the King's minister by naming their youngest son Cromwell Lee.

Thomas Cromwell had also been the chief patron and protector to Sir Thomas Wyatt, and, with the fall and execution of Cromwell in 1540, Wyatt was at the mercy of the many enemies he had made at Court. He was arrested on a charge of treason in January 1541 and taken bound and handcuffed to the Tower. Allington Castle was cleared on the orders of the Council, and from an inventory of persons residing there, it is clear that the Lee children, now numbering at least four – Henry, Robert, Thomas and Cromwell – had already moved. As Anthony Lee had come into his inheritance at Quarrendon on the death of his father Sir Robert Lee on 23 February 1539, it is reasonable to surmise that his growing family had reassembled there.

How much of this the young Henry Lee would have known is conjectural. He was seven when he left Allington, the eldest child in a highly politicized family. If he knew little at first hand, family experience would have warned him that royal service was rife with pitfalls, jealousy and rivalries, and that the financial returns were far from guaranteed. Lee's uncle, Sir Thomas Wyatt, was released from the Tower and rehabilitated into royal service by 1541, but he died in debt, many miles from home and was buried in a stranger's vault in Sherborne, Dorset, in 1542. It may have been Lee's awareness of this, as well as his family pride in his uncle's achievements, that led him in 1609 to leave money in his will for a tomb to be constructed for Sir Thomas Wyatt at Quarrendon. The order was never carried out.

The prosaic but more profitable virtues of land ownership and development came from the Lee family traditions, and Henry Lee knew that, as first-born son, he would eventually inherit the entailed Lee estates. The acknowledged founder of Lee's landed fortunes was his grandfather, Sir Robert Lee. The Lee family had begun to feature as leaseholders of the manor of Quarrendon

---

4   *LP*, XII, ii, p. 870.
5   BL, Harleian MS 282, f. 208.

from 1438, and it became their property by a grant of socage in 1512.[6] After pursuing an interesting if somewhat unprofitable career at Court in his early years, Robert Lee inherited the freehold of Quarrendon in October 1516 and was knighted in 1522. Sir Robert chose to turn his back on the Court, choosing the less flamboyant but more lucrative path of landholder and sheep-farmer. If Sir Robert Dormer, a near-neighbour, could be described by Henry Machyn as 'the grete shepe-master in Oxfordshyre', the same might well have been said of Sir Robert Lee in Buckinghamshire who, like many gentleman graziers, was busy enlarging and consolidating his lands.[7]

Quarrendon, Sir Robert's principal manor, was held in knights' service to the Crown, and by 1526 he had acquired land at nearby Burston, Weedon, Hardwick and Fleetmarston where the Lees already had interests.[8] Quarrendon was prime pasture land, and Sir Robert Lee followed the contemporary custom of converting arable land to pasture. With rising prices for wool, there was an ever-present temptation to enclose land and, despite Wolsey's commission of enquiry in 1517 which mentioned Robert Lee twice in this context, Fleetmarston and Quarrendon itself were enclosed.[9] Sir Robert later obtained a licence to export wool to Calais in 1533, laying the foundations for solid family income and possessions.

It was also from his grandfather that Henry Lee derived the inestimable advantage of good family connections (see Appendix 2 for details). Sir Robert Lee married twice. After the death of his first wife, he used his Court connections in 1521 to marry Lettice Penistone, widow of Robert Knollys and mother of Sir Francis Knollys who married Katharine Carey, daughter of Mary Boleyn. This was the most advantageous marriage the Lees ever made and it eventually linked Sir Henry Lee not only with the Knollys and Carey families at Court, but also to Lord Hunsdon, Queen Elizabeth's cousin, and to the Queen herself. Through the usual Court web of nuptial connections, the Lees later became connected to the Earls of Essex and the Earl of Leicester.

The Lees were also linked by marriage to the Cookes, a relationship which would bring them into kinship with the Cecils, the Hobys and the Killigrews, influential families at the Court of Queen Elizabeth. Sir Robert's first marriage had produced a son and heir, Anthony. His second marriage would produce a son and two daughters. It also had the effect of keeping Anthony Lee and his family away from Quarrendon until his father's death.

---

[6]   Oxfordshire Record Office (hereafter ORO) DIL X/a/1–13 (court rolls of Quarrendon).

[7]   Henry Machyn, *The Diary of Henry Machyn – Citizen and Merchant-Taylor of London (1550–1563)*, ed. J.G. Nichols, Camden Old Series XXXXII (London, 1848), p. 22.

[8]   ORO, LEE II/1 and LEE II/7. The precise details of the Lee estates in Buckinghamshire are discussed in Chapter 5 below.

[9]   *The Domesday of Inclosures, 1517–1518*, ed. I.S. Leadam, 2 vols (London, 1897), I, pp. 161, 170.

Anthony Lee, like his father before him, had followed a somewhat limited Court career, but was knighted in 1539 and rode with other knights to receive Anne of Cleves between Blackheath and Greenwich in January 1540.[10] On his father's death in February 1539, Anthony had inherited the manor of Quarrendon, and Lettice, as his father's widow, received a life interest in Burston, which she later returned to her stepson.[11] Sir Anthony Lee was happy to retire with his family to his Buckinghamshire estates, and John Leland described Quarrendon as standing in 'the myddle parte of the vale of Ailesburie … fruitful for pasture … where Mr Leigh hath a goodly house with Orchards and a parke'.[12] Although Sir Anthony preferred to remain at home, he was still described as the King's servant in 1542 and sat as member of parliament for Buckinghamshire in the parliaments of 1542 to 1545 and of 1547 to 1549.[13] As one of the leading county gentlemen, he took musters for the Aylesbury hundred of Buckinghamshire and provided great horses, light horses, demi-lances, archers and arquebusiers for the King's service.[14]

Sir Anthony Lee also generated more complications for his future heirs. He had four sons – Henry, Robert, Thomas and Cromwell – by Margaret Wyatt. At what point Margaret Wyatt died is unknown, but by the time of Anthony Lee's second marriage in May 1548 to Anne Hassall, he already had two illegitimate sons by her, Richard and Russell alias Hassall. Sir Anthony also had four daughters, but it is unclear from his will who was their mother. When Sir Anthony Lee died on 24 November 1549, he made provision for all his children but left his lands and 'all my horses, greyhounds, spanyells, geldings and mares' to 'Harry Lee my sonne'.[15] At sixteen, Henry Lee was already identified as someone with a marked preference for an active and sporting life. Thus, if Lee inherited both an appetite for royal service and knowledge of its pitfalls from his Wyatt lineage, it was from his Lee inheritance that he gained the highly profitable estates that would finance his aspirations at Court.

By the terms of Sir Henry Wyatt's will of 1536 Henry Lee had received 'yerely during his nonage tenne poundes, and in lykewyse unto Robert Lee his brother

---

[10]   *LP*, XIV, ii, p. 572.

[11]   An entangled court case over detention of deeds ensued between Sir Anthony and his stepmother. See The National Archives, Public Record Office (hereafter TNA, PRO), C1/847/7 and C1/1024/17–18. The twice-married Lettice did not stay a widow long. After the death of Sir Robert Lee, she married Sir Thomas Tresham of Rushton, Northants, later the first Prior of the restored Order of St John of Jerusalem. This gave Sir Henry Lee a longstanding link with the staunchly Catholic Tresham dynasty.

[12]   John Leland, *The Itinerary of John Leland the Antiquary*, ed. Thomas Hearne, 9 vols (Oxford, 1710–12), II, p. 110.

[13]   *LP*, V, p. 686; VI, p. 32; VIII, p. 9; XVII, p. 641.

[14]   *LP*, p. 6 (20 February 1548).

[15]   TNA, PRO, PROB 11/33 (17 October 1550).

during his nonage yerely tenne markes towards and for to fynde them to scole'.[16] Where Henry Lee received his education is uncertain. Although he wrote to Sir Robert Cecil in 1594 that 'I was once a student at New College, in Oxford', it is difficult to prove conclusively that he had followed the normal pattern of having earlier attended Winchester College.[17] For this period few documented cases exist of New College students who were not Wykehamists, but unlike their Lee cousins from Maids Moreton, Buckinghamshire, neither Henry nor Robert appear on the scholars' list for Winchester College.[18]

The society in which Lee grew up was influenced and informed by the popular conduct books circulating at the time, but without information on Sir Henry Lee's library, it is impossible to know what precise effect they had upon his values and youthful aspirations. Lee, having resided for at least six years in the literary household of Sir Thomas Wyatt, grew up with the notion that books were a necessary part of a gentleman's possessions. If it is impossible to prove that Henry Lee read Sir Thomas Elyot's *The Boke named The Gouvernor* and Baldassare Castiglione's *Book of the Courtier,* he was at least raised in a society influenced by their precepts. Peter Burke omits Sir Thomas Wyatt from his list of readers of the *Courtier* 'for lack of evidence', but it is difficult to believe neither he nor Lee ever read it.[19]

Sir Thomas Hoby, the first English translator of the work in 1561 confessed in his preface that 'this Courtier hath long strayed about this Realm'.[20] George Bull, a more recent translator, comments that 'the kind of behaviour recommended to Italian courtiers became the accepted standard for English gentlemen'.[21] Not only was Hoby a cousin of Lee, but when his English translation was published, Lee had already spent several months in Italy. He was clearly conversant with the language as he used it during his later travels in 1568 and 1569. Similarly, in the light of Lee's subsequent career, it would be unusual if he had not come into contact with Caxton's editions of Mallory's *Morte D'Arthur* and Ramon Lull's

---

[16]   TNA, PRO, PROB 11/26. Young Robert Lee appears to have been born in Hatfield, Yorkshire before 1536, and lived there most of his adult life. The only family connection is the fact that Sir Henry Wyatt was Constable of nearby Coningsburgh Castle, which office subsequently passed to his son, Sir Thomas Wyatt.

[17]   HMC, *A Calendar of the Manuscripts of the Most Hon. The marquis of Salisbury, K.G., preserved at Hatfield House, Hertfordshire* (hereafter HMC *Salis.*), 24 vols (London, 1883–1976), IV, p. 529 (13 May 1594).

[18]   T.F. Kirby, *Winchester Scholars* (London and Winchester, 1888). I am grateful to Caroline Dalton, archivist at New College for these details.

[19]   Peter Burke, *The Fortunes of the Courtier: The European Reception of Castiglione's Cortegiano* (Cambridge, 1995), p. 163.

[20]   Baldasarre Castiglione, *The Courtier*, trans. and ed. George Bull (London, 1967), p. 2.

[21]   Ibid., p. 13.

Order of Chivalry.[22] It is possible to link the latter especially with the chivalric themes of loyalty, obedience and military prowess found in the Ditchley Manuscript[23] – themes that had a major influence on Lee's life.

It was perhaps Henry Lee's guardian, Sir William Paget, who was responsible for many of his early expectations and his initial steps towards a career at Court. Lee was still a minor when his father died in 1549, and, as Quarrendon was held in socage from the Crown, his wardship and marriage were available for purchase. It is unclear what the relationship between Sir Anthony Lee and Paget had been, but Paget was named as one of the executors of Lee's will, receiving some 'threescore fatte weathers' in payment.[24] Paget was an ambitious man who had risen from lowly beginnings in London to become Secretary of State under Henry VIII and one of the most powerful office-holders in the kingdom. With six daughters and three sons to provide for, he took a keen interest in the profitable purchase of wardships and obtained Henry Lee's in December 1549. S.R. Gammon suggests that Paget's second daughter, Anne, was already betrothed to Henry Lee, and at least three more of Paget's wards became his sons-in-law.[25]

Although there is no evidence that Paget ever abused his position, the dating of Henry Lee's wardship coincides almost exactly with the time of greatest complaint against the system. Bishop Latimer preached before Edward VI in March 1549 that 'there was never such marrying in England as is now ... I hear of stealing of wards to marry their children to. This is a strange kind of stealing, but it is not the wards, it is the lands they steal.'[26] Lee was no more than eighteen when he married Anne Paget, who was even younger. His father-in-law, in a letter to William Cecil on 31 July 1551, stated: 'I mynd vppon Monday to remove to my soone Lees house there to take clene ayer for a sevenught.'[27] Lee's wife Ann bore him three children in all, a girl and two boys. Paget wrote to the Countess of Bath on 24 June 1558 that 'my daughter Lee ... was brought to bed

---

[22]   Ramon Lull, *The Booke of the Ordre of Chyualry*, trans. and printed by William Caxton, 1484, ed. Alfred Byles (London, 1926).

[23]   The Ditchley Manuscript consists of a collection of documents related to Sir Henry Lee stored at Ditchley Park. The documents were acquired by the British Library when the house was sold. They can be found at British Library Additional Manuscript (hereafter BL Add. MS) 41499A and B.

[24]   TNA, PRO, PROB 11/33 (17 October 1550).

[25]   S.R. Gammon, *Statesman and Schemer: William, First Lord Paget, Tudor Minister* (Newton Abbot, 1973), p. 22. Paget already had the lucrative wardship of Thomas Kytson and that of two illegitimate sons of the wealthy Mayor of London, Sir John Alleyn.

[26]   J. Hurstfield, *The Queen's Wards: Wardship and Marriage under Elizabeth I* (London, 1958), p. 25.

[27]   B.L. Beer and S.M. Jacks (eds), 'Letters of William, Lord Paget of Beaudesert', *Camden Miscellany*, XXV, pp. 1–141, Camden Society, 4th Series XIII (Cambridge, 1974), p. 123.

of a goodly boye ... and was moche weakened but now thankes be to God doth fele her self moche amended'.[28] Both the boys, John and Henry, died in infancy and Lee's daughter Mary died in the early 1580s.

In the long run, the circumstances of Lee's early marriage had a major effect on his career. At that time, a minor had little choice but to marry whomever the holder of his wardship chose. Lee lost any chance to benefit materially by marrying an heiress, and any advantages he gained from his association with Lord Paget rapidly ceased when Paget fell from power in 1559. Lee's early marriage could explain not only his failure to take a degree at New College, Oxford – not in itself uncommon for a gentleman – but also his failure to spend time at the Inns of Court in London, a practice that was rapidly becoming a prerequisite for a position in government service. Lee's inclinations may have been against a career in administration in his younger days but, without at least some legal experience, he stood little chance when he sought a Court appointment after his retirement as 'Queen's Champion' in 1590. Most importantly, Lady Lee failed to give him a son who lived beyond a few months and, although she herself lived until 1590, she was, by her own admission, prone to melancholy. Her Catholic beliefs became problematic, as did the increasingly treasonable practices of her brothers. There had been little in Sir Henry Lee's early life to convince him that marriage should include either devotion or felicity, and he rapidly tired of his wife.

The Beginnings of a Court Career, 1553–1558

Although Henry Lee gained little in material terms from his marriage, he did benefit from the opportunities Paget could create for him at Court after 1553. Lee was old enough to appreciate the vicissitudes of Court politics which had affected Paget's career. Paget had been a leading member of the Privy Council under Henry VIII, but despite being created Baron Paget of Beaudesert in December 1549, he was forced to resign many of his offices in that year. He was arrested in October 1551 on charges of corruption and stripped of his Order of the Garter. Paget was later pardoned, and his political fortunes were restored with the accession of Queen Mary in 1553. There were benefits for his family: his son and heir Henry Paget was created a Knight of the Bath at the coronation on 1 October 1553, and two of his wards and sons-in-law, Henry Lee and Christopher Alleyn, were among the eighty knights dubbed by Henry Fitzalan, Earl of Arundel, the next day.[29] On becoming a knight, Lee was deemed to have achieved his majority and came into full possession of his own lands. The new

---

[28]   Ibid., p. 138.
[29]   Machyn, *Diary*, p. 22.

Sir Henry Lee rapidly acquired his own political acumen. When his cousin, the younger Sir Thomas Wyatt, led a rebellion against Queen Mary in 1554, Lee had the good sense to maintain his distance, and there is no further recorded contact between the Lees and the Wyatts until the last decade of the century.

There is one tantalizing incident that, if proven, could give us an invaluable clue to Lee's early experience as a courtier. From 20 May to 10 June 1555 Paget travelled to Gravelines, attempting unsuccessfully to negotiate a peace treaty between the Holy Roman Empire and the French at Marck. He did not go alone: the State Papers Venetian relate that Lord Paget's son and son-in-law came to Brussels to see the Court on 4 June 1555. The two young men had not come in any official capacity. Paget's heir, Henry, was eighteen at the time, and it would appear that his father had simply given them a chance to see the most magnificent court in Europe at the Coudenberg Palace in Brussels. On 8 June

> ... the Emperor [Charles V] gave orders for refreshments to be sent to Lord Paget's son and son-in-law, and as they had not asked to kiss hands, his Majesty gave them to understand ... that he wished to see them before their departure, as he did, showing them many marks of good will. [30]

This appears to have caused not a little consternation. The Emperor was granting very few audiences at this time and had earlier refused to meet the Plantagenet loose cannon, Sir Edward Courtenay. The case for Lee being the son-in-law is strong. Paget's only other son-in-law at the time was Sir Christopher Alleyn of Ightham Mote in Kent. Although now a wealthy knight, Alleyn was the illegitimate son of a London merchant with little experience at Court. Sir Henry Lee, on the other hand, was a third-generation courtier on both sides of his family and already familiar with court practices. Lee's uncle, Thomas Wyatt, would have been well known to Charles V, and, at twenty-three, Lee was more of an age to be a companion to the young Henry Paget than the older Alleyn. If this is more than conjecture, one can well imagine the deep impression made on Lee by the Coudenberg Palace with its magnificent tiltyard and possibly court reminiscences of the 1549 Magnificences at Binche. These Magnificences were legendary for their extravagance. In August of that year the Holy Roman Emperor, Charles V, moved his Court from Brussels to the Walloon town of Binche. To welcome her brother and his nephew, Philip of Spain, his sister, Mary of Austria. staged these extraordinary 'Triumphes of Binche' between 23 and 30 August. At some point and somewhere, Lee acquired his taste for foreign courts and the tournament, and the Imperial Court in Brussels would have been an impressive place to start.

---

[30]   *Calendar of State Papers Relating to English Affairs in the Archives of Venice* (hereafter *CSP Venetian*), VI 1555–1558, pp. 121, 127 (4–8 June 1555).

It is possible that it was through his connection with Sir Henry Paget that Lee formed his long friendship with Lord Robert Dudley. Dudley's father, John Dudley, Duke of Northumberland, had been executed in 1553 for his attempt to place Lady Jane Grey on the throne, and his sons owed their reinstatement at Court in no small part to the influence and friendship of Lord Paget. Later Lord Robert Dudley, as Earl of Leicester, informed the third Lord Paget that 'he loved his father and brother as dearly as any friends I ever had'.[31] Lee and Dudley, much the same age, shared not only a love of the tournament, but also the experience of an early marriage that they had rapidly outgrown.

Lee had other formative experiences of government policy-making. On 16 October 1555 he was present at the burning of the Protestant divines, Hugh Latimer and Nicholas Ridley in Oxford. John Foxe tells us that, immediately prior to execution, Master Ridley 'gave away divers other small things to gentlemenne standynge by ... to Syr Henrye Lee he gaue a newe grote, and to diuers of my Lord Williams Gentlemen ... some nutmegs and rasins'.[32] Lee was standing in a prime position near the stake, but it is not recorded whether this was because he was officially part of the armed guard provided by Lord Williams of Thame, an Oxfordshire nobleman frequently used by Queen Mary in a military capacity. However, Lee was named as someone of note in the first edition of Foxe's *Acts and Monuments* in 1563, thus being singled out in print. There is no indication whether he shared Williams' distaste for the task or how he viewed the sight, especially of Ridley's prolonged sufferings. Lee did, however, develop a marked and lifelong tendency to sympathize with the numerous unfortunate individuals who would later rely on him for support when sentenced to death, such as the Duke of Norfolk at his execution in 1572.[33] By 1555 Lee was taking up his responsibilities as one of the principal landowners in Buckinghamshire, for he was named as a magistrate in that year and, despite his relatively tender age, was elected as a knight of the shire in the two parliaments of 1558.[34]

Paget's position on the Privy Council as Comptroller also gave Sir Henry Lee his first opportunity of soldiering in the service of the commonweal, an aspiration of many young gentlemen in this period. In 1558 the Regent of Scotland, Mary of Guise, was attempting to ravage the border lands with French troops, and Lee was appointed by the Council to lead 300 men to join the

---

[31]   Staffordshire Record Office (hereafter SRO), Paget MS X/12 (12 May 1574).

[32]   John Foxe, *Acts and Monuments* (London, 1563), p. 1377. *RSTC* 11222. See also the version edited by S.R. Cattley (London, 1838). I am indebted to Tom Freeman for the suggestion that the source was probably Shipside, Ridley's brother-in-law and that Lee would have been standing near the stake, not merely with the crowd.

[33]   See Chapter 6 below.

[34]   The parliaments were held 20 January–7 March 1558 and 5–17 November 1558.

English army on the Scottish border in January 1558.[35] Holinshed recounts in his *Chronicles* that 'Sir Henrie Lee, Captain Read and others, beyng in the battell, behaved themselves very stoutly, causing the footmen to staye and boldly to abide the enemy'.[36] He added that, but for this, 'it might have turned very euil to the English'. In a letter to Queen Mary from Warkworth, dated 30 April 1558, the Earl of Northumberland commented that 'on Thursday night with Sir Henry Lee and other captains of your garrisons there, my brother passed over at Norham and burnt the town and took a great booty of cattle'.[37] Lee was appointed to serve at Berwick-upon-Tweed by force of the Council's letter, 28 June 1558, with a warrant for £100 for victuals for his men.[38]

If it was unusual for a young Buckinghamshire gentleman with no known military experience to be given a command on the Scottish border, it was even more unusual for him to be singled out for inclusion in a harp song composed for the occasion. A single manuscript in the Bodleian library, Oxford, preserves a thirty-six-line ballad, 'Within the north country', which celebrates the heroes of the campaign – Lord Dacre, Sir Harry Percy and Sir Richard Lee.[39] Alongside this illustrious host

> ther ys also Sr harry ley
> who dar both fight and fray
> w[he]ther it be be [*sic*] night or day
> I dar be bold to say
> he wyll not rone a way
> he ys both hardy & frae

The young Lee had made his mark in good company. On 17 October 1558 he was called home, with orders 'to leave in good order his charge with his lieutenant for this wynter season'.[40] If Lee's initial appointment had been the result of highly placed Court connections, his conduct showed him to be adept at soldiering. In the next thirty years he would seize what limited opportunities there were to exercise a military role, short of mercenary service on the Continent.

---

[35] *Acts of the Privy Council of England*, ed. John Roche Dasent (hereafter Dasent, *APC*), New Series, 46 vols (London, 1890–1964), VI, p. 244 (1556–58).

[36] Raphael Holinshed, *The firste volume of the chronicles of England, Scotlande, and Irelande* (London, 1577), p. 485. *RSTC* 1358.

[37] Norham Castle was across the border into Scotland. *Calendar of State Papers, Domestic Series* (hereafter *CSPD*), *Addenda 1547–1565*, (London, 1872), p. 474 (30 April 1558).

[38] BL, Harleian MS 7457, ff. 6, 12, 20 (wrongly numbered in the catalogue).

[39] Bodleian MS, Ashmole 48, f. 101; Andrew Taylor, 'The Sounds of Chivalry: Lute Song and Harp Song for Sir Henry Lee', *Journal of the Lute Society of America*, XXV (1992), pp. 1–23.

[40] Dasent, *APC*, XVII, p. 415; BL, Harleian MS 7457, ff. 12–20.

With the accession of Elizabeth I in November 1558, Paget's authority and influence at Court declined rapidly and with it, Lee's early hopes of a flourishing Court career. Before his retirement, however, Paget secured Lee's first appointment from the new Queen. In September 1558 a commission had been made out for the Lord Chancellor William Lord Howard of Effingham, Sir Nicholas Throckmorton, the newly appointed resident ambassador in Paris, and Dr Nicholas Wotton to travel to the French Court, escorted by Sir Henry Lee, Sir Robert Rich and John Smythe. Although Queen Mary died in November 1558, Elizabeth was persuaded to reappoint her sister's commissioners to travel to Paris in May 1559 for the ratification of the Treaty of Cambrai.[41] The peace treaty, concluded at Câteau-Cambrèsis in April 1559 and marking a general cessation of hostilities in Europe, had left certain matters between England and Scotland unsettled. These were the subject of a treaty signed at Upsettlington in May 1559 which needed ratification by 'King and Queen Dauphin' of France, Mary Stuart and her husband François, as *de jure* rulers of Scotland.

On 3 May 1559 letters were sent to Lee, Rich and Smythe, instructing them 'to be here at Court upon Sunday next, so as they may be ready the day following to attend the Lord Chamberlain and others whom the Queen presently sends to the French King'.[42] The three young men were of much same age and with similar talents. Lee was a personable young courtier of proven military skill, Robert Rich was the son of the first Baron Rich and accustomed to the ways of the Court and John Smythe was a gentleman who had fought as a volunteer in France and the Low Countries. Ambassadorial escorts who could dance as well as they could fight were useful diplomatically. We only know of Lee's initial summons to Court. Although he is not mentioned again by name, presumably he was among the many people who participated in the official entry into Paris, and in the jousts and courtly entertainment that followed the formal ratification of the treaty on 28 May. After the formalities, Howard and Wotton left Paris with their entourage on 30 May, bearing the proclamation of a tournament to be held at the French Court on 28 June 1559 – a tournament that would cost the life of King Henri II.

On his return from Paris, Sir Henry Lee received no further commissions from the new Queen. With the change of monarch and with Paget's retirement from office and subsequent death, Lee's potentially promising Court career temporarily ground to a halt. There were many young gentlemen at Court vying for advancement and Elizabeth showed a marked preference for those who had shown her conspicuous loyalty in earlier years. Lee was not only marked by his

---

[41]   Paget, from his sickbed, had been offering advice to Cecil on these peace negotiations in 1559, and doubtless Cecil was happy to include Paget's son-in-law and his own kinsman on the embassy.

[42]   Dasent, *APC*, VII, p. 99 (3 May 1559).

association with the previous reign, but also lacked influential patrons and had little distinctive to commend him to Elizabeth. It was to be ten years before he received any further recognition from her.

Rebuilding a Court Career through Travel and High-level Reporting, 1559–1569

Although Lee was fortunate in that, as a wealthy landowner, he had no financial necessity to seek office, at the age of twenty-five the life of a country gentleman was not going to satisfy him. It was a popular aspiration among such young gentleman of means in Tudor England to travel abroad to acquire the cosmopolitan polish and competency in languages that were necessary for a diplomatic career or preferment at Court. The courts of Italy were the chief attraction, and even Sir William Cecil sent his son and heir Thomas Cecil to Italy in 1561 to 'have the French or Italian tongue'.[43] Another aspiration of young gentlemen was to gain military experience. Opportunities for this were few in Elizabeth's England, and the government was conscious that a long peace would lead to a lack of experience in the very class that was needed to provide military leadership in the shires. By 1559 Sir Henry Lee was no *ingénue*, travelling abroad with a tutor for his education, and seeking youthful excitement in foreign skirmishes. He had already tasted both foreign travel and battle, and if he was to rebuild a court career, he needed to make both his travels abroad and his soldiering of practical use to the new Elizabethan regime. There is little to suggest that Lee deliberately set out to work his way into royal favour: his wealth permitted him the freedom to follow his own wishes. But, as he 'gave himself to Voiage and Travaile into the florishinge States of France Itally & Germany … gracinge the Courts of the most renowned princes [with] Skill and Proofe in Armes', he was becoming an accomplished courtier who might attract the attention of Elizabeth.[44]

Prolonged warfare in Europe had curtailed non-essential travel abroad, but the Treaty of Câteau-Cambrèsis in 1559 created new possibilities. Lee took the opportunity of peace in Europe to visit foreign courts, especially in Italy, and to see at first hand the tournaments and armour used abroad. We know little of Lee's attitude to the new Elizabethan regime at this time, but the survival of a private letter written during a visit to Venice and Naples in spring 1561 raises some interesting questions. Lee, while abroad, was corresponding with

---

[43]   L. Stone, *Crisis of the Aristocracy 1558–1641* (Oxford, 1965), p. 693.

[44]   From Lee's *memoriae sacrum* in E.K. Chambers, *Sir Henry Lee: An Elizabethan Portrait* (Oxford, 1936), p. 304.

Francis Yaxley, a man of dubious political loyalties.[45] Yaxley, initially a protégé of Sir William Cecil and a Clerk of the Signet until 1558, developed a taste for diplomatic meddling, and on the accession of Elizabeth, displayed firm Catholic beliefs and an indiscreet tongue. In January 1561, while corresponding weekly with Lee, Yaxley was briefly imprisoned in the Tower of London for speaking too freely of the Queen's possible marriage to Lord Robert Dudley. His papers were later seized, and they included correspondence with leading Catholics who had been imprisoned in 1561 for hearing Mass. Lee's letter of March 1561 to Yaxley, confiscated with the others, mentioned that Lee had also been writing to his Buckinghamshire neighbour, the Catholic peer Lord Loughborough, Master of the Horse under Mary.[46] Loughborough was arrested in April 1561 with 'divers persons for unlawful practices in religion'.[47] He was later released, and as with other leading Catholics of proven loyalty, his religious affinities appeared to do him little harm as long as he was discreet.

Lee was probably seeking Loughborough's aid over some local Buckinghamshire matter and. on the evidence of Lee's later letters, it appears entirely out of character that he was writing on religious matters. Throughout his life there was little to suggest he had Catholic sympathies. The incident illustrated, however, how warily one had to tread in the changing religious climate of the early years of the new reign. There was nothing in Lee's letter to Yaxley from Venice to suggest that he was using his travels abroad for any ulterior political or religious motive: he was merely passing on a factual report of an imminent conflict between Philip II of Spain and the Turks, and of the rebellion of the second son of Sultan Suleiman against his father. It is difficult to see how Yaxley could have put it to any real political advantage. Lee probably saw himself as part of the information-gathering service for Dudley, with whom he was also in correspondence in 1561.[48]

On his return from Italy, Lee leased a London lodging at the Savoy in February 1563 and developed a network of highly influential friends, including Sir William Cecil, the Queen's Secretary. Lee's friendship with the Queen's favourite Lord Robert Dudley, now Earl of Leicester also developed and in

---

[45]   TNA, PRO, SP70/19/1, f. 05. The internal evidence in the letter confirms that this correspondence was two-way and weekly.

[46]   *Calendar of State Papers, Foreign Series, of the Reign of Elizabeth 1561–1562* (hereafter *CSP Foreign*), ed. J. Stevenson, 23 vols (London, 1863–1912), p. 7 (4 March 1561); TNA, PRO, SP70/19/1, f. 05.

[47]   *CSPD*, XVI, p. 49; *CSPD, Addenda*, XI, p. 510 (8 April). Loughborough's imprisonment was brief, and he continued to serve actively as a Knight of the Garter until his death in 1572.

[48]   *Household Accounts and Disbursement Books of Robert Dudley, Earl of Leicester*, ed. S. Adams, Camden Society 5th Series, VI (Cambridge, 1995), p. 78. In 1561 Lee was not corresponding directly with Dudley.

February 1566 Lee welcomed him to his home at Quarrendon.[49] Lee may have supported Leicester's aspirations as a royal suitor, as he had Sir Thomas Smith's *Dialogue on the Queen's Marriage* copied for his library.[50] Lee's connections gave him the beginnings of a standing at Court. In an uncalendared letter from Sir Nicholas Throckmorton to Leicester on 9 May 1567, Throckmorton referred to a recent disagreement between the Earl and the Queen, but stated that 'I do judge by Sir H. Lee she meaneth to send your Lordship a token and some message'.[51]

When Lee next departed for Italy in June 1568, ostensibly in a private capacity, he conducted a somewhat safer correspondence with Cecil and Leicester. Although the ten letters Lee sent home from June 1568 to March 1569 are full of immediate and pertinent news from the Continent, it is not clear if his reports had any official standing. The flow of letters was two-way: Lee refers to letters he received from Cecil, although these have not survived. The indications are, however, that Lee's letters were sufficiently useful to Cecil for him to reply regularly.

For the first part of his journey to Italy, Lee travelled with his Buckinghamshire neighbour, Edward, Lord Windsor, the newly appointed ambassador in Italy. In Antwerp, the two men found time to have matching portraits painted by King Philip's former master painter Antonis Mor.[52] In this, the first portrait we have of Lee (see Ill. 1), he is shown as a handsome, athletic man, with disproportionately wide shoulders, betokening his skill with the lance and sword. The portrait is rich in the enigmatic symbolism typical of Lee's later portrait collection and indicates that by 1568 Lee could afford the fees of a notable artist.

There were, however, more pressing matters than portraits in the Netherlands in June 1568. In 1567 Philip II had sent the Duke of Alva to the Netherlands as captain general to subdue what was perceived as heretical unrest. In September 1567 Alva had instigated the punitive Council of Troubles in Brussels, and when the Regent, Margaret of Parma, departed in December 1567, Alva was appointed as Governor-General. Lee's first letter to Cecil, sent from the relative calm of Antwerp, was very detailed and suggests that Lee was attempting to prove his usefulness.[53] After giving military news from Friesland, he described the recent actions of Alva who

---

[49]   TNA, PRO, SP12/39/105 (20 February 1566).

[50]   Item 21, Taylor Medieval and Renaissance Manuscripts (Princeton University). This was formerly in the library of Viscount Dillon.

[51]   Reference is made to this in the introduction to *CSPD, Addenda 1566–79*, p. xv.

[52]   This portrait is analysed below in Chapter 6 with others in Lee's portrait collection. Lee's portrait now hangs in the National Portrait Gallery, London. The much-damaged matching portrait of Windsor is privately owned.

[53]   TNA, PRO, SP70/104b/36–38 (6 June 1568). The list of names is accurate with the exceptions of the Seigneur de Backerzeel and Antoon van Stralen, Burgemeester of Antwerp, who

... no what abstaynathe from his fyste begone course, but with more cruelte to the utter dysmeyng of all this contry. On twesday laste he begane his execusyon, on whyche day in Bryssealles dyed XXII gentellmen, on wensday III and yesterday beyng satterday Count d'Egmunt and Count Horne.[54]

Lee enclosed the names of twenty-five gentlemen, marking with crosses seven who were shriven by friars before death. He made no personal comment on the proceedings, other than noting that all the victims were gentlemen or nobles. The last execution on the list was on 5 June in Brussels. By the next day, Lee was forwarding a professionally inscribed list to Cecil from Antwerp, suggesting that Lee was not just the amateur bystander he claimed to be. Lee's letters, unlike official missives, always included useful gossip and rumour along with precise information, and he included a lively description of a dinner-table fight in Antwerp involving his former travelling companion John Smythe.

Lee then continued alone to Augsburg, sending Cecil and Leicester virtually identical letters about the hospitality he had received from the Prince of Orange, the military dispositions of the Elector Palatine and his son Casimir, the reaction among German princes to Alva's actions and the rumours of Emperor Maximilian II's condemnation of the executions in Brussels.[55] Lee was in a position to visit some of the leading courts in Europe and, unlike Windsor who had an official ambassadorial position, he could go anywhere the 'port ... and countenance of a gentleman' could take him. At thirty-five, he was a personable character, with confident, easy manners, and, from the evidence of his letters, many ranks of men were prepared to talk to him. Later letters show that Lee's sporting prowess made him a welcome guest at the many princely courts of Europe – prime places in which to gather news. From Florence, for example, he reported in December 1568 that he had frequently spoken to the Prince 'and since coming in his company, I have been twice or thrice a-hawking'.[56] The *entrée* into court circles accorded to sporting gentlemen was a recurring refrain throughout Lee's career.

It appears that Lee's initial role in Italy was to forward to Cecil 'advices', the confidential *avvisi* or handwritten newsletters that had a very limited circulation within diplomatic circles. He made his base in Venice, well positioned to receive the *avvisi* from Constantinople, which he mentioned in his letter from Venice sent on 21 August 1568. Lee was also eager to include his own observations, and in his early letters he took pains to stress both his kinship and loyalty to Cecil, begging him 'to command me as one that desyerath to searve

were executed on 24 September 1568.

54   TNA, PRO, SP70/104b/36–38 (6 June 1568).

55   HMC *Pepys* I, p. 119, TNA, PRO, SP70/98/41. See also SP70/102/90 (Padua); SP70/103/73–74 (Venice); SP70/104a/17 (Florence); SP70/106/133 (Venice). See also ORO, DIL XXI/12.

56   TNA, PRO, SP70/104a/17.

you ... withowt double dealyng'.[57] Lee wrote from Venice, Padua, Florence and Rome – principally of political events, such as rumoured royal marriages and alliances throughout Europe – and included details of the military movements in France of the Protestant princes, Casimir, William of Orange and the Prince of Condé.

In retrospect, his information was highly accurate. Many of the enclosures, the 'advyces from Constantynople', have not survived, but the advices from Rome to *All'Illustre S[ign]or et padrone mio Colend[issi]imo S[ign]or Arigo Leaa, cavallliero inglese*, 9 October 1568, have.[58] On this occasion, Lee forwarded three pages of detailed political information, some of it encoded. Lee's informant appears to have had a very precise knowledge of papal policy towards the Italian states; towards Alva and Philip II; to the Spanish in Naples; and to both the French King and the Emperor. It also mentioned the ample *denari* that could be sent from Rome to Catholic armies in France and Flanders. It is written from the inevitable conviction that papal opinion was central to all events in Europe, and possibly came from inside the Vatican itself. It is not clear whether Lee was the anonymous author of any other 'advices' now in the State Papers.

One recurrent issue which Lee reported home to Cecil, apart from the widespread effects of Alva's actions in the Low Countries, was the Catholic reaction to Emperor Maximilian II's granting the people of Hungary and Lower Austria permission to use the *Confessio Augustana*, the Lutheran Augsburg Confession, in August 1568. Lee referred to it in his letter from Padua in September, and the consternation it was causing in the Vatican was a major topic in his advices from Rome in October. In the same month Lee reported from Venice that the 'papal troops [are] to ... hinder the growth of the confession Augustana'.[59] In December 1568 Lee wrote from Florence to say that the Duke's son-in-law had been given the command of a papal army of 5,000 to determine 'the overthrowe of all contrary relygons', and also reported that the Florentine 'chieffe captayns of credyte' were flocking around him, offering support for his policies.[60] Given the international standing of Florentine banking, this was interesting news, especially in relation to events in England.

In Florence, where Lee had resided for several weeks, the Piazza Santa Croce was the scene of great public tournaments, as was the Strada Nuova in Genoa. Venice, from where Lee sent many of his letters, still holds the biennial Marostica, a medieval chess game with real people and horses, devised in the

57 TNA, PRO, SP70/102/90 (Padua).

58 TNA, PRO, SP70/103/35–37. To my knowledge, this has not been retranslated since Cecil's day; neither the HMC *Calendars*, nor Dillon and Chambers attempted a translation. I am grateful to Mel Marshall and Leofranc Holford-Strevens for their assistance with this.

59 TNA, PRO, SP70/103/73–74 (31 October 1568 from Venice); SP70/147/342 (20 November 1568 from Venice).

60 TNA, PRO, SP70/104a/17 (4 December 1568 from Venice).

fourteenth century to avert bloodshed between two jealous suitors, Venice was the home of the Compagnie della Calza who organized all the *spettacoli cittadin* (spectacles of the citizens).[61] The Palio in Sienna is still known worldwide: less well known is the annual Tilt of the Saracens still held in Arezzo. If these medieval public festivals are still celebrated in the twenty-first century, how much more prominent would they have been in the time of Sir Henry Lee? Perhaps it is no coincidence that when Lee returned to England he had the capability to devise the Accession Day tournaments as great public festivals in honour of his Queen.

In late December 1568, somewhat uncharacteristically, Sir William Cecil ordered the seizure of Spanish ships in the English Channel carrying money borrowed from Genoese bankers to pay Alva's army in Flanders. As Wallace MacCaffrey has rightly observed, Cecil's view of the international scene was changing, and his opinions were summed up in his official paper of January 1569 'A short memorial on the state of the realm'.[62] In this, Cecil outlined his conviction that there was a growing European Catholic crusade, in obedience to the Pope, directed against Protestants in the Low Countries, in France and especially in England. If the precise information Lee was relaying from Italy was typical of the 'advices' Cecil was receiving, his change of policy at this time is very understandable.

Lee's last Italian letter from Venice in March 1569 reported that, although the Pope had committed 11,000 horsemen and 12,000 foot soldiers to help the French King, the 'bruits of Italy' (i.e. rumours) were that Elizabeth would not willingly have wars against Spain. Lee was correct; war was averted, but he confessed that 'the fame of the warres wyll make me draw homeward sooner than I had ment ... to searve her majestie ... and my contre'.[63] If there was any possibility of England's going to war, Lee wanted to be part of it, as much out of personal inclination as for patriotism. He travelled home via the Imperial Court, again indicative of the level at which he was gathering his information.

Sir Henry Lee's letters from 1568 to 1569, as well as revealing much about his own aspirations and interests, clearly illustrate the machinations of Cecil's intelligence-gathering service. In his biography of Sir Horatio Palavicino, Lawrence Stone gives a graphic description of how Cecil and Elizabeth's spy-master, Sir Francis Walsingham, both came by their foreign information.[64] News came from a variety of sources – from official ambassadors in neutral

---

[61]   *The Elizabethan Garden at Kenilworth* (English Heritage, 2014), p. 5.1 offers evidence from the work of the Italian painter Zuccaro that knowledge of their nature had reached England.

[62]   W.T. MacCaffrey, 'Cecil, William, First Baron Burghley (1520/21–1598)', *Oxford Dictionary of National Biography* (Oxford, 2004), at: http://www.oxforddnb.com/view/article/4983; C. Read, 'Queen Elizabeth's Seizure of the Duke of Alva's Pay-Ships', *Journal of Modern History*, V (December 1933) pp. 443–64.

[63]   TNA, PRO, SP70/106/133 (5 March 1569).

[64]   L. Stone, *An Elizabethan: Sir Horatio Palavicino* (Oxford, 1956), p. 234.

and friendly countries, from Protestant leaders such as William of Orange and Henry of Navarre, and from international merchants whose business interests depended on knowledge of the current political situation. There then remained the murky world of the professional spies – what Stone calls the 'leaky and unreliable vessels as sources of military and political intelligence'.[65]

A major problem with Tudor espionage was the difficulty in assessing whether the information was reliable. This suggests that Cecil was using such information as Lee sent back to corroborate other sources. Lee frequently admits in his letters that Cecil is 'better advertysed by others', and there is little evidence to suggest he was acting in any official capacity.[66] To Sir William Cecil, Lee was a free source of information, a loyal kinsman he could trust, an experienced traveller with a keen military eye who could express himself well on paper and one who had the social *entrée* into many varied milieux. The effort Cecil put into conducting a two-way correspondence was a small price to pay.

Even though Lee does not mention it specifically in his letters, we know that many of the places he visited, especially Augsburg, would have served to enhance his developing interest in tournaments both as a public spectacle and as a way of preparing for participation in military conflicts. Indeed, when Lee passed through Augsburg in June 1568 his contemporary interest in tilting was indicated by his commission of a suit of armour at significant cost from the master craftsmen there.[67] Lee then retraced his steps from Italy in March 1569 through Germany, believing he was returning to an England at war.

Lee's Domestic Military Activities and his First Royal Appointment, 1569–1573

Although war with Spain failed to materialize, in November 1569 Lee arrived home in time to join the royal army sent to subdue rebellion in the north of England. It was a gentleman's duty to serve his monarch and the commonweal in a military capacity, but the government of Elizabeth and Sir William Cecil was reluctant to commit itself to war, and the years between 1564 and 1586 saw few opportunities for nobles and gentlemen to fight on the battlefield. Paul Hammer has observed that:

---

[65]   Ibid.

[66]   TNA, PRO, SP70/102/90.

[67]   Deutsches Historisches Museum, Berlin (hereafter DHM), *Monatsbild Januar-Februar-Marz*, Jörg Bren, 1531 (DHM 1990/185.1).

> ... in an age which placed an enormous premium upon martial exploits, wars were a necessary part of political and social life, while prolonged peace ... represented stagnation, moral decline and the loss of opportunity to display skill and courage.[68]

Gentlemen might serve in mustering troops in their counties, but many sought active military service. Some, like John Smythe, went abroad to fight as volunteers in France and in the Low Countries while others, like Sir Henry Lee, seized what few opportunities arose at home.

The 'Rising of the Northern Earls' had been precipitated by a conspiracy hatched in the spring of 1569 to overthrow Cecil and marry the Duke of Norfolk to Mary Stuart, the Scottish Queen, who was a prisoner in the north of England. Although the conspiracy had collapsed when Norfolk confessed all to Elizabeth, his co-conspirators, the Earls of Westmorland and Northumberland rose in rebellion at Durham in November 1569. The President of the Council of the North, Thomas Radcliffe, Earl of Sussex, was slow in dealing with the situation, and the Queen sent her cousin Baron Hunsdon north, rapidly followed by the Earl of Warwick and Baron Clinton with a royal army of some 20,000 men. This was the army that Sir Henry Lee and other loyal gentlemen joined as volunteers. Once again, Lee wrote letters home to Cecil, acknowledging that he was in no way supplanting the official reports, but substantiating suspicions about Sussex harboured by many in the Privy Council.

Sussex, approached initially by Norfolk's agent in spring 1569, failed to inform Cecil of the plot. When the northern earls rose in rebellion, Sussex was criticized by the Council for letting Northumberland escape from captivity and for being slow to raise an army. Cecil at this point had reason to exercise some caution and doubtless welcomed the first-hand opinions of a kinsman with military experience. On 14 December 1569 Lee wrote to Cecil from the military camp at Wetherby, saying:

> ... here be with our Lords many willing hearts; more of experience and counsel would do no hurt. The most of Lord Sussex's dealings that I mislike is that such as are known both for religion and dutiful zeal to her Majesty have less trust committed to them, and the contrary, more credit.[69]

Lee's military opinion was apposite; Sussex's loyalty was unimpeachable, but both Hunsdon and Warwick had seen more military action and few of the troops were experienced. Lee was sufficiently secure in his relationship with Cecil to commit his opinion to writing, criticizing not only his social superior, but also his commanding officer.

---

[68] P.E.J. Hammer, *Elizabeth's Wars* (Basingstoke, 2003), p. 10.
[69] *CSPD, Addenda 1547–80*, p. 151.

By 1569 Lee's letters revealed a growing confidence in his own opinions and his position vis-à-vis men of authority. His relationship with Sir William Cecil had developed into a friendship that lasted for the rest of their lives and would extend to Cecil's son, Robert. Lee had also achieved some favour with the Queen. In 1570 he had some undisclosed business in the court of the Archbishop of Canterbury, Matthew Parker, and the Queen wrote to the Archbishop 'in his favour'.[70] Cecil also wrote to Parker on the same matter, stressing 'how heartily I do love Sir Henry Lee for many good causes'.[71] By January 1571 Lee was being described as 'the Queen's servant' and in the same year he was first seen tilting at Court.[72] Later in 1571 Lee purchased Edward Dyer's patent as steward of the Queen's manor at Woodstock and established himself as the *de facto* administrator of the property.

Re-established in royal favour and with a potentially promising Court career in view, Lee would have been quite justified in retiring from any military involvement. The fact that in 1573 he felt himself free to volunteer to fight at the siege of Edinburgh Castle is indicative of his desire to serve his Queen and country on his own terms. Lee was a man of forty with private means who, despite his responsibilities at Woodstock, chose to retain some freedom of action. This was not unattractive to Elizabeth, who admired chivalric prowess in her male courtiers. In later years Lee would take pride in his role with the army, and it militated against claims that tournaments were merely courtly posturing by those with no genuine military experience. At the siege, Lee not only acquitted himself with distinction, but once again sent his private opinions home to Cecil, now Lord Burghley, 'synce I am on the stage a bistander'.[73]

The situation in Scotland had been volatile and confused for several years. After the collapse of the Northern Rebellion in 1569, the northern earls had fled into Scotland, making common cause with supporters of the exiled Mary Stuart, led by William Maitland of Lethington. The head of the regency government in Scotland, the Earl of Moray, had entrusted the nation's greatest stronghold, Edinburgh Castle, to Sir William Kirkcaldy of Grange, an experienced commander who had fought in France for Henri II. Moray himself was assassinated in 1570, and Maitland persuaded Kirkcaldy to defect to the Marian rebels. Together, they held Edinburgh Castle for Mary, with its ordnance, Crown jewels and State Papers in what became known as the 'Lang Siege'.

In 1573 Sir Henry Killigrew, Elizabeth's agent in Scotland, brokered an agreement between the new regent, the Earl of Morton and other Marian rebels,

---

[70]   John Strype, *Life and Acts of Matthew Parker*, 4 vols (London, 1711), IV, i, p. 527.

[71]   Parker, M., *Correspondence of Matthew Parker DD, Archbishop of Canterbury*, ed. J. Bruce and T. Perowne for the Parker Society (Cambridge, 1853), p. 354 (24 September 1569).

[72]   TNA, PRO, C66/1076. Lee's role at Woodstock is discussed below in Chapter 3.

[73]   BL, Cotton MS, Caligula CIV, ff. 91–2.

leaving Kirkcaldy and Maitland isolated in Edinburgh Castle. The possibility of French aid to the besieged castle finally galvanized Elizabeth into action, and in April 1573 Sir William Drury, commander of the English garrison at Berwick, was ordered to take Edinburgh Castle with some 1,500 men and thirty-three pieces of artillery. Regent Morton joined him with 500 Scots troops, ranged against a castle garrison of only 150 defenders.

Drury's force was joined by a certain number of 'gentlemen of name', who 'serve[d] at their own free wile', including Sir Henry Lee. Henry Killigrew, himself a veteran of the attack on Boulogne in 1563, had little regard for the military capabilities of these 'newly-come courtiers' and thought them better suited for dancing attendance on the Queen than enduring the rigours of war.[74] The composition of this group, ranging from men in the prime of life to excitement-seeking youths, illustrates the aspirations of a cross-section of Elizabethan courtier-gentlemen. Sir Henry Lee was one of the older members of the group; he also had the most military experience and his own company of recruits. Others, such as the Queen's cousin Sir George Carey, William Knollys and Burghley's son Thomas Cecil, had seen action against the northern rebels in 1569. There was a number of inexperienced young courtiers: William Killigrew, younger brother of the ambassador, Edward Dyer and the future Master of the Revels, Edmund Tilney.[75] Together, they had youth, enthusiasm, experience in the tiltyard, chivalric aspirations and a certain *esprit de corps*. They also demonstrated how eager Elizabeth's young lions were to prove themselves in the crucible of war, and how difficult it was to find the opportunity.

Lee was first to admit to Burghley that he had little ideological commitment to the action, '[these] being causes not pertaining to me', and his letters reflect the fact that the predominant sympathy of the English officers appeared to be with the besieged Maitland and Kirkcaldy.[76] Regent Morton was 'wise and wily', whereas 'Kirkcaldy [is] well-beloved here of all sorts ... for his valour and wisdom'.[77] Lee reserved his chief scorn for the Scots in general, 'in appearance only religious but in effect traitorous'. As allies, he failed to understand or trust them.

> Ys not Scotland a poor, barren and ne[e]dy contry, full of people rather cravyng increase than able to spare any thyngs? Wyll the[Scots] nobles and gentellmen, in who was never truth nor constancy, newly reconcyled ... suffer us, being

---

[74]   TNA, PRO, SP52/25/42 (Killigrew to Burghley).

[75]   Holinshed, *Chronicles*, V, p. 669.

[76]   Maitland, a former friend of Burghley's had been instrumental in securing Henry Killigrew's release from a French prison in 1563; Kirkcaldy had a longstanding friendship with Sir William Drury, and his professionalism, military abilities, chivalry and valour were respected by all.

[77]   BL, Cotton MS, Caligula CIV, ff. 91–2 (11 May 1573).

strayngyers ... to spoyll that place of wealth wherin the honour of this contry lyeth [the castle].[78]

Lee feared for the English ordnance, suspecting that the Scots 'will covet ... that which they so much need', leaving the English forces 'in hazard'.[79]

Nevertheless there was a job to be done, and the volunteer gentlemen were welcome. Drury began his attack on the castle on 4 May 1573, personally commanding the battery opposite the castle's principal fortification. The other sides of the castle were bombarded by batteries on four mounts, commanded by Lee, George Carey, Regent Morton and Thomas Sutton, a seasoned English captain.[80] Lee's expertise might have been with armour and cavalry, but on this occasion he showed his competence in commanding cannon. Killigrew reported to Burghley by 22 May that Sir Henry Lee's breach was 'in more forewardness', and on 26 May, during a feigned assault at Lee's breach, Drury stormed the main entrance. Much of the castle was reduced to rubble, occasioning a major reconstruction of the buildings. Strenuous efforts were made by Drury to save the lives of Maitland and Kirkcaldy after the surrender, but Lee was percipient when he wrote of the Regent, 'the fear he hath to the aforenamed two will make him thruste more greedily after their bodies, that he may live hereafter more qui[et]ly'.[81] Maitland, already sick, died in captivity on 9 June, and Kirkcaldy was hanged in August 1573.[82]

At the end of the siege, Lee's position of favour with the Queen proved useful to Sir William Drury. He and Killigrew had sent efficient official military and diplomatic accounts of the action to Cecil, but something more personal was required for Elizabeth. Lee had not only the military credibility, but also the innate courtliness and imagination to act as personal raconteur. On 31 May 1573 Drury sent Lee to the Queen, advising Burghley that 'the particularities of winning the Castle are referred to Sir Henry Lee, who saw the experience thereof'.[83] Lee gave a good account of the action, and on 8 June the Queen wrote to Drury, stating:

---

[78]   BL, Cotton MS, Caligula CIV, ff. 91–2 (11 May 1573).

[79]   BL, Cotton MS, Caligula CIV, ff. 91–2 (11 May 1573).

[80]   *Calendar of State Papers relating to Scotland and Mary, Queen of Scots,* (hereafter *CSP Scotland*), vol. IV: 1571–74, ed. William K. Boyd (London, 1905), p. 568.

[81]   BL, Cotton MS, Caligula CIV, ff. 91–2.

[82]   It was Elizabeth herself who ordered Drury to turn over Maitland and Kirkcaldy to Regent Morton. On 31 May Morton told Burghley that the fate of the prisoners 'rests now in her majesty'. At the end of July Morton finally received advice from Queen Elizabeth that she would leave 'the judgment and ordering of those matters to him': *CSP Scotland*, 1571–74, pp. 575, 582.

[83]   Ibid., p. 276.

... by the lively report of our trusty servant, Sir H. Lea, knight, who like a very good gentleman, has had his part therein, we do most certainly understand the continuance of your labours and dangers to have been such that none could be more.[84]

Paul Hammer makes the salient point that the Queen recognized that 'going to war would require her to delegate her royal authority to distant commanders and weaken her control over events'.[85] Elizabeth was sensitive to the fact that, as a woman, she would never emulate her father and lead the army herself: any detailed information that enabled her to believe that she was still au fait with the military situation would make her look favourably upon the messenger. At a time when most courtier gentlemen could only aspire to military experience and tournaments were mocked as mere posturing, Lee's commendations on the battlefield provided solid evidence of his practical expertise and his loyalty to Queen and commonweal. One consequence was that in November 1573 Lee was rewarded with the reversionary lease to the lieutenancy of Woodstock, his first major royal appointment.[86]

Some Initial Reflections on Lee's Early Life

This account of the early life of Sir Henry Lee raises an obvious question: how significant were his early activities to his later life? Leaving aside the fact that Lee was thirty-five before his first royal appointment, his early life and experiences made him the man he was – the man who eventually found favour with Elizabeth. His family had been armigerous for several generations, so the vain pursuit of a coat of arms through documents fabricated by the heralds was not for him. He had the assurance of a man of considerable property; he had been tested on the battlefield and found his courage to be more than adequate; he had visited the courts of Europe and acquitted himself well. He had much to offer his Queen and commonweal, and the experience and freedom of action to choose how he would serve.

Lee waited a long time to return to royal favour. If he had been too young to appreciate the career of his uncle, Sir Thomas Wyatt, he was old enough to learn from the example of his father-in-law, Lord Paget, and experienced for himself the vicissitudes of Court life. Courts were splendid places; gentlemen might become ennobled, but favour was fickle. Knights of the Garter could be made

---

[84]   Ibid., p. 581. Lee maintained his interest in northern events and on 25 February 1581 sat on a parliamentary commission on the bill to fortify the frontier with Scotland.

[85]   Hammer, *Elizabeth's Wars*, p. 59.

[86]   See Chapter 3 below.

and unmade on a whim: a royal councillor could find himself in the Tower facing a ruinous fine, and a change of monarch could signal the end of a promising career. Elizabeth's Court was a place for back-biting, gossip and slander. A young courtier gentleman might be dazzled by its energy and dangled promises, but Lee, as an older man, preferred to serve his Queen at some distance. By 1573 he had found his own solution to the problem. In future years he would receive and entertain the Queen lavishly at the royal manor of Woodstock when she came to him on progress, and he would devise the Accession Day tournaments in her honour, where he himself would determine the action.

Chapter 2

'The Queen's Knight': Sir Henry Lee and the Elizabethan Tournaments

By the late sixteenth century tournaments, for long the premier entertainment in European courts, were rapidly becoming outmoded as firepower replaced naked steel in the technology of war. In Elizabeth's England, however, tournaments enjoyed something of a renaissance, thanks to the Queen's own enthusiasm for the sport and the efforts of Sir Henry Lee. He instituted the Accession Day tournaments, held annually on 17 November, to commemorate the Queen's accession on that day in 1558. Although Lee has popularly been known as the 'Queen's Champion', it was not a title he himself claimed, nor was it in the Queen's gift to bestow. The hereditary dignity of Champion of England or 'King's Champion' was held by the Dymoke family of the manor of Scrivelsby, Lincolnshire. Sir Robert Dymoke had delivered the Loyal Challenge at the coronations of Richard III, Henry VII and Henry VII, and his son Sir Edward Dymoke had filled the same role at the coronations of Edward VI, Mary I and Elizabeth I. By tradition, Sir Edward's son Robert should have inherited the position after his father's death in 1566. However, he had been imprisoned as a Catholic recusant, suffered a stroke and died in 1580. In the absence of a legal claimant, Sir Henry Lee assumed the *de facto* role of personal champion to the Queen at tournaments, issuing the formal challenge to anyone who would dispute her honour, proudly wearing the Queen's colours and leading out the Challengers onto the tiltyard against the Defenders. He exercised this role until his retirement in 1590, when the Queen accepted George Clifford, Earl of Cumberland, as her champion.

The Tournament Traditions Inherited by Sir Henry Lee

The earliest concept of the tournament was as a brutal practice for even more brutal warfare, fought à *l'outrance* with sharp-edged weapons and resultant carnage and loss of life. The tournament as an expensive chivalric Court entertainment, fought à *plaisance* with rebated or blunted weapons, was developed in the mid-fifteenth century at the court of René of Anjou and at the Burgundian courts of Philip the Good and Charles the Bold. It became widely adopted throughout Europe, with chivalric literature, festival books, elaborate scenery and dramatic programmes. England's own tournament traditions had already been codified by John Tiptoft, Earl of Worcester, who formulated the first rules of jousting in English in 1466. The Burgundian tournament genre was first seen in England in 1467 when the negotiations for the marriage of Margaret of York, sister of Edward IV, to Charles the Bold occasioned an initial tournament between the Burgundians and the English at Smithfield in London. The actual marriage in 1468 was marked by a magnificent *Pas d'armes de l'Arbre d'Or* in the marketplace at Bruges, and Sydney Anglo points out that the allegorical references to 'Florimont, knight of the Golden Tree', which ran throughout the eight days of jousting, in no way detracted from 'the consummate artistry of the exercises and feats of the necessary disciplines of Arms'.[1] This was jousting that required genuine skill, not merely the symbolic breaking of lances that Anglo claims was the norm in the late Elizabethan Court. It set a high standard for any subsequent tournament devisers.

It was Henry VII who did most to introduce the Burgundian tradition of tournament into England, with the arrival of Katherine of Aragon to England in November 1501 as the bride of Arthur, Prince of Wales. Katherine's sister, Juana, had married Philip the Fair of Burgundy in 1496, and Henry VII wished to emulate the celebrations of the most fashionable court in Europe with a great spectacle, marking the first foreign marriage for the new Tudor dynasty. William Cornish devised the festivities, and a distinct narrative thread ran through the action, with knights in pageant-cars fashioned as dragons, ships or castles, fantastical pavilions and a tree of chivalry. Gordon Kipling makes the point that only the lack of a literary text to accompany the action distinguishes these tournaments from those of the Elizabethan Accession Days organized by Lee.[2] The spectacle, however, was for private Court entertainment: only Katherine's entry into London was public.

The high point of the English tournament was reached in the reign of Henry VIII, with the King himself leading some forty recorded jousts between 1509 and 1529. Whereas many were simply Court entertainments to celebrate Christmas or Shrovetide, some were great triumphs. The tournament of February 1511 that marked the birth of Henry's short-lived son cost some £4,000, nearly twice the cost of his warship, the *Great Elizabeth*, and was celebrated in The Great Tournament Roll of Westminster. In June 1520 the meeting of Henry VIII and Francis I of France at the Field of Cloth of Gold was marked by jousts, tourneys and barriers.

---

[1]   S. Anglo, 'Anglo-Burgundian Feats of Arms: Smithfield June 1467', *Guildhall Miscellany*, II, 7 (1965), pp. 271–83.

[2]   For a full description, see G. Kipling, *The Triumph of Honour: Burgundian Origins of the Elizabethan Renaissance* (The Hague, 1977), pp. 72–95; S. Anglo, *Spectacle, Pageantry and Early Tudor Policy* (Oxford, 1969), pp. 56–92.

Sir Henry Lee's family had long been associated with these spectacles. His grandfather, Sir Henry Wyatt, had organized the finance for many of the tournaments and at the Christmas Revels of 1524–25, Lee's uncle, Sir Thomas Wyatt, was among the jousters defending the 'Castle of Loyalty'. A new tiltyard was built at Whitehall for the coronation of Anne Boleyn in 1533, but tournaments declined after Henry VIII's spectacular fall during a tournament in 1536 had left him unconscious for more than three hours. This marked the end of the King's personal participation in the sport, and no triumphs marked the birth of Henry VIII's son Edward in 1537 as the Queen, Jane Seymour, died very shortly after. There was little reason to impress foreign ambassadors, and the King's own declining physique made him unwilling to hazard the tourney or watch younger, fitter men excel at a sport he had once made his own.

Tournaments under Edward VI were tailored more for the King's tender years. The traditional coronation tournament was held in 1547, but full participation in the sport was not allowed until a youth had reached his majority. Notwithstanding this, the young king participated enthusiastically in the training exercises for boys – 'running at the ring' – or 'the Justes of the hobihorses', held on New Year's Day 1553.[3] When Edward's sister, Mary I, came to the throne later that year, she had little enthusiasm for tournaments, but her Spanish husband, Philip, a long-time *aficionado* of the sport, was eager to reintroduce them at Court for his own reasons. Relations between his Spanish gentlemen and those English gentlemen detailed to serve him were often fraught: it was reported that 'not a day passes without some knife-work in the palace between the two nations', and Philip saw the tournaments as a way of bonding his bellicose servitors.[4] The King, with his Spanish retainers, had treated the Court to a display of traditional Spanish cane-play or *jeugo de canãs* on 25 November 1554, but this had failed to impress the English.

Nothing loathe, Philip issued a challenge for a tournament on 18 December 1554. The tilting list for the tournament reveals that the King led a team of Challengers drawn from both nations, whereas the Defenders were dominated by the three Dudley brothers: Ambrose, Robert and Henry.[5] All three had been implicated in their father's plot to place Lady Jane Grey on the throne in 1553, but the rising had failed, and John Dudley, Duke of Northumberland, was executed. His sons were imprisoned for some time in the Tower, but Philip's need to include English tilters in his tournament gave the Dudley brothers a chance to restore themselves in royal circles. The tournament itself was so successful that it was repeated on four other occasions before Philip's departure

---

[3]   Henry Machyn, *The Diary of Henry Machyn – Citizen and Merchant-Taylor of London (1550–1563)*, ed. J.G. Nichols, Camden Society Old Series XXXII (London, 1848), p. 7.

[4]   *Calendar of letters and State Papers relating to English affairs principally in the archives of Simancas Spanish*, Volume XIII of XX, July 1555–November 1558, pp. 60–61 and 74 (20 October 1554).

[5]   College of Arms (hereafter CA) MS, Portfolio of Tournament cheques, ILL3b.

for Brussels in September 1555, giving many young English courtiers their first experience of tilting.

Queen Elizabeth's own obvious enthusiasm for Court spectacles saw a new flowering of tournaments after her accession in November 1558, and she, as much as Lee, can be credited with the revival of interest in the sport. The two-day tournament to celebrate her coronation in January 1559 was postponed, but three other tournaments were held that year with Robert and Ambrose Dudley as leading Challengers.[6] Tiptoft's fifteenth-century Ordinances were re-adopted in 1562, and these gave the occasions a greater degree of formality. What actually happened in an Elizabethan tournament had deep historical roots. Sir Henry Lee inherited a tournament structure that had remained largely unchanged in England for several centuries, and it was upon this that he built the allegorical rhetoric and courtly spectacle that characterized the Accession Day tournaments. The practical running of the tournament was handled by the Heralds of the College of Arms, who derived much of their income from the activity. The College had been reorganized in 1555 under the Duke of Norfolk as Earl Marshal, and the heralds' tournament duties more clearly codified. Initially, a Challenge or 'cartell' would be proclaimed by the heralds. This was often written by the knights themselves. Lee himself wrote 'A cartell for a challenge', Sir Henry Lee's Challenge before Shampanie'.[7]

In the case of international tournaments, these 'cartells' would be issued several weeks or even months ahead, and the heralds would make lists of those knights who agreed with the Challenge – the Challengers – and those who refuted it – the Defenders. The Crown was responsible for the upkeep of the four tiltyards in London at Westminster, Whitehall, at Greenwich near the Almain Armourers' workshop and at Hampton Court. The majority of Elizabethan tournaments were held at Whitehall, with Hampton Court being kept for practice or for when the plague struck in London. In the days immediately prior to the tournament, the tilt rail, the judgehouses, the stands for spectators and the temporary stairs leading to the Queen's windows were erected at the Crown's expense, and these are clearly illustrated in contemporary pen-and-ink sketches (see Ill. 2).[8]

As Elizabeth's tournament Champion, Sir Henry Lee was naturally conversant with *imprese* and *imprese* shields. These latter were the pasteboard shields, presented to the monarch by the participating knights. William Segar of the College of Arms erroneously complained that 'emblems devices poesies [*sic*] and other Complements were lost'. However, in Tudor times many of the *imprese* shields were hung in the Shield Gallery at Whitehall Palace, something

6   CA, MS, Portfolio, 4A, 4b, 4c, 5a, 5b, 5c.
7   BL, Add. MS 41499, f. 1.
8   TNA, PRO, E.351/3204–3229.

which was seen and commented upon by several visitors and recorded by Thomas Platter, Lupold von Wedel and even Samuel Pepys. The Shield Gallery took its name from the shields offered to the monarch on the occasion of the tournaments in the Whitehall Palace tiltyard that started in 1559. The Queen ordered these to be held twice a year, the first on her birthday and the second on 17 November, the anniversary of her ascent to the throne.

Lupold von Wedel also offered his readers a detailed description of an Accession Day tournament. When the Queen and Court had assembled, the knights, by tradition twenty-four, would enter the tiltyard with their entourages and pasteboard *imprese* shields. Everybody who wished to take part had to ask the Queen's permission. Once this had been granted, the knight offered his pasteboard *impresa* shield to the Queen, who ordered it symbolically to be hung up initially on a specially constructed 'Tree of Chivalry', a relic of the medieval Burgundian *Arbre d'Or*, for eventual transfer to the Gallery.[9] The creation of a suitable *impresa* with its enigmatic devices and classical mottoes, obliquely referring to their hopes and aspirations, often taxed the ingenuity of a knight more than the actual jousting. In 1593, in a letter to his wife, Sir George Carey commented on 'euery gallants best employed witts, best to shew themselfs at the cowrs in the filde, witty in theyr shilde deuises and pleasinge in the choyse of theyr presents'.[10]

The tournament itself consisted of three parts: the joust, where a knight would break six lances with his opponent across a tilt barrier; the tourney, or *grand mêlée*, where all the knights fought on foot simultaneously with swords; and barriers, which was one-to-one combat on foot across a barrier, often fought with staves (see Ills 2, 3(a) and 3(b)). The whole contest was governed by the rules of chivalry and adjudicated by the judges who sat at a little distance from the tilt barrier. The College of Arms in London holds a unique collection of score cheques or tilting tables, on which the scores of the knights were kept by the heralds either by marking the number of broken lances or pricking the sheet with a pin (see Ill. 4).[11]

In the evening, the Queen awarded symbolic prizes to the knight who 'hath justid best of all'.[12] Knights were responsible for their own armours, horses and accoutrements, but items of armour such as vamplates and the staves and lances

---

[9]   Lupold von Wedel, 'Journey Made through England and Scotland in the Years 1584 and 1585', *TRHS*, New Series IX (1895), p. 236.

[10]   Berkeley Muniments, General Series, Letter Bundle 4, reproduced in Katherine Duncan-Jones, 'Christs Teares, Nashe's "Forsaken Extremities"', *Review of English Studies*, 49, 194 (May 1998), pp. 167–80.

[11]   CA, MS, M4 bis, ff. 1–58b; CA, Portfolio of Tournament cheques; S. Anglo, 'Archives of the English Tournament: Score Cheques and Lists', *Journal of the Society of Archivists*, II, 4 (1961), pp. 153–62.

[12]   CA, MS, Portfolio of Tournament cheques.

used were supplied by the Tower of London Armoury. Many knights maintained their expensive armour at the Tower, and Sir Henry Lee was later appointed Master of the Armoury, a position traditionally filled by a good exponent of tournament skills.

Although one had to be at least of gentry status to participate in the 'triumphs' at Court, the sixteenth-century score cheques held at the College of Arms suggest that a very open attitude pertained as to who could or could not participate.[13] Prowess at the sport was the overriding criterion. Mere gentlemen tilted against peers of the realm and known Catholic adherents tilted alongside men of extreme Protestant views. Some jousters were members of the aristocracy; some were drawn from the ranks of the Gentlemen Pensioners; and many, like Lee, were courtier gentlemen, eager to show their ability. There were also professionals: score cheques reveal the continued presence of Robert Alexander, alias Zinzan, and later his sons Henry and Sigismund, of Hungarian extraction, who were employed to provide training and skilled opposition for aspiring tilters at Court.[14]

Lee's Tournament Experience

Lee is first recorded as tilting in 1571, as one of the 'four knights errant' who challenged some twenty-seven 'excellent men of armes … late fallen asleep from any kynde of expertise'. Clearly, this was not Lee's first excursion in the sport; by that date, he was thirty-eight, jousting alongside renowned tilters such as Charles Howard and Christopher Hatton and acquitting himself exceptionally well. The score cheque for the occasion and the 'tilting table' show that Lee and Edward de Vere, the young earl of Oxford, were the two highest-scoring participants, both breaking thirty-two lances out of a possible forty-two.[15] Tilting at this level entailed a great deal of practice and expensive equipment. Experience could be gained in the royal tiltyards in London: some great houses, such as Kenninghall in Norfolk and Kenilworth, boasted their own tiltyards. Lee is not recorded as having participated in the tournaments held by King Philip in the winter of 1554–55, or in the coronation tournament of 1559, but not all tournament score cheques have been preserved. A good jouster was always in demand, if only for practice sessions, and many young court gentlemen gained their initial experience and expertise in this way.

---

[13]   CA, MS, M4 bis; CA, MS Portfolio of Tournament cheques.

[14]   Lee's later letters show he maintained a close relationship with both father and son, commending Robert to positions after the latter's retirement. See Cecil MS 78.32 (HMC Salis., XI, p. 156), (Lee to Sir Robert Cecil, 3 April 1601).

[15]   CA, MS, M4 bis, f. 1, Bodleian Library (hereafter Bodl.), MS, Ashmole 845, f. 164.

It is possible that Lee gained tournament experience in 1568 and 1569, during his travels in Germany and Italy where the sport was popular. The itinerant Imperial Court staged great spectacles, as did the Estes in Ferrara, and he could have seen public tournaments in the Strada Nuova in republican Genoa and at the Piazza Santa Croce in Florence. Lee's letters to Cecil make no reference to tournaments during his travels, but Lee's first suit of armour gives us a possible clue. The *Almain Armourer's Album*, held at the Victoria and Albert Museum in London, is a folio collection of water-colour sketches of armours made at Greenwich from around 1555 until 1588, many by Master Armourer Jacob Halder. Included in the album is an illustration of Lee's first armour, inscribed 'Sir Henrie Lee. This feld armor was made beyond see' (see Ill. 5(a)).[16] Where exactly was this made? During the sixteenth century some of the finest armour came from Augsburg, and Halder himself trained there until his move to England in 1557. Alan Williams observes that Augsburg and Greenwich technologies are very similar and it is often difficult to know in which armoury different parts of an armour were made.[17] Certainly, an armour created in Augsburg could have added to in Greenwich. Not surprisingly, Augsburg was a centre for tournaments; the four superb *Monatsbild* painted panels executed by Jörg Breu the Elder in 1531 show a lavish tilt and tourney proceeding in the central square there.[18] Lee passed through Augsburg in June 1568; he could well have participated in a public tournament and commissioned a suit of armour from the master craftsmen there.

Lee retraced his steps from Italy in March 1569 through Germany, believing he was returning to an England at war. Wherever Lee purchased his first armour, the cost must have been significant, and the purchase sufficiently important to Lee to warrant it. The *Armourer's Album* also shows that Lee's armour had additional pieces or garniture essential for tournament purposes, and the illustration bears the inscription 'Thes tilte peces wer made by me Jacobe' (see Ill. 5(b)). The garniture must have been made in England because Halder had been in Greenwich since 1555. By 1569 Lee was sufficiently sure of his ability as both soldier and tilter to spend a substantial sum on the best foreign armour, confident that he could acquire the matching garniture in England.

Tournament experience could also be gained in foreign royal courts since the organizers of international tournaments often requested the participation of English tilters. On 30 November 1570 the French ambassador La Mothe Fénelon presented a request for '*un ambassade extraordinaire au roi et aux*

---

[16]   Victoria and Albert Museum (hereafter V & A), *An Almain Armourer's Album*, D664 and D664A (1894).

[17]   A. Williams and A. de Reuck, *The Royal Armoury at Greenwich, 1515–1649* (London, 1995), p. 99; A. Williams, *The Knight and the Blast Furnace* (Leiden and Boston, MA, 2003), p. 361.

[18]   DHM, *Monatsbild Januar-Februar-Marz,* Jörg Bren, 1531 (DHM 1990/185.1).

seigneurs anglais d'assister au tournoi ... en France' to celebrate the marriage between Charles IX and Elizabeth of Austria in March 1571.[19] There is no proof that Lee was among these gentlemen, but the request suggests that there were opportunities for gentlemen of ability, presence and courtliness to acquire tournament skills at the highest level.

In Elizabeth's reign there were four distinct types of occasion on which tournaments were held, and Sir Henry Lee participated in the majority of them from 1570 until his retirement in 1590. First, tournaments were used as Court entertainment – to mark events such as a coronation, Twelfth Night, Shrovetide or visits from foreign notables – and the cost of these would be borne by the Exchequer. Lee took part in a tourney held by torchlight on 14 June 1572 to entertain the Duke of Montmorency, an ambassador from Charles IX, sent to ratify the Treaty of Blois.[20] Other foreign dignitaries were similarly entertained. Sir Henry Lee issued the Challenge before le Sieur de Champagny in February 1576, as the 'straunge knight ... in hewe of greene', and Duke John Casimir of Heidelburg was welcomed with a tournament in February 1579.[21] The Duke of Anjou watched the Accession Day tournament in November 1581 and then participated in the tournament held in January 1582. On 1 December 1584 a *hastiludum*, a joust between ten married men and ten bachelors was held for the entertainment of the Court, with Lee competing against the brother of his future mistress, Thomas Vavasour.[22]

Second, individual courtiers often staged tournaments to celebrate family weddings, and even though these were held at Whitehall, the cost was borne by the families. A three-day celebration was held in November 1565 to mark the marriage of Ambrose Dudley, Earl of Warwick, and Anne Russell, and on 17 December 1571 jousts were held for the marriage of the Earl of Oxford to Burghley's daughter, Anne Cecil.[23] As Burghley's friend and Oxford's tilting partner, Lee took part in the latter occasion.

The third type of occasion, and the one that was most controversial, was the tournament staged entirely by private individuals for the exclusive entertainment of the Queen and the Court. These spectacles, where the instigator bore all the expenses, were few and costly, suggesting that those who staged them had ulterior political motives and were taking an expensive gamble in an effort

---

[19]   *Correspondance Diplomatique de Bertrand de Salignac de la Mothe Fénelon Ambassadeur de France en Angleterre de 1568 à 1575*, ed. J. Teulet, 7 vols (Paris and London, 1838–70), III (Depesche du dernier jour de novembre 1570).

[20]   BL, Cotton MS, Titus C10, f. 16a.

[21]   BL, Add. MS, 41499A, f. 1; TNA, PRO, 31/3/27 (preparation of the tiltyard and Accession Day tournaments).

[22]   Bodl. MS, Ashmole 845, f. 168.

[23]   CA, Portfolio M6, 8a–8c 1565; CA, M4, ff. 4a, 7, 5a. This latter, in the hand of the Clarencieux Herald, Robert Cooke, is misdated 17 December 1572.

to influence the Queen. The entertainment itself needed an authored text to make the argument clear, and this would usually be printed and circulated with some speed to reach a wider audience. There was always the risk that the Queen might take offence at the message implied. The Earl of Leicester set something of a precedent for this type of entertainment, combining a tilt and tourney with *Gorboduc*, a dramatic presentation performed first at the Inner Temple and then at Court in January 1562. In 1565 he staged a tournament at Court, followed by a masque in which the goddesses Juno and Diana debated the virtues of marriage as opposed to chastity. Guzmán de Silva, the Spanish ambassador, reported that 'the Queen turned to me and said "this is all against me"'.[24] In 1575 the entertainment Leicester staged during Elizabeth's visit to his home at Kenilworth had originally included a tournament, but this was cancelled when the Queen cut short her visit.

In 1581 Philip Howard, son of the fourth Duke of Norfolk, issued and published *The Earl of Arundel's challenge by Callophisus*.[25] The Norfolk title had been rendered extinct by the fourth Duke's treason and execution in 1572, but Philip Howard inherited his grandfather's title, *jure matris*, on the death of Henry Fitzalan, Earl of Arundel, on 24 February 1580. Howard's title to the earldom was questioned before the Privy Council, and his expensive and lavish tournament staged on 22 January 1581 was an attempt to win the Queen's favour. Howard tilted against the Earl of Oxford, Philip Sidney, Lord Windsor and Fulke Greville, and although Lee did not participate in this contest, the manuscript preserved at Lee's home at Ditchley contains several pages of unpublished text from the triumph, suggesting that he had contributed to its planning.[26]

The most spectacular of the privately funded tournaments was the 'Fortress of Perfect Beauty', depicting Elizabeth as Queen and woman under siege from the 'Four Foster Children of Desire', Philip Sidney, Lord Windsor, Fulke Greville and Arundel. The entertainment clearly referred to the Queen's impending marriage to the Duke of Anjou and was staged on 15 and 16 May 1581 before the Court and the French commissioners sent to negotiate the matter. The tournament was accompanied by music and a full dramatic text, which was immediately printed by Henry Goldwell.[27] The four did not perform alone: their Challenge was met by twenty-one Defenders, including Sir Henry Lee, who entered 'in the midst of the running as Unknown'.

---

[24] *Calendar of letters and State Papers relating to English affairs preserved principally in the archives of Simancas Spanish* (hereafter *CSP Spanish*), 4 vols (London, 1894), Eliz. 1558–1567, p. 404.

[25] *RSTC* 4368.5. The Challenge was printed and circulated in London on 16 January 1581.

[26] CA, MS, M4, f. 22a–b; BL, Add. MS 41499, f. 6a.

[27] Henry Goldwell, *A brief declaration of the shews, devices, speeches and inventions performed before the Queen's majestie & the French ambassadors* (London, 1581), *RSTC* 11990.

The political purpose and efficacy of the piece, which eventually showed the Queen to be an impregnable fortress, resistant to siege by the Children of Desire, has long been debated. Katherine Duncan-Jones voices the conventional thesis that this lavish two-day spectacle was funded entirely by Leicester, Sidney's uncle, in opposition to the Queen's marriage with Anjou.[28] Susan Doran disagrees, arguing that 'there can be little doubt that this production was commissioned by the queen, and therefore an official statement of policy and not merely another public relations exercise by opponents of the match'.[29] Philippa Berry is sceptical about this explanation.[30] The Privy Council was divided over the French match, as were the 'Four Foster Children' themselves in private life. The spectacle was originally scheduled to be staged in April 1581 and was delayed twice at the Queen's request, suggesting that Elizabeth and many other members of the Court were far from making up their own minds over the French marriage.

In 1595 Robert Devereux, Earl of Essex, extended the personal use of the tournament to a wider audience when he staged the scripted drama of *Erophilus* or *Love and Self-Love* during the public Accession Day tournament of that year, holding up the tilting action for twenty minutes while the crowd grew impatient. George Peele recorded that Cumberland, who had entered the tiltyard first as Queen's Champion, stood 'impacient of Delaie, awayting there his friendly foes approache'. When Essex continued his *Erophilus* drama in the evening in place of the barriers, Elizabeth was not amused and retired to bed, saying 'if she had thought their had bene so much said of her, she wold not haue bene their that Night'.[31] It would appear that while the Queen welcomed praise and laudation of herself in public, any attempt to give counsel or criticism was best kept for a private occasion.

The fourth type of occasion marked by tournament, and the one most closely connected with Sir Henry Lee, was the anniversary of the Queen's accession on 17 November. These annual public contests came to dominate the tournament scene in England and from 1588 they replaced all other tournaments. The occasion often marked the Queen's return to London from her annual progress and her chambers were prepared in Whitehall, 'her highness comynge thether to see the Triumphe and Running at the tilt'.[32] Sir William Segar, in both his *Booke*

  [28]   K. Duncan-Jones, *Sir Philip Sidney, Courtier Poet* (London, 1991), p. 204.
  [29]   S. Doran, 'Juno versus Diana: The Treatment of Elizabeth I's Marriage in Plays and Entertainments, 1561–1581', *The Historical Journal* (hereafter *HJ*), XXXVII (June 1995), pp. 257–74.
  [30]   Philippa Berry, *Of Chastity and Power: Elizabethan Literature and the Unmarried Queen* (London, 1989), p. 113.
  [31]   A. Collins, *Letters and Memorials of State … [of the Sydney family]*, 2 vols (London, 1746), I, p. 362.
  [32]   TNA, PRO, E351/542 (Woodstock), f. 31v, November 1581 (Accounts of Sir Thomas Heneage, Treasurer of the Chamber).

of honor and armes (1590) and in *Honor Military and Civill* (1602), suggested
that it was at the commencement of Elizabeth's reign in 1558 that Sir Henry Lee

> ... voluntarily vowed (unlesse infirmity, age or other accident did impeach him)
> during his life, to present himselfe at the Tilt armed, the day aforesayd yeerly,
> there to performe, in honor of her sacred Majestie the promise he formerly made.[33]

Despite Segar's claim, the existing evidence suggests that 'these annual exercises in
Armes' began later in the reign. David Cressy has made the plausible suggestion
that the defeat of the northern rebels in 1569 had sparked off spontaneous
rejoicing, with bell-ringing, bonfires and national celebrations that were rapidly
adopted as annual festivities for what came to be called 'Crownation Day'.[34] In
London, the celebrations took the form of church services, followed by the
public Accession Day tournament at Whitehall.[35] The Exchequer records are
unclear whether preparations for the first November tournament were made in
1569 or 1570, but as Lee was still with the army in Wetherby in November 1569,
the latter date is more feasible.[36]

The November tournament rapidly became an annual event. The French
ambassador La Mothe Fénelon recorded in 1572 that on 17 November tilts were
usually held at Court, and his successor M. de Castelau refers to a November
tournament in letter to Henri III of 24 November 1577.[37] Score cheques exist
for 1574 and 1578, indicating no month but having the same format as those for
later Accession Day tournaments.[38] A tournament was held on 17 November
1580, and from November 1581, an unbroken set of score cheques gives clear
evidence that Accession Day tournaments were held annually. From 1588
the occasion became a two-day affair – extended to include 19 November,
St Elizabeth's Day – to commemorate England's deliverance from the Spanish
Armada.

The Accession Day tournaments differed in many ways from other 'triumphes'
held at the English Court, or anywhere else in Europe. They were held on a fixed
date, 17 November, and the verses in the Adam Ottley manuscript, attributed

---

[33]   Segar, *Honor Military and Civill*, p. 197.

[34]   D. Cressy, *Bonfires and Bells: National Memory and the Protestant Calendar in Elizabethan
and Stuart England* (London, 1989), pp. 50–57.

[35]   In 1576 a special liturgy was added to the Prayer Book for 17 November.

[36]   Exchequer records TNA, PRO, E.351/3204 run from 1567 to 1572, and are unclear
whether preparation of the tiltyard took place in 1569 or 1570.

[37]   Fénelon, *Correspondance Diplomatique*, V, pp. 203–4; TNA, PRO, 31/3/27.

[38]   See TNA, PRO, E351 series for preparations to the tiltyard at Whitehall; also TNA,
PRO, E351/542 – Sir Thomas Heneage's accounts for 'making ready for her Matie ... against the
running'. Score cheques CA, MS M4, f. 4 (1574) and CA, MS M4, f. 3 (1578) show the year and
running order but not the month.

to Philip Sidney, show that even if 'her day on which she entred' fell on a Sunday, the 'Sainte of the Saboath' was still entertained with triumphs.[39] The tournaments were annual, only being cancelled twice because of the plague in 1582 and 1592, and postponed once because of bad weather in 1599.[40] The tournaments were also public: members of the Court, invited dignitaries and ambassadors had seats on the erected stands, but the occasion was open to all the citizens of Elizabeth's England who could afford the 12d entry fee. Lupold von Wedel, a Swiss traveller, gives us an eyewitness account of this during the 1584 tournament. He describes 'thousands of spectators, men, women and girls ... not to speak of those who were within the barrier and paid nothing'.[41] Von Wedel's account suggests that the tournaments followed the relatively fixed format of tilt, tourney and barriers, but with an increasing emphasis on spectacle and pageantry. The knights themselves entered the tiltyard with their servants 'disguised like Irishmen, with hair hanging to the girdle like women ... the horses equipped like elephants'. The pages approached the stairs to the Queen's window and, as the mouthpiece of their masters, would flatter and amuse the Queen with extravagant speeches and present a costly gift. Von Wedel painted a vivid picture, but his details were not always correct: for example, he credited the Earl of Oxford and the Earl of Arundel with the overall victories in 1584. In fact, neither tilted that year, as Oxford was in disgrace with the Queen and Arundel was in the Tower.

The financing of the Accession Day tournaments is far from clear. The tiltyard itself and the erection of the tilt, judgehouse and stairs to the Queen's window were clearly paid for by the Exchequer but, by and large, this was all the Crown paid for. The Master of Revels received a payment to attend the occasion and prepare a festival book, but played no role in the tournament itself. [42] Some payment was made to the College of Arms and to the heralds themselves who ran the tournaments, and by tradition the heralds were allowed to claim any item that dropped to the ground as part of their fee, but these would have been ransomed by individual knights. The contestants themselves paid for their own armour, horses, equipment and entourage as well as for a present for the Queen and this could run into several thousand pounds. In November 1580 Philip Howard, Earl of Arundel, paid *'tout la despence qui est fort grande'* for the tournament and had earlier, in 1578, been accused by his family of wasting

[39]   P. Beal, 'Poems by Sir Philip Sidney: The Ottley Manuscript', *Library*, 5th Series, 33 (1978), pp. 284–95. The Adam Ottley manuscript is held at the National Library of Wales, and the poems AT19, AT21 and ATOt are quoted in full in H. Woudhuysen, *Sir Philip Sidney and the Circulation of Manuscripts* (Oxford, 1996), pp. 413–15.

[40]   CA, MS M4, ff. 54v–55v.

[41]   von Wedel, 'Journey Made through England and Scotland', pp. 258–59.

[42]   Albert Feuillerat (ed.), *Documents relating to the Office of the Revels in the time of Queen Elizabeth* (London, 1908), p. 391.

'a great part of [his] Estate … by profused expences of great Summs of money in diverse Tiltings & Tourneys made upon the anniversary dayes of the Queen's Coronation'.[43] Londoners paid an entry fee to view the proceedings, ranging over the years from 'the spence of a few pence' to 12d in later years, but who benefited from these fees is uncertain: clearly, it was not the jousters. The Accession Day spectacles became the only tournaments to be held at Court after 1587, and an increasingly parsimonious Queen relied on them to entertain foreign ambassadors. It was reported in 1590 that 'these sports were great and done in costly sort, to her Majesty's liking and their great cost'.[44]

Lee's Role in the Accession Day Tournaments

In 1590 Sir William Segar claimed that Lee was the instigator of the Accession Day tournaments, and in an undated tournament speech Lee described himself as the 'first Celibrater in this kind of this sacred memorie of that blessed rayne'.[45] Lee had no official salaried role like the traditional organizers of Court events in the Office of Revels. The inception of the Accession Day tournaments in 1570 coincides with the time when Lee first came into royal favour, and the internal evidence of existing sources confirms that Lee played a major role in deciding the content of the tournaments. It is highly significant that Lee was the principal Challenger in the majority of tournaments between 1570 and 1590, acting as the Queen's Champion and fighting for her honour.

In 1605 Joshua Sylvester gives a retrospective description of Lee in his prime as:

> … hardy Laelius, that great Garter-Knight,
> Tilting in triumph of Eliza's right
> (Yearly the day that her dear reign began)
> Most bravely mounted on proud Rabican
> All in gilt armour, on his glistring mazor
> A stately plume of orange mixed with azure,
> In gallant course, before ten thousand eyes,
> From all defenders bore the princely prize.[46]

---

[43]   TNA, PRO, 31/3/28, f. 203a; H.G. Fitzalan-Howard, *The Lives of Philip Howard Earl of Arundel and of Anne Dacre, his Wife* (London, 1857), p. 7.

[44]   Edmund Lodge, *Illustrations of British History*, 3 vols (London, 1791), II, p. 419.

[45]   BL, Add. MS, 41499A, ff. 1–1v.

[46]   Joshua Sylvester, *Bartas, his Devine Weekes and Workes* (London, 1605). Laelius was the name given to Lee by Sidney in his *New Arcadia*, identified in J. Hanford and S. Watson, 'Personal Allegory in the Arcadia: Philisides and Laelius', *Modern Philology*, XXXII (August 1934),

'Laelius' was the name given to Lee by Sir Philip Sidney, when Lee makes a brief appearance in Sidney's *New Arcadia* (see Appendix 5). 'Rabican' was the name of Astolpho's horse in *Orlando Furioso*, but its use here was probably more a literary compliment to Lee than an accurate reflection of the name of Lee's horse. George Peele, in *Polyhymnia* describes Lee as 'Knight of the Crown' and gives a vivid picture of Lee at the start of his retirement tilt of 1590: [47]

> Mightie in Armes, mounted on a puissant horse,
> Knight of the Crown in rich imbroderie,
> And costlie faire Caparison charg'd with Crownes,
> Oreshadowed with a withered running Vine
> As who would say, My Spring of youth is past;
> In Corslet gylt of curious workmanship,
> Sir Henry Lea, redoubted man at Armes
> Leades in the troopes.

We also have a glimpse of how Lee appeared from the brightly coloured folios of the *Almain Armourer's Album*, which show three of Lee's suits of armour and their garniture.[48] His first suit of armour was decorated with gilt chevrons and eagles reaching for bright suns (see Ills 5(a) and 5(b)). His second suit, made some time after 1580 when he became Master of the Armoury, was decorated with bands of etched and gilt strapwork linked with quatrefoils and shows a lanneret holding a heron's leg (see Ills 6(a) and 6(b)). His third suit of armour, probably made around 1586, was field armour (see Ills 7(a) and 7(b)). This still exists virtually complete in the possession of the Armourers' and Brasiers' Society (see Ill. 8). Despite the illustration shown in the *Album*, there is no sign that the one currently in existence has ever been decorated, and no tournament garniture was recorded as having been made for this suit. Lee would have been mounted on 'great horses', and a later letter refers to his 'saddles of tawny velvet'.[49]

Lee was more than just the instigator of, and leading Challenger in, the Accession Day tournaments. He also acted as impresario, putting together or collaborating with other participants to devise an entertainment for the Queen that reflected loyalty, chivalric values, sporting prowess, Renaissance allegory and good humour. The chief evidence for Lee's role, apart from later laudatory accounts, is the miscellany of texts that were obviously used at the Accession Day

---

pp. 1–10. Sylvester's use of the name in 1605 would suggest that its association with Lee was recognised by contemporaries.

[47]   George Peele, *Polyhymnia, describing the honourable Triumph at Tylt* (London, 1590), *RSTC* 260.

[48]   V & A: Lee's first Armour with garniture is D599 and D599A, Lee's second armour isD604 and 604A, Lee's third armour is D610 and 610A.

[49]   BL, Lansdowne MS 89, f. 160. no. 82.

tournaments, preserved for centuries in manuscript at Lee's home at Ditchley, Oxfordshire.[50] In his twenty years of influence over the event, the tournaments increasingly combined chivalric sport with the use of tournament texts and addresses to the Queen.

Frances Yates sees Lee weaving a 'chivalrous romance' around the Queen from his entertainment for her at Woodstock in 1575, through the tournament texts to his Ditchley entertainment in 1592.[51] The texts in the Ditchley manuscript are, however, mostly undated and can only occasionally be put into context by internal evidence. Nor is it clear that Lee himself was the author of the texts. Yates and other writers, such as Alan Young, are prepared to affirm that Lee was the author without offering any actual proof.[52] A more satisfactory suggestion is that many of the 'tiltyard devices', including Arundel's Challenge as Calliphisus and Sidney's 'Fortress of Perfect Beauty', were the result of collaborative efforts.

It is also unclear whether Lee's innovations were the result of collaboration with Philip Sidney and Edward Dyer, both courtiers, poets and protégés of the Earl of Leicester. Lee and Edward Dyer had worked together at Woodstock from 1572, when Lee obtained the reversion of Dyer's patent as Steward. Both were heavily involved in the entertainment for the Queen's visit to Woodstock in September 1575, and there is evidence that both not only contributed to its text, but also took part in the dramatic action. Philip Sidney was in the Queen's entourage on that occasion, and this may have been his first meeting with Lee and Dyer. Dyer became a member of what Sidney termed the Areopagus with Sidney's boyhood friend Fulke Greville, writing poetry together from the late 1570s.

Lee had travelled with Sidney, Greville and Dyer on embassy to the court of Emperor Rudolf II in Prague in spring 1577, and, despite the age difference, friendships developed on that journey. Lee appears to have been not a little influenced by the charismatic younger Sidney and, unlike on his earlier travels, there is no evidence that Lee kept Burghley privately abreast of events on the journey.[53] In subsequent years Sidney and Lee tilted together, Sidney gave Lee a manuscript copy of his *Old Arcadia* and they shared a lodging at Theobalds

50   BL, Add. MS 41499A.

51   Frances Yates, *Astraea: The Imperial Theme in the Sixteenth Century* (London, 1975), pp. 96 7.

52   A.R. Young, *Tudor and Jacobean Tournaments* (London,1987), pp. 152–4.

53   J.M. Osborn, *Young Philip Sidney 1572–1577* (New Haven, CT, 1972) pp. 478–9. At forty-four, Lee was probably chosen by Burghley as a more mature, steady companion to accompany the impressionable twenty-three year-old Sidney and his friends, and the absence of Lee's letters is interesting. It is possible that Lee even concealed things from Burghley. Languet, Sidney's mentor and former tutor in France suggested that Sidney was attempting to marry the sister of John Casimir of the Palatinate and 'Monsieur Ley was privy to the scheme'. Sidney's marriage into a foreign ruling house would have been anathema to Elizabeth.

during the royal progress in 1583.[54] After Sidney's death at the Battle of Zutphen in 1586, it was Lee who would stage the first public English tribute to him at the Accession Day tournament that same year.[55]

A Conjectural Case Study of the Tournament Entertainment, 16–17 November 1577

Lee has not left an orderly collection of documents describing how a collaborative entertainment was devised, but if one puts together miscellaneous sources possibly relevant to the 1577 November tournament, a picture emerges which, if only conjectural, can give us a fair indication how a tournament entertainment might have been assembled under Lee's hand.

The score cheque held by the College of Arms and dated 1577 in the contemporary hand of Robert Cooke, Clarencieux King of Arms is usually considered to be the first one existing for an Accession Day tournament and the first to name Philip Sidney as making his debut as a tilter (see Ill. 9).[56] On closer inspection, it becomes clear that this document, like several others, has been wrongly dated by Cooke and is in fact the missing score cheque for the 'Fortress of Perfect Beauty' tilt in May 1581. What has not been previously noted is that, if the score cheque was correctly dated, the 'earl of Arundel' listed would, in 1577, would have been the seventy-five-year-old Henry Fitzalan, a little old for tilting even by Lee's standards, who himself tilted until the age of fifty-seven.[57] We do, however, have proof that a November tournament was held in 1577. The French ambassador M. de Castelau, writing to Henri III on 24 November, mentioned that the 'Sieur de Havré, brother of the Duc d'Ascot' had just watched the '*ung tourney de gentilz-hommes qui couroyent en lice*' ('a Tourney of gentlemen, who ran in the lists').[58]

We have no proof that Philip Sidney tilted on this occasion, but at some point around that date he would have made his debut in the tiltyard, and it was typical of what we know of Lee that he would have had some care of novices. Sidney drew on his early experiences when he wrote *New Arcadia* sometime after 1580, in which Philisides tilts against the older Laelius in the tournament (see Appendix 5).[59] Laelius, identified as Lee,

---

[54]   Cecil MS, 140.31.

[55]   BL, Add. MS 41499A, f. 7.

[56]   Young, *Tudor and Jacobean Tournaments*, p. 154; Woudhuysen, *Sir Philip Sidney*, p. 275.

[57]   Henry Fitzalan, born in 1502, was Earl of Arundel until his death on 24 February 1580, when his grandson, Philip Howard, inherited the title.

[58]   TNA, PRO, 31/3/ 27. The 'Duc d'Ascot' was Philipe de Croÿ, Duke of Aarschot, Governor-General of Flanders.

[59]   Philip Sidney, *The Countess of Pembroke's Arcadia,* ed. M. Evans (Harmondsworth, 1977), II, 21, pp. 351–5.

... was known to be second to none in the perfection of that art, ran ever over his head – but so finely, to skilful eyes, that ... he showed more knowledge in missing than others did in hitting.

By 1584, the only year for which a score cheque exists definitely showing Lee tilting against Sidney, Sidney had ceased to be a novice in need of fostering care. This suggests that Sidney first tilted against Lee at some point between 1577 and 1580. As a friendship had developed between Sidney, Dyer and Lee during the embassy to Prague in 1577, there is no reason why they should not have collaborated to devise the November tournament of that year.

A study of the tournament texts which are still extant adds to the picture. In the Ditchley Manuscript there is an unpublished text of an entertainment much in the same style as that held at Woodstock in 1575.[60] The whole tale is too long for use during an actual tournament, and the reference to 'tilting on the morrow' suggests that it was an entertainment held the day before the tournament, perhaps as a Saturday evening entertainment at Court on 16 November. The simple tale is full of asides, which again suggests it was intended for a specific audience who would understand innuendoes lost on the general public. There is, for example, reference to the Queen as 'such a Jewell ... (with the best eies besides that happened to see it)'. In their private correspondence, Elizabeth often referred to her favourite, Leicester, as 'her eyes', and as Leicester frequently acted as a judge for the Accession Day tournaments, it would suggest that he was at Court beside the Queen to see the entertainment.

The tale is narrated to the 'most excellent princesse' by a hermit on behalf of a 'homely rude Companye ... of Shepherds & heardsmen, breaders of Cattell & followers of the plough', led by 'a worthy Knight as Constant in Faith as variable in fortune ... clownishly clad'. Dyer had already played the hermit in 1575 at Woodstock, and Lee's own motto, *Fide et Constantia*, would identify him as the knight, as does the later reference to his vow. The knight, we are told, had become disenchanted with the Court despite his love for 'the Mistress of the place' and took himself away to the 'simple hermitage' of the narrator. Later, he withdraws 'in a little lodge': by 1577 Lee held four lodges at Woodstock, with High Lodge as his main house.

The knight's rustic neighbours later come to him with news of 'a holidaye wich passed all the pope's holidays & that shold be kept the seaventeth day of Noueamber'. The Knight 'rememberinge then the vowe he had made ... to sacrifice yearly the strength of his arme, in honor of her that was Mistress of his hart' would have hurried towards the Court had he not been stopped by his neighbours, 'makinge merye with this homely melody' and desiring to accompany him. They claimed that 'so shall we see for the Spence of a few pence the godliest ladye ... so shall we see Justinge and we will just too'. When the knight tells them that 'this noble exercise apperteynes not to men of your birth', they reply, 'we know not of pedigrees, perhaps we come as gentle blood as some of them'.

This was possibly a humorous reference to the current practice of obtaining fabricated pedigrees from the College of Arms – even Sir Henry Sidney, Philip Sidney's father, had been prepared to pay for a pedigree proving Sidney's descent from the fictitious 'Sir William de Sidenie'.[61] The rustics then insist that the hermit accompany them to put their petition case to the Queen, that 'they might have leave to morowe, among the noble gentlemen, to rune if they cannot Tilt ... at the Quintyne'. The quintain was a rustic version of tilting at a stuffed Turk's head, and Elizabeth had seen local countrymen running at the quintain during her stay at Woodstock in 1575.

The rustic characters in this play reoccur in the poems in the Adam Ottley manuscript, recognized as Sidney's and designed to be used during a tournament.[62] The poem 'Philisides the Sheapheard good and true' was 'to be said by one of the Plowmen after that I [Sidney?] had passed the tilt with my rusticall musick'. The line 'Sing neighbour sing, here you not say this Sabboth day' confirms that the poem could have been written for 17 November, which, in 1577, was a Sunday. The only other relevant occasion when 17 November fell on a Sunday was in 1583, when Sidney definitely did not tilt.[63] Even if this reconstruction of the events of 16–17 November 1577 is erroneous, it nevertheless gives a template for the tilt in Sidney's *New Arcadia,* a fictitious representation of a tournament with its origins in reality.

The Multiple Purposes of the Accession Day Tournaments

Under Lee's benign aegis which lasted until 1590, the Accession Day tournaments retained their initial purpose of good sport and good public entertainment in the Queen's honour. From 1588, however, a number of factors were combining to change the nature of the tournaments, and these reflected the increasing domination of the event by the Queen's new favourite, the Earl of Essex. Elizabeth was notoriously reluctant to change the old guard of her advisers at Court, and many of the rising younger generation at Court who had taken part in the Armada emergency now found they had no further outlet for

---

[61] Centre for Kentish Studies (hereafter CKS) (Penshurst Papers) U1475 E93, T4/1–25; U1475 E93, F15.

[62] Poems AT19, AT21 and AT Ot. See Beal, 'Poems by Sir Philip Sidney'.

[63] CA, MS M4 bis, f. 30a.

their military aspirations or even their new armour. For some, the tournament was the only arena in which both could be aired in public.

Several of these tensions showed themselves in the spectacular tournament in November 1590 that marked Lee's retirement, and it says much for Lee's powers of showmanship that he withstood the competition from the younger generation for self-promotion. Sir Henry Lee, his courses run, remained silent until the end of the tournament. Then, in a pageant full of allegory and music, he offered up gifts and his own armour to the Queen, 'beseeching she would take the earl of Cumberland for her Knight, to continue the yeerely exercises.'[64] Yet Lee and Cumberland, despite the Queen's gift of magnificent Greenwich armour, were close to being upstaged by the young Earl of Essex.[65] Essex rode high in Elizabeth's favour, but the discovery of his secret marriage to Sir Philip's Sidney's widow in 1590 had landed him in temporary disgrace with his monarch. At the tournament, he appeared

> ... all [in] Sable sad,
> Drawn on with cole-blacke steeds of duskie hue;
> In stately Chariot full of deepe deuice
> ... this great Champion
> Young Essex, that thrice honourable Earle
> Yclad in mightie Armes of mourners hue. [66]

Whether Essex was still in mourning for the death of his friend, Philip Sidney, or for the loss of his own popularity with the Queen was not clear. Certainly, he resented Cumberland being named as 'the Queen's Knight' instead of himself; a later Hilliard miniature depicts Essex with the Queen's favour, her glove, tied to his arm over his armour. Another of the Essex coterie was also drawing attention to himself on 17 November 1590. Sir Charles Blount, lover and later husband of Essex's married sister, Penelope Rich, was wearing her colours very prominently in the tiltyard, and he is described in *Polyhymnia* as 'Rich in his colours, richer in his thoughts / Rich in his fortune'. Adoration of the Queen on her special day did not appear to be a priority among this younger group of courtiers.

---

[64] J.C. Nichols, *The Progresses, Public Processions etc. of Queen Elizabeth*, 3 vols (London, 1823; New York, 1967), III, p. 49. Lee's authorship of the poem that marked his retirement tilt in 1590 'My Golden lockes are to silver turned' is agreed on by many; see Thomas Clayton, 'Sir Henry Lee's Farewell to the Court: The Texts and Authorship of his "Golden Locks Time Hath to Silver Turned"', *English Literary Renaissance*, 4, 2 (1974), pp. 268–75.

[65] The Queen's gift of armour to Cumberland, one of the finest ever produced by the Greenwich armourers, is now in the Metropolitan Museum of New York (hereafter MMNY) 32.130.6.

[66] Peele, *Polyhymnia* (*RSTC* 260).

From 1590 Essex dominated the tournaments, especially those held on 19 November, to commemorate England's victory over the Armada. On 19 November 1594, and again in 1596, Essex single-handedly challenged all eighteen opponents. Essex's attempt to promote himself before the Queen by staging an entertainment during the 1595 tournament was received badly, but it is indicative of how he viewed both himself and the occasion that he believed it acceptable to delay the jousting on the Queen's Accession Day tournament for his own ends. Essex made the tournament popular with other younger members of the peerage, with the effect of driving up the cost of participation as they vied with each other for self-promotion. Sir Henry Lee, by royal command, continued to attend the tournaments on 17 November as a judge, on one occasion appearing as 'a pore faythfull feeble knight yet once yor fellowe in Armes'.[67] Accession Day tournaments continued to be held on 17 November until 1603, when the accession of a new monarch changed the date to 24 March. They then became an increasingly outdated form of entertainment at Court and ceased to be held after 1624.[68]

Given the vast fortunes that could be spent on them, it has long been accepted that most tournaments could be, and were used as, a vehicles for political propaganda, thus copying those Lee had witnessed on the Continent.[69] Monarchs used them for entertaining and impressing visiting foreign dignitaries, for underlining dynastic occasions and for demonstrating the chivalric prowess of their nobility. Individuals could use them to gain the attention of their monarch or to make political points. The Accession Day tournaments, however, were somewhat different, in that they were great public events not necessarily directed or financed by the Crown. They involved several thousands of people, actively participating in the combat, organizing the event, watching from the Court areas or merely being part of the appreciative crowd. Any one tournament could conceal a variety of agendas. Even the crowd of London citizens had their own reasons for being there – they were good days out and, unlike the public theatre which was rapidly gaining popularity, the Accession Day tournaments were the only occasions when the people could pay to be entertained by members of the Court. Courtiers were very aware of this: the Earl of Essex, for example, exploited it to raise popular support for himself, although other less agile courtiers were careful not to make complete spectacles of themselves before the common crowd. So what were the various purposes of the Accession Day tournaments, and to what extent did they change over time?

Sir Henry Lee's overt intention each 17 November was to honour his Queen and celebrate her Accession Day. A close reading of Lupold von Wedel's account

---

[67]   BL, Add. MS 41499A, ff. 1–1v.

[68]   See scored and unscored cheques in CA MS M4bis.

[69]   See Chapter 1 above.

of the 1584 Accession Day tournament shows that it was an exuberant public spectacle, the ultimate celebration of the Queen's Day and a superlative London reflection of the hundreds of smaller celebrations that were being held all around the country. In this massive display of public diplomacy, Elizabeth herself only played the passive role of observer. Von Wedel's account dwells far more on the crowd and the participating knights than on the Queen's actions.[70] Lee's purpose each year was to stage an entertainment to amuse and praise his Queen. As her champion, he would defend her honour – not that anyone at the tournament would have dreamt of impugning it. In 'leading in the troops' for the tournament, traditionally the monarch's role, Lee took care not to usurp the Queen's position as the focus of the occasion. The laudatory phrases that abounded while Lee was in charge, however, tended to be nationalistic – 'this English holiday or rather Englands happie daye' – rather than any ode to a Fairie Queen.[71]

As Accession Day tournaments were great public affairs, the government of Elizabeth I was well aware of their value for propaganda purposes. As the threat from Spain became more imminent, Burghley was quite prepared to use any public opportunity to foster loyalty to the regime and to the Queen personally. Roy Strong and Frances Yates initially suggested that a deliberate cult was fostered by Elizabeth's government, using portraiture, literature and Court pageantry, with Lee and the Accession Day tournaments playing a major role in the creation of this cult.[72]

Other historians have taken issue with this view. Carole Levin has seen the Queen as 'the master-builder of her own public image', while Susan Frye sees the creation of the royal image as the result of interplay between the Queen and her subjects, not necessarily at public tournaments. Helen Hackett has correctly suggested that much of the evidence for a cult comes from late in the reign and Susan Doran, on the evidence of portraiture, argues that the term 'cult' is inappropriate and denies an orchestrated campaign of image-making for propaganda purposes.[73] Evidence to support the ideas contained within these varying theories therefore exists, but there is no evidence that the 'cult' was deliberately sponsored by the government or by the Queen herself. Indeed, if this did occur, it appears likely to have been in the last decade of the reign when

---

[70]   See Appendix 3.

[71]   BL, Add. MS 41499A, f. 1.

[72]   See Yates, *Astraea*, pp. 88–111; R. Strong, *The Cult of Elizabeth* (London, 1977), pp. 129–34.

[73]   C. Levin, *The Heart and Stomach of a King: Elizabeth I and the Politics of Sex and Power* (Philadelphia, 1994), p. 27; S. Frye, *Elizabeth I: The Competition for Representation* (Oxford, 1993); H. Hackett, *Virgin Mother, Maiden Queen*, 2nd edn (Basingstoke, 1996), p. 8; S. Doran, 'Virginity, Divinity and Power: The Portraits of Elizabeth I', in S. Doran and T. Freeman (eds), *The Myth of Elizabeth* (Basingstoke, 2003), pp. 171–200.

national unity was paramount, the succession was in doubt and the Queen was attempting to control public images of herself.[74]

What cannot be doubted is that Lee created an occasion that could be used for propaganda, if the Queen and her councillors so desired. The overall spectacle of the cream of the Queen's knights, sumptuously dressed with accompanying trains which they themselves funded, jousting in the Queen's honour in front of an immense crowd of loyal Londoners demonstrated national loyalty and martial skill to the invited foreign ambassadors and visitors. But if the government was deliberately making propagandist use of the event, it was strangely amateur in doing so. Despite the great crowd that came to watch, the government put little money into the event. Elizabeth herself did not process or show herself in public during the tournament, as she did on entering her capital after a summer progress or opening Parliament, two of the other activities usually undertaken in November. She merely watched the tilting from the window of her chambers with her ladies, and was visible to very few.

On the Continent, court tournaments had always been held for specific propaganda purposes, publicizing events such as coronations, weddings and christenings, which reinforced the continuity of the dynasty. Lavish tournament books were printed before the event, often reflecting activities that never actually took place, reinforcing the political message of the occasion. In England, tournament books were certainly produced. In 1588, when Edmund Tilney was the Virgin Queen's Master of the Revels, Burghley certainly used the fame of the participants for propaganda purposes. At the height of the Armada crisis that year, a 'Copie of a letter' was published in England and on the Continent, purporting to have been sent to the Spanish ambassador Bernardino Mendoza by an English Catholic informant giving a 'true' account of the defeat of the Spanish Armada from English eyes.[75] The real author was Lord Burghley himself, and the account showed that, much to the 'surprise of the Catholic writer', the majority of the aristocracy and gentry of England had risen to defend the country against the Spanish. Among the named heroes are many that appear on the tournament score cheques of 1585, 1586 and 1587 – the Earl of Cumberland, Thomas Gerard, Thomas Vavasour, Charles Blunt, Henry Nowell, William Hatton, Robert Carey, and Arthur Gorges and William Harvey 'not to me known but here about London spoken of with great fame'.

This account contains many inaccuracies – it claims that Burghley's son Robert Cecil fought against the Armada – but it does show that Burghley was prepared to use the fame of the jousters to drive home his point that all the

---

[74]   Dasent, *APC*, I 1596–97, p. 69.

[75]   William Cecil, *The copie of a letter sent out of England to Don Bernardin Mendoza, ambassadour in France for the King of Spaine* (London, 1588), *RSTC* 15412; BL, Lansdowne MS 1157.

gentlemen of England were loyal to the Queen, even the Catholics. Overall, the Accession Day tournament was sufficiently important to the government for it to be chosen in an extended form as the permanent commemoration of the victory over the Spanish in 1588.

Individual jousters derived a marked degree of personal satisfaction from their participation in the sport, an element that cannot be easily evaluated and is seldom discussed. The ultimate occasion for it was the November tournament, when some twenty-four knights rode out before the Queen, the Court and a crowd of more than 8,000 spectators. What it must have been like to have been one of that number is seldom chronicled; Philip Sidney comes closest to giving us a description in *Astrophil and Stella*. This was something to which the courtier gentleman aspired. Excellence at the tilt was advocated in the best courtship manuals, and young gentlemen sought to emulate the heroes of chivalric romance, from Mallory's *Morte D'Arthur* to Ariosto's *Orlando Furioso*.[76] The cult of chivalry was venerated in European courts in general in the sixteenth century as 'an honour cult that promoted jousts, tournaments, portraiture and literature of knightly romance'.[77] Not every man at Court had the ability to tilt, and to be one of the exclusive group who rode out on 17 November was, if only momentarily, to be among the gods.

Other advantages the jousters enjoyed were the strong sporting camaraderie that existed among them and the *entrée* into privileged circles that the sport gave them. Lee, a courtier gentleman with few direct family connections to the aristocracy, jousted alongside the cream of the peerage and developed lifelong friendships. In 1571 Lee tilted with Charles Howard, the future Lord Admiral, and Christopher Hatton, the future Lord Chancellor. By 1572 he had developed a personal relationship with Thomas Howard, Duke of Norfolk and Earl Marshal of England. For example, Lee received visits as a friend at Quarrendon from Robert Dudley, Earl of Leicester; tilted at Dudley family weddings; acted as godfather for Leicester's illegitimate son, Sir Robert Dudley; and frequently hunted with Leicester at Kenilworth. These friendships probably arose through their mutual association with the tournaments. Tilting as he did until the age of fifty-seven, Lee enjoyed personal connections with several generations of young courtiers, including Sidney and Essex.

The jousting fraternity could be a somewhat volatile group, composed as it was of ambitious young warriors, and Richard McCoy sees Elizabethan tournaments as a 'class safety valve, allowing a socially sanctioned and carefully regulated

---

[76]   Castiglione wished his courtier 'to be an accomplished and versatile horseman ... he should put every effort and diligence into surpassing the rest just a little in ... the tilt and joust [and] in tourneys'. B. Castiglione, *The Courtier*, trans. and ed. George Bull (London, 1967), p. 63.

[77]   J. Adamson (ed.), *The Princely Courts of Europe* (London, 1999), p. 19.

release of aggressive energies'.[78] This was more true of later tournaments. Under Lee's aegis, antagonism between tilters did not appear to spill over publicly into the Accession Day tournaments. The tilting fraternity was no easy group to keep in line, but the quarrel between the Earl of Oxford and Philip Sidney of August 1579, for example, did not prevent them tilting side by side in January 1581. Arthur Gorges' quarrel with Lord Windsor in 1580, which saw him sent to the Marshalsea prison for brawling in the Presence chamber, did not prevent them tilting at the same tournament that year. Oxford and Thomas Knyvett tilted together in 1581, despite a deadly quarrel over Oxford's seduction of Knyvett's cousin Anne Vavasour.

Tournaments could give courtier gentlemen a momentary opportunity to present themselves to the Queen in public, as a persona of their own choosing. Lee himself appeared as Elizabeth's personal tournament champion, a role that existed solely in the fantasy world of the tiltyard. His favourite personae were military: he appeared as 'a straunge forsaken and dispayringe knight ... in hewe of greene' in 'Sir Henry Lee's Challenge before Shampanie' in 1576 and as the black knight who escorted the 'wanderinge knights' who had been absent from the tournament a year before in November 1584.[79] In 1590 he adopted the role of soldier-turned-hermit from Ramon Lull's *Ordre of Chyualry*, and later appeared at the tilts as the hermit who instructs the younger knights in the 'order of chivalry'.[80] This latter role was not mere play-acting for Lee: he fulfilled it in a practical demonstration of his knowledge of the tenets of chivalry.

Despite the markedly Protestant nature of the Accession Day celebrations and church services, the 17 November tournaments gave another specific group of courtier gentlemen a unique opportunity to present themselves in public as loyal knights of the Crown. The Court included a number of gentlemen who were either openly Catholic, or who had Catholic affiliations, and a surprising number of these jousted. Lord Windsor and Philip Howard, Earl of Arundel, were notable for this, although Arundel eschewed the sport after his conversion to Catholicism. William Tresham jousted in 1581 before his flight to Paris in 1582 to join other recusants, and the names of other known Catholics, Arthur Gorges and William Cornwallis, appear on the score cheques. Thomas Gerard, brother of the Jesuit John Gerard, jousted on fourteen occasions between 1584 and 1602. Everard Digby, with a father imprisoned for recusancy and a son who would be implicated in the 1605 Gunpowder Plot, jousted seven times between 1581 and 1591. Other known Catholics such as George Gifford jousted six

---

[78]   R.C. McCoy, *The Rites of Knighthood: The Literature and Politics of Elizabethan Chivalry* (Berkeley, CA, 1989), p. 24.

[79]   BL, Add. MS 41499A, f. ii.

[80]   R. Lull, *The Booke of the Ordre of Chyualry*, trans. and printed by William Caxton, 1484, ed. Alfred Byles (London, 1926). See also Chapter 3 below.

times; Henry Nowell eleven times; and Thomas Vavasour, with Catholic family affiliations, was a frequent jouster when not in active military service abroad.[81] Attitudes to religion at Elizabeth's Court were mixed, and changed depending on the threat from Spain. As a general rule, Catholics who were known to be loyal to the Crown were tolerated. Degrees of loyalty could vary within one family, however, and many Catholic gentlemen welcomed the chance to distance themselves in the Queen's eyes from their recusant relations. The tournaments were one arena in which they could publicly declare their allegiance.

Overall, the cost of participation to individual jousters, arising from their need for armour, horses, an entourage and a present for the Queen, exceeded their potential material gain. Most tilters received no obvious reward other than the symbolic prizes for 'him that justid best'. Sir Christopher Hatton received a suit of armour from the Queen in 1564, but he enjoyed a special relationship with Elizabeth. Cumberland received his stupendous suit of Almain armour from the Queen in 1590, but his position as Queen's Champion after Lee's retirement contributed more to his debts than his fortune. It would appear that the ordinary courtier gentleman gained little financially and could spend much.

The Accession Day tournaments were also of value to other groups of people. One such was the College of Arms. A major part of the College's income derived from its jurisdiction over tournaments, and any increased popularity in these events would be to its benefit. At that time, the College was the subject of much criticism from the aristocracy, in that the heralds were providing the much sought-after coats of arms for newly risen gentlemen, often fabricating an armigerous descent from fictitious forebears. The Duke of Norfolk, as Earl Marshal, had introduced unpopular innovations in 1568 to stop this practice, but Norfolk was executed for treason in 1572, and the College faced accusations of inefficiency and disorganization.

In 1571, shortly after the Accession Day tournaments began, Richard Lee, first cousin to Sir Henry Lee, became Portcullis Pursuivant, progressing to Richmond Herald in 1585 and Clarencieux King of Arms from 1594 to 1597. He was therefore perfectly positioned to liaise with his cousin and to encourage public tournaments, which would enhance the reputation of the College of Arms. Another member of the College who promoted both the propaganda value of the tilts and Lee, was Sir William Segar, who rose from Portcullis Pursuivant to Somerset Herald in 1589, Norroy King of Arms in 1597 and Garter King of Arms by 1604. It was Segar who produced the first printed account of Sir Henry Lee's vow to initiate the Accession Day tournaments in his *Booke of honor and armes* in 1590. By that date, Lee was well established as the leading proponent of the tournament, and Segar's descriptions of his chivalric virtues could well have been an attempt to reflect glory on to the College by association. Segar's

---

[81]   CAMS Portfolio of Tournament Cheques, CAMS M4bis.

later *Honor Military and Civill* in 1602 coincided with criticisms of the heralds' practices from Norfolk's brother, Lord Henry Howard.

Another effect of the Accession Day tournaments was to keep the military aspects of life in the public eye, to provide a purpose and income for the armourers during the long years of peace, as well as giving courtier gentlemen at least the illusion they could acquit themselves adequately on the battlefield. Traditionally, tournaments were seen as training for combat. Lee himself defined their purpose as 'treininge the Courtier in those exercises of Armes that keepe the Person steeled to Hardinesse, That by Softe Ease Rusts & Weares'. Lee always regarded himself as a soldier 'having had the use of Arms both in earnest and sport all the days of my life'.[82] His contemporaries were divided over whether or not tournaments were genuinely any training for warfare. Segar was an advocate of 'the ordinary exercises in Armes'; Francis Bacon, despite assisting Essex with his entertainment in 1595, believed that nobles should be ornaments of the Court rather than commanders of armies. He was sceptical about tournaments, writing that 'these things are but toys to come among serious observations ... since princes will have such things, it is better they should be graced with elegancy rather than daubed with cost'.[83]

Present-day historians are also divided over the military efficacy of tournaments, with Sydney Anglo, Richard Barber and Juliet Baker dismissing them as mere ceremonial theatricals, and Malcolm Vale and Roy Strong emphasizing their usefulness as training for war.[84] Helen Watanabe-O'Kelly argues that the skills demonstrated in the later sixteenth-century tournaments were vital to the changing nature of warfare across Europe. The increasing use of firepower and handguns, for example, called for greater skill in controlling lighter, better-trained horses on the battlefield, and this argument is borne out by the contemporary interest in horsemanship among jousters.[85]

Leicester, as Master of the Horse from 1559 to 1581, imported foreign strains to improve native horse-breeding and brought the Italian Claudio Corte to England, to train and exercise horses 'for skirmish, for battell and for combate ... [which] standeth him in steed for the exercise of the turneie and all other feates of arms'.[86] Corte's *Art of Riding* was published bound together with John Astley's *Art of Riding* in 1584, at the behest of Henry Mackwilliam,

---

[82]   Cecil MS 117.3. (HMC *Salis.* XIV, p. 182), 29 July 1601 (Lee to Sir John Stanhope, Vice-Chamberlain to the Queen).

[83]   Francis Bacon, *The Works of Francis Bacon* (London, 1819), II, P. 345.

[84]   Anglo, 'Archives of the English Tournament'; R. Barber and J. Barker, *Tournaments: Jousts, Chivalry and Pageants in the Middle Ages* (Woodbridge, 1989); R. Strong, *Art and Power: Renaissance Festivals 1450–1650* (Woodbridge, 1984), p. 12.

[85]   Helen Watanabe-O'Kelly, 'Tournaments and their Relevance for Warfare in the Early Modern Period', *European History Quarterly*, XX (1990), pp. 451–63.

[86]   Claudio Corte, *The Art of Riding* (London, 1584), *RSTC* 5797.

former jouster, Gentleman Pensioner and owner of one of the most spectacular armours in the *Almain Armourers' Album*.[87] Like Corte, the Italian riding master, Malatesta, writing in 1600, saw no distinction between cavalry riding in war and riding in tournaments. Leicester's nephew, Philip Sidney, expert at the joust and eager for battlefield experience, made frequent reference to horsemanship in his sonnets (see Appendix 4) and Elizabeth's three masters of the horse, the Earls of Leicester, Essex and Worcester, were renowned jousters.

Even if jousting was not direct training for warfare, many jousters saw themselves as soldiers and were eager for military action. It is also possible that the Accession Day tournaments were a way of 'showcasing' themselves as possible military commanders in order to win lucrative commissions. Many of the Gentlemen Pensioners of Elizabeth's Court jousted, and many named on the tournament score cheques also saw active military service. Sir Henry Lee and at least four of his companions who served with him at the siege of Edinburgh Castle in 1573 jousted. Philip Sidney died as a result of wounds received at the battle of Zutphen in 1586, and Edward Denny, who saw active service in Ireland from 1574 to 1588, jousted in tournaments from 1578 to 1587. Edward Norris, one of the six soldier sons of Rycote, jousted from 1578 to 1584, following an earlier family tradition set by his brothers William and Henry. Ralph Lane, who jousted in 1583, became the disastrous military governor of Roanoke Island, Virginia. Lord Willoughby de Eresby, who jousted in 1583 and 1584, led the celebrated English cavalry charge at Zutphen in September 1586 where he unhorsed the general of the enemy horse and took him prisoner.

Friendships begun in the tiltyard continued on the battlefield. Philip Sidney resigned his governorship of Bergen op Zoom 'to my lord Willoughby, my very special friend' in 1586 and later, as Elizabeth's commander-in-chief in the Netherlands, Willoughby befriended and promoted Thomas Vavasour, who had tilted with him in 1583, and on four other occasions. Vavasour led a company of Yorkshire men to the Netherlands in 1585 and served at Brill until 1591. For several regular jousters, like Vavasour, absence from the Accession Day tournaments was caused only by active military service abroad.

It was Essex who actively attempted to bring the tournament to the battlefield. On the English expedition to Portugal in 1589 he offered to fight all-comers in Lisbon in honour of his mistress, Elizabeth, and at the siege of Rouen in 1591 he challenged the enemy commander to single combat. Dutch historian Jan Dop gives an interesting view of 'Eliza's Knights' on the battlefield, claiming that their admiration for knightly heroism made them unsympathetic to the new breed of professional soldiers fighting in the Low Countries.[88] He

---

[87]   John Astley, *The Art of Riding* (London, 1584), *RSTC* 884.

[88]   Jan A. Dop, *Eliza's Knights – Soldiers, Poets and Puritans in the Netherlands, 1572–1586* (Alblasserdam, 1981).

argues that Leicester's failure to achieve success there reflected the gulf between military practice and the 'courtly ideals of heroism' and quotes Philip Sidney's romanticized, but severely misplaced, heroism on the battlefield at Zutphen in 1586 as illustrative of 'how disastrous a sudden transition from games of war to the real thing could be'.

Attempts were made by Leicester and Sidney to make political points before the Queen and Court and to use tournaments for political purposes, but they met with little success. The public Accession Day tournaments were emphatically not the place for political comment, as the noisy circumstances in which they were staged militated against engaging in political argument. This makes the events of the Accession Day tournament of 1581 puzzling, and if a political point was being made, it still remains obscure.

The impending marriage between Elizabeth and the Duke of Anjou made 1581 a year of tensions at Court, and Lee had already been involved in the private tournaments staged by Arundel and Sidney. Anjou himself arrived in England on 31 October, and on 17 November he was watching the tournament with the Queen from her window. A list of tilters exists in the Bodleian Library, clearly marked by Robert Cooke, Clarencieux King of Arms, as 'Thys be the names of the noblemen and gentlemen that for the honor of the Queene's ma[jes[tie did their endevors at the Tylt at Westminster on the xvij day of November ... the xxiiij yeare of the reigne of queene Elizabeth'.[89] Thirteen couples were due to tilt, and the list gives the names of the first four couples as the Earl of Arundel and Lord Windsor, Henry Grey and Henry Windsor, Sir Henry Lee and Philip Sidney, and Fulke Greville and Ralph Bowes. The clear implication is that all eight had intended to tilt; indeed, Lee had a major responsibility for the event.

A similar list held at the College of Arms, however, tells a different story. The list is annotated in a hasty, different hand, crossing out names, and it is clear that Arundel, Lord Windsor, Grey, Lee, Sidney, Greville and Edward Norris withdrew from the lists at the last minute (see Ill. 10).[90] The College also holds an obviously hastily compiled score cheque for 1581, showing the first couple who actually tilted as Thomas Perott and Thomas Ratcliffe (see Ill. 11).[91] This list rapidly deteriorates into jottings, and Sir Henry Lee's name appears again, crossed through. Cooke again annotated the score cheque: 'Al these on bothe papers dyd Rone on the Quenes day the xvij November of 1581.'

Clearly, something unusual was happening. Individual knights did occasionally withdraw during a tournament with injuries, but if seven of the principal tilters withdrew, it would have been unprecedented in the whole run of score cheques. Apart from the obvious expensive preparations that would

---

[89]   Bodl. MS, Ashmole 845, f. 165.

[90]   CA, MS M4, i.

[91]   CA, MS M4, vi.

have been made, such actions would have incurred a financial penalty. Was a political point being made? The fact that the Duke of Anjou was to be present at the tournament had been known for weeks and, as he and the Queen merely sat at the window of her apartments, their proximity would not have been obvious to the crowd. The 'Four Foster Children of Desire', all of whom scratched from the tournament, had made an earlier presentation in May 1581. Also, Arundel and Lord Windsor favoured the French match even if Sidney and Greville did not. The Queen gave Anjou a ring in token of betrothal, but this was not until 22 November, and all sources agree that the move was unexpected.[92] The gesture could not have been foreseen on 17 November.

The explanation could lie in an event other than the proposed French marriage. The Jesuit priest Edmund Campion had arrived secretly in England in June 1580, only to be arrested on 17 July 1581. Campion was incarcerated in the Tower of London, and was questioned secretly in Leicester House by Leicester and members of the Privy Council, possibly in the presence of the Queen, in an effort to make him recant his Catholicism. When he refused, Campion was returned to the Tower and was repeatedly racked. He underwent numerous interrogations, some of them public, and valiantly defended his faith. On 14 November he was again racked and arraigned on a charge of conspiracy to overthrow the Queen. There was much indignation at Campion's treatment: Leicester tried to improve Campion's lodging in the Tower, and Sidney, who had met Campion in Prague in 1577, asked Anjou to intervene, a request that was ignored. Arundel, watching Campion's public interrogation at the Tower, became converted to Catholicism. Lord Windsor, already a Catholic, was sympathetic to Campion. On 20 November Campion was found guilty at his trial, and eleven days later was hanged, drawn and quartered at Tyburn.

If the last-minute withdrawal from the tilt on 17 November was a protest against the treatment of Campion, the actions of Sidney, Arundel, Lord Windsor and even Greville, who was Sidney's closest companion, are understandable. The reasons for the withdrawal of Henry Grey and Edward Norris of Rycote are less obvious, but the withdrawal of Lee, as Queen's Champion, is very strange. Lee had been with Sidney in Prague in 1577 and may have met Campion, although there is no evidence whatsoever that Lee had Catholic sympathies. Possibly Lee's very atypical action was influenced by the charismatic Philip Sidney. Alternatively, Lee might have been attempting to deflect possible royal wrath at the hasty actions of Sidney and the young tilters by showing that their opinions were also held by older men. Tilters with known Catholic affiliations such as George Gifford, Everard Digby and William Tresham did not withdraw from the tilt: perhaps the question of joining a protest against the treatment of

<hr>

[92]   M.P. Holt, *The Duke of Anjou and the Politique Struggle during the Wars of Religion* (Cambridge, 2002), p. 161.

Campion came a little too close to home for them. Ironically, Sir Henry Lee was present officially as Master of the Armoury at Campion's execution on 1 December 1581. His conformist acceptance of the conditions of his official position is typical of his actions, but makes his refusal to tilt on 17 November even more of an aberration.

To date, the incident defies explanation. It has never been mentioned in print and deserves more detailed research. It is possible that Cooke's comment on the score cheque signified that all the tilters did, in fact, run, although what arguments were put to them have been lost. Of course, a simpler explanation might be that Robert Cooke, yet again, mislabelled his paperwork, as he had with score cheques for 1572 and 1577.

Another purpose for the tournaments, argue historians such as Mervyn James and Richard McCoy, was to act as an outlet for thwarted aristocratic pride, a 'resolution of the conflict between obedience to the monarch and aristocratic militarism and autonomy'.[93] If these arguments are genuinely relevant to the tournaments, they refer to those held after Lee's retirement in 1590 and to nobles such as the Earls of Essex and Southampton, rather than courtier gentlemen like Lee. For many years, very few members of the peerage tilted in public. If one looks at the score cheques for tournaments between 1571 and 1581, the majority of the tilters were not even knighted – in the 1579 February tilt, fourteen of the sixteen participants are named as 'Mr'. Sir Henry Lee stands out as one of the few knights participating, with usually the Earls of Oxford and Arundel, and Lord Windsor representing the upper echelons of the nobility. In 1583 the aristocracy was solely represented by the Earl of Cumberland and Lord Willoughby de Eresby, and Lee was the only knight.

The remaining twenty-one tilters were untitled, hardly supporting McCoy's claim that tournaments were for the glorification of 'aristocratic militarism and traditional notions of honor and autonomy'.[94] The Earl of Essex first appears on the tilting lists with Cumberland from 1586. Changes were occurring at Court and while Lawrence Stone's reference to 'a whole generation of high-spirited young aristocrats in open rebellion against the conservative establishment in general and Lord Burghley in particular' is somewhat sweeping, it is true that the later tournaments were increasingly dominated by members of the peerage including the Earls of Essex, Southampton and Bedford who had been Burghley's wards.[95] From 1590 a greater number of nobles appear on the November tournament cheques.

---

[93]   McCoy, *Rites of Knighthood*; M. James, *Society, Politics and Culture: Studies in Early Modern England* (Cambridge, 1986).

[94]   McCoy, *Rites of Knighthood*, p. 3.

[95]   L. Stone, *The Crisis of the Aristocracy 1558–1641* (Oxford, 1965), p. 265.

In 1590 Essex, Cumberland, and Lords Strange, Burke and Compton ran with four knights and fifteen untitled gentlemen. By 1594 Essex was joined by the Earls of Sussex, Southampton and Shrewsbury, with Lords Mountjoy, Compton, Sandys and Norris. In 1597 seven peers were tilting, with seven knights and eight untitled gentlemen. The growing number of knights possibly reflected Essex's predilection for creating knights on the battlefield, with a personal loyalty to him and against the Queen's wishes. The Accession Day tournaments, held before an immense London crowd, afforded Essex his greatest public platform for exposure as a popular hero, if only for a few hours.

Whether his behaviour there, and that of the other peers was, as McCoy claims, 'a cultural resolution of ... the conflict between honour and obedience ... and duty to right royal majesty' is highly dubious.[96] If such a conflict existed, it had little to do with Lee. Lee was no member of the peerage – he came from a long line of land-owning gentry, and social advancement for both his mother's and father's families had come from service to the Tudors. He was keenly aware of his standing as a knight and a gentleman, but did not labour under the aspirations or frustrations of those who, like Sidney and Essex, sprang from more noble blood.

The Accession Day Tournaments: Some Concluding Observations

Overall, Lee's twenty-year influence over the Accession Day tournaments, this much debated form of Court entertainment, was clearly substantial. Few others did as much to influence the development and character of the Elizabethan tournament. Lee, to his monarch's obvious enjoyment, ensured the continuation of the tournament in England long after it had become outmoded on the Continent. The Accession Day tournaments, amateur in the best sense of the word, stand in marked contrast with Catherine de Medici's government-funded Magnificences in an increasingly war-torn France. Can the tournaments organized by Lee therefore be interpreted as anachronism or a forward-looking development on an earlier theme? Their military use might be debatable given the growing use of artillery firepower, but tournaments generally looked back to a more chivalric 'golden' age which still appeared to hold Western Europe in thrall even in the late 1590s. The concept of rules and manners on the battlefield still held an appeal. The argument still rings true, that *Don Quixote*, in which 'Cervantes smiled Spain's chivalry away', would not have received such universal acclaim in 1606 had the spectacle of tilting knights not enjoyed such a wide currency in Europe.[97]

---

[96]   McCoy, *Rites of Knighthood*, p. 3.
[97]   W. Byron, *Cervantes: A Biography* (London, 1979).

And what did Sir Henry Lee get out of the tournaments? It is difficult to believe that he was operating entirely from self-serving motives. In the early 1570s Lee's prowess in the tiltyard brought him into favour with the Queen, and his creation of the Accession Day tournaments brought initial rewards from her, culminating in his appointment as Master of the Armoury in 1580. However, participation in the tournament, even for a man trained from youth, required physical fitness, strength, agility and considerable financial outlay. Although he might not have known it, by 1580 Lee had received all the material benefits that he was going to get and, at forty-seven, he would have been quite justified to rest upon his laurels. Yet Lee continued to 'lead out the troops' for another ten years, which cannot really be explained in terms of financial reward.

His participation in the sport probably cost him more financially than he gained in royal favour, but his personal satisfaction appears to have been great. The annual Accession Day tournaments gave him both a very public outlet for his creative and sporting abilities and an occasion to come to Court when he personally was one of the main attractions. His influence over the event brought him into contact with at least two generations of courtiers of all ranks, the majority of whom he could number as personal friends. It is interesting that when he was elected as a Knight of the Garter in 1597, long after he had retired from the sport, many of the votes he received were from friends with whom he had tilted.[98] Lee created an annual occasion in the Queen's honour that, despite the changing demands on ceremonial at the Elizabethan Court, was both enjoyable to all and celebrated the growing confidence of the Elizabethan political and social elite in their society.

---

[98] See Chapter 3.

The Relationship between Sir Henry Lee and Elizabeth I, 1570–1603

The tradition of service to the Crown, beyond the usual expectations that a gentleman would serve his monarch and the commonweal in his locality as an MP and JP, ran strongly in Sir Henry Lee's family, and Lee showed every indication of wishing to continue it. At some point around 1569, Lee came into favour with Elizabeth I, and he remained in her service as 'the Queen's well-beloved and faithfull subject and servant' until 1603.[1] Initially there were many signs of royal favour. He became Steward of the Queen's Manor at Woodstock in 1572 and Master of the Armoury in 1580, as well as receiving several financially advantageous patents. Although he retained these appointments until his death, no further public offices were forthcoming after 1580, and by the last decade of the reign Lee was actively complaining about the cost of his commitments. Lee's attitude to his Queen and his service to her over some thirty years can be gleaned from the way in which he fulfilled his responsibilities, from his letters on the subject to a variety of courtiers and from the various entertainments he prepared for Elizabeth at Woodstock. It is also possible to glimpse the Queen's attitude to Lee and other gentlemen in her service and compare the progress made by Lee with other courtier gentlemen whose careers were more successful.

In the first decade of Elizabeth's reign there had been little opportunity for Lee to serve at Court, and it was only after his return from Italy in 1569 that he was singled out for royal favour with concomitant rewards. What caused the change in his fortunes? The most obvious answer is that by 1569 Sir Henry Lee was exactly the type of courtier who appealed to the Queen. If the evidence of the 1568 Antonis Mor portrait (Ill. 1) is reliable, Lee was an attractive, athletic man, outstanding at the hunt and the tilt. His foreign experience had made him at ease with royalty and nobility, he had some literary skill and he was both a capable and amiable courtier who was an asset in any social scene. He was well connected at Court and, like many other favoured courtiers, was related to the Queen, through the Knollys family. He had independent means and made few obvious demands for a lucrative position at Court. Any hint of association with

---

[1] Lee is so described in *Calendar of Patent Rolls* (hereafter *CPR*), 13 Eliz. I, Part VI, no. 2056; TNA, PRO, C 66/1076 and in TNA, PRO, DL/42, f. 102 – his 1575 patent to manumit villeins.

the previous reign had long been lived down, and Lee's willingness to abandon a wife in Buckinghamshire was no less than the Queen expected. There were many young courtier gentlemen who could claim some of these virtues, but by 1569 Lee was a man in his prime, attractively described in his *Memoriae Sacrum* as having returned from Italy 'charged with the Reputation of a well formed Travailour & adorned with those flowers of Knighthood, Courtesie Bounty & Valour'.[2] The Antonis Mor portrait (Ill. 1) gives us another clue to his popularity with the Queen. Among the motifs shown on Lee's shirt is the armillary or celestial sphere. In addition to being an astronomical instrument, the device was used symbolically in many ways, including as a symbol for the courtiers revolving around the Queen as their sun and deity and as a symbol of the tournament. It was used as such by Lee in his famous Ditchley portrait of 1592 and in the miniature portrait of Cumberland as Queen's Champion. Its depiction on Lee's shirt in 1568 would be a graceful statement of his devotion to Elizabeth, even if the portrait was intended for private use. Lee probably came into favour with the Queen because she enjoyed his courtly virtues, coloured, as they were, by foreign experience and the muscular flattery of his Accession Day tournaments.

Gentlemen of Lee's social status could advance themselves at Court by seeking positions within the royal household, although in a predominantly female establishment these opportunities were few. They could also join the elite band of Gentleman Pensioners, the Queen's personal bodyguard. There is no evidence that Lee ever sought either mode of service, and he lacked the training and inclination to pursue a career in government on the basis of legal and administrative expertise, as had Nicholas Bacon or William Cecil. Lee would never achieve the same relationship with the Queen as Robert Dudley, Earl of Leicester, or, in later years, Robert Devereux, Earl of Essex, but men of Lee's rank were achieving great favour and position in Elizabeth's Court.

Thomas Heneage, son of a Lincolnshire landowner, became Steward of Hatfield in 1561 and a Gentleman of the Privy Chamber around 1565, receiving offices, lands, leases and reversions almost every subsequent year. Camden described him as 'a man for the elegancy of life and pleasantness of discourse born ... for the Court'.[3] Heneage became Treasurer of the Queen's Chamber around 1570, was knighted in 1577 and eventually in 1587 became Vice-Chamberlain of the Queen's Household. Thomas Sackville was the son of the immensely wealthy Sir Richard Sackville, a Privy Councillor, and rose to become Lord Buckhurst and eventually Earl of Dorset in 1604. Christopher Hatton, the son of a modest gentleman with moderate resources, was, like Lee, a notable tilter and participated with Lee in the 1571 tournament. He became Keeper of

---

[2]   E.K. Chambers, *Sir Henry Lee: An Elizabethan Portrait* (Oxford, 1936), p. 304.

[3]   P.W. Hasler, *The History of Parliament: The House of Commons, 1558–1603*, 3 vols (London, 1982), II, p. 292.

the Parks at Eltham Palace, and Gentleman of the Privy Chamber in 1572. Like Heneage, he received very tangible rewards for his service at Court, eventually becoming a Privy Councillor and Lord Chancellor. The advancement of all three men depended on their personal relationship with the Queen, and just how far they would go was as yet uncertain in 1569. Whether Lee saw himself among their ranks is unknown, but clearly there were opportunities for courtier gentlemen to advance themselves.

Before 1570 there is no evidence that Lee was actively seeking royal appointments that would bring in financial rewards. On 5 October 1570, however, Lee lost more than 3,000 sheep in a great flood, and this forced him to search for a remunerative position.[4] The financial loss of his livestock was quoted as the Queen's reason for granting him a licence to export wool in January 1571, and this was the first document that described Lee as 'the Queen's well-beloved & faithfull subject and servant'.[5] On 10 August 1572 Lee received a personal gift from the Queen, mentioned in a letter from Lord Burghley to Leicester:[6]

> I here send your Lordship a bill signed by the Queen's Majesty for Sir H. Lee which the Q[ueen's] Mai[es]tie meaneth to bestow upon him unawares to himself and therefore recommend me to take some care that it might be sealed and so her Mai[es]tie might have it to give him.[7]

The nature of this bill is unknown. It is possible that it was the licence Lee received that year to export 500,000 woolfells for ten years. This may have been a profitable gift but was hardly the token of personal favour planned by Elizabeth for Lee that Burghley's phraseology suggests. In the absence of a better explanation, one possibility is that this was the royal warrant necessary for Lee to use the Almain Armourers at Greenwich. Lee's first suit of armour had been a plain harness made in Germany. The decoration and garniture making it more suitable for tournament use were added later in Greenwich by Jacob Halder, later to be Master Armourer.[8] Ian Eaves, on the evidence of the chronological

---

[4] Raphael Holinshed, *The firste volume of the chronicles of England, Scotlande and Irelande* (London, 1577), *RSTC* 1358, IV, p. 257; Thomas Knell, *The declaration of such tempestuous and outrageous fluddes as hath been in divers places of England 1570* (London, 1571), *RSTC* 15032. This is discussed below in Chapter 5.

[5] TNA, PRO, C66/1076. *CPR* 13.Eliz.I Part VI. no. 2056.

[6] *Calendar of State Papers, Domestic Series, of the Reign of Elizabeth, 1581–1603*, 7 vols (London, 1865), SP12/89/3. In Elizabeth's reign it was possible for noblemen to have armour made at Greenwich, although this needed a warrant under sign manual (personally signed by the sovereign).

[7] *CPR* 69-72. no.3359; TNA, PRO, C66/1093.

[8] V & A, *Almain Armourer's Album,* D599 and D599A (1894).

arrangement of the armour in the *Almain Armourer's Album*, places the modification of Lee's first armour in the period 1571–75.[9]

Lee continued to receive financial favours and patents throughout the decade, although in practical terms it is debatable whether many of these were immediately profitable. The Queen was always prepared to use patents and licences to reward her favourites financially, but the implementation of these favours was very much in the hands of their recipients. The more sensible courtiers often sold them to a third party for the ready money needed to maintain appearances at Court.

Lee and the Administration of Woodstock

Lee's principal appointment as a royal servant was therefore as Steward and Parker at the Queen's manor of Woodstock, Oxfordshire, a royal manor since the reign of Ethelred II (978–1016). Its proximity to the forest of Wychwood meant that hunting was the main attraction for the monarch, and its healthy location ensured that it was often used when plague was rife in London. Tournaments had been held there in medieval times, and remnants of the tournament ground may have survived to Lee's time.[10] Henry VII had ordered a major rebuilding of the house, although when Elizabeth was imprisoned here in 1554–55, in the custody of Sir Henry Bedingfield, Woodstock was said to have been 'for many years decayed and prostrated'.[11] The famous graffito she scratched on a window, 'Much suspected of me, Nothing proved can be', became an object of curiosity in Lee's time and was later noted by both Thomas Platter and Duke Bracciano.[12] Despite her earlier imprisonment there, Woodstock was a favourite residence for Elizabeth on summer progress and she visited it with her Court on five occasions between 1566 and 1592.

Lee lived at Woodstock from 1571 when he purchased the patent of Steward of Woodstock originally granted to Sir Edward Dyer in 1570.[13] On 28 November

---

[9]   I. Eaves, 'The Greenwich Armour and Locking Gauntlet of Sir Henry Lee in the Collection of the Worshipful Company of Armourers and Braziers', *Journal of the Arms and Armour Society*, XVI,3 (1999), p. 153.

[10]   *The Victoria County History of Oxfordshire*, (hereafter *VCH Oxon*), IV, p. 436 mentions the death of John, Earl of Pembroke, in a jousting accident in 1389, quoting *Polychronicon Radulphi Higden* (Rolls Ser.), IX, pp. 219–20.

[11]   H.M. Colvin (ed.), *The History of the King's Works*, 6 vols (London, 1982), IV, p. 351.

[12]   Thomas Platter and Horatio Busino, *The Journals of Two Travellers in Elizabethan and Early Stuart England*, ed. Peter Razzell (London, 1995), p. 226; Cecil Papers 82.80 (HMC *Salis.* X, p. 427 (2 December 1600)).

[13]   The patents for this had originally been granted to Sir Edward Dyer in 23 June 1570, but Dyer, perennially short of money and out of favour with the Queen from 1571 to 1573,

1573 the Queen granted him a reversionary lease of the offices of Steward and Lieutenant of the manor of Woodstock for life, with the office of Keeper of all the parks and woods on the manor. His position gave him an annual exchequer fee and considerable perquisites, which grew as he acquired additional offices. Lee's thirty-eight year stewardship of the whole property was one of the longest and most formative in its history. His activities as Steward are documented in a virtually unbroken set of annual exchequer returns, duplicated by those of the Woodstock Comptroller, George Whitton.[14] Lee's duties at Woodstock were threefold: he administered the house and estate for the purposes of royal hunting; he dealt with problems with manorial tenants and, most importantly, he received the Queen when she visited there, providing lodging, sustenance and entertainment for the Court.

Lee's 'exile' to Woodstock seems a strange move for an ambitious courtier who knew that advancement relied on proximity to the monarch. Both Hatton and Heneage held similar positions at the royal houses of Eltham and Hatfield respectively, but both chose to delegate their practical administration to subordinates. For a man of Lee's temperament and talents, the decision to administer Woodstock personally was, in the early 1570s at least, understandable. Woodstock was one of the ten favoured royal residences, and its stewardship had always been an office coveted by courtiers. Lee welcomed the Queen and Court there on the summer progresses of 1572, 1574 and 1575, and it was not obvious until several years later that Woodstock would not enjoy regular royal visits.

The outdoor life suited Lee better than the corridors of Whitehall. Woodstock, some fifty miles from London, was blessedly plague-free throughout Elizabeth's reign and sufficiently close to the capital for her to receive the Privy Council and foreign ambassadors there.[15] Hunting was a passion of Elizabeth's, and one she shared with Lee. At Woodstock she could hunt in Wychwood and also in Woodstock's own deer park which Lee developed and enlarged.[16] Above

---

had allowed them to pass by purchase to Lee until Dyer's death or his forfeiture or surrender of the patents. The reversionary lease of 1573 meant that they would eventually pass to Lee in his own right. Dyer lost his offices at Woodstock in 1603 at the accession of James I, and the patent passed outright to Lee. See Chapter 5 below for a full discussion of Lee's finances in relation to Woodstock.

[14] TNA, PRO, E101/671.

[15] 'Chaucer's House' on the edge of the park at Woodstock, was leased by St John's College as an alternative residence when plague came to Oxford, which it did for more than a year, in 1571–72.

[16] Elizabeth's ability to overstretch the rules of hospitality became legendary after she outraged Lord Berkeley by hunting most of his deer during her stay at Berkeley Castle in 1574. Lord Berkeley threatened to destroy his herd himself so that the Queen could not have the pleasure of doing so. See Mary Hill Cole, *The Portable Queen: Elizabeth I and the Politics of Ceremony* (Amhurst, MA, 1999), p. 149.

all, the stewardship of Woodstock afforded Lee intimate informal contact with Elizabeth when on progress – something that was granted to very few courtiers in London. Residence at Woodstock did not cut Lee off from friends at Court. It was near enough to Leicester's estates at Kenilworth to exchange visits, and the manor was a convenient staging post for royal officials travelling between London and Ireland or Wales.[17] It was also conveniently linked by Akeman Street to Lee's own lands at Quarrendon. Lee was not necessarily resident at Woodstock for the whole year; he joined the Queen on summer progress each year, maintained his lodgings at the Savoy in London and came to Court for the tournaments and to fulfil commitments as Master of the Armoury.

Lee's primary role at Woodstock was the maintenance of the manor and the deer park. Woodstock was a royal residence capable of housing the Court and comprised a substantial set of buildings, with chapels, stables, tennis courts and outbuildings which appeared to be in constant need of repair and reconstruction. Within the park were four lodges, High Lodge, Bladon Lodge, New Lodge and Gorrel Lodge. By 1577 these were all held by Lee. As Woodstock's main purpose was for royal recreational hunting, imparking or enclosing manorial land to extend the deer park had been practised for several decades. In 1576 Lee enlarged an area of park near High Lodge known as the Straights, which he then imparked by building a stone wall at a cost of £309, the new enclosure being known as Queen's Park. In 1577–78, Lee felled forty oaks on the estate for fencing.[18]

The well-being of the deer herd itself was of paramount importance, and Lee maintained a herd of some 2,000 to 3,000 to provide sport for the Court and venison for its table.[19] There appeared to be a well-established policy of exchange between deer parks. In November 1577 Lee received some thirty-six live red deer of various ages from Leicester's park at Kenilworth, which had in turn received stock from Lee's brother Robert at Hatfield Chase, Yorkshire.[20] The newly fashionable red deer were unpopular with the residents of New Woodstock, who later complained they were overrunning the countryside.[21] Local cooperation

---

[17]   See, for example, HMC de Lisle and Dudley I, pp. 262, 263 – stable accounts of Sir Henry Sidney, 12 October 1574, 21 December 1574. Woodstock appeared to be a convenient night's stop between Ludlow and Kingston.

[18]   *Calendar of the manuscripts of the Most Honourable the Marquess of Salisbury, K.G., ... : preserved at Hatfield House, Hertfordshire* (London, 1883–1976) (hereafter HMC *Salis.*), II, p. 390 (draft to Lord Treasurer for payment of £309 for building a wall enclosing certain additions to Woodstock Park, 9 July 1576).

[19]   TNA, PRO, SC6/Eliz. 1/1825, (Special Collections: Ministers' and Receivers' accounts and General Accounts of crown lands). Lee probably also had some responsibility for the breeding of hunting dogs and deer herds for royal gifts or for stocking other royal parks. Lee's brother Robert exercised a similar position at Hatfield Chase, Yorkshire.

[20]   CKS (Penshurst Papers), U1475 E.93, ff. 12v, 17v.

[21]   TNA, PRO, E101/670, f. 28.

was important – in the harsh winter of 1579 the Privy Council instructed Lee to buy stover or fodder locally 'for the nourishing of the deer ... where it might best be spared without the great hurt of many, especially the porer sort'.[22]

Awareness of local sensitivities was vital to Lee in his second role at Woodstock, that of dealing with the problems that arose on the manor, especially with the tenants. Lee's family had long been highly successful landowners in Buckinghamshire, and Lee was prepared to use all his experience in the Queen's interests. Unlike the majority of Court appointees, Lee did not view his position as a sinecure and he was the first steward for some time prepared to make the administration of Woodstock his main priority. The stewardship had been held largely *in absentia* by three generations of the Chamberlayne family from 1508 to 1570, and certain situations had developed that Lee found impossible to reverse.[23] In addition, irregularities on a royal property were often referred to a higher authority and Lee's decisions could be overruled by Burghley. Lee, as Steward, had immediate responsibility for manorial demesne land that was retained by the lord of the manor for his own use. Much of the manorial land outside the demesne was let out to freehold or leasehold tenants in villages and townships within the manor, and these latter tenants tended to be better educated and more outspoken on the subject of their rights.

Lee's problems with Woodstock's township tenants began in 1576 when a common was enclosed and a road diverted. Some forty or fifty tenants travelled to Windsor to make their complaints known to the Queen and appealed noisily to her as she passed by in public. Not unnaturally, the Queen was offended and commanded the men to depart or be punished. As Lee had not dealt with this problem, it fell to Burghley to hear the tenants' complaints and make a judgement.[24] Burghley's inquiry revealed the existence of a more complicated problem. As on most English manors, in addition to demesne and leasehold or freehold land, a third category of manorial land existed at Woodstock – the bury land. This was demesne land, temporarily surplus to the lord's requirements and rented out to tenants for a short period of time. In 1576 Lee discovered that the Queen's tenants were encroaching on the bury lands in a more permanent way than manorial practice permitted, and took steps to remove the offenders. The tenants themselves claimed they had been awarded bury land in the past, as compensation for freehold and leasehold land lost by a previous imparking.

---

[22]   Dasent, *APC*, XI, p. 45 (9 February 1579).

[23]   Sir Edward Chamberlain, Steward from 1508 to 1543, was accused in the Star Chamber of extorting money from the tenants. His son Sir Leonard Chamberlain, who shared the office from 1532 and held it until his death in 1561, pursued an extensive military career which included holding the governorship of Guernsey. His son Francis Chamberlain held the office from 1561 to 1570, while also being active elsewhere. The office was granted to Edward Dyer in 1570, but he was more ambitious for a Court career.

[24]   HMC *Salis*. II, p. 141.

On 26 January 1577 six named tenants sent a written petition directly to Burghley, challenging Lee's authority 'as well for themselves as for other of their neighbours'.[25] They complained that 'her Majestie's tenants ... have been lately discharged from the occupation of ... the burrye land' and that they had held 'the said Burrie land ... jointlie with their sayd customarie land ... time oute of mind'. Burghley asked Lee to prepare a legal case, and Lee sent the Woodstock accounts on 13 February 1577, showing that, by custom, the bury land had been kept in hand or let out at will by the Steward.[26] He also itemized the encroachments on the bury lands. Certain tenants had done very well out of their allegedly illegal activities – Lee claimed that 'the cause of the welthe of such as be riche is the bury land and the great poverty of the rest is that they have none or very little therof'. As a result, Burghley ordered an independent survey of the manorial lands to be drawn up, which was duly presented in November 1577.[27] In January 1578 the tenants at Woodstock protested their readiness to obey Burghley and they sent their title to the bury lands to him in February 1578.[28] Lee suggested that Burghley consult George Whitton, Comptroller of Woodstock since he and his family had held that position for more than a century.

The affair dragged on tediously. In March 1579 Burghley obtained the offices of keeper of the garden and the meadows at Woodstock for Lee, possibly in an attempt to placate him, but by May 1579 Lee's patience was wearing thin. He sent six men to speak in person to Burghley, protesting that he had 'spent his time and consumed much ... I complain to few though I might complain more'.[29] He listed the damage done by the tenants' encroachments:

> ... on the bury grounds they will have no tree standing ... [they are] destroying the quick mow that no show thereof appear ... [they have] sawn great trees clean by the roots ... they claim the yard land as many acres as pleaseth them besides the copyhold land and bury land, they will enclose the great wastes as pleaseth them without lease or order. They will till up demesne land at their pleasure never before plowed, to the great hindrance of the rest of the poor inhabitants which were wont with their cattle to have relief there.

---

[25]   BL, Lansdowne MS 25, no. 91, f. 191. Chambers suggests that the imparking mentioned was Lee's 1576 imparkment of the Straights. The tenants' letter makes it clear that this was not the case, and their claim springs from a much earlier imparkment 'time out of mynde'.

[26]   BL, Lansdowne MS 25, no. 96, f. 199.

[27]   BL, Lansdowne MS 25, no. 92, ff. 191–192 – the survey of Thomas Moryson, Clerk to the Pipe in the Exchequer.

[28]   BL, Lansdowne MS 27, no. 46, f. 190.

[29]   BL, Lansdowne MS 25, no. 96, ff.196–197v; BL, Lansdowne MS 27, no. 45, ff. 94–5. Yard land in this context was probably the land around the manorial buildings. Poor tenants had the right to graze animals on bury land between Michaelmas and Martinmas each year.

Typically, Lee protested that 'they offer her Majesty great wrong in claiming that [land], that seemeth her just inheritance'. The six men sent to Burghley gave a good account of themselves. In 1580 Burghley decided to grant bury lands to the occupiers for reasonable fines, and Lee was forced to accept this.[30]

In seeking 'the perservacyon of her Majestie's inheritance and the performance of that duty', Lee had exercised his office at Woodstock far more rigorously than had previously been the practice.[31] He himself had been enclosing demesne land for the development of the deer park but was incensed at any attempt by the tenants to do likewise with the bury lands. Lee himself, even as a private landowner of twenty-five years' experience, had had little experience in dealing with recalcitrant tenants. Buckinghamshire was sheep-rearing country, and Quarrendon itself had been enclosed by Lee's grandfather and by 1563 contained only four families. Even Quarrendon's own 'Berryfield' was usually only leased to one tenant for grazing purposes.[32] Lee's apparent ineptness in dealing with the Woodstock situation illustrates that practices varied across the country with the type of landholding, and a conscientious newcomer would do well to tread carefully, even when safeguarding the Queen's rights.

No sooner was this problem resolved than Lee was faced with another result of the Chamberlains' lax stewardship, although on this occasion he had the support of Burghley and the Privy Council. The long absence of an efficient steward and lieutenant at Woodstock had meant that Woodstock's Comptroller had enjoyed great power and influence, and the coming of a new resident steward with close Court connections was viewed unfavourably. The comptrollership had been held by the Whitton family for at least four generations and, in Lee's time, was held by George Whitton, lord of the manor of Hensington, near Woodstock. Lee and Whitton worked together amicably over the problem of the bury lands, but relations between the two men deteriorated and in December 1580 Whitton's resentment of what he saw as interference by a Court favourite resulted in his bringing an official complaint against Lee.[33]

Whitton was also prepared to rake up old quarrels. In a letter to the Privy Council, Whitton referred to a ten-year-old quarrel over a stolen buck and some pasties, and declared that Lee had said he would 'make me weary of my office'. Whitton also itemized more recent injustices. Lee, he claimed, had kept him from the lucrative wardship of the Spelsbury woods for six or seven years and withheld allowances due to him as Comptroller. Lee had shown much malice, he wrote, and he had been forced to bear various quarrels with Lee's servants 'on account of Sir Henry's great countenance'. Lee was quite prepared to answer

30 *VCH Oxon*, XI, p. 276.
31 BL, Lansdowne MS 25, no. 96, ff. 196–197v.
32 ORO, DIL X/h/1.
33 *CSPD, Addenda 1580–1625*, pp. 26–7. The original in SP12 is badly damaged.

what he regarded as libellous clamours with chapter and verse, and did so in a reply to the Privy Council.[34] George Whitton had earlier complained about the influence of men like Lee who had powerful friends at Court and should not have been surprised when he found himself committed to the Marshalsea prison 'for exhibiting a complaint against sir Henrey Ley, Knight'.[35] The case went before the Privy Council who, although ruling against Whitton, requested that Lee, as the Queen's servant, should 'content himself with the imprisonment of the said Whitton ... and his submission [apology], which their lordships, tendering very much the credytt of the said Sir Henry, thincke to be sufficient'.[36] In the circumstances, it is interesting that Lee sat on a parliamentary committee on the bill against slanderous libelling in February 1581.

Such was the notoriety of the case that in 1584 it was quoted in an attack on the Earl of Leicester. In *A copie of a letter*, usually referred to as *Leicester's Commonwealth*, Leicester was erroneously accused of forcing George Whitney [*sic*] 'to forgo the Controllership of Woodstock [on] ... behalf of Sir Henry Lee'.[37] The anonymous author obviously recognized the relationship between Leicester and Lee, and while listing Leicester's many alleged transgressions, quoted not only the Whitton case, but that of the bury lands at Woodstock. Despite numerous wrangles between Lee and Whitton, both men continued to serve at Woodstock until Whitton's retirement in 1600, when his nephew replaced him at Lee's request.[38] It might have been these two arguments that prompted Lee to seek his own property in the vicinity of Woodstock in May 1581, and by 1583 he had bought the nearby manor house at Ditchley.[39]

Welcoming Queen and Court to Woodstock

A more enjoyable aspect of Lee's work at Woodstock was his duty to welcome the Queen and her Court to her own manor, and to provide suitable entertainment. Elizabeth had already visited Woodstock on 26–31 August 1566, as well as staying there on two occasions in 1572, on 27 August and 7–19 September, and Lee was at pains to make the palace more comfortable before her visit during the period 24 July to 2 August 1574. New windows were cut in the Queen's Presence Chamber and Privy Chamber, and there was enough work to be done in modifying and improving the manor for Woodstock to maintain its

---

[34]   *CSPD*, 1547–80, p. 691.

[35]   Dasent, *APC*, XIII, p. 93 (20 June 1581).

[36]   Ibid.

[37]   *Leicester's Commonwealth: The Copy of a Letter Written by a Master of Art of Cambridge. (1584) and Related Documents*, ed. D.C. Peck (Athens, OH, 1985), pp. 122–3.

[38]   Cecil MS, 69.9 (HMC *Salis*. XVIII, p. 356).

[39]   ORO, LEE 1/3a (9 May 1581).

own resident stonemason.[40] There was much to recommend Woodstock as a convenient stopping place. It was the Queen's own property, she was not there as a guest, and Lee ran the manor solely for her convenience and delectation. Lee's wife never made an appearance at Woodstock so there was no danger of a hostess antagonizing Elizabeth.[41] Lee knew how to combine the skills of the countryman with the accomplishments of the courtier. In addition to hunting, he provided flattering, but not sycophantic, dramatic entertainment. Woodstock's more relaxed, predominantly male ambience made the manor a favourite with Elizabeth.

Many of these factors can be identified in Elizabeth's visit to Woodstock from 29 August until 3 October 1575. The Queen's progress that summer, the longest of the reign, had been in the planning stage since February, with Shrewsbury being chosen as the final destination. The highlight of the progress was the Queen's visit, between 9 and 27 July, to Kenilworth Castle, home of her favourite, Robert Dudley, Earl of Leicester. In 1575 the war in the Netherlands and the possibility of a French marriage for Elizabeth made the political situation tense, and Leicester was eager to use the Queen's visit to further his own political and matrimonial ambitions.

Over eighteen days, he presented entertainments in what Susan Frye describes as 'nearly every allegorical, narrative and festive form conceivable', written for the occasion by George Gascoigne and others.[42] Despite the expense lavished on the hospitality, the 'intense Dudley-centred devices' did not please the Queen, and the last two entertainments were severely curtailed. Gascoigne published the entire text of the entertainments immediately after the Queen's visit, and it appears that the masque of *Sir Bruse sans Pitie* had originally included a military skirmish, for which Leicester had commissioned a new suit of armour from Greenwich.[43] In the event, neither this military spectacle, which possibly

[40]   TNA, PRO, E101/670, f. 26. Anthony Damary was the resident stonemason at Woodstock from c.1570 until 1605.

[41]   Lady Anne Lee would either have been at Quarrendon or with her mother at West Drayton.

[42]   S. Frye, *Elizabeth I: The Competition for Representation* (Oxford, 1993), p. 62. Gascoigne collaborated with William Ferrers, William Hunne and William Patten in producing the texts.

[43]   E. Blakeley, 'Tournament Garniture of Robert Dudley, Earl of Leicester', *Royal Armouries Yearbook*, 2 (1997), pp. 55–63. Gascoigne published all the entertainments originally planned for the visit in *The Princely Pleasures at the Courte at Kenelworth* (London, 1575), and we also have an account known as *Laneham's Letter* (London, 1575) *RSTC* 15190.5, likewise published immediately after the Queen's visit. See also Elizabeth Goldring, 'Portraits of Queen Elizabeth I and the Earl of Leicester for Kenilworth Castle', *Burlington Magazine*, CXLVII, 1231 (October 2005), pp. 654–60; Frye, *Elizabeth I*, pp. 56–78; J. Wilson, *Entertainments for Elizabeth I* (Woodbridge, 1980), pp. 119–42; R.C. McCoy, *The Rites of Knighthood: The Literature and Politics of Elizabethan Chivalry* (Berkeley, CA, 1989), pp. 43–46.

reflected Leicester's military ambitions in the Netherlands, nor the *Masque of Zabeta*, which advocated marriage, was performed. Elizabeth left Kenilworth early, with the unfortunate Gascoigne running alongside her coach, on the Earl's command, attempting to deliver 'some Farewel worth the presenting'.

The Queen's progress then took her west, but she got no further than Sudeley Castle in Gloucestershire when plague in Worcester forced her to turn homewards. The first recorded date when Woodstock was mooted as a stopping place on the 1575 progress was 15 August; it appears that Lee did a formidable job in preparing for the royal visit in a bare fourteen days.[44] Plague was also rife in London, so the Queen and Court remained at Woodstock from 29 August until 3 October, and were joined by the new French ambassador, Michel de Castelnau, Sieur de la Mauvissière and the outgoing ambassador, Bertrand de Salignac de la Mothe Fénelon. Burghley and other members of the Privy Council journeyed to Woodstock and Leicester hastened to be near what he called 'our heaven on earth'.[45]

As well as arranging the hunting, Lee was expected to put on some kind of entertainment for the Court. Here, he had to tread a fine line between his devotion to the Queen and his long friendship with Leicester, as Lee had witnessed the embarrassing curtailment of Leicester's planned devices at Kenilworth. In the event, Lee chose a format he knew well – a chivalric display. There is evidence that a tournament had originally been planned at Woodstock for May Day 1575, and a proclamation had been drawn up by the Heralds, on behalf of 'two strange knyghtes', possibly Dyer and Lee, to challenge 'all nobellmen and gentyllemen at Armes ... to Tylt, cours of the fiels, Turnoy and barryers' ... at your maujestyes royall palace of Woodstocke'.[46] This tournament was never held, but by the time the Queen and Court reached Woodstock on 29 August, it had been subsumed into the entertainment that Lee offered to his sovereign. At Kenilworth, the military skirmish promoting Leicester as the chivalric hero had been cancelled. Did this result in Lee showing how a narrative framework for chivalric display should be couched, or merely, at short notice, utilize trappings unused by Leicester?

The first day of Lee's entertainment told the tale of Hemetes the Hermit, and was one of a number of 'devices' performed during the stay.[47] As the Queen

---

[44]   *CSPD*, 1547–80, p. 502 (15 August 1575). I am grateful to Simon Adams for making this point at the 'Kenilworth Revisited' conference at Kenilworth in September 2005.

[45]   *CSPD*, 1547–80, p. 503 (6 September 1575).

[46]   CA, Portfolio of Tournament cheques, 23a. The precise wording suggests that a chivalric challenge was included in whatever entertainment had been offered to Elizabeth during her ten-day stay in 1574, and also that Lee was already sufficiently confident of his tenure at Woodstock and his tournament prowess by 1574 to issue such a challenge for the following year.

[47]   The Ditchley manuscript is usually known as 'Sir Henry Lee's Devices, etc. before Queen Elizabeth I', BL, Add. MS 41499A. The text for this analysis is taken from ff. 4a–5b and BL,

approached Woodstock, she came across a scene of combat between two knights, Contarenus and Loricus, who battled before Gaudina, daughter of Occanon, Duke of Cambia. On Elizabeth's appearance, the fight was stopped by a blind hermit, Hemetes, who brought the group before her and narrated the story. The two extant manuscript copies of the entertainment both begin at the same line, 'he speaketh to two Knights that foughte there', and clearly some formidable display of arms preceded the narrative.[48] The Queen sat in 'a fine Bower ... covered with greene Ivie, and seates made of earthe with sweete smelling herbes', while a simple tale of thwarted love and chivalry unfolded.

Two star-crossed lovers, Gaudina and Contarenus, had been parted by Gaudina's father until Contarenus 'should fighte with the hardyest Knighte and see the worthiest Ladie of the world'. Deprived of her lover, Gaudina travels to the grotto of Sibylla the prophetess, where she meets Loricus, a knight played by Lee himself, who in vain loved a matchless lady, 'a pearle, as his heart onely esteemed'. Gaudina and Loricus also meet the blind hermit, Hemetes, possibly played by Edward Dyer, once 'a knight of renown', but now 'cast into a corner', by a Lady in 'the shape of a tygresse'. Sibylla prophesizes that all will be resolved when the three travellers reach 'a place, wheare men were moste stronge, women moste fayre, the countrey most fertyll, the people most welthy, the government most just and the Princes most wourthy'. There, two knights will fight and 'the most virtuous lady in the world shal be theare to look on ... a ladie in whome enhabiteth the most vertue, learnyng and beawtie'. Hemetes then proclaimed that the prophecies had indeed just come true: Contarenus had fought Loricus, 'the hardyest Knighte', and the Queen's arrival, as the 'worthiest Ladie of the world', had fulfilled the last condition. In the play, the lovers Gaudina and Contarenus are reunited before Elizabeth and Hemetes regains his sight. The message offered by Woodstock was simple – the mere presence of Elizabeth was enough to resolve all dilemmas.

If the spotlight is turned away from the Queen and the entertainment as a whole, and on to Loricus who appears to gain nothing, what clues can be gathered as to the character and motivation of his alter ego, Lee himself? One assumes that Lee took the part of Loricus willingly, there being no indication of any duress, and he already had a major role as host at Woodstock. Was Lee merely presenting an entertainment or was he taking the opportunity to fashion

---

Add. MS 41499B, Dillon's Victorian transcription. I am grateful to Gabriel Heaton for making his transcriptions of the 1575 Woodstock and 1592 Ditchley entertainments available to me in advance of their publication in the new edition of J. Nichols, *The Progresses and Public Processions of Queen Elizabeth I* (Oxford, forthcoming).

[48]   BL, Add. MS 41499A and BL, Royal MS 18A, XLVIII, ff. 1–37, quoted in J.C. Nichols, *The Progresses, Public Processions etc. of Queen Elizabeth*, 3 vols (London 1823; New York, 1969), I, pp. 553–82. The later 1592 Ditchley entertainment, referring to this production, comments that 'the rest were Iusts & feats of armed knights', BL, Add. MS 41499A, f. 13r.

a role by which he wished to be known to Elizabeth? Did Lee devise the piece himself?

The precise reasons for the entertainment and its authorship have long been debated. A.W. Pollard, in the first modern printed version of the piece in 1910, asserted that it was 'contrived at Leicester's behest in order to allay the overbearing marriage suit made at Kenilworth'. J.W. Cunliffe contested this, stating that the Woodstock devices were directed not by or for Leicester, but against him. Charles Baskervill argued that many of the devices and speeches used at Kenilworth were echoed at Woodstock, and suggested that it was 'designed to restore Leicester to the Queen's favour through evidence of a more self-effacing spirit'. More recently, Susan Doran has agreed that this was an entertainment prepared by Leicester, 'supervised by Leicester's client, Sir Henry Lee'. George Gascoigne, the principal author at Kenilworth specifically denied authorship when he presented the transcribed text to the Queen in 1576.[49]

The oldest manuscript copy remained in Lee's home at Ditchley Park until 1932, and Frances Yates asserts that Lee was indeed the author.[50] As an experienced host, Lee knew what message he wanted to put across, and what was most appealing to the Queen, but whereas certain other poems are definitely attributed to Lee, recent scholarship has shown that the text of *The Tale of Hemetes* was probably the work of Robert Garrett, Reader of Rhetoric at St John's College, Oxford.[51] Given the limited time span Lee had to prepare everything for the Queen's visit, it is highly likely that he delegated the creation of the actual text to the nearest candidate and one from a college with which Lee had close links. But if the words themselves were Garrett's, the deviser of the piece must nonetheless have been Lee, given his close identification with Loricus.

The Tale of Hemetes is the earliest datable text associated with Lee, and Gabriel Heaton makes the convincing suggestion that Lee used it to deliberately present himself in his self-constructed role of Queen's personal tournament Champion.[52] In the entertainment text, Loricus is not afraid to describe himself

---

[49]   *The Queen's Majesty's Entertainment at Woodstock, 1575*, ed. A.W. Pollard (Oxford, 1910), p. 24; J.W. Cunliffe (ed.), 'The Queenes Majesties Entertainment at Woodstocke', *Proceedings of the Modern Language Association*, XXVI (1911), pp. 130–31; C.R. Baskervill, 'The Genesis of Spenser's Queen of Faerie', *Modern Philology*, XVIII, 1 (May 1920), pp. 49–54; S. Doran, *Monarchy and Matrimony: The Courtships of Elizabeth I* (London, 1996), p. 69. Gascoigne's manuscript transcription is BL, Royal MS, 18A XLVIII, ff.1–37 and is reproduced in Nichols, *Progresses ... of Elizabeth*, I, pp. 553–82. The first printed version of the text appeared in 1585.

[50]   F. Yates, *Astraea: The Imperial in the Sixteenth Century* (London, 1975), p. 97.

[51]   G. Heaton, 'The Queen and the Hermit: The Tale of Hemetes, 1575', in P. Beal and G. Ioppolo (eds), *Elizabeth I and the Culture of Writing* (London, 2007), pp. 87–115. Lee's brother, Cromwell Lee, was a fellow of St John's, as were three of Lee's later chaplains at Ditchley.

[52]   Ibid.

as 'the hardyest knighte', as befits the Queen's Champion. He confesses that he 'loved a Ladie' and desired that 'he mighte but love her without lokinge for rewarde'. Finding no favour, he 'made a straunge assay', turning to one of the Queen's attendants, 'a new mistress that lived every day in her eye', in an attempt to provoke jealousy from his true Lady. Thereafter, 'he lefte his owne country and betooke himself to travel and to armes', a reference to Lee's Italian journey and his recent military service in Edinburgh. Loricus's only aim was 'to deserve that reputation, as this greate and noble mistress wold but think hym worthy to be hers thoughe she woule never be none of his'.

If Loricus genuinely wished to serve his lady without looking for reward, his desires were fulfilled, at least in the entertainment. While Hemetes regained his sight, and the lovers Gaudina and Contarenus found each other, Loricus's only reward in the play was some good advice from Hemetes. 'Knight' he was counselled, 'prosecute thy purpose, it is noble, learning ... not to fear ... to take paine, remembering nothing notable is woon without difficulty.'

If Lee created the role of Loricus for himself, he also created a role for the Queen as the matchless unattainable lady he wished to serve. The success of the piece relied on the Queen accepting both her role and Sir Henry Lee as her knight. Lee had already seen at Kenilworth that the Queen could refuse to accept the message of an entertainment, but on this occasion Elizabeth was charmed with the tale of Hemetes. Unlike other entertainments offered to her, it bore no reference to her marriage, her religion or her foreign policy, and Lee's implied request merely to serve her typifies the very undemanding nature of the relationship between Lee and his Queen. Lee's role as Queen's Champion thereafter became central to his career, and he would 'lead out the troops' in her name on 17 November each year until 1590.

What remains unclear is whether this was the first time that Lee had put forward the imaginative proposition that he should be the Queen's tournament champion? The 1575 Woodstock visit marks the first occasion where a text survives of a major entertainment staged by Lee for the Queen and her Court: if an entertainment had been staged for the royal visit in 1574, no record survives other than the tournament challenge. The texts in the Ditchley manuscript are undated and make it difficult to see whether he had claimed the role of champion on an earlier occasion. The position could have been implied by Lee's actions in an Accession Day tournament, but the entertainment at Woodstock in September 1575 gave him the perfect opportunity to put his request directly to the Queen before the whole Court. The milieu of Woodstock was more conducive to a request from Lee than a public tournament in London in November, where the principal focus was on the jousting.

By 1575 Lee was sufficiently confident of his supremacy at the tilt to make his claim in superlative terms as 'the hardieste knyght'. The entertainment, which Heaton suggests had a more complex chivalric frame than anything before associated with Lee, was played before a Court conversant with the allegorical references.[53] The Queen, in holiday and possibly even birthday mood, viewed a simple entertainment specifically designed to flatter her in the sunshine of a September day, and Lee, in his privileged position as her host, could believe it would find royal favour. Lee also revealed his confidence in his position by including oblique references to circumstances known only to the Court. When the Woodstock entertainment appeared later in pamphlet form, the preface advised that 'if you mark the words with this present world or were acquainted with the state of the devices, you shoulde finde no lesse hidden then uttered'. Lee's reference to his having a possible mistress from among the Queen's ladies 'that lived every day in her eye' was bold and shows that Lee was sufficiently in favour to risk mentioning these things before the Queen.[54]

Lee's direct dramatic involvement as Loricus ended with Hemetes' tale; what was said later was of little concern to him, except in his role as overall host. The entertainment continued, and at the end of the first day, Hemetes led the Queen to the new banqueting house, built around the trunk of an oak, which was hung with garlands for the Queen's ladies and many curious pictures. The narrator did not include an explanation of the allegorical references in the pictures, which intrigued the visiting French ambassadors and 'were hard to understand without some knowledge of the inventors'. The 'Queen of the Fayrys' appeared to Elizabeth as she feasted, the first definite sighting of this key character in Elizabethan literature.[55] As Elizabeth left for her lodgings after dinner that night in 1575, she heard a song 'of greate inuention', possibly composed by Edward Dyer, coming from inside the oak tree.[56]

The entertainment on the second day was in a far different vein from the simple tale of the hermit. Now the reunited lovers Gaudina and Contarenus agreed to renounce their love for reasons of state, declaring that 'you must regard the common weales good plight and seek the whole not onely one to saue'. Gaudina returned home, and Contarenus requested that he might go abroad to seek knightly quests elsewhere. Susan Doran contends that Leicester, having

---

[53]   Ibid., p. 91.

[54]   Lee gave no clue whatsoever who this court lady might have been, and there is no reference to any liaison before his long-term affair with Anne Vavasour after 1590 – see Chapter 6 below. Chambers suggests that it could have been Lady Susan Bourchier, who was present at Woodstock. If so, the affair was amazingly discreet.

[55]   Chambers in *Sir Henry Lee*, p. 269 suggests that the undated 'message of the damsel of the Q of fayries' in BL, Add. MS 41499A, ff. 1v–2 refers to an earlier entertainment for Elizabeth at Woodstock in 1572. See also Chambers, *Sir Henry Lee*, p. 88; Matthew Woodcock, 'The Fairy Queen in Elizabethan Entertainments', C. Levin, J. Eldridge Carney and D. Barrett-Graves (eds), *Elizabeth I: Always Her Own Free Woman* (Aldershot, 2003), pp. 97–119.

[56]   Bodl. MS, Rawlinson, Poet. 85, f. 7 ascribes the lines to 'Mr. Dier'; in BL, Harleian MS 6910, f. 169, they are anonymous; see also Chambers, *Sir Henry Lee*, p. 90.

renounced his desire to wed Elizabeth for the sake of his country, was pleading to be allowed to lead an army to the Low Countries.[57] Although the second day's entertainment seems to have been well thought of, Chambers dismisses it as 'a tedious piece', and it certainly had little in common with the simple tale of Hemetes. The Queen had requested that the Hermit's tale 'should be brought to her in writing', and this was rapidly seized upon by George Gascoigne as a way of restoring himself into royal favour after his Kenilworth debacle. Gascoigne's transcription of the entire entertainment was presented to the Queen on New Year's Day 1576, together with his somewhat pretentious translations into Latin, French and Italian.[58]

Clearly, the first day's entertainment was the more acceptable, but one doubts whether Cunliffe was right to suggest that it was inspired by hostility to Leicester, Lee's long-time friend. A far simpler explanation is that Lee devised the tale of Hemetes for his own ends, giving Leicester the opportunity in the second day's entertainment to show himself in a more 'self-effacing' light. Historiographical arguments may rage over the meaning of the second entertainment, but Lee's message had gone forward on the first day.[59]

After the 1575 visit, the Queen continued to favour Lee. In 1577 he was included in the embassy sent to the Emperor in Prague and in 1580 he became Master of the Armoury at the Tower of London. Shortly before 1580 he received a substantial loan from the Queen, which he possibly used to purchase Ditchley in 1583. From 1576 onwards Lee's name appears on the rolls of the New Year's gifts the Queen gave to select courtiers. In return, Lee gave the Queen a series of intricate gifts that often made imaginative reference to his service. In 1576, after the triumph at Woodstock, he gave the Queen 'A booke of golde, with leaves in it of paper and parchment'. In 1577 he gave a 'cap of vellate with xlviij pence of gold'; in 1578 'a juell, beinge a garlande of golde with leaves, and the walnutts in the myddes, with a betterfly pendant of sparks of ophalls and rubyes'. His 1581 gift was 'a launce-staff of goulde, sett with sparkes of dyamondes and rubyes' and in 1585 'a bodkin of golde, with a pendant, being a hunter's horne, and a buck in the midest of it'.[60]

If Lee shared Loricus's desire to love the Queen 'without lokinge for rewarde', he would have his wish in the long run. After 1575 Elizabeth did not return to Woodstock for seventeen years, although this cannot have been a deliberate snub

---

[57] Doran, *Monarchy and Matrimony*, p. 69.

[58] Gascoigne's presentation copy is BL, Royal MS 18A, XLVIII, ff.1–37.

[59] See the debates over the Kenilworth and Woodstock entertainments in Frye, *Elizabeth I*, pp. 56–78; Doran, *Monarchy and Matrimony*, p. 69; S. Doran, 'Juno versus Diana: The Treatment of Elizabeth I's Marriage in Plays and Entertainments, 1561–1581', *HJ*, XXXVII (June 1995), pp. 257–74.

[60] New Year's gifts are listed from various sources in Nichols, *Progresses ... of Elizabeth*, II, and also in Chambers, *Sir Henry Lee*, p. 267.

to Lee as she made no summer progresses whatsoever between 1578 and 1591. Lee merited no mention in official documents after 1580 until his appointment in December 1587 as General of the Horse in the north of England under the Earl of Huntingdon. He continued to lead out the knights as the Queen's Champion each Accession Day and received New Year's gifts from the Queen, but these were largely formulaic 'gifts of plate' and seldom came from the Queen's own hands. After his appointment at the Armoury, Lee gained neither promotion nor favour from the Queen, but his lack of advancement was reasonably typical of the way in which Elizabeth treated her servants, especially those in the gentry.

Simon Adams points out that the Queen used office as a reward rather than as a means of advancement. Once a courtier was appointed to a position of royal service, he was expected to continue there, often at his own expense.[61] This was certainly true of Lee. However generous the Queen might have been to Lee in earlier years, he was still expected to fulfil his positions decades afterwards. Only in his self-appointed role as her champion was he allowed to retire, and even then at the somewhat advanced age of fifty-seven.

It is striking that at the tournaments, Lee frequently adopted the image of a knight divorced from the Court. Rejection of the Court and its corrupt values for the purer virtues of the country was a constant trope in Renaissance literature and Lee, based as he was at Woodstock, had more right than most to appear as the outsider. In the texts recorded in the Ditchley manuscript, he appears as the loyal servant who returns to Court only once a year to fulfil his vow to tilt in the Queen's honour.[62] In 1571 and in 1576 he appeared as 'the green knight', a reference to his hunting persona or to the classic opponent of Sir Gawain. In the entertainment possibly staged on 16 November 1577 Lee, a 'knight … constant in faith', flees the Court for the wilderness, where

> … ther was … no whisperinge of lie to breed or feed factions … no odd fellowes or intelligencers, that carye all newes in ther bosomes & bees in ther brayenes … no sarvants to Ambition, that intangle themselves oft in ther owne snares.[63]

This was a somewhat pointed criticism in an entertainment intended for the Court.

On other occasions he appeared as the 'straunge, forsaken and dispayringe knight' or as 'a knight that warrs against hope and fortune'. This recurring image suggests that it was Lee's own choice, possibly reflecting how he saw his relationship with the Queen. Gabriel Heaton suggests that Lee's tournament

---

[61]   Simon Adams, 'Eliza Enthroned?', in C.A, Haigh (ed.), The Reign of Elizabeth I (Basingstoke: Macmillan, 1984), p. 28.

[62]   BL, Add. MS 41499A, ff. 1–16.

[63]   BL, Add. MS 41499A, ff. 1–16.

personae revealed his frustration at having no greater reward for royal service than his position at Woodstock.[64] Lee's choice of role, however, continued after his appointment as Master of the Armoury, and it is more probable that Lee genuinely preferred to serve the Queen as a soldier, as the organizer of her hunting or at the tournament, even though it curtailed his advancement.[65] His lack of patience with the Court is a recurring theme, and the condemnation of certain types of courtiers in the 1577 entertainment suggests that Lee had sufficient confidence in his own position at Woodstock to voice it.

The role that Lee gives the Queen in the tournament texts is also interesting. Although Elizabeth was cast in roles possessing all possible virtues in the private Court entertainments, it is noticeable that in the texts directly associated with the public November tournaments the tone is less personal. She is naturally addressed as 'most noble ladye', but few compliments are addressed to her personally: the emphasis is more on national celebration and loyalty. There is reference to 'this English holiday, or rather England's happie day', celebrating 'yr highness entrance into government'.[66] Elizabeth is the 'most honoured owner of all trew englishe harts'. Lee proclaims that 'his hart is at libertie to paye the homage of his love', but the stress is on the devotion of the knights, not the nature of its recipient. The texts associated with the tournaments, however, were created for one hearing only, with the main focus of the occasion being the jousting. Also, it was fundamental that the entire day was in Elizabeth's honour.

Lee's Relationship with the Queen as 'Goddess', 1591–1603

Until 1590 there is little evidence in the texts associated with Lee that he endorsed the concept of 'the cult of the Virgin Queen': his addresses to Elizabeth were little more than what would be expected to a reigning monarch. In Lee's last tiltyard entertainment in 1590, however, and in his 1592 entertainment at Ditchley, the imagery that Strong and Yates associate with the 'cult of Elizabeth'[67] began to appear. Elizabeth was addressed as 'Goddess' and there were references to the sacred powers of her virginity. Although Lee never used the names, the literary and artistic association of the Queen with the mythical figures of Cynthia, Diana, Astraea and Bellophoebe date from this time. We also begin to see a deeper dimension to Lee in these later texts. We

---

[64]   G. Heaton, 'Images of a Champion: The Tiltyard Personae of Sir Henry Lee', unpublished paper presented at Courts, Courtiers and Courtliness in the Tudor Age Conference, Kingston University, 9 September 2004.

[65]   Lee's appointment as Master of the Armoury is discussed below in Chapter 4. This necessitated visits to London but not residence at Court.

[66]   BL, Add. MS 41499A, f. 1.

[67]   R. Strong, *The Cult of Elizabeth* (London, 1977); Yates, *Astraea*.

have seen him as soldier, as countryman, as jouster and as deviser of tournament spectacles, but the imagery associated with these two entertainments reveals a Lee who had knowledge at his fingertips of contemporary symbolism, emblems and iconography. It is a dimension of Lee that was also found in his gardens and portrait collection.[68]

On 17 November 1590 Lee staged his retirement from his position as Queen's Champion. This took place during the Accession Day tournament. Too wise a showman to attempt a dramatic presentation while the jousting was actually in progress, he remained silent until it had ended. Then, as a bonus for the onlookers and with all eyes upon himself, he caused a pavilion of white taffeta to arise from the tournament ground, 'like unto the sacred Temple of the Virgins Vestall'.[69] Within the pavilion was an altar, tended by three virgins – the fourth virgin being Elizabeth herself.[70] A crowned pillar, 'embraced by an eglantine tree', stood before the door of the temple and bore a script that addressed Elizabeth as *Felicissimae Virgini*. While all attention was on the scene, Lee caused Mr Hales, one of the Queen's musicians, to plead his case before the Queen in a song of Lee's own composing.[71]

> His golden locks, time hath to silver turned
> (Oh time too swift, and swiftness never ceasing),
> His youth 'gainst age, and age at youth have spurned;
> But spurned in vain, youth waneth by increasing.
> Beauty, strength, and youth, flowers fading bene,
> Duty, faith, and love, are roots and ever green.
>
> His helmet, now, shall make a hive for bees,
> And lover's songs shall turn to holy psalms:
> A man-at-arms must now serve on his knees,
> And feed on prayers, that are old age's alms.
> And so from court to cottage he departs,
> His saint is sure of his unspotted heart.

---

[68] See Chapter 6 below.

[69] W. Segar, *Honor Military and Civill* (London, 1612), *RSTC* 22164. Nichols, *Progresses ... of Elizabeth*, III, p. 49.

[70] The reference to Elizabeth as a vestal virgin was implied in the portrait *Queen Elizabeth with a Sieve* by Quentin Metsys the Younger, c.1583. In Plutarch's *Triumph of Chastity*, Tuccia, one of the four vestal virgins, proved her purity by carrying water from the Tiber to the shrine of Vesta in a sieve.

[71] T. Clayton, 'Sir Henry Lee's Farewell to the Court: The Texts and Authorship of his "Golden Locks Time Hath Turned to Silver"', *English Literary Renaissance*, 4, 2 (Spring 1974), pp. 268–75.

And when he sadly sits in homely cell,
He'll teach his swains this carol for a song,
Blest be the hearts, that think his sovereign well,
Cursed be the souls, that think to do her wrong.
Goddess, vouchsafe this aged man his right,
To be your beadsman now, that was your knight.

These verses precisely expressed Lee's situation and devotion to the Queen and were rich in imagery. The crowned pillar supporting an eglantine rose had long been a favourite device symbolizing devotion to the Queen and was a frequently used trope for Elizabeth. Leicester had used it as an *impresa* in 1559 as *Te Stante Virebo*: 'With you standing, I shall flourish.'[72] The reference to a 'helmet [which] now shall make a hive for bees' would have been recognized by the cognoscenti as an image used in the popular Alciati's *Emblemata* and also in Geoffrey Whitney's recently published *Choice of Emblems*.[73] Lee addresses the Queen as Goddess: before this, he had cast her as the fairest Queen but had hesitated to confer divinity upon her. At the end of the song, the three vestal virgins offered to the Queen Lee's costly gifts, including a 'vaile of white' again betokening sacred virginity. Lee symbolically offered up his own armour at the foot of the crowned pillar, relinquishing his right to fight, and humbly beseeched the Queen to take the Earl of Cumberland for her new Champion. Lee then donned the habit of a hermit, adopting the well-known image in Lull's *Ordre of Chyualry*.

In 1592 Lee used this new persona when, after a long absence, Elizabeth and the Court came on progress to Woodstock from 18 to 23 September. During this stay, Elizabeth visited Lee's own home at Ditchley, four miles from Woodstock, and what Chambers calls 'the Ditchley entertainment' was staged over two days.[74] Despite the longstanding claims by subsequent owners of Ditchley that Elizabeth actually stayed there, Sir Thomas Heneage's accounts

---

[72]   CA, MS M6, f.56b. The device first appeared in Claude Paradin's *Devises Heroiques*, published in 1551 and expanded in 1557.

[73]   Andrea Alciati, *Emblemata* (Augsburg, 1531) was republished in many popular editions in the sixteenth century; see Geoffrey Whitney, *A Choice of Emblemes* (London, 1586), p. 138. *RSTC* 25438.

[74]   Unlike the earlier 1575 Woodstock entertainment, the principal part of the text remained only in manuscript until 1936. Some parts of it were included in *The Phoenix Nest* (1593) *RSTC* 21516. The principal source is the Ditchley MS (BL, Add. MS 41499A) and Dillon's nineteenth-century transcription (BL, Add. MS 41499B). Short extracts from the text also exist in the Ferrers MS transcribed by William Hamper, 1821, reproduced in Nicholls, *Progresses ... of Elizabeth* and in Inner Temple Library, Petyt MS, 538, XXXIII, ff. 299–300. Text drawn from all three was first printed in Chambers, *Sir Henry Lee* (1936) and in Wilson, *Entertainments*, pp. 119–42. Here I have quoted from Dillon and a new transcription by Gabriel Heaton for the new *Progresses ... of Queen Elizabeth I*.

in his role of Treasurer of the Chamber suggest that it is highly unlikely that the Queen did any more than dine there and see part of the entertainment. If the Queen was to reside at a house, it was standard practice for Simon Bowyer, Gentleman of the Chamber and a team of eight yeomen and grooms to spend eight days preparing her apartments, at a cost to the Chamber of £8 17s 4d.[75] This was done for Woodstock in September 1592. 'The said Simon Bowyer' was, however, only given two days 'for making ready a dinner house at Sr Henrie Leyes at Ditchley' at a cost of 39s 4d, with no mention of apartments being prepared. At the same time, Bowyer and his team were paid 39s 4d 'for the making ready a standing at Sr Henrie Leyes for the hearing of an oration for her Ma[jes]tie' and a similar amount for a standing for Woodstock. This confirms the view that the entertainments were held at the two locations.

The Ditchley entertainment was more involved than the brief narrative that followed Lee's retirement tilt, and both the text and the portrait of Elizabeth that was integral to the performance were rich in the imagery of her as Virgin and Divine Being. The theme of the entertainment was the struggle between Constancy and Inconstancy, and if it lacked the innovative narrative and freshness of the 1575 Woodstock entertainment, it was full of riddles and allegorical references to amuse an older, wiser and perhaps more sedentary Queen. In many ways, it can be regarded as a sequel to the earlier entertainment, and several hands appear to have contributed to the text. Richard Edes, an Oxford cleric associated with Lee, is named as the author of the specific dialogue between Constancy and Inconstancy, but the heart of the entertainment contains phrases reminiscent of those used by Lee in both his tournament texts and his letters. The subject matter on both days was intensely personal to Lee to the point of self-indulgence: he himself played a major role as the Old Knight, and there is little doubt that he devised the piece. It tells us much about the relationship between Lee and his Queen that he saw an entertainment based largely on his own career as acceptable to Elizabeth and the Court.

Indeed, much of this was daringly autobiographical. Lee had long been estranged from his wife, and Lady Lee had died in 1590. By then, Lee had begun his long-term liaison with his mistress Anne Vavasour, formerly one of the Queen's gentlewomen of the chamber, who had given birth to the Earl of Oxford's son in the maids' chamber at Court in 1581. It is not known when their relationship started, but by 1590 Anne was a permanent fixture at Ditchley, although it seems improbable that she would have been present during the Queen's visit.[76] On the first day of the entertainment, the Queen was led through a magic grove where knights had been turned into trees and their ladies into leaves on account of their inconstancy. She then came across an old knight cast into an enchanted

---

[75] TNA, PRO, E351/541, f. 166v (Thomas Heneage's accounts).
[76] For a full discussion of Lee's relationship with Anne Vavasour, see Chapter 6 below.

sleep as a result of his disobedience to the Fairy Queen. Here, Lee, as the Old Knight, recalled the entertainment of 1575 when 'the fayrie queene the fairest queene saluted' and continued its tale. A principal feature in *The Tale of Hemetes the Hermit* had been the 'enchanted pictures' which hung around the hermit's cell. The Fairy Queen had commanded the Old Knight to keep the pictures all together, acting as their guardian in that place, 'euer to tarry neuer to depart'. But Lee, as the Old Knight 'whome in elder tyme she dearly loued' confesses that he, too, had been inconstant in his devotion:

> but loe unhappie I was ouertaken
> by fortune forst a straunger ladies thrall
> whom when I saw all former care forsaken
> to fynd her out I lost meeself & all
> through which neglect of dutie 'gan my fall.[77]

Lee was an expert on *imprese*, and the last of the Latin mottos in the Dirchley portrait gives a clue to the whole entertainment. This Latin *impresa* has been variously construed as 'She gives and does not expect', 'In giving back she increases' and, perhaps more significantly, 'She can but does not take revenge'. Was Lee, while stressing his devotion to his Queen, also emphasizing that he had no real intention of relinquishing his illicit mistress who lived with him at Ditchley until his death in 1611? Despite his misalliance there is little evidence that Lee was in disgrace with the Queen in 1592; indeed, the royal visit to Lee's home in Ditchley would argue against this. Lee made his fault the main import of the first day's entertainment, deliberately putting the Queen in a magnanimous and miraculous light. He made it clear that the Queen could have exacted revenge for his wrong-doing, and was therefore twice as glorious for disdaining to do so. He also pre-empted any adverse reaction on the part of the Queen by claiming:

> So kind is loue, then being once conceaued
> It trusts agayne although it wer deceaued.

By the evening of the first day's entertainment, the 'captive Ladies, captive Knights' had been freed by the quick wits of the 'Heavenlie Goddesse' and the portrait, as often happened in the Queen's progresses, remained *in situ* as a vivid memorial to an ephemeral event.

The second day's entertainment was again heavily autobiographical. Lee reverted to his 1575 persona of Loricus, and a chaplain narrated what had happened to him since that date. It appeared that Loricus had

---

[77] Text taken from sources listed at footnote 74 above.

... consorted with coragious Gentlemen, manifesting inward joyes by outward
justes, [giving] the yearly tribute of his dearest loue', [and spending] the florishe
of his gladest dayes, crauing no rewarde els but that he might loue and might be
knowne to loue. [At last] he retired his tyred lymmes ... in this Countrye ... where
he kept a [verie] Court in his owne bosome.

Lee was quick to draw attention to 'the miserie of his bodie, whos roof was
rough with the moss of gray hayers'. Exactly the same age as Elizabeth, Lee
frequently contrasted his decrepitude with the perennial youth of the Queen.
The chaplain was relating that Loricus was dying when, suddenly, his page
appeared with news that the Queen's presence had brought about his master's
recovery, hence endowing Elizabeth with godlike-powers over death. On his
recovery, Loricus presented a 'simple Legacie' to the Queen. Lee had learned an
important lesson from Leicester's entertainment at Kenilworth in 1575. When
the Lady of the Lake had attempted to give Elizabeth the castle and all its lands,
the Queen had replied somewhat tersely that she thought she already owned
it. Lee now bequeathed to Elizabeth not Woodstock, which she owned, nor
Ditchley, which was his, but 'The Whole Manor of Love', not geographically
delineated, but with 'meadowes of greene thoughtes, pastures of feeding fancies,
rivers of flowing fauers, orchards stored with apples, fishing for daintie kisses'
and 'spanniells of kindenes'.

How far did these texts, presented to Elizabeth over the span of some twenty
years, genuinely reflect Lee's attitude to the Queen? It is well to remember
the circumstances in which they were conceived. The texts were not designed
for publication or even for circulation and study over several years. Texts of
entertainments that found a printer, such as Gascoigne's *Princely Pleasures at the
Courte at Kenelworthe* or the Earl of Hertford's 1591 Elvetham entertainment
did so because their patrons wanted to disseminate their political point as
widely as possible, and often they did not accurately reflect what had occurred.[78]
The 1575 text of *Hemetes* was unique in that it was presented to the Queen in
manuscript form at her specific request, and it was Gascoigne who sought to
benefit from it, not Lee. The full text of Lee's 1592 Ditchley entertainment had
to wait until 1936 to appear in print, and most of the tournament texts still
remain in manuscript.

Texts designed for Court entertainment would usually have been performed
once, for a quite specific audience and for a specific occasion and location.[79] As

---

[78] George Gascoigne published *The Princely Pleasures at the Courte at Kenelworthe* (London,
1576). A unique copy of this was destroyed in 1879, but the text was reprinted in *The whole workes
of George Gascoigne Esquire* (London, 1587).

[79] *Gorboduc*, first performed at the Inns of Court in 1562, was unusual in that it was
subsequently performed at Court.

they were topical, many of their references are lost to us now and their recovery is only speculative. These texts do not rival Sidney's *Arcadia*, Spenser's *Faerie Queene* or Shakespeare's plays, and laboured attempts to subject them to detailed literary criticism is to mistake their very ephemeral nature. Lee's message to the Queen throughout the texts was simply one of fidelity, devotion and service. His private sentiments appear to be equally straightforward. There is no indication that he ever corresponded with the Queen personally, although he mentioned her often in his seventy private letters that do survive, and in all but one, discussed below, the sentiments he voiced echoed those in the literary texts. His attitude to the Queen was largely unchanging over some thirty years and leaves little doubt that what he said in public genuinely echoed his private thoughts.

Despite the success of the 1592 visit, the Queen never returned to Woodstock. She did, however, order a major programme of modernization to be carried out on the property from September 1593 until May 1595, and this was overseen by Lee. The building work was organised by a William Spicer, although Burghley decreed that Spicer would 'in noe sorte medle with the money'.[80] Much of the £800 laid out on the two-year programme was spent on the fashionable new plasterwork in the principal rooms and Privy Chamber, for which Spicer recruited local Oxford craftsmen, and even Lee's High Lodge was given a new hall at this time.[81] Although documentary evidence indicates that Lee was heavily involved in this work, the Queen's continued absence from Woodstock explains why he chose to spend more time at Court in London after 1595.

Many Elizabethan courtier gentlemen, having achieved a certain standing in their younger days at Court, later opted to devote more time to their own estates if the Queen would allow it. Lee reversed the practice, spending more time in London after his retirement and seeking a more lucrative Court position. Promotion was rare in the last decade of Elizabeth's reign, but the deaths of two prominent office-holders in the Queen's household created rare opportunities for advancement. The great pluralist Sir Thomas Heneage died on 17 October 1595 leaving vacant his positions as Treasurer of the Queen's Chamber, Keeper of the Records at the Tower, Keeper of Waltham Forest, Vice Chamberlain and Chancellor of the Duchy of Lancaster. These attracted much speculation and lobbying among prospective contenders, and Lee's candidature was backed by Burghley and Sir Robert Cecil. The gossip at Court caused contemporaries some amusement. Rowland Whyte, London agent for Sir Robert Sidney, brother of the late Sir Philip, wrote to his master at Brill on 19 October 1595

---

[80]   TNA, PRO, AO1/2483/300, Roll 300 of Sir Henry Lee, Keeper of Woodstock House covering 24 September 1593–31 May 1595. See also TNA, PRO, E351/3363; Colvin, *King's Works*, IV, II, p. 353.

[81]   C. Gapper, 'Plasters and Plasterwork in City, Court and Country 1530–1640', doctoral thesis (University of London, 1998).

confirming Heneage's death and reporting that there were 'many great sutors' for his positions.[82] Sir Robert Cecil, he reported,

> ... stands for the chancellorship of the duchye; [Sir John] Stanhope, [Sir Walter] Rawleigh, who is come in secret neare the Court ... [and] Sir Hen. Leigh wold be Vice-Chamberlain, and ... my Lord Essex desires Waltham forest. I doe not know who shall have the treasurership of the chamber.

The last position was rapidly filled by Stanhope, but the other positions remained vacant. On 27 December 1595 Whyte reported to Sydney that:

> I was at Court this morning, where nothing is so much thought upon as dancing and playing. Some are there, hoping for preferment, as my Lord North and Sir Henry Leigh. They play at cards with the Queen, and yt is like to be all the honor that will fall unto them this yeare.[83]

On 19 July 1596 Sir Francis Knollys, Treasurer of the Household, died, and his son Sir William Knollys, soon complained to Cecil, on 26 July 1596, that, despite his assiduous lobbying, the Queen had decided to award his father's position to the card-playing Lord North.[84] Rumour had it that she was minded to make Knollys Vice-Chamberlain and appoint 'Sir Harry Lea' to the position of Controller of the Household, which had been vacant since 1590. Knollys protested that he would rather be Controller than Vice-Chamberlain, 'for as I desire to continue my father's place if it be possible, so will I ... shun to be Vice-Chamberlain'. In the event, North became Treasurer of the Household, Knollys became Controller and the office of Vice-Chamberlain remained vacant. In February 1598 Rowland Whyte again informed Robert Sidney in code that:

> Sir Henry Leigh came to Court 7 days ago, and was private with 900 [Burghley] and 200 [Cecil]. I hear he is encouraged to stand to be Vice-Chamberlain. Lord Essex ... may not be against Sir Hen. Leigh.[85]

Once again, Lee was destined to be disappointed – the office of Vice-Chamberlain was to remain vacant for another three years when it was filled

[82] HMC de Lisle and Dudley, II p. 175; A. Collins, *Letters and Memorials of State ... [of the Sydney family]*, 2 vols (London, 1746), I, p. 175.

[83] HMC de Lisle and Dudley, II, p. 205; Collins, *Letters*, I, p. 386; HMC *Salis*. V, p. 523. Lord North's household books often record the amounts that he lost to Elizabeth playing cards – 'Lost at play with the Queen £32' – and he never failed to present her with a New Year's gift of £10 in gold in a silken purse; see Lady F. Bushby, *Three Men of the Tudor Time* (London,1911), p. 105.

[84] HMC *Salis*. VI, pp. 287–88.

[85] HMC de Lisle and Dudley, II, pp. 321–22; Collins, *Letters*, II, p. 89.

by Stanhope. Although it is interesting to see what patronage Lee enjoyed, one wonders whether, at sixty-five, his candidature was serious. The work could be onerous, but the previous two vice-chamberlains, Sir Christopher Hatton and Sir Thomas Heneage, had enjoyed considerable royal favour to the point of friendship. The position guaranteed access to the Queen in the Privy Chamber, a seat on the Privy Council and a prospect of considerable financial gain – all of which were attractive to Lee. His efforts to secure a position had necessitated greater attendance at Court, and in 1598 he was named at the head of a list of '58 principal Gentlemen of value and service that have ben and are usually in Court'.[86] He also headed a similar list for Buckinghamshire, of the same date, of 'principal gentlemen that dwell usually in their contreis'.

Lee's increased attendance brought him into contact with the brightest star in the late Elizabethan Court, Robert Devereux, Earl of Essex. Essex, stepson to Lee's long-time friend, the late Earl of Leicester, had made his first appearance on the tournament field in 1586 and had dominated the Accession Day tournaments after 1590. In many ways, Essex, high in royal favour, filled the place left in Lee's affections by the death of Sir Philip Sidney, as the chivalric hero of the tournament and a young man of considerable promise. Lee followed Essex's military career closely, and his letters to him reveal personal warmth. Lee also continued his long friendship with Lord Burghley and his son Sir Robert Cecil, notwithstanding a degree of rivalry between Cecil and Essex. In 1596 Burghley proposed Lee as a member of the Order of the Garter, and although Lee received only Burghley's vote that year, he received nine out of the ten votes of nobles in the Order in 1597.[87] The Knights of the Garter might elect a candidate to join their ranks, but the Queen had the last word on the matter and could use her veto. The ever-busy Rowland Whyte wrote to Sir Robert Sidney on 27 April 1597 that:

> ... there were 5 knights of the Order made, the Duke of Wurtemberg, Lord Hunsdon, Lord Montjoy, Lord Th. Howard and Sir Ha. Leigh. Lord Essex, as I have heard, was earnest with his companions for the election of Sir H. Leigh; then had much ado to bring the Queen to consent.[88]

Lee was undoubtedly a gentleman, a knight and a royal servant of long standing, but membership of the oldest chivalric order in Christendom was limited to twenty-four and rarely included men who had no noble blood or had not been

---

[86]   TNA, PRO, SP12/269, f. 46; Penry Williams, 'Court and Polity under Elizabeth I', in John Guy (ed.), *The Tudor Monarchy* (London, 1997), pp. 372–5.

[87]   BL, Add. MS 36768 (Register of the Order of the Garter).

[88]   HMC de Lisle and Dudley, II, p. 271; Collins, *Letters*, II, pp. 45–6.

ennobled.[89] The Queen allowed few honours in the last decade of her reign and, having a keen sense of social precedence, she was only reluctantly persuaded to award Lee this highest chivalric accolade. Frances Yates makes the salient point that Elizabeth, at least in the early years of her reign, used membership of the order to bind members of the nobility to her.[90] Clearly, in the Queen's eyes, by 1597 there was very little more to be gained from appointing Lee to the honour.

Lee's election to the ranks of the Garter Knights elevated his standing high above other courtier gentlemen of his time and, at sixty-four, he made the most of the occasion. The annual St George's Day ceremonies had developed into a great public spectacle: the 'splendid cavalcade' of new knights would ride to Windsor for the feast on 22 April, followed by the investiture of the new knights in St George's Chapel and the procession of the Queen and her knights around the castle courtyard on 23 April.[91] Sir Henry Lee rode from Charing Cross to Windsor with a train of 200 retainers, all dressed in blue, and was duly invested on 23 April. This led to him commissioning Marcus Gheeraerts to paint a new portrait of him in his Garter robes (see Ill. 13). This was the pinnacle of his chivalric career, and it was a matter of great personal regret to him that his health, which forced him to leave Windsor immediately after the investiture, allowed him to attend so few of the Garter feasts after 1600.

Lee was also an observer of the somewhat turbulent relationship between Essex and the Queen. Essex, the royal favourite and a man of great ambition, was becoming increasingly frustrated by his lack of military success against Spain and what he saw as his diminishing influence on Elizabeth in the Council. In a famously stormy debate in the Council Chamber in July 1598, Essex turned his back upon the Queen, provoking her to box his ears. He reached for his sword in the royal presence, only to be held back by Lord Howard, and left the room after forcibly speaking his mind. Essex acrimoniously withdrew from Court, and Lee was among the many who wrote to him on this occasion.

Letters often reveal more about the writer than the subject, and if the spotlight is turned away from Essex and his quarrel, what Lee wrote tells us much about his own attitude to the Queen.[92] It is therefore worth looking at Lee's letter of August 1598 as a whole (see Appendix 6). It is interesting to compare it with the more famous missive to Essex from the Lord Keeper, Sir Thomas Egerton.[93] Egerton was a lawyer and argued like one; he reminded the Earl that he was failing in his 'indissoluble dutie which you owe to your most gratious soveraigne, a dutie imposed upon you not by nature and policie only but by religious and

---

[89]   One of the few was Sir Christopher Hatton, Lord Chancellor of England, who was made a Knight of the Garter in 1588.

[90]   F. Yates, *The Rosicrucian Enlightenment* (London, 1972), p. 8.

[91]   Strong, *Cult of Elizabeth*, p. 173.

[92]   BL, Add. MS 48126, f. 97.

[93]   BL, Add. MS, 48126, ff. 99–99v.

sacred bond'. He quoted advice from Seneca and pointedly commented that 'the difficultie, my good Lord, is to conquer yourself'.

Lee's letter to Essex is more personal and reveals greater intuition in handling both an intransigent peer and a Tudor monarch. He acknowledges, like Egerton, that Essex's 'honour is more deare unto you than yor life', but clearly understands the Queen, both in her body politic and body natural. He reminds Essex that:

> ... she is your sovereigne, with whom you may not treate uppon equall conditions ... consider ... how great she is with whome you deal, how willing, with how little yielding, to be conquered; what advantage [you have] by yielding when you are wronged.

Lee here demonstrates a keen knowledge of the female psyche. Essex had formerly castigated the Queen's female qualities in government; now Lee is subtly showing him how to play on them.[94] Lee's arguments are varied: Essex was ambitious for Court preferment, and Lee reminds him, after the recent death of Burghley on 4 August, 'what opportunities [the Queen's] late loss and the State's present necessity maye give you'. Lee's closing sentence again shows his understanding of Elizabeth as a woman when he writes 'whatsoever peace you make ... use no means but yourself, w[hi]ch will be ... more acceptable to her'. This is one of the longest and the most personal of Lee's letters and demonstrates both considerable affection for Essex and an appreciation of his damaged pride. It is also one of the few surviving letters in which Lee presumes to give any kind of advice.

In his role as mediator, Lee also wrote to Cecil on 27 August 1598, asking for his 'love and friendship to a man of more worth [Essex]: now is the time for you to show and he to accept'.[95] Lee had already informed Essex how Cecil had 'made reporte of your lordships good service in counsel' and was keen for both men to 'leave circumstances apart'. Regrettably, unlike Essex's spirited reply to Egerton, no letter to Lee has survived.[96] It was, however, Essex's physical weakness rather than his political arguments that occasioned reconciliation. In September 1598 Essex succumbed to a bout of fever, and Elizabeth seized the opportunity more as a woman than as a monarch. She sent her own physician to tend her turbulent favourite, and Essex returned to Council on 10 September, having an audience with the Queen two days later.

---

[94] In 1597 Essex had told the French ambassador de Maisse that he 'laboured under two things at Court, delay and inconstancy, which proceeded chiefly from the sex of the Queen': de Maisse, *A journal of all that was accomplished by M. de Maisse, Ambassador in England*, trans. G.B. Harrison and R.A. Jones (London, 1931), p. 115.

[95] Cecil MS, 63.70 (HMC *Salis*. VIII, p. 320).

[96] T. Birch, *Memoirs of the Reign of Queen Elizabeth, From the Year 1581 till her Death*, 2 vols (London, 1754), II, pp. 384–7.

In 1600 Lee himself was driven to display an opinion of the Queen far removed from his usual deference. The Queen's insistence on a royal progress that summer had been unpopular with many members of the Court, and Lee wrote irascibly to Cecil on 13 June, complaining that:

> ... her Majesty threatyns a progress, and her comyng to my houses ... I wolde be most proud as oft before tyme, if my fortune answered my desire, or part of her hyghness many promises [had been] performed ... my estat withowt my undoyinge cann not bere yt, my contynionce in her Cowrt has bin long, my charge grete, my lands sowld and debts not small, how this wyll agree with the entertaining of such a prynce, y[ou]r wisdom can best judge.[97]

Although Lee was not alone in attempting to avoid the burden of a royal visit, the letter is very uncharacteristic, especially since Woodstock was the Queen's own property. At the time, Lee was heavily in debt through his building programme at Ditchley and Quarrendon, and had failed to obtain the lucrative position of vice-chamberlain at Court, the very office which was responsible for royal progresses. Moreover, he was now sixty-seven and suffering badly from gout, as his other letters testify. The letter appears to reflect more a momentary fit of pique than a considered opinion, but Lee escaped lightly. The Queen went elsewhere on progress, and Rowland Whyte informed Sir Robert Sidney from Oatlands on 30 August 1600 that:

> ... this gracious souverayne of ours ... meanes to kill many stags and buckes er she remove from these hunting cowntreis. Her body endures more travel than they can that attend her.[98]

Lee had warned Essex in his letter of August 1598 that if he caused the Queen 'to forgett her powers and yeild [*sic*] in her affection to that w[hi]ch she is unwilling to doe, your peace cannot be without a matter of newe difference, in always as she will hardlie forgett to what unequal conditions you brought her'. [99] Lee's advice proved percipient. Essex failed to secure the late Lord Burghley's Mastership of the Court of Wards, and his appointment as Lord-Lieutenant of Ireland and his military activities there in 1599 was dogged with disaster. When he deserted his command in Ireland and burst into the Queen's chamber at Nonsuch Palace on 28 September 1599, his fall became inevitable. Later the same day he was arrested and, although the terms of his confinement were eased in the succeeding months, he had lost the Queen's favour. Denied

---

97   Cecil MS, 80.24 (HMC *Salis.* X, p. 180).
98   HMC de Lisle and Dudley, II; Collins, *Letters*, IV, p. 280.
99   BL, Add. MS 48126, f. 97.

access to Elizabeth and facing financial ruin, Essex and his group of followers embarked on an attempt to raise London to his cause on 8 February 1601. Essex was arrested, tried for treason on 19 February and executed on Tower Green on 25 February 1601. No letter from Lee to Essex during these unfortunate eighteen months survives, if one was ever written. Indeed, Lee was more taken up with his unsuccessful attempts to keep his own unfortunate cousin, Thomas Lee, out of trouble.[100]

Lee's relationship with the Queen in her last years seems to have been more affected by his own poor health than by any association with Essex. He seldom came to Court, and only referred to Elizabeth's passing in March 1603 in a letter to Sir Robert Cecil, describing his 'grieved and wandering spirits ... since the calling from us of our most dread and gracious sovereign'.[101] The Queen's personal Champion, always at pains to stress her youthfulness compared to his twisted old age, was to outlive his sovereign by some eight years.

Some Reflections on a Very Singular Courtier

Sir Henry Lee, like Heneage and Buckhurst, was what Steven May terms 'a working royal servant' as opposed to the largely ornamental courtier of the type practised by Edward Dyer and the Earl of Oxford.[102] He was not a royal favourite in the mould of Leicester, Essex or Hatton: he was a courtier gentleman who enjoyed the Queen's favour, especially in the decade from 1570 to 1580. After 1580 he fell more into the conventional category of having achieved a position in royal service and being expected to remain there with no more pecuniary favours. The substantial financial benefits he received in the early years had largely ceased by 1580, and by 1600 Lee was in no doubt that his service had cost him more than he had gained. He was aware that, like many of the Queen's servants, he could ruin himself financially in the Queen's service without recompense. Despite his attempts to secure the vice-chamberlainship somewhat late in life, Lee appears to have been well satisfied with his roles at Woodstock and at the Armoury, which he administered personally and with some relish. He was unique in that he personally created a role for himself as the Queen's tournament Champion, and decided how best to serve his Queen, in positions he found conducive.

In his public relationship with Elizabeth, Lee comfortably subscribed to the Petrarchean and Platonic trope of the constant lover who remained ever faithful, although he loved in vain. In his 1575 Woodstock entertainment, rejection of

---

[100] See Chapter 6 below.

[101] Cecil MS 99.56 (HMC *Salis*. XV, p. 9) (Lee to Cecil 27 March 1603).

[102] S. May, *The English Courtier Poets: The Poems and their Contexts*, 2nd edn (Columbia, MO, 1999), p. 63.

Loricus by his Lady had already been scripted in. Within the concept of courtly love, the Queen was the unattainable mistress, goddess and saint. Obedience and devotion to such a one could allow proud men to accept the demands and control of a female monarch while maintaining their self-respect in a patriarchal society.[103] The relationship between male courtiers and the Queen was multi-layered and complex. John Guy has defined the 'essence of Elizabethan politics' when he wrote that 'to succeed at Court, politicians had to pretend to be in love with the Queen'.[104] While this is a somewhat cynical view, many men at Court fundamentally saw the Queen as a female in need of masculine advice and guidance.

There were a few, like Burghley or Cecil, who were prepared to accept her as a female employer and some, like Egerton, found it easier to see her as the monarch *per se*. Lee, no politician and one of the least demanding of her courtiers, could also see her essentially as a woman, and the intuition he reveals in his advice to Essex in 1598 is an indication of his age and maturity. Given how little evidence there is of Lee enjoying female company before his relationship with Anne Vavasour, it might also be indicative of the education he himself had been receiving since 1590.

In private, Lee was an accomplished courtier to whom the Queen was accustomed and with whom the Queen had grown old. They were both born in 1533 and shared many of the inherent prejudices, manners, memories and habits of an earlier age. Decades of service created a comfortable if undemanding relationship between them, which availed Lee little financially but ensured that he was welcome to join the Queen at cards. Lee might declare himself in public as the knight 'whome in elder tyme she dearly loued', but it was probably his sheer longevity that made him an agreeable companion to the Queen as they mutually moved towards their seventh decade. Elizabeth enjoyed the company of young men around her, but still remained more comfortable with the families she knew well. Elizabeth's lovers could and did age: she would remain ever young.

> Times yong howres attend her still
> And her Eyes and Cheekes do fill
> With fresh youth and beautie;
> All her louers olde do growe
> But their hartes they do not so
> In their Loue and duty.[105]

---

[103]   Hackett, *Virgin Mother*, p. 79.

[104]   J. Guy, 'The 1590s: The Second Reign of Elizabeth I?' in J. Guy (ed.), *The Reign of Elizabeth: Court and Culture in the Last Decade* (Cambridge, 1995), p. 3.

[105]   Francis Davison, 'To Cynthia' in *A Poetical Rhapsody* (London, 1602), p. 119. *RSTC* 6373. The verses were sung at the 'shew on horseback' presented by the Earl of Cumberland, on May Day 1601 or 1602.

During Lee's retirement the Queen would play cards with him, accept his company, deny him any promotion and begrudge his appointment to the Order of the Garter. It was no wonder that he grew uncharacteristically tetchy when threatened with yet another royal visit. But the best testimony to Lee's private attitude to the Queen comes from his 1598 letter to Essex, where he unerringly credits Elizabeth not only with the greatness of a Queen, but also with the human qualities of a woman.

What was it, then, that made Lee act as he did, and in what way could his career be assessed to have been 'successful'? A simple answer is that what ultimately separated him from other courtier gentlemen of his status was his election to the Order of the Garter in 1597. Yet this was more an accolade that came from the acclaim of the peers of the realm than from a reluctant Queen, and above all from the connections he had made through his organization of, and participation in, the Accession Day tournaments. Financially, he benefited little from royal service: he received no titles, and his most famous role was self-made. His experience in this regard was not untypical of others who made their careers in royal service, although his loyalty and uncomplaining devotion to his royal mistress lasted longer than most. Perhaps Lee, in his alter ego as Loricus had already grasped the reality of the situation when he entertained Elizabeth in 1575. Hemetes gives 'this advyse ... Loricus, thy end wilbe reward, at least most reputation, with noblest women'. The message was clear: Lee, in serving his mistress, must appreciate that service was its own reward. His recompense was honour and reputation, but little else.

Chapter 4

Master of the Armoury, 1580–1611

On 9 June 1580 Sir Henry Lee received his patent as Master of the Armoury following the death of Sir George Howard, and he held this position until 1611. As with his stewardship at Woodstock, Lee chose to exercise his authority in practical terms, accepting the responsibilities of an office which, in other hands, could have become merely ceremonial. Although this gave him wide powers over armour provisions throughout the country, he also inherited major and often intransigent problems that typified Crown service in late Elizabethan England. Many Crown officials with whom he dealt were poorly paid and relied on entrenched corruption and peculation (that is, embezzlement) to supplement their wages. The London guilds had vested interests and entertained high expectations of royal servants associated with their trade. Above all, Lee experienced the Queen's notorious reluctance to spend money on the upkeep and development of her armoury at a time when not only was the nature of warfare fundamentally changing in Europe but England was actively engaged in conflict.

The Work of the Armoury

The Office of the Armoury and the Ordnance Office had been created in the early fifteenth century from the Privy Wardrobe, with both organisations accommodated in the Tower of London. The first Master of the Ordnance was appointed in 1414, and an official solely responsible for personal armour appeared in 1423. It was not until 1462 that the position was given the title of Master of the King's Armoury. This position rose in importance when Henry VIII established the royal armoury workshops at Greenwich in 1515. Under the Tudor monarchs, men who had distinguished themselves in warfare and in tournaments were usually appointed to the office. Sir Richard Guildford, who held the post from 1485 until 1506, and his son and successor Sir Edward Guildford were both responsible for the military logistics of provisioning wars against France, and Sir Edward acted as Master of Ceremonies for Henry VIII's tournaments. Sir John Dudley, soldier, admiral, expert tilter and later Duke of Northumberland, was Master of the Armoury from 1533 to 1544, and Sir George Howard, a veteran jouster with military experience in France and Scotland held this position from

1559 until his death around 1580.[1] Sir Henry Lee, with both military and tournament experience, admirably fitted the career profile of his predecessors.

The Master of the Armoury was responsible for maintaining stores of armour and small weapons in the south of England, sufficient to equip an army both against the growing threat of invasion and for service abroad. The premier southern arsenal was the Tower of London, and Lee's own Exchequer accounts described the task as:

> ... yssuing and defreyinge ... in provyson of Armes, for kepinge and repayringe the armoure and other habiliamentes remayninge in the Severall stores within the Tower of London, ... Hampton court, the castle of Windsore and at Portsmouth ... repayring of arms sent to her Ma[jes]ties shippes ... and repayring the Armoury made at Grenewyche.[2]

The Master, who had his main office in the White Tower, was assisted by a deputy who carried out the day-to-day administration. There was a clerk of the Armoury and some eighteen armourers at the Tower, while the smaller armouries had their own keepers. The office carried an Exchequer fee, with additional payments for the armoury at Greenwich and rents for various tenements adjacent to the Tower.[3] The Master had accommodation near the Tower, and Lee made regular visits to London, although it is unclear how much of his time was spent in the Armoury. Little actual armour was made at the Tower, and the armourers were mainly occupied in maintaining both the existing stores and the expensive tournament armour deposited there by the monarch and various noblemen.

Lee was thorough in the performance of his duties as Master. The Armoury accounts from May 1580 were well kept for Elizabeth's first time in the reign and rendered each Michaelmas and Easter. Over a period from 1 May 1580 to 31 December 1610 they record the issuing of arms and personal armour to the army:

> ... corseletts, jackes of plate, morryons & other sortes of Armour ... the provysion of swordes with gardes and hangers and carradge therof by land and sea for furnishinge of the forces in Ireland late servinge her highness there at severall tymes.[4]

---

[1]   Sir George Howard owned one of the expensive tilting armours in the *Almain Armourer's Album*. Sir Thomas Darcy was Master of the Armoury from 1544 to 1553, followed by Sir Richard Southwell, who was persuaded to relinquish the position in 1559.

[2]   TNA, PRO, E351/2963 III, 1580–1601 and IV, 1601/2–1610. Also TNA, PRO, AO1/2299/3; AO1/2299/4. Hull, a safe distance from the border, served as the premier arsenal for the north of England.

[3]   BL, Harleian MS 6064, f. 7457.

[4]   TNA, PRO, E351/2963. See the glossary for technical terms and definitions of items of armour.

Materials for repairing and cleaning armour at the Tower included 'nyppers, piches, foundheaded nayles, mollheaded nayles, coffer buckles, greate buckles, mydle buckles, small buckles, oyle'.[5] The Armoury also furnished certain articles for use in the Court tournaments, such as tilt staves, vamplates, coronels and some swords. As Master of the Armoury, Lee was responsible for the armour stored in the Great Gallery and Green Gallery off the tiltyard at the Royal Palace in Greenwich.

Most of the equipment that the Armoury supplied to the common soldier, other than that purchased abroad, was produced by the Armourers' Company in London, and the Master of the Armoury had a close working relationship with it. The Armourers' Company, while not being among the twelve big city companies entitled to provide a Lord Mayor, had a long and illustrious history. Dating from at least the beginning of the fourteenth century, it received its royal charter in 1453 and soon came to control the manufacture of the ordinary armour used in the country.[6] Ian Archer defines the company as existing to exercise 'the maximum control over their trade, the elimination of outside interference and the maximization of employment prospects for members'.[7] As Master of the Armoury, Lee found himself expected to endorse the Armourers' Company's petitions to Parliament, protect its rights and privileges as outlined in their ordinances, and steer lucrative contracts in their direction.[8]

The Master of the Armoury also had jurisdiction over the Almain Armourers in the royal workshops at Greenwich. Until 1515 high-quality field and tilt armour had traditionally been imported from the Continent. However, in that year Henry VIII invited nine German and Flemish craftsmen to start armour production at Greenwich under the Master Workman Martin van Royne to compete with the *Hofplattnerei* of Emperor Maximilian and the armour mill of James IV at Linlithgow, Scotland. The Greenwich workshops initially engaged in the production of fine armour for the King, but, later, any courtier who had both a royal licence and the money to commission a suit of armour from

---

[5]   Ibid.

[6]   Unfortunately, little of it before the seventeenth century can be positively identified today. See A. Williams and A. de Reuck, *The Royal Armoury at Greenwich 1515–1649* (London, 1995), p. 26.

[7]   I.W. Archer, 'The London Lobbies in the Later Sixteenth Century', *HJ*, 31, 1 (1988), p. 19.

[8]   Lee obviously did the job to the company's satisfaction, as the close connection still continues today. Lee's third armour is preserved in the Armourers' Hall, as is the locking gauntlet of his second armour. The Gheeraerts portrait of Lee in Garter robes hangs in the Armourers' drawing room alongside the De Critz portrait of Anne Vavasour. It may be that the activities of Viscount Dillon, himself made an honorary member of the Armourers' Company in 1905, ensured that Sir Henry Lee's memory would remain evergreen at its Hall at 81 Coleman Street, London (see Ills 8 and 13).

them could do so.[9] By custom there were usually twenty-two workmen at the Greenwich workshops under a master workman; these included hammermen, millmen, locksmiths, labourers and one poorly paid gilder, whose use of mercury in the gilding process inevitably rendered his life nasty and short.[10]

The Armourers' Company had shown considerable resentment of the profitable royal patronage given to the technologically more advanced and better-paid foreigners, and locating the workshops at Greenwich had been an attempt to put the Almains beyond the jurisdiction of the London guilds.[11] The two groups, however, soon began to work in reasonable harmony, and the Armourers' Company admitted 'forren' workmen into their brotherhood. As a result, by Elizabeth's reign English names were appearing on the Almain payroll and its third master workman was the Englishman John Kelte (1567–76).

Lee worked first with Master Workman Jacobe Halder (1576–1608), who was German. Halder was first recorded as a hammerman at Greenwich in 13 July 1559, and the Register of the Armourers' Company records that on 4 August 1561 'Jacobe Halder, servant unto the quenes maiestie dwellinge at greneche was sworn a brother with vs in this haull'.[12] Halder had a good relationship with Lee and made the garniture for Lee's first armour and the whole of his second and third armours. The costly suit of armour Lee gave to the young Prince Henry around 1606 also has the hallmarks of Halder's workmanship.

A certain amount of ceremonial attendance was required from the Master of the Armoury, including the less pleasant duty of accompanying the axe when it left the confines of the Tower of London, principally for executions on Tower Hill. Lee had already performed this duty *ex officio* on 2 June 1572 when Thomas Howard, Duke of Norfolk, was executed on Tower Hill, and Norfolk's cousin Sir George Howard, then Master of the Armoury, was noticeable by his absence on that occasion. It is not known why Lee was deputizing for him, but his presence was not unwelcome. John Strype relates that, on the scaffold, Norfolk whispered some message into Lee's ear and 'so with Sir Henry Lee staying him by the left arm', knelt and asked the Queen's forgiveness.[13] At that date Lee exercised no

---

[9]   There is little evidence that Greenwich ever made armour for the army.

[10]   Williams and de Reuck, *Royal Armoury*, p. 28 gives the names of the master workmen from 1515 to the dissolution of the Royal Armoury in 1649. Examples of names of Greenwich workmen and their wages are to be found in Royal Armouries Tower of London (hereafter RATL) RAR 0–244.

[11]   The company frequently petitioned the Crown for protection for the home market. See C. Blair, 'The Armourers' Bill of 1581: The Making of Arms and Armour in 16th Century London', *Journal of Arms and Armour Society*, XII (1986), pp. 20–53.

[12]   Guildhall Library (hereafter GL) MS 12,079 I, v. 45.

[13]   John Strype, *Annals of the Reformation and Establishment of Religion during Elizabeth I's Reign*, 8 vols (London, 1824), II, p. 461; William Camden, *The history of the most renowned and victorious Elizabeth, late Queen of England* (London, 1615), p. 178. Wing C362.

office at the Tower of London and had no recorded relationship with England's premier duke save the fact that Norfolk, Lee and Sir George Howard were all notable jousters. As Norfolk had specifically requested the support of his good friend and old tutor John Foxe, the martyrologist, Lee's presence might also suggest a personal friendship.

When Lee became Master of the Armoury in 1580 he was again called upon to accompany the axe for the execution of Edmund Campion. In that year Campion had come with his brother Jesuit Robert Parsons on a mission to England. He had been arrested in July 1581 and was eventually sentenced to be hanged, drawn and quartered at Tyburn on 1 December 1581. Such was the reputation of Campion, who was subsequently canonized, that every detail of his execution was noted, including the presence of Sir Francis Knollys, Lord Howard and Sir Henry Lee as official witnesses.[14] It is not recorded whether Lee was present at other executions.

Lee's Initial Difficulties in Fulfilling his Duties, 1580–1587

After Sir Henry Lee had received his patent as Master of the Armoury, it is clear that he was confronted by a number of difficult problems and an organisation in some disarray.[15] He had not been included in the commission created on 26 August 1580 under Sir Owen Hopton, Lieutenant of the Tower, to review the state of the Armoury, but wrote an undated letter to Burghley from his Savoy lodgings on 1 November, presumably in 1580, voicing his disquiet at the state of things:

> [I have] come hith[er] to the towre to know your plesuer and atende your ... offyce of the armoury of w[hi]ch as yet I have reseved no charge ... [I have found] many a hande prancke played by shuche as have bene longe suffered synce the dethe of Sir George Howwarde yea and synce my going in to the contry, as conveying

---

[14] Thomas Alfield, *A true reporte of the death & martyrdome of M. Campion Iestuite* (London, 1582), pp. 8–9. *RSTC* 4537; R. Simpson, *Edmund Campton: A Biography* (London, 1867).

[15] C.J. Ffoulkes, *Inventory and Survey of the Armouries of the Tower*, 2 vols (London, 1916), I, p. 46. It is unclear precisely when Lee took over as Master of the Armoury at the Tower of London. The exact date of Sir George Howard's death is not known, but a privy seal docket book records both a last payment to him as Master of the Armoury in May 1580 and the appointment of Sir Henry Lee in the following month. A warrant had been issued to Lee on 7 July 1578 for the repair of houses near the Tower held by him 'as Master': see E.K. Chambers, *Sir Henry Lee: An Elizabethan Portrait* (Oxford, 1936), p. 109. The book, *A View of Valyaunce* was dedicated to 'Sir Henry Lee, Knight, Master of the Armourie' by Thomas Newton, 20 June 1580. *RSTC* 21469.

> & carrying owt of the tower shuche furnyture ... as they myght wth less susspysyon carry.[16]

Despite such habitual pilfering, Lee assured Burghley that:

> wth your lordships goode helpe [it] may easyly be corrected and altogether amended and thoffyce brought to as good if not a better order then ever heretofore.

Lee was destined to be disappointed and his initial assessment turned out to be false.

Fundamental problems existed at the Tower, which proved to be insoluble throughout Lee's long period in office. The most intransigent of these was the close association of the Armoury with the Office of Ordnance. As Master of the Armoury, Lee's responsibilities were quite distinct from those of the Master of the Ordnance, Ambrose Dudley, Earl of Warwick. Lee's department handled small arms and armour, whereas the Ordnance's remit covered a much wider range of materiel than the heavy ordnance from which it took its name, including gunpowder, firearms and even buckets and shovels for military use. The annual regular allowance for the Armoury was only £400 a year, compared to the £6,000 a year allowed to the Ordnance Office. More significantly, the development of new weapons created a grey area of administration between them. Although the two departments shared the same accommodation at the Tower, Lee soon discovered that whereas he enjoyed a considerable degree of autonomy as Lieutenant at Woodstock, this was not the case at the Armoury.

The major problem was that the Ordnance Office was notorious for peculation and corruption throughout Elizabeth's reign and was manned by individuals prepared to put their own interests before loyalty to commonweal or monarch.[17] It was far from unique in this, and many of its problems were inherent in the systems of late Tudor government administration.[18] The official salaries of most Crown officials were poor, and there was a contemporary expectation that

---

[16]   RATL, RAR 0–99. 'Furniture' usually referred to articles of armour, but in this case it was used generically, and could have referred to almost any article in the Tower armouries. This was the only letter of Lee's to remain at Ditchley through to 1932, and, as there is no evidence that Lee ever retained copies of his letters, one wonders whether it was ever sent.

[17]   R. Ashley, 'Getting and Spending: Corruption in the Elizabethan Ordnance', *History Today*, XL (November 1990), pp. 47–55; R. Ashley, 'War in the Ordnance Office: The Essex Connection and Sir John Davis', *Bulletin of the Institute of Historical Research* (hereafter *BIHR*), LXVII, 164 (October 1994), pp. 337–45.

[18]   See also G. Elton, 'The Elizabethan Exchequer: War in the Receipt', in S.T. Bindoff, J. Hurstfield and C.H. Williams (eds), *Elizabethan Government and Society: Essays presented to Sir John Neale* (London, 1961), pp. 213–49; J.D. Alsop, 'Government, Finance and the Community of the Exchequer', in C. Haigh (ed.), *The Reign of Elizabeth I* (Basingstoke, 1984), pp. 101–25.

a substantial proportion of one's wages would come from the perquisites of the job. In the case of the Ordnance Office, this included profiteering from contracts, pilfering of military equipment and falsification of records. The opportunities for peculation in the Ordnance increased in time of war when new contracts for a vast array of war materials were being granted and equipment was delivered to a variety of stores in the Tower and other arsenals.

Many minor government servants held their positions for life, and consequently they were exceedingly difficult to remove, even when corruption was proved. Reversionary leases also existed on many positions in the Ordnance, making new appointments very difficult. Although leading Crown officials such as Lee might not be guilty of peculation, few of them were equipped to prevent it. Moreover, the Queen often kept major offices untenanted for several years and day-to-day administration was usually delegated to a deputy.[19] Roger Ashley correctly points out that while there were technical experts such as gunners and armourers at the Tower, the principal Crown officials, as elsewhere, were gentlemen amateurs with little training, least of all in accountancy.[20]

When Lee became Master in 1580, a major conspiracy to defraud had just been uncovered at the Tower. The principal malefactor was one William Painter who, from 1560 to 1581, was not only Clerk of the Ordnance, but Clerk of the Armoury as well. Painter was superbly placed for financial embezzlement, being responsible for issuing supplies from the various stores at the Tower and listing the return of unused items. He also compiled the permanent books of accounts, and Richard Stewart rightly points out that 'the very complexity of the supply process and overlapping systems of indentures, ledger books and official responsibilities created loopholes for the clever and industrious cheat'.[21] Investigations in 1579 revealed that William Painter had been using his dual clerkship to defraud the Queen ever since 1560, in collaboration with the Surveyor of the Ordnance. Such highly placed corruption over a long period of time affected not only the Ordnance, but also the condition of the Armoury when Lee inherited it, and gives a clear context for Lee's letter to Burghley in 1580.

The conspiracy appeared to be well known in the Tower, but an anonymous letter from an employee in the Ordnance received by Burghley in June 1578 suggests that corruption was so entrenched that workers there feared to speak out.[22] The writer, while outlining

---

[19]   There was no Master of the Ordnance between Warwick's death in 1590 and the appointment of Essex in 1597, key years in Lee's mastership of the Armoury.

[20]   Ashley, 'Getting and Spending'.

[21]   R.W Stewart, *The English Ordnance Office, 1585–1625: A Case Study in Bureaucracy* (Woodbridge, 1996), p. 33.

[22]   BL, Lansdowne MS 26, no. 27, ff. 64–65. The scheme suggested by the anonymous writer involved an investigation of the amount of gunpowder brought into the Tower and 'foreign

... a way the abuses of the affair of th'ordnance may be found out ... [had] sought all the means possible to refforme these abuses but I know not what course to take for indangeringe my selfe. For ... if any suspytio[n] should growe unto me ... I should surely be murthered wher I goe.

He named the chief culprits as being 'the Clerke', William Painter and John Powell, the Surveyor, with the connivance of the Lieutenant of the Ordnance. The scheme he proposed for discovering the miscreants clearly showed an intimate working knowledge of the department. Burghley obviously found the scheme both believable and workable, as a footnote appended to the letter states that 'this course was accordingly taken by the Lord Treasurer'.

Charges of misappropriation were finally brought against Painter in 1581, and he was removed at least from his clerkship of the Armoury. The Council attempted reform with a 'List of Orders for the Ordnance' published in 1584, but the case against Painter and Powell continued until 1587, when it threatened to engulf the Master of the Ordnance, Ambrose Dudley, Earl of Warwick. The charges were rapidly dropped, and Painter was not removed from the Ordnance Office until 1595.[23]

The case, developing over some thirty-seven years, affected the Armoury as well as the Ordnance, and many of Lee's problems in building up and maintaining an adequate supply of armour originated in Painter's financial machinations. The absence of Painter's Armoury accounts between 1561 and 1580 makes it difficult to ascertain what money had been spent equipping the Armoury, but in correspondence with Burghley and Walsingham, Lee showed that he was only too aware of the poor quality and quantity of armour at the Tower, especially in time of war.[24] The country's fighting forces needed arms and armour, and with a monarch notoriously reluctant to spend on either, what money there was had to be husbanded. Lee handled government contracts for weapons procurement, but had only been allotted an annual sum of £400 in December 1580 for the upkeep of the Armoury which was barely sufficient for the armourers' wages. The clerkship of the Armoury remained vacant from 1580 to 1589, and Lee himself signed the accounts, although it is unlikely that he drew them up.

---

powder' which never arrived and was charged for. When Painter was again investigated in 1593 by George Hogge, Clerk of Deliveries, the specific charges made against him by Hogge related to accounts drawn up in 1575 and 1576 concerning gunpowder. One wonders if the suggestions of the anonymous writer of 1578 eventually served to incriminate Painter.

23   BL, Lansdowne MS 5, no. 19, ff. 67–71. Painter's Armoury accounts of 1561 are later annotated 'William Painter, Clark of the Armoury Discovery of his Receipts and Deceits 1561'. The accounts are so closely written as to need a trained Tudor accountant to decipher them. Only Painter's armoury accounts from March 1556/7–December 1561 exist as TNA, PRO, E351/2962.

24   *CSPD* 1581–90, p. 623 (Lee to Walsingham, 3 October 1589).

Lee needed subordinates in whom he had confidence, and it was a typical practice in late Elizabethan bureaucracy for a gentleman to extend what patronage he could to his own kinsmen. In 1589 Lee attempted to obtain the clerkship for his cousin John Lee, but the position went to a Mr Sugden.[25] Armoury accounts were now maintained by Sugden, but Lee continued to sign them until 1610 and the Armoury escaped the constant investigations for corruption experienced by the Ordnance Office. Although Sir Henry Lee could only obtain the post of yeoman at the Greenwich arsenal for his cousin, John Lee occupied the Armoury house there and acted as Lee's deputy at the Tower on a day-to-day basis from 1589.

Another problem that faced Lee was his relationship with the Armourers' Company of London. Claude Blair describes the Master of the Armoury as the 'head of the Crown organization that provided the members of the Armourers' Company with much of their employment'.[26] Lee was therefore involved in the various machinations of the company. One of the chief duties of livery companies, such as the Armourers' Company, was the protection of the quality of the goods produced by their craft, but the amalgamation of smaller companies with the principal ones in the City of London widened the scope of products for which they claimed responsibility. The Armourers' Company, originally the Helmers' Company, had enlarged its remit to include all armour by 1453 and, on amalgamation with the Bladesmiths Company in 1515, it asserted jurisdiction over all bladed weapons, a claim hotly disputed by the Cutlers' Company. By 1570 the Armourers were claiming jurisdiction over the making of crossbows and guns.

The rapid developments in gun technology in the sixteenth century and the great variety of guns being produced caused conflict as to which London companies could claim responsibility for them and thereby gain lucrative government contracts.[27] To ensure their success, companies sought to promote bills advantageous to them through Parliament, approaching leading men at Court and on the Council with suitable inducements.[28] Such bills, however, were subject to the many vagaries of the Elizabethan parliaments, and considerable time and money could be wasted.

These problems can be seen in the ill-fated Armourers' Bill of 1581, and it illustrates the frustrations that beset Crown officials like Lee who worked with the London guilds. All livery companies claimed the right of search for

---

[25]   *CSPD*, 1581–90, p. 604 (2 June 1589).

[26]   Blair, 'The Armourers' Bill of 1581'.

[27]   As the livery companies originated from the medieval guilds, the two terms were used interchangeably during the sixteenth century.

[28]   Ibid. The Armourers' Company promoted bills in 1576, 1581, 1584–85 and in 1597–98, dealing with the right of search of imported armour and the assaying, marking and quality of weapons. None of these became statutes.

defective or substandard wares belonging to their craft, sold within three miles of London. The right of search, apart from being a quality control, was exceedingly profitable to the guild – everyone searched had to pay a small fine to the company concerned, and those caught with defective wares were substantially fined. The transition to firearms for personal use, and specifically the development of the caliver as the principal firearm in the army, occasioned a demarcation dispute with the Blacksmiths' Company.[29]

In 1581 early in his appointment to the Armoury, Lee was asked to promote a parliamentary bill enforcing the Armourers' claim that its right of inspection of all armour and weapons should include guns, especially calivers. The bill had already been put before the Speaker and Recorder of 'the parlament howsse' in January 1581 for a first reading; now the Master and officials of the company were lobbying the Lord Chancellor and Sir Walter Mildmay for a second reading. The *Armourers' Court Book* gives a detailed account of the campaign, noting that:

> Sir Henry Leie was a hellper of us to set forward our bill ... He had to dinner at his lodgings in the Saveoie [numerous named Members of Parliament] ... and caussid us to bring our boucks, grauntes and exambepelles with us to shewe and make the best prove we cowld unto them ... they promosid to stand with us the best they could.[30]

The story then degenerates into farce. The Speaker promised the bill would be read 'upon Monday next', but a subsidy bill took its place. On the following Friday, when 'Sir Henry Leye' had mustered a goodly number of members in Parliament to support the bill, the Queen sent for the Speaker on another matter. The following Saturday, Lee and his friends 'could not be ther', but the Speaker advised the company to rally its support in Parliament for the next Monday, which Lee promptly did. The Armourers' records related:

> ... then comithe ij bills frome the quenes majestie again that must neades be read that daie ... so our bill was putt of.[31]

The Master of the Armourers' Company then importuned the Lord Chancellor, who agreed to speak to the Queen and promote the bill in Parliament, but

---

[29] *CSPD, Addenda 1547–65*, p. 78 (19 June 1569) stated with regard to musters, 'the men to be recruited, with firearms ... as many as can be to be calivers'. The Blacksmiths' Company had claimed the right of search on calivers in 1571.

[30] GL, MS 12071/2, ff. 412–415, 538, 539–40, 584. For a full transcription and account of the bill, see Blair, 'The Armourers' Bill of 1581'.

[31] One of these was the bill for the defences of the North, on which committee Lee had sat earlier.

... then comithe the French Imbassadors so his honor whent to St. Jamesis ... then
the parlament beganne to drawe to an end.

The Armourers' Renter Warden accounts record the full incidental costs of
the action, which Blair reckons to have been one-seventh of the company's total
income in that period. There is no mention of any inducement given to Lee for
his services, but 'xiijs' was paid on 'the furst of March for one Lame [lamb] and ij
capons which was geven to Sir Harry Lee', presumably for the dinner at his Savoy
lodgings.[32] The politics of the domestic production of arms continued to involve
Lee throughout his time as Master of the Armoury, with petitions being put to
Parliament in 1585, 1589 and 1590.[33] The links forged between the company
and Lee, however abortive in 1581 and in 1585 when an Armourers' bill again
failed in Parliament, stood the company in good stead in 1589 and 1590. These
bills were successful and illustrate Ian Archer's point that a company's plight that
was frequently brought to the attention of those in authority would eventually
receive a sympathetic hearing.[34]

War with Spain and in Ireland: Lee and the Armoury, 1584–1561

As war with Spain became imminent from 1584 onwards, the demands on
the Armoury increased, and its accounts record the costs for 'furnyshing the
Queenes Maiestie's shippes set forth for the seas for the better defence of the
Realme, 26 November 1587'.[35] Four separate defensive armies had been created
by 1588: the first to shadow the Spanish fleet in the Channel and prevent a
landing; the second under Lord Hunsdon to protect London; the third under
the Earl of Leicester to guard Kent and Essex; and the fourth under the Earl of
Huntingdon to guard the north of England. The manpower for these armies
came from the trained bands,[36] and the servants and tenants of nobility, gentry
and clergy. Armouries at different locations were called upon to supply body
armour and weapons. The Armoury at the Tower of London was also involved
in a healthy

... sale of provycons & armour out of the store [to] noblemen and other persons
for the pryce of armoure sold to them for their better furniture to attende the

---

[32] GL, MS 12065/2, f. 25v.

[33] TNA, PRO, SP12/8/2, f. 3. The Armourers were petitioning for the City to hold an
annual show of armour, as this would increase sales from their company. The petition was
unpopular with the other companies and was rejected in Parliament.

[34] Archer, 'The London Lobbies', p. 40.

[35] TNA, PRO, E351/2963, III, 1580–1601.

[36] Most cities had 'trained bands' for their defence, drawn from apprentices and volunteers.

defence of her Ma[je]tie's person upon the Spanish invasion in Somer 1588 viz. armors complete for launce, corselettes, burgonettes, spanish moryans, sleeves of mayle, in all solde by warrante of the Lords of the Councill dated iiij day of august 1588.[37]

As securing the return of loaned armour was a perennial problem for the Armoury, direct sale was often more practical.

The Greenwich armourers were also busy furnishing expensive field armours to leading courtiers between 1585 and 1587. The *Almain Armourer's Album* appears to group its illustrations in chronological order, although it neglects to date each armour. Eric Eaves draws attention to a group of five illustrations at the end of the *Album* that appear on a gathering of sheets rather than separately, and suggests that these armours, more suitable for field use than tournaments, were all produced at the same time.[38] In each case there was a good reason why often unlikely combatants would have purchased armour around 1585–87. Sir Christopher Hatton had long since ceased to appear at tournaments but, as a leading courtier, he had commissioned new armour in 1585. The armour was loaned to his friend Leicester on 29 November 1585 and used when the latter was appointed head of the army guarding Kent and Essex. Hatton's appointment as Lord Chancellor in 1587 necessitated a less combative approach.[39] Privy Councillor Lord Buckhurst had no aspirations to a military role, but was appointed Lord-Lieutenant of Sussex in 1586 and exercised his position with great zeal. Lord Cobham, a key player in the diplomacy surrounding the Armada, was appointed Knight of the Garter in 1586 and probably believed this and his position as Lord-Lieutenant of Kent warranted an expensive armour. The wealthy Italian merchant Horatio Palavicino was granted letters of denization in November 1585, was knighted by the Queen in November 1587 and volunteered for service against the Spanish in 1588. All these things would justify the purchase of a suit of Greenwich armour. Sir Henry Lee's third suit of armour is the fifth illustration in this group, and the inclusion of long tassets, more suited for riding than jousting, would seem to confirm that this

---

[37]   Ibid.

[38]   V & A, D586 1894 and D586A (1894)–D614 (1894) and D614A (1894) (*Almain Armourer's Album*); I. Eaves, 'The Greenwich Armour and Locking Gauntlet of Sir Henry Lee in the Worshipful Company of Armourers and Brasiers', *Journal of the Arms and Armour Society*, XVI, 3 (1999), p. 153.

[39]   Williams and de Reuck, *Royal Armoury*, p. 98; *Household Accounts and Disbursement Books of Robert Dudley, Earl of Leicester*, ed. Simon Adams, Camden Society 5th Series, VI (Cambridge, 1996), p. 339. A portrait in Sion House shows Leicester wearing Hatton's new armour.

was commissioned for field use (see Ills 7(a), 7(b) and 8).[40] These armours were not cheap, and their purchase around this time shows how seriously the leading men of Elizabeth's Court took the threat of Spanish invasion and their own responsibilities to Queen and commonweal.

Lee's new suit of armour was not just for show. Despite his responsibilities at the Armoury and his fifty-five years, he was not prepared to miss an opportunity for active military service. In December 1587 Lee was appointed as General of the Horse in the North of England under the Earl of Huntingdon. Lee's colleague at the Tower of London, Lieutenant of the Ordnance Sir Robert Constable, was General of the Foot.[41] Although neither man took up his position until May 1588, it is still an interesting question what two major figures with responsibilities at the Tower were doing away from their posts at the height of the Spanish emergency that summer. A possible explanation is that the majority of provisions had already been allocated by May and deputies were performing the day-to-day work. Lee's earlier apprehension over both the quality and quantity of armour provisions was rapidly justified. When Lee and Constable travelled to Doncaster in May 1588 to train the raw recruits for a month, Huntingdon wrote to Secretary of State Sir Francis Walsingham stressing that:

> ... we must continue to make the necessary provisions, and then we may with better spirits commit the success to God. Her Majesty shall find as good service in these parts ... (if war do come) if necessaries are provided.[42]

Lack of 'necessaries' and confusion in national preparations for war were evident throughout the whole campaign. Lee reflected the general state of affairs in a letter to Walsingham of 28 July 1588 from Sheffield:

> I am here a cypher ... I desire to be set to work, no more a looker on in so general a need. [I wish] I may know ... what Her Ma[jes]tie will have me do and that where most needed and peril is [but] my horses are in one place, my saddles, furniture and armour in another and myself in a third.[43]

---

[40]   Ibid. Williams and de Reuck date the Scudmore armour (not shown in the *Almain Armourer's Album*) as being made around 1587 (MMNY 11.128.1). They suggest the same date for the Buckhurst armour (probably that in the Wallace collection, London, A62). They date Lee's second armour around 1585 (RATL IV.43) and his third armour shortly after. See Chapter 6 below for further debate on the personal implications of Lee's third armour.

[41]   *CSP Border*, I, 1560–1594, p. 289 (3 December 1587).

[42]   *CSP Border*, I, 1560–1594, p. 323 (15 May 1588).

[43]   TNA, PRO, SP12/213/95 (*CSPD*, 1581–90, p. 515).

Lee's personal logistical problems appeared to be symptomatic of the whole enterprise: even Leicester himself begged the Queen to assemble her forces rapidly and not to risk defeat by delays.

Lee's worst fears on the state of the Armoury were confirmed when Leicester wrote to Walsingham on 1 August 1588 that:

> ... ther ar here aryved a nombre of burgonetts fr[om] the tower but not ane man wyll bye one, but [is] a shamed to wear yt, I never saw ye lyke. I wyll send yo some of tha[m] & return the rest & for gods sake let her Ma[jes]t[ies]s Armory be better looked unto or elles save the charges of yt.[44]

Huntingdon likewise wrote to the Privy Council from 'Hartyllpoole' on 17 August 1588, protesting that at the general musters at Durham, he had found 'many able bodies fit for service but in effect all naked [unarmed] without furniture'.[45] Lee was fortunate that, while he was journeying south to inform the Council of the difficulties, the national emergency passed without any call being made on the northern army. He returned to Court in late August 1588 to give the Queen a personal account of the military actions in the north of England and, as Master of the Armoury, he accompanied her to St Paul's to give thanks for England's deliverance from the Spanish Armada.[46]

Lee was also swift to present a memorandum to Walsingham, itemizing the North's major defence needs, although he, of all people, knew how unlikely these were to be met.[47] Although both Lee and Constable had been absent from the Tower in the summer months of 1588, it is difficult to see how their presence would have made a difference. Years of neglect and corruption had left the Armoury and the Ordnance Office barely able to equip four major defensive armies in the first war since 1564. In eight years, with entrenched hostility among several of the staff at the Tower and very little money, Lee had been unable to bring the armour up to the standard required. The crisis in summer 1588 passed, but from this point until 1604 Lee faced demands on the Armoury from a country both at war and facing rebellion in Ireland.

Major changes were needed in the Armoury, and the appointment of a new clerk and a new deputy in 1589 was a step in the right direction. The demands of 1588 had taken a heavy toll on the military supplies in general and the Armoury store in particular. In addition to the usual problem of reclaiming armour once the danger was passed, there were now new demands for military supplies for

---

[44]   TNA, PRO, SP12/214/1.

[45]   *CSP Border*, I, 1560–1594, p. 329 (17 August 1588). 'Furniture' was used as a generic term for all military equipment.

[46]   TNA, PRO, SP46/125/175 (27 August 1588); Nichols, *Elizabeth*, II, p. 537.

[47]   *CSP Border*, I, 1560–94, p. 331 (23 August 1588).

Ireland.[48] The Queen therefore requested a review of the whole state of armour and weapons throughout her realm.

In a graphic letter to Walsingham dated 3 October 1589, Lee described the Armoury as

> ... not only much unfurnished and full of wants, but ... out of all order' [as] my self have oft and sundry times complayned ... not only to her Ma[je]tie but also set down the same in writing. [My offer] to make such supply & good armour ... was little harkened unto, and such as is in the tower [is] in such plight, delivered unto me as I was ashamed to see and most pity it should be in the armour of so great a princess. Our former toil, charge and travail hath been bestowed upon nothing, [as armour had been] delivered over in to sundry countryes, much sent to and fro to the shipps, a great deal lost and through negligence and the force of salt water, made so thin that the virtue was clean taken away ... the charges and trouble hath been exceeding great in transporting armour from one place to another, [leaving] other forces unfurnished.[49]

Lee himself lacked the finances to make frequent trips to London and requested that he might deal with the situation at the Armoury when he came to London for the November tournament, hence 'stop[ping] two gaps with one bush'. Lee's financial embarrassments appear to have been typical of many officials at the Tower. For example, Sir Owen Hopton, Lieutenant of the Tower from 1570 to 1590, resigned with substantial financial problems deriving from the tenure of his office.[50]

Lee's complaints about the state of the Queen's armoury were also reiterated by the Armourers' Company. On 13 July 1589 the company had directed a petition to the Council 'to have leave to furnish the State with what armour is wanting and upon what terms'.[51] The company's prime objective was to secure work for its own members, but the petition did raise the very pertinent question of the state's dependency on imports of foreign arms for its defence. When, at her accession in 1559, the Queen had thought it prudent to purchase large quantities

---

[48]   HMC *Salis*. III, no. 863, p. 409 (3 May 1589). Walsingham sent demands to Constable and Lee for a supply of munitions, morrions, oil for armour and other necessities for Ireland, from the Ordnance and the Armoury.

[49]   *CSPD*, 1581–90, p. 623 (3 October 1589).

[50]   As is obvious from the Loseley Papers at the Surrey History Centre, some of the financial embarrassments on death or resignation resulted from monies being paid personally into the hands of officials and then reclaimed from their estates. See Surrey History Centre (hereafter SHC), LM/64 'Account of money owed to the Crown by Henry Lee esq. as heir and executor of Sir Henry Lee, KG. late Master of the Armoury for the period Jan. 1602 – Dec 1610. Residue of monies received into the hands of Sir Henry Lee KG'.

[51]   BL, Lansdowne MS 63, no. 5, ff. 19–20.

of arms, her agent Sir Thomas Gresham had procured them from Germany and the Low Countries. Paul Hammer observes that Gresham's shopping list shows England's dependency on imports for virtually every item needed for war, including essential components for making gunpowder.[52] There is little to indicate that matters had changed substantially by 1589. An elegantly produced document created by the Armourers laid out their case succinctly. They had been at great charge in

> ... enterteynin and keping foreyn men from beyond the seas to learne and practice the making of Armour [but] ... at this tyme we make ... better armor then that is w[hi]ch cometh from beyond the seas ... and fearing that for lack of sale ... of the same we shall not be able to kepe and maynteyne the number of our apprentices and servants which are very well practysed in making all sorts of armours.[53]

They requested that:

> ... we may be appointed to bring unto her Ma[jes]tie's store at reasonable price monthly the Armour that we shall make till her Ma[jes]tie's store be furnyshed ... it is a means to set a great number of her Ma[jes]tie's subjects to work ... it will furnish this land with skilful men to make and fytt armours to mens bodies ... and we shall be free from those dangers which may onset by the great nombers of bad and insufficient armourers which are now brought unto this land by unskilled men.

This petition was endorsed by Sir Henry Lee's deputy at the Armoury, John Lee, who concurred that the Armouries at this point were 'very weakly furnished ... [and] the armour that is made here is accounted far better than that which cometh from beyond the seas'. On this occasion, the Armourers' petition met with greater success than had their earlier ones.

Whereas good armour could be made in England, the best metal was usually procured from overseas. Apart from one experiment in 1540, when English ore had been sent to Nuremburg to be tried, English armour manufacture had always used imported ore from Germany, and both the Armourers' Company and the Greenwich workshops preferred this arrangement. Before his death in 1590, Sir Francis Walsingham set in train an inquiry into the use of Shropshire iron, and Lee reported to Burghley on the subject on 12 October 1590.[54] He had, he wrote, together with his cousin John Lee and the Lieutenant of the Ordnance,

---

[52]   P.E.J. Hammer, *Elizabeth's Wars* (Basingstoke, 2003), p. 68.

[53]   BL, Lansdowne MS 63, no. 5, ff. 19–20.

[54]   *CSPD*, 1581–90, p. 692; H.A.L. Dillon, 'A Letter of Sir Henry Lee, 1590, on a Trial for Armour', *Archaeologia*, LI, 1 (1885), pp. 167–72.

Sir Robert Constable, attended a 'trial of iron for armour', of 'certayne ierne metell w[hic]h grewe [*sic*] or was made in Sropshere. A new brest[plate] beyng sent owt of the contry' was tested with one 'of the very same wayght' newly made in the Greenwich workshop. Lee took 'a good and stronge pystolle', an identical weight of powder and equal charge and 'tryed fyrste the one and then the other'. The breastplate made in Greenwich and of 'mettell of Hungere' held out with a little dent; that made in Shropshire was 'clene shotte thereowe. Thus muche for this Yenglyshe metal'.[55] Despite Lee's willingness to undertake an empirical experiment, the test merely confirmed the superiority of foreign ores, and an opportunity to encourage a domestic metallurgy industry was missed.

Lee was also prepared to lend his voice to that of the Armourers in preventing freelance workshops developing outside London. Not only was Lee 'gratified' in 1590 to the tune of £50 by the Armourers' Company for hindering one Stanley from setting up as an armourer, but he also made a plea to Burghley for the 'whole compene of the Armourers, beynge very many that lyve on that trade with ther wyves and chyldren'.[56] He pointed out the dangers of armour-making being put into unskilled hands, 'where warres may happen as well by sea or land', and hoped that 'suficient armour of good shape and good stuffe' may be had within the realm, presumably from the Armourers' Company.

The Armoury continued to supply body armour, helmets, shields and swords to the English soldiers in Ireland throughout the decade, and Lee directed several lucrative contacts to the Armourers' Company. In 1596 a warrant was made out to Sir Henry Lee, for £2,000 3s to be paid to the Armourers' Company for '449 cuirasses, 433 lances, 96 cuirasses of proof, 62 targets of caliver proof, 59 targets of pistol proof and armour complete'.[57] Lee was prepared to extend Armoury patronage to the Cutlers' Company, and in 1599 he was instructed to pay both companies a total of £1,031 8s for 3,000 swords and £29 8s 8d for 'theire carriadge ... into Irelande'.[58]

Lee's relationship with the Armourers' Company was not unusual among Crown officials who had dealings with the City. Regardless of what his own attitude to the Company's trade practices might have been, Lee's main priority in the thirty-one years he was Master of the Armoury was to ensure a smooth working relationship between the Armoury, the Greenwich workshops and the Armourers' Company. The state needed a reliable supply of armour and personal

---

[55] Ffoulkes makes the salient point that it was hardly fair to place armour made by a provincial blacksmith against that made by the Queen's finest Armourers'. See C. Ffoulkes, 'The Armourers' Company of London and the Greenwich School of Armourers', *Archaeologia*, LXXVI (1927), pp. 41–58. 'Metal of Hungere' usually denoted German metal.

[56] Ibid. and *CSPD*, 1581–90, p. 692.

[57] *CSPD*, 1595–97, p. 295 (19 October 1596). See the Glossary for description of weapons.

[58] TNA, PRO, E101/64/11 (duplicate of the account of Sir Henry Lee, Master of the Armoury), 16 January 1598 and 30 June 1599; BL, Sloane MS 1519, ff. 209, 216.

weapons, and an England at war with Spain was no place to make far-reaching experiments in weapons procurement.

The Armoury in the Last Decade of Elizabeth's Reign

In the last decade of Elizabeth's reign, the Armoury was increasingly overshadowed by the Ordnance Office, as the expansion of firearms made its basic products relatively insignificant. The Department of Ordnance was not a pleasant place in which to work. George Carew, Lieutenant of the Ordnance in 1594, described it as

> ... this troublesome place where I have found at no time either profit or ease ... and my fellows in office so corrupt and of such malicious spirits as but in hell I think their matches can hardly be found ... hope did persuade me that as their falsehoods were discovered and proved they would be displaced, but that hope is lost.[59]

Things did not improve and, as there was no Master of the Ordnance from 1590 to 1597, the department was under almost constant investigation. During one such investigation in 1600, the new Clerk of the Ordnance Stephen Riddleston confessed himself to be 'over-wearied with a company of wayward and malignant spirits', and in 1601 an investigation of the 'discovery and reform of the deceits, forgeries and abuses in that Office in her majesty's reign' estimated that, during some four decades of corruption, some £60,000 had been embezzled.[60]

As Master of the Armoury, Lee felt that the larger office was taking advantage of his advancing years. His complaints were many. In 1594 he wrote to Sir Robert Cecil complaining that the house in Greenwich belonging to the Armoury and occupied by his deputy John Lee had been taken over by another minor government official.[61] In 1598 Lee again complained to Cecil that 'there were some that would cunningly intrude themselves into my office', and when attempts were made in 1600 to encroach on a tenement held by the Armoury near the Tower, he appealed yet again to Cecil 'to defend me in my aged absence from such greedy procurers ... especially in the matter of small offices in my gift as Master of the Armoury'.[62] The truth was that, with the demands of foreign war and Irish rebellion, and with the increasing use of new weapons, the Armoury

---

[59] HMC *Salis*. IV, p. 555 (George Carew to Robert Cecil 30 June 1594).

[60] Cecil MS 251.11 (HMC *Salis*. X, p. 244); Cecil MS 90.111 (HMC *Salis*. XI, p. 551).

[61] HMC *Salis*. IV, p. 576.

[62] Cecil MS 68.2 (HMC *Salis*. X, p. 18) (29 January 1600). See also TNA, PRO, E133/10/1492.

was having difficulty maintaining its autonomy. Its claim to be the sole provider of basic equipment, such as swords, was regularly undermined as the Council and even Essex bought swords for overseas use from sources other than the Armoury. Stewart makes the point that the fact that Lee had to write to Cecil in 1598 and again in 1601, specifically pleading that swords should be supplied by the Armoury, indicates that the 'delineation of tasks between the ordnance and the armoury was no longer clear'.[63]

The example of an incident in 1601 not only illustrates how fiercely Lee was prepared to fight for Armoury rights, but also reveals his anachronistic attitudes. In that year a warrant was sent to the Tower for swords and armour to be supplied 'jointly' by the Armoury and Ordnance Office. Lee immediately appealed for the warrant to be made 'severally', to preserve the reputation of his department.[64] The Privy Council had authorized George Harvey, Deputy Lieutenant of the Ordnance, to supply arms for Ireland, including swords. Lee had stated that the provision of swords was the Armoury's responsibility, but the Privy Council had excused itself on 28 July 1601, claiming that since a large supply was needed in some haste, they had appealed to Harvey since they 'did require the healp of a man of some credite and of skill [so] we thought him a fitter person than a merchant to deale in it'.[65] Stewart again makes the telling point that this did not speak well of the Council's opinion of Lee's ability to organize a supply of arms.[66]

Lee immediately sent a letter to Sir John Stanhope on 29 July 1601, complaining of what he regarded as an insult to himself and his office.[67] He deeply resented the Council's support of George Harvey, and wrote that 'for skill I will neither give place to him nor any other, having had the use of arms both in earnest and sport all the days of my life'. Lee subsequently gave full range to his anger on many fronts. For example, he was enraged that the armour of Henry VIII that had been displayed in a room off the Green Gallery at Greenwich since the King's reign had been 'thrown into a corner ... thrown upon heaps and without my knowledge ... a wrong to the dead and to her Majesty'. However, the main import of Lee's letter to Stanhope was to warn him that too little armour was being maintained at the Queen's houses for her defence.

The armoury at Windsor Castle and at Hampton Court had been run down since 1580, and the Tower supplies were poor. Lee quoted the precedent of the danger posed to Queen Mary in 1554 when there was insufficient armour in Whitehall to defend her from Wyatt's rebellion, and implied that 'if God had not provided better', the situation might have been repeated during Essex's recent

---

[63] Stewart, *The English Ordnance Office*, p. 125; HMC *Salis*. X, pp. 550–51.
[64] Cecil MS 90.107 (HMC *Salis*. XI, p. 551).
[65] Dasent, *APC*, 1601–4, 108–9 (28 July 1601).
[66] Stewart, *The English Ordnance Office*, p. 124.
[67] Cecil MS 117.3 (HMC *Salis*. XIV, p. 181).

rising in February 1601. Overall, the letter illustrates Lee's bitter resentment of the decline of both his influence and his budget, as well as his conviction that respect for himself and armour in general was a thing of the past. His convictions were probably accurate. In 1601 Sir John Peyton, Lieutenant of the Tower, wrote to Sir Robert Cecil, stating he considered that the office of Master of the Armoury was in his gift and regretted it was 'otherwised disposed of'.[68]

Some Observations on Lee's Handling of the Armoury

If Lee was not exactly handed a poisoned chalice in 1580, he was certainly appointed to a department where it was going to be difficult to succeed. The armour he inherited in 1580 was in poor condition. In peacetime the Armoury cared principally for ornamental tournament armour; very little money had been invested in field armour since the Le Havre expedition in 1562–63, and what little had been allocated appears to have been embezzled. Lee's meagre budget of £400 a year had barely begun to bring the Armoury up to standard when it was called upon to equip four major defensive armies, and then provide arms and armour for war with Spain and rebellion in Ireland.

Many of the practical problems that Lee was experiencing in the Armoury were corroborated in 1591 by his former travelling companion, Sir John Smythe, in his *Instructions, Observations and Orders Militarie*.[69] Smythe, like Leicester, observed that:

> ... in the camp and armie at Tilbury 1588 ... I did see and observe so great disorder and deformitie in their apparrell to arme withall as i saw but very few of that army that had any inconvenience of apparel and chieflie of doublets to arme upon ... many did weare their armors verie uncomlie and uneasilie.

Like Lee, Smythe was of the opinion that:

> ... the long peace that we have had till within these 15 or 16 [y]eares past did bring a great decaye in armors and weapons throughout the Realme but that armours and weapons of late yeares brought and provided in all the shires of england by the Muster orders were reduced ... verie few or none of the corslets of all the shires throughout England are Augsburge or newremburg which are the best stuffe.

---

[68]   Cecil MS 181.142 (HMC *Salis.* XI, p. 169).

[69]   John Smythe, *Certen Instructions, Observations and Orders Militarie* (London, 1594), *RSTC* 22884; BL, Harleian MS 135, f. 96. A letter sent by Leicester during the Armada crisis suggests that Smythe was too sick to take part at Tilbury, TNA, PRO, SP12/213/94.

Notwithstanding the petty jealousies that existed between government departments, and the opportunism of younger men prepared to take advantage of an aging Master, the fundamental problem was that armour itself was declining in importance and, with it, the role of the Armoury. When, in 1590, Lee had assured Burghley that 'the worlde ... is lykelye to use more [armour] hereafter than in the tyme paste', he was voicing an understandable but anachronistic judgement of a situation which left many of his contemporaries equally confused.[70] Lee's main area of expertise was with ceremonial tournament armour. The annual Accession Day tournaments served to keep the armourers in business for another two decades after peace with Spain in 1604, but, by then, tournaments were becoming outdated as a mode of Court entertainment.

The nature of warfare had been changing rapidly during the final decades of the sixteenth century and Lee, nearly seventy years old by 1600, would have been unusually prescient to have appreciated the technical innovations needed in weaponry. He missed opportunities to encourage the development of English steel for armaments, but a country at war was no place to nurture a young industry through its teething troubles, and the credit for any successful innovation would probably have been taken by the Ordnance Office. Lee was also hampered by the vested interests of the Armourers' Company, which was more interested in strengthening defensive armour and preserving the status quo than in fundamental change. Increasingly, the work of the Armoury as a supplier of swords, lances and corseletts was taken over by the Ordnance Office. Stewart convincingly argues that the decline in the Armoury is even more obvious when one looks at its expenditure.[71] From 1590 to 1594 it spent £2,087, only marginally more than the £400 per annum allotted to it for those five years. Between 1595 and 1603 it needed to spend substantially more – some £11,000, mainly on providing swords and armour for Ireland. From then on, with small exceptions, the Armoury spent only its allowance of £400 a year. One cannot help but conclude that although Lee continued as Master of the Armoury until his death in 1611, by then he was presiding over an office whose time had passed.

---

[70]   *CSPD*, 1581–90, p. 692 (12 October 1590). The title Master of the Armoury was abolished with the office in 1671. However, Lee's descendant Viscount Dillon became the first modern part-time curator of the Royal Armouries from 1895–1912, and voluntarily classified, cleaned and reassembled much of the armour then at the Tower of London. When Charles Ffoulkes was appointed as full-time curator in 1910, the ancient title of Master of the Armouries was revived, though with rather different responsibilities.

[71]   Stewart, *The English Ordnance Office*, p. 125 from Lee's accounts TNA, PRO, AO/1/2299/3 and AO/1/2299/4. 2300/6-9.

1   *Sir Henry Lee* by Antonis Mor, 1568, National Portrait Gallery,
London/The Bridgeman Art Library

2   The tiltyard. By permission of the Kings, Heralds, and
Pursuivants of Arms at the College of Arms

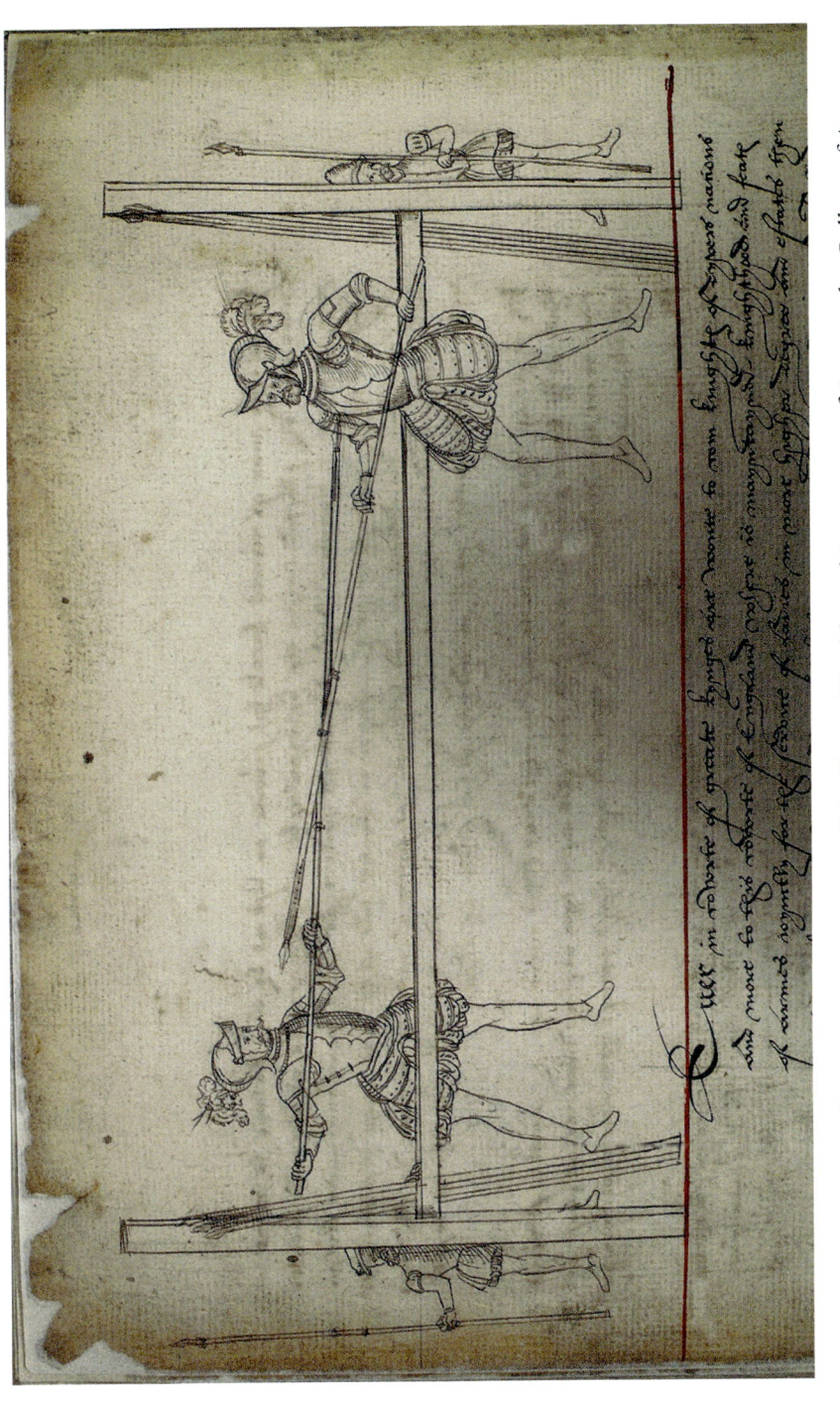

3(a)   Tourney and barriers. By permission of the Kings, Heralds, and Pursuivants of Arms at the College of Arms

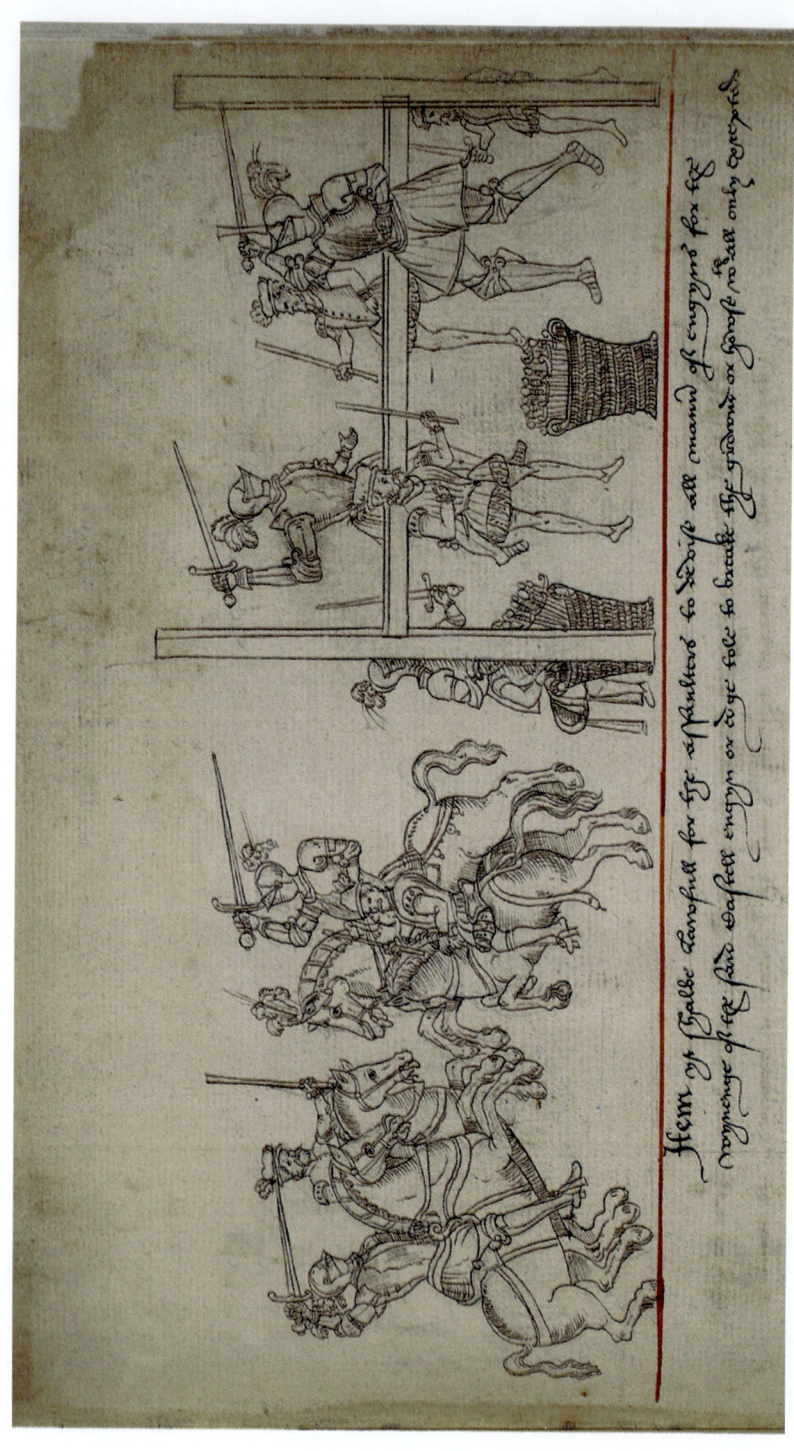

Item yt shalbe Lawfull for the assistans to devise all maner of engyns for the wynnynge of the said engyn or to se hoe to breake the grovnd no all onby onely exceptd

3(b) Barriers. By permission of the Kings, Heralds, and Pursuivants of Arms at the College of Arms

4   Score cheque, 1584. By permission of the Kings, Heralds, and Pursuivants of Arms at the College of Arms

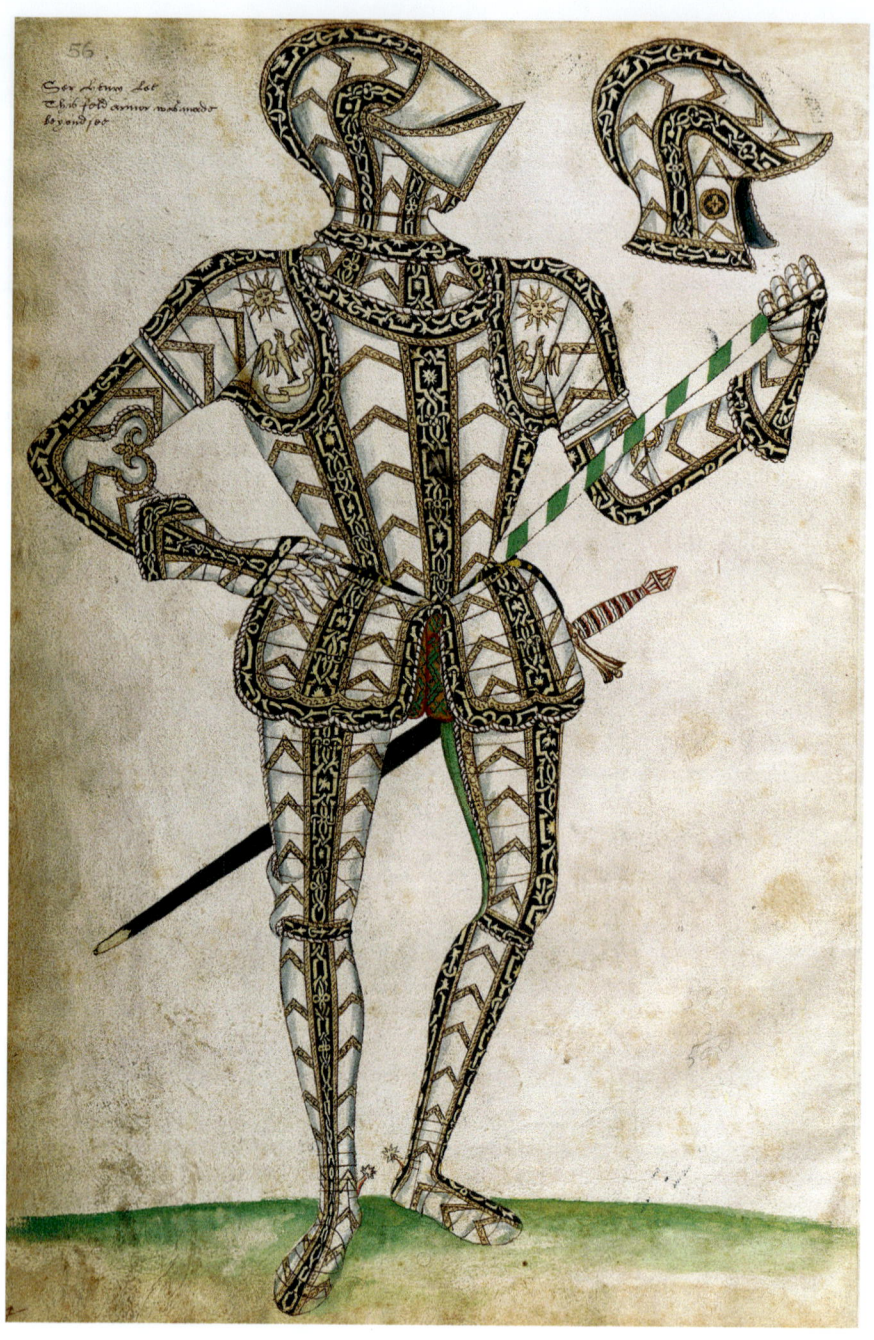

5(a)   Lee's first armour. Fom the *Almain Armourer's Album*. Victoria and
Albert Museum, London/The Bridgeman Art Library

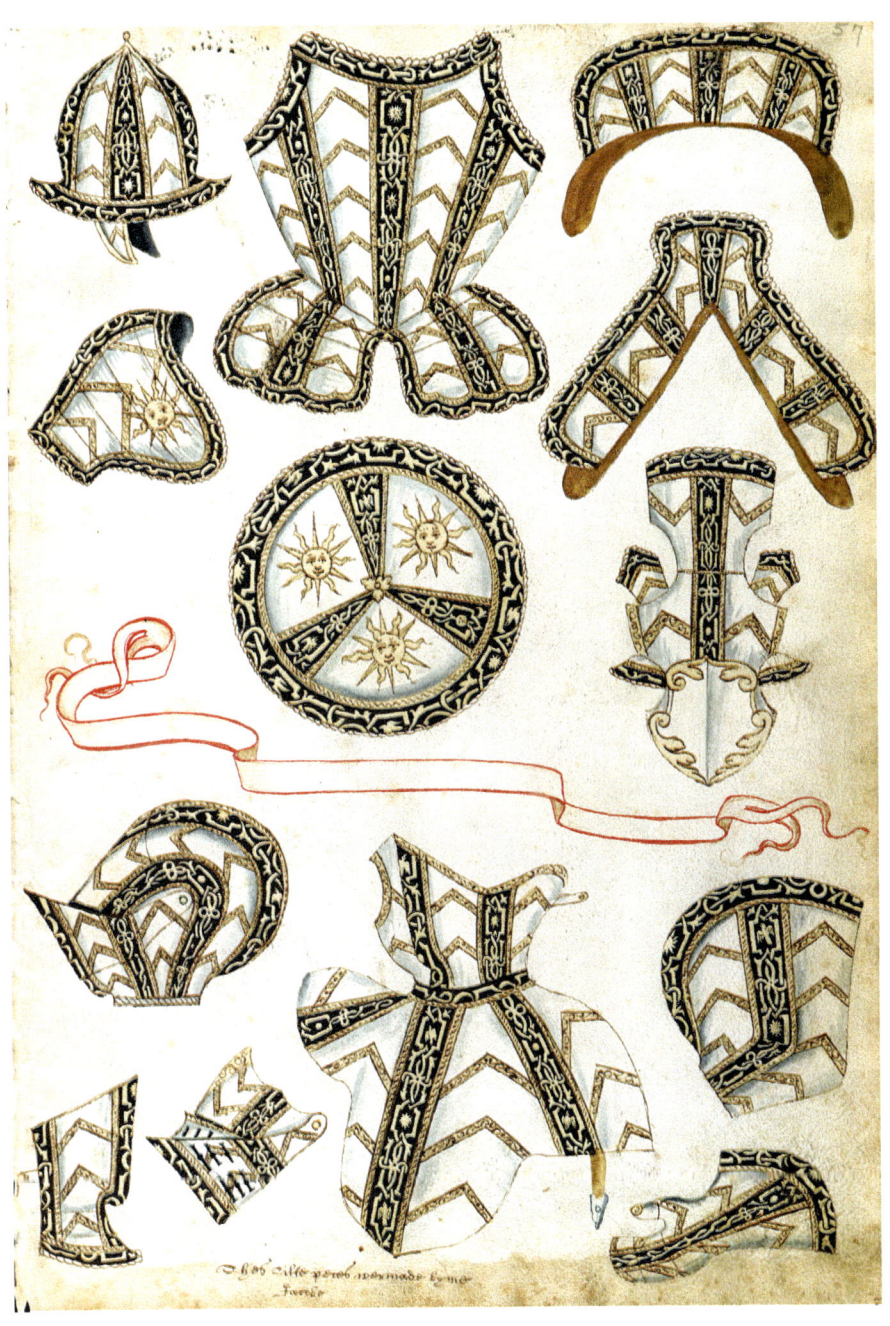

5(b)   Lee's first armour – garniture. Victoria and Albert Museum,
London/The Bridgeman Art Library

6(a)   Lee's second armour. From the *Almain Armourer's Album*.
Victoria and Albert Museum, London/The Bridgeman Art Library

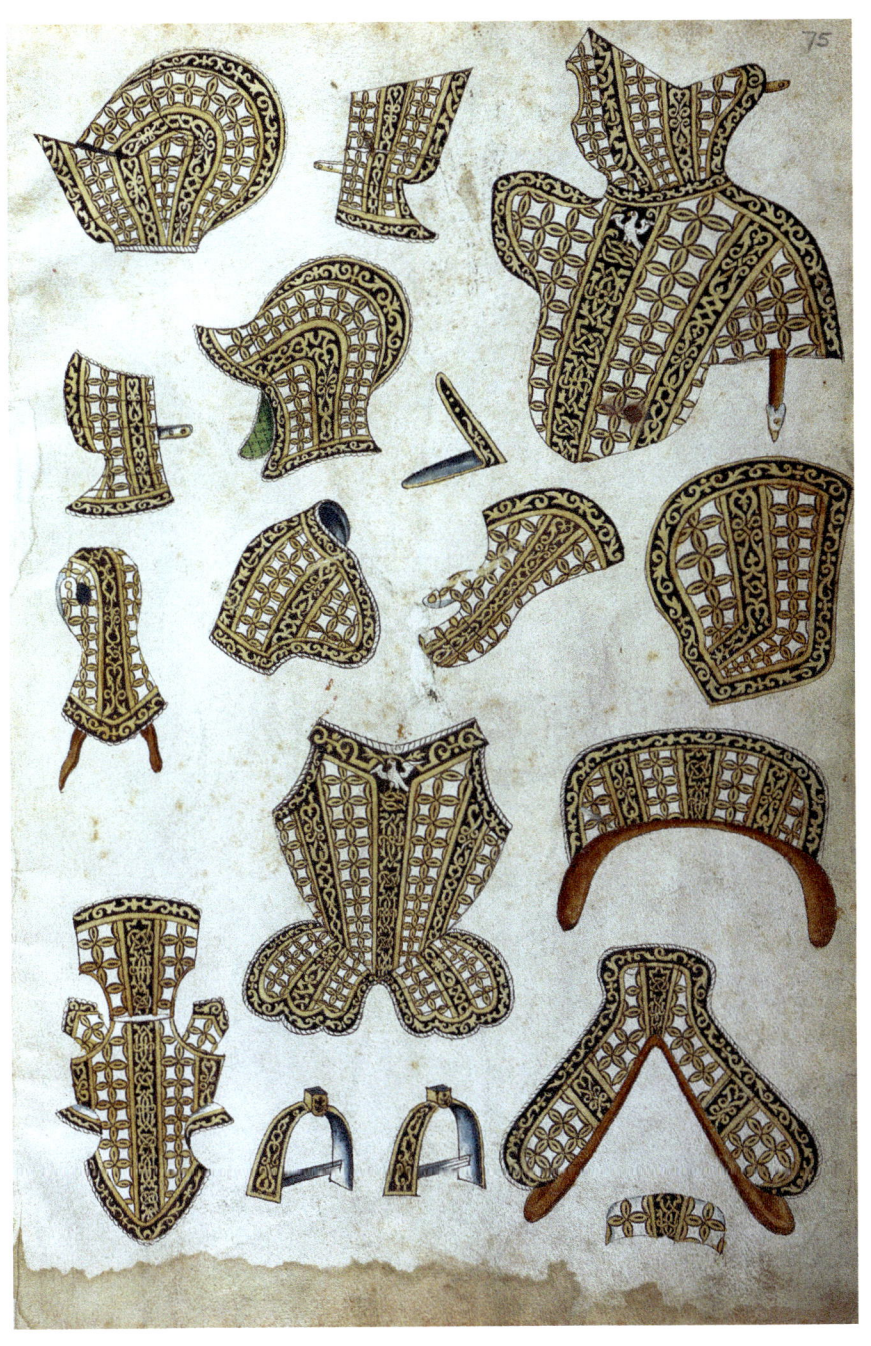

6(b)   Lee's second armour – garniture. Victoria and Albert Museum, London/The Bridgeman Art Library

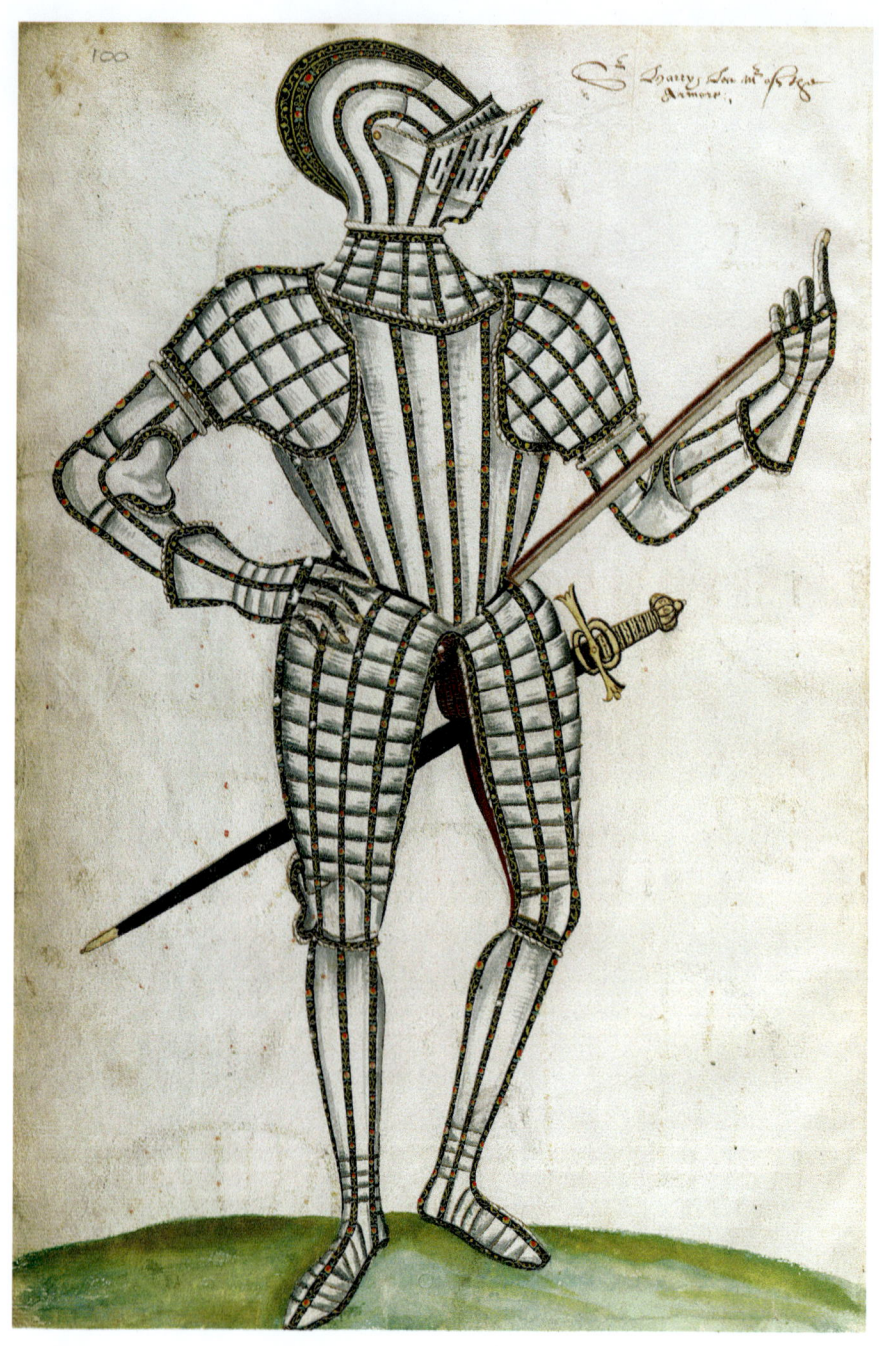

7(a)   Lee's third armour. From the *Almain Armourer's Album*.
Victoria and Albert Museum, London/The Bridgeman Art Library

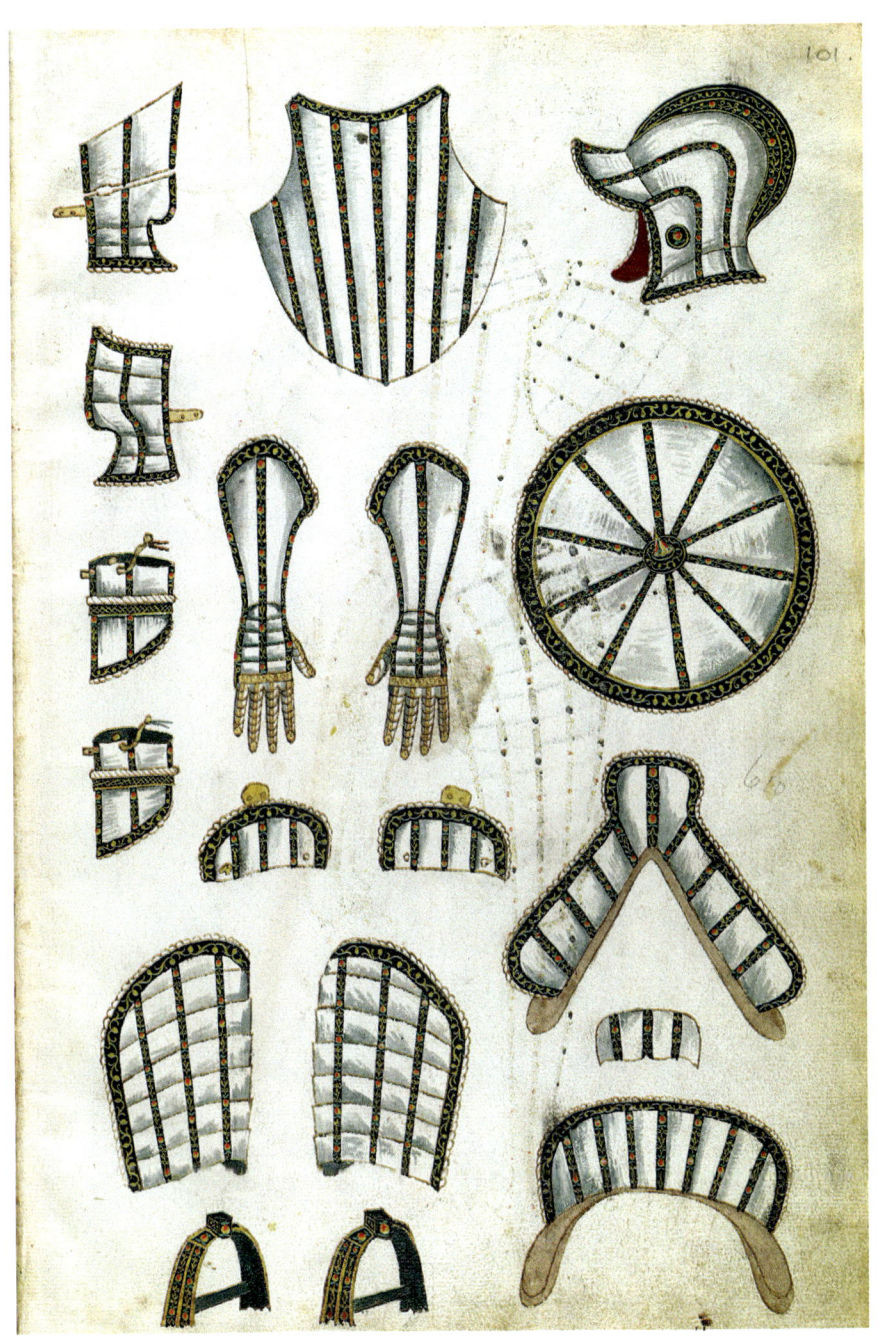

7(b)　Lee's third armour – garniture. Victoria and Albert Museum, London/The Bridgeman Art Library

8 Lee's third armour at the Armourers and Brasiers Hall, London. By kind permission of the Armourers and Brasiers Company, London

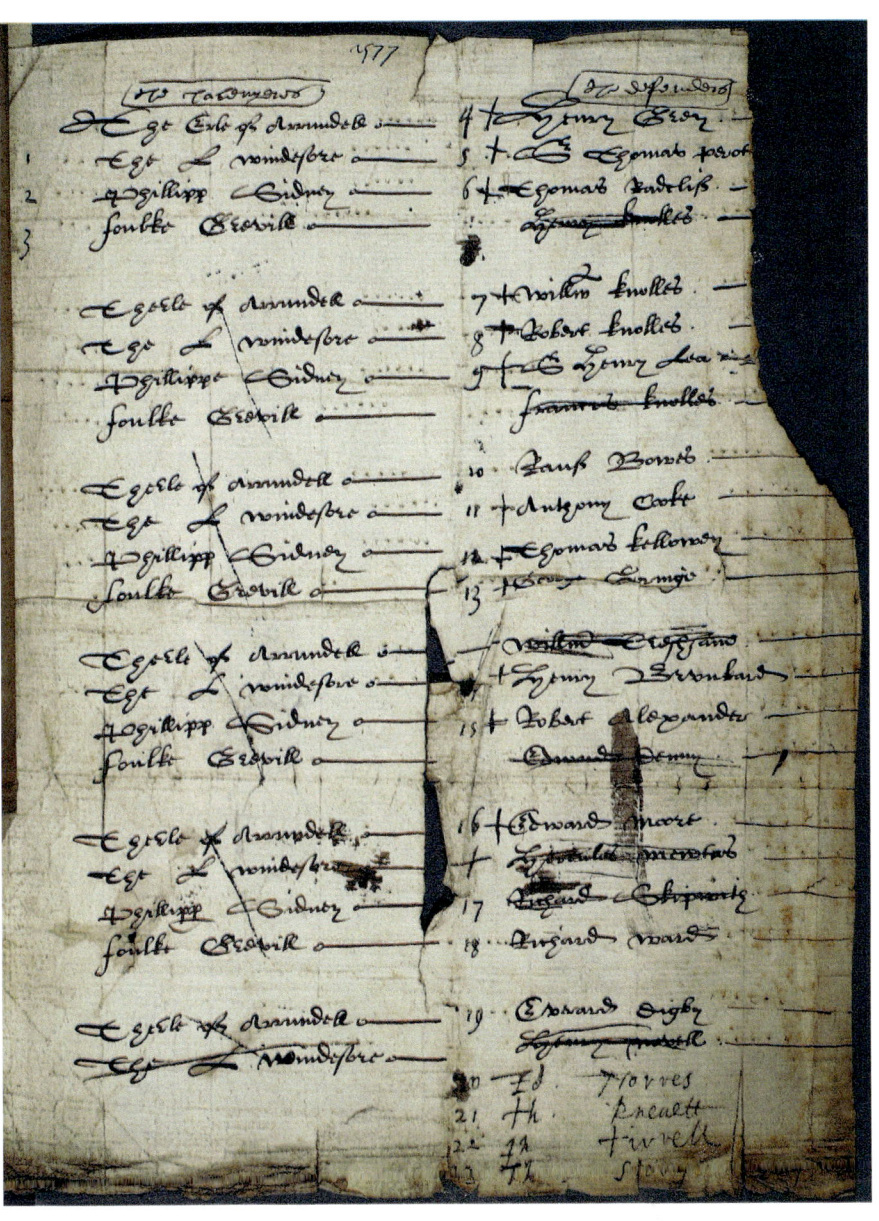

9   Score cheque, 1577. By permission of the Kings, Heralds,
and Pursuivants of Arms at the College of Arms

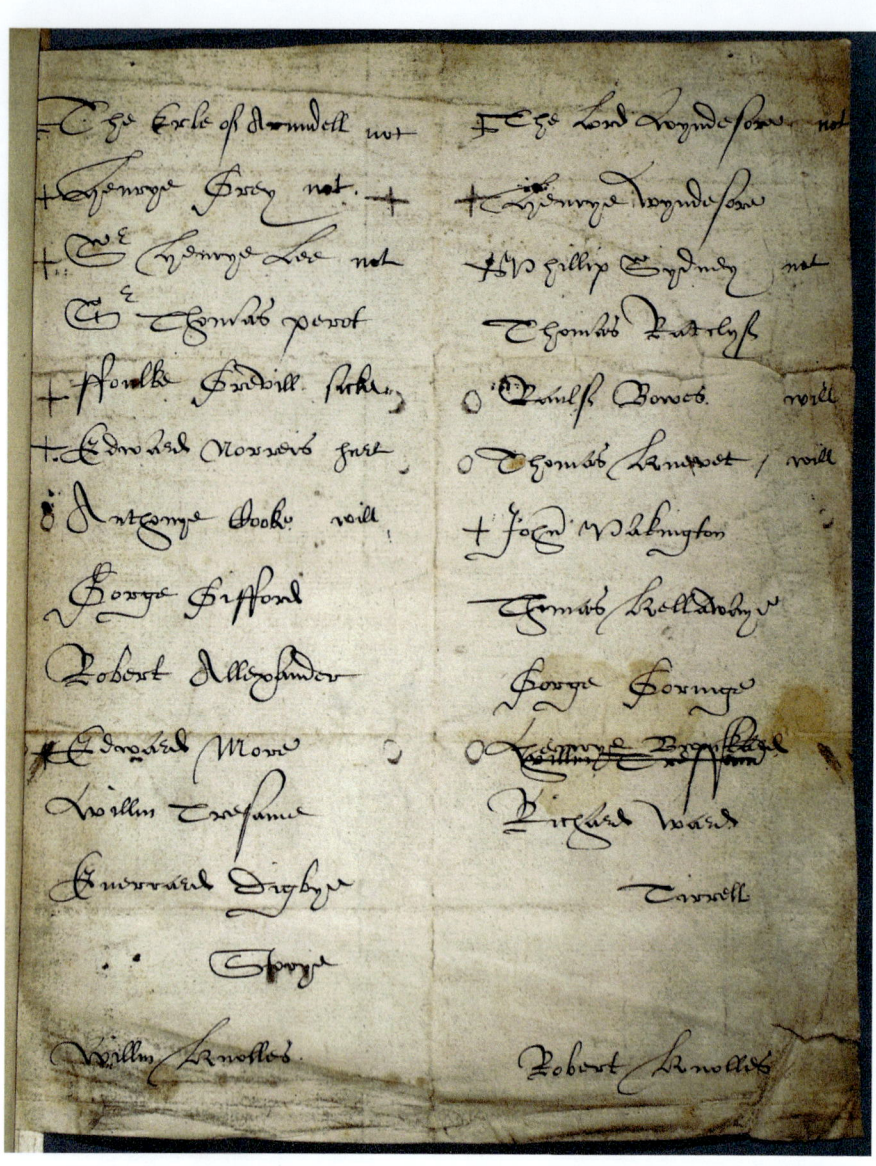

10   Tilting list, 1581. By permission of the Kings, Heralds,
      and Pursuivants of Arms at the College of Arms

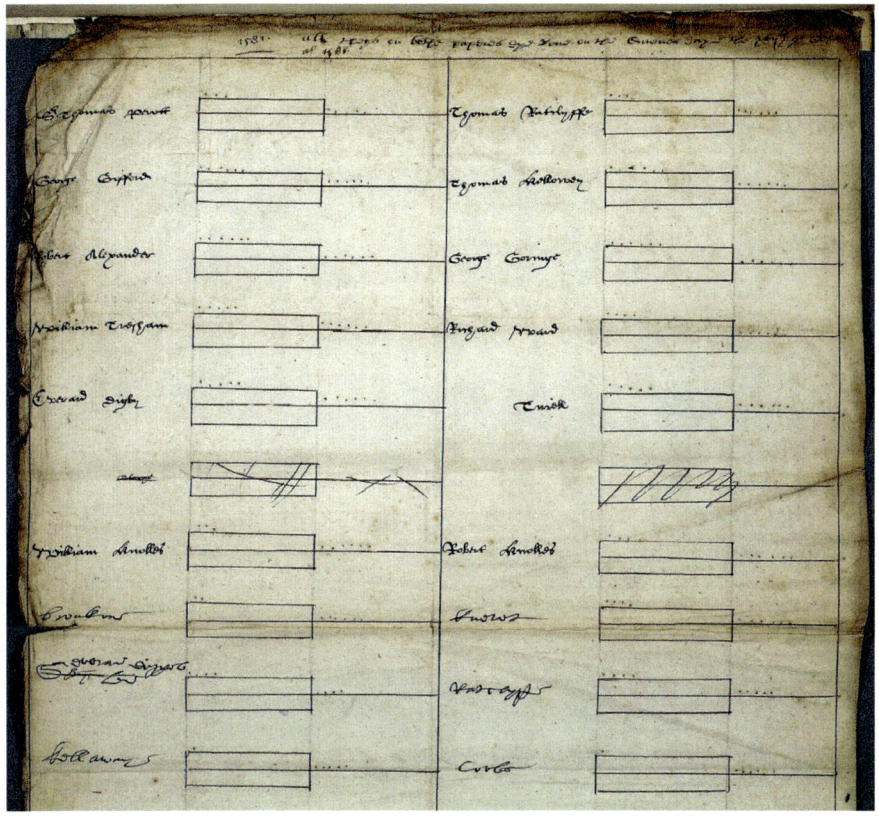

11   Revised score cheque, 1581 (detail). By permission of the Kings, Heralds, and Pursuivants of Arms at the College of Arms

12   The Ditchley portrait of Elizabeth I, by Marcus Gheeraerts
the Younger, c.1592. National Portrait Gallery, London.
© Stefano Baldini/The Bridgman Art Library

13 Sir Henry Lee in his Garter robes, by Marcus Gheeraerts. By kind permission of the Armourers and Brasiers Company, London

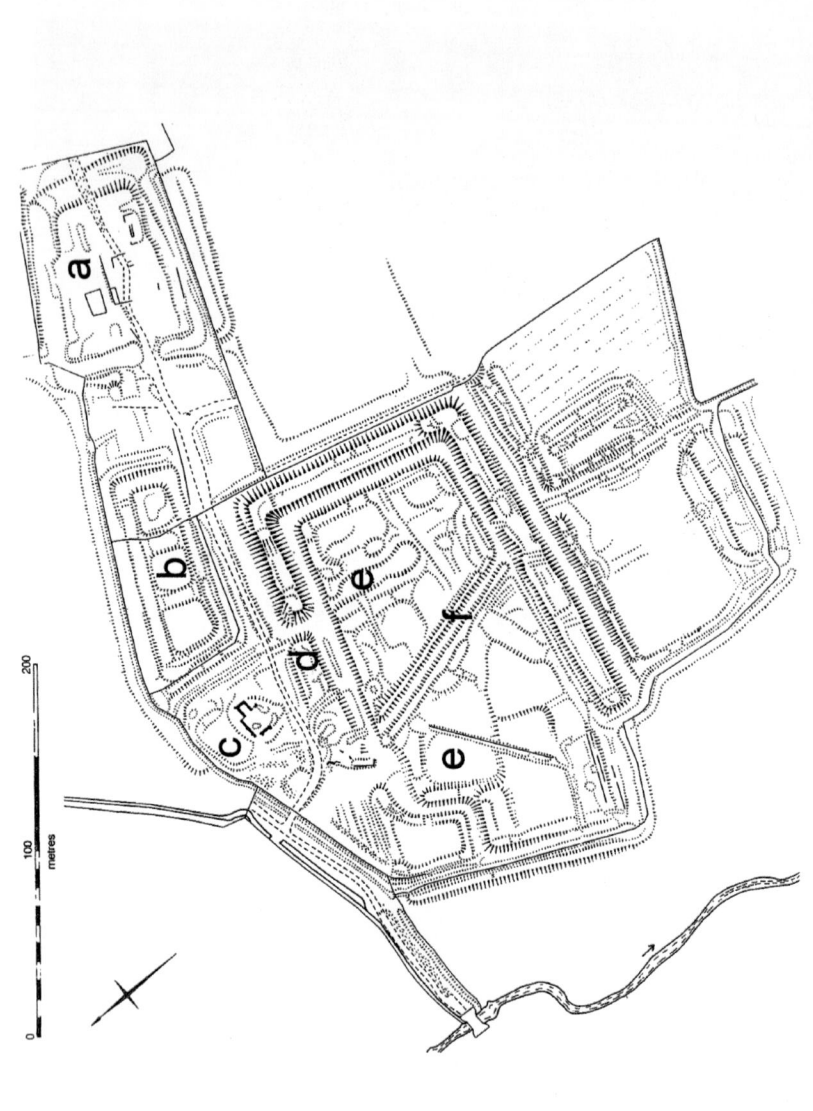

14   RCHME's surveyed plan of Quarrendon in 1990 (including six reference points a–f). © Crown Copyright, EH

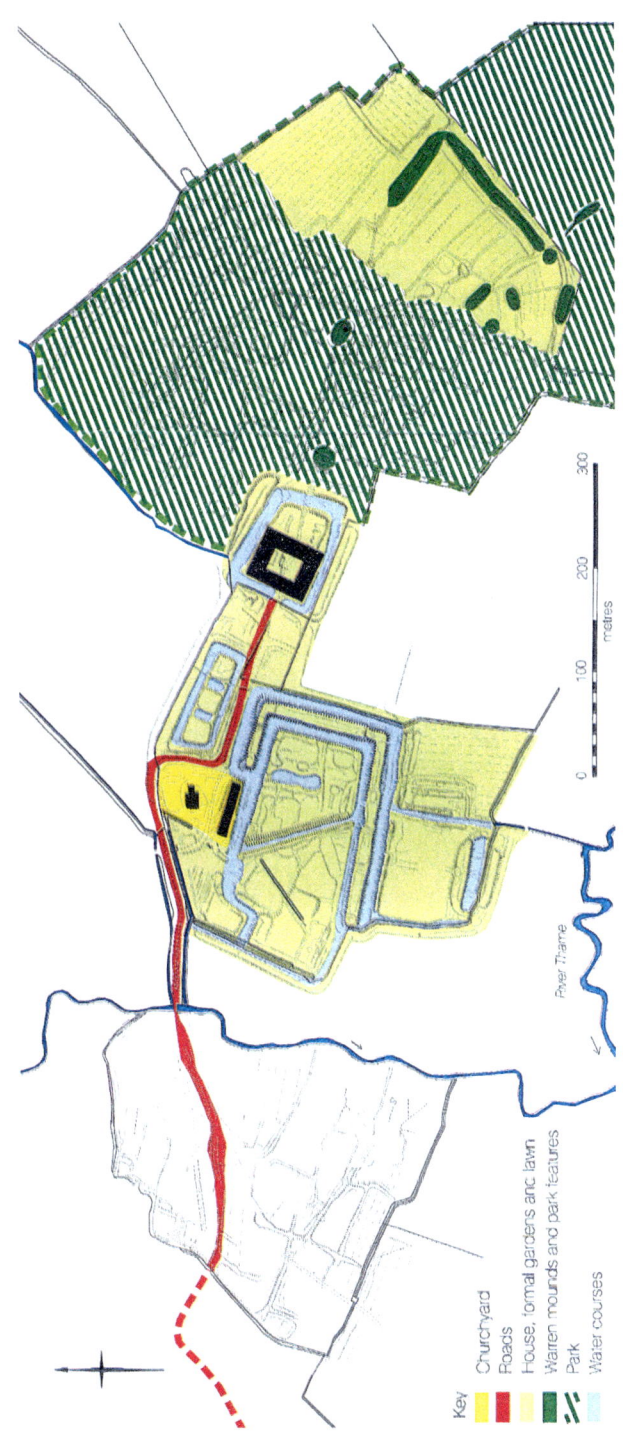

Key

- Churchyard
- Roads
- House, formal gardens and lawn
- Warren mounds and park features
- Park
- Water courses

River Thame

metres

0   100   200   300

15   Colour plan of Quarrendon. Reproduced by kind permission of Bucks Archaeological Society and Paul Everson

16   Aerial photograph of Quarrendon.
Cambridge University Collection of Aerial Photography

17   Sir Henry Lee with dog, by Marcus Gheeraerts, c.1595.
By permission of The Fitchley Foundation

18   Anglo-Netherlandish School, Robert Dudley, Earl of Leicester
(1532–1588), c.1564. Waddesdon, The Rothschild Collection
(Rothschild Family Trust). © The National Trust, Waddesdon Manor

19   Unknown Lady in Fancy Dress by Marcus Gheeraerts.
Hampton Court Palace, Middlesex, UK/The Bridgeman Art Library

20   'Dangers averted' medal. Fitzwilliam Museum,
University of Cambridge, UK/The Bridgeman Art Library

Chapter 5

The Life of a Tudor Gentleman: Lee's Personal Estates and Financial Position

Sir Henry Lee, like many Elizabethan gentlemen in public service to the Queen, also enjoyed a rich private life with lands, family, friends and other private interests. To his close associates, he was Sir Harry Lee, a sobriquet that even found its way into the State Papers. He owned extensive sheep-rearing estates at Quarrendon, close to Aylesbury in Buckinghamshire, the revenues from which afforded him freedom from constantly importuning for a lucrative position at Court, as was the lot of many of his contemporaries. Although the care of his inherited estates was to some extent subordinated to his stewardship of the Queen's manor at Woodstock, Lee had the time and finance after 1583 to acquire and develop a new private estate at Ditchley, Oxfordshire, which became his principal home.

Lee left no direct heir, and very few of his personal papers appear to have been preserved by later incumbents of Ditchley. Those that do exist are usually in the collections of other men and contain few financial details. However, the extent of Lee's lands is recorded, as are the patents granted to him, the salaries he received for official positions and the occasional loans he obtained from the Queen. Other than that, his financial position can only be pieced together from circumstantial evidence. It is interesting to compare his economic activity with comparable gentry families who did leave a record, such as the Dormers of Oxfordshire and the Treshams of Northamptonshire. Lee was a landowner for some fifty-six years, and a study of this aspect of his private life offers an opportunity to see how an Elizabethan gentleman dealt with the vicissitudes of the wool trade and the practical economies of funding a career at Court.

Lee's Lands and Finances

The main financial priority for a private Elizabethan gentleman was the accumulation and consolidation of his landholdings. The latter frequently involved their conversion to pastoral farming. Sir Henry Lee himself was fortunate that by 1540 the hard work of establishing the family estates in the rich Buckinghamshire pastureland had already been done by his grandfather, Sir Robert Lee, at a time when the expansion of sheep farming and enclosure of common land were at their height. Although his principal estates were at Quarrendon, he also had land in Over Upping and Little Marston. A recent RCHME/English Heritage archaeological survey of Quarrendon reveals that the Lees lived in a substantial moated manor house, built in the first quarter of the sixteenth century. They had a formal garden and courtyard within the moat, a two-acre toft called Pondecroft and an ancient church near the house.[1] In 1540 the manor of Quarrendon itself comprised 355 acres – twenty-five acres around the manor house itself and 330 acres of pasture called the Berryfield, the whole being valued at £44 18s 0d.[2] In addition to this, there were seventy-three and a half acres of land appertaining to the manors at Bierton, Aylesbury and Bellinger and 330 acres of woods. The total annual value of these was £58 9s 10½d. Sir Robert Lee also leased land from four nearby manors – at nearby Fleetmarston with Blackgrove, at Weedon from New College Oxford, and Hardwick and Burston – some 960 acres of pasture in all. His son Anthony Lee added Little Marston, additional land at Fleetmarston and the manor of Oving, and also continued his father's lease of tithes from Quarrendon and Bierton from the Dean and Chapter of Lincoln Cathedral.[3]

In 1553, after five years in wardship, Sir Henry Lee inherited these extensive, well-ordered and consolidated estates of rich pasture in the highly profitable Midlands sheep-rearing area, which throughout the later sixteenth century produced some of the best-quality wool and heaviest fleeces in the country. Quarrendon had a long record of exporting wool to the Continent, and, despite the collapse of wool and cloth prices on the foreign market in 1551, Buckinghamshire remained important as a source of long combing wool for the booming domestic worsted industry of Berkshire and Hampshire.[4] Lee was well placed to take advantage of this, and even without detailed estate accounts, it is reasonable to assume that for the first twenty years of his ownership of Quarrendon, he was a man of considerable means. Like his father, Lee added small parcels of land as the occasion arose, although the existence of other moieties and reversions of leases created court cases that seem to have been commonplace among Elizabethan landholders.[5]

---

[1]   Royal Commission on the Historical Monuments of England (RCHME) survey 1989–1990, taken for English Heritage. See P. Everson, 'Peasants, Peers and Graziers: The Landscape of Quarrendon, Buckinghamshire Interpreted', *Records of Buckinghamshire*, XXXI (2001), pp. 1–45.

[2]   ORO, DIL X/b/2c, 'A breve declaration of the Inquisition found for ... the Mannor of Quarrendon now in the holding of Sir Anthonie Lee Knight'.

[3]   ORO, DIL X/f/1, 2.

[4]   P.J. Bowden, *The Wool Trade in Tudor and Stuart England* (London, 1962), pp. 41–76. Sir Robert Lee had received a licence to export wool to Calais in 1533.

[5]   See arguments with William Hawtrey over Fleetmarston in *The Victorian County History of Buckinghamshire* (hereafter *VCH Bucks*, IV, p. 74. John Lord Mordaunt brought an action against Lee in 1559 for wrongfully detaining the premises of 'the Manor place' at Burston.

Like many other gentleman landholders in Buckinghamshire, Lee's prosperity was based on enclosures and the depopulation of hitherto arable land. These practices produced unrest among the tenants and local workers, resentment from neighbours and investigations by government commissioners. The land Lee inherited had long been converted to sheep-farming and although he was in a position to benefit, he did not appear to be personally responsible for the depopulation of Quarrendon, which had twenty resident families in 1524 and only four by 1563.[6] His grandfather, Sir Robert Lee, had enclosed Fleetmarston and Quarrendon, and while he had been exonerated from legal infringement at Quarrendon by Wolsey's enclosure inquiry of 1517, he was held responsible for the depopulation of Fleetmarston.[7]

Prior to the enclosure inquisition for Buckinghamshire in 1566, the Earl of Leicester stayed with Sir Henry Lee at Quarrendon and wrote to Burghley on 20 February describing the state of affairs as he saw them in the county generally: 'I never saw in so rich a soyll so many miserable and poor people. Hir ... some have all and greate numbers nothinge.'[8] No criticism was voiced directly at Lee and later, in 1577 and 1578, Lee was appointed by the Privy Council to sit as one of the twelve commissioners investigating complaints against enclosures in Buckinghamshire and Oxfordshire.[9] Bowden observes that the administration of Tudor statutes against depopulation and enclosure was usually put into the hands of those most opposed to the statutes, but Lee's letters make no personal comment on enclosures.[10]

Lee's marriage to Anne Paget in the early 1550s had brought him little material gain except the advowson of Aylesbury Church, but he did have the use of Paget House, his father-in-law's residence on the Strand.[11] After Lord Paget's fall from office in 1558 and death in June 1563, Lee obtained the lease of an apartment at the nearby Savoy, which became his main London lodging until 1608.

See also Centre for Buckinghamshire Studies (hereafter CBS) for details of Lee's smaller land purchases, D-LE/1/12 (bargain and sale, 30 May 1561); D-LE/1/15 (exemplification of recovery, 15 November 1561); D-LE/2/22 (lease, 1561–62); D-LE/5/9 (fine, 8 July 1557).

[6]   Everson, 'Peasants', p. 17.

[7]   Fleetmarston was reduced from fifty persons and eight ploughs in 1500 to a manor house and five cottages for shepherds by 1540.

[8]   TNA, PRO, SP12/39/105 (20 February 1566).

[9]   *CPR*, 19 Eliz. I, Part VI, p. 292 (17 April 1577); Dasent, *APC*, IX, pp. 323–4; *APC*, X, p. 155; *VCH Bucks*, IV, p. 9. By 1636, Quarrendon was described as 'an ancient enclosure and depopulated', *VCH Bucks*, IV, p. 100.

[10]   Bowden, *Wool Trade*, p. 110.

[11]   Paget House was bought by the Earl of Leicester for £2,500 around 1570, becoming, first, Leicester House and, later, Essex House.

By the latter part of the 1560s, therefore, Sir Henry Lee was established as one of the most prosperous sheep farmers in Buckinghamshire, well travelled, with influential friends at Court and in growing favour with the Queen. The latter was a fortunate development as a considerable part of his livelihood was swept away in the great floods of 1570. Quarrendon occupied a low-lying position adjacent to a tributary of the river Thames, and Lee's lands were vulnerable. Thomas Knell, in his *Declaration of such tempestuous and outrageous fluddes* described the damage done by the major floods, gales and high winds that shook the east coast of England on 5 October 1570, wreaking havoc from Hull and Lincolnshire to Sussex. There was a tidal wave in the Thames, and flood waters reached as far east as Oxfordshire.

Knell correlated the death toll of people, sheep, horses and cattle in the fourteen counties affected. The greatest named loser in his whole account was 'Sir Henry Ley, [who] lost by the flouds of water the number of III M sheep, besides horses and other cattell a great number'.[12] How large a percentage of Lee's total livestock was lost is unknown, but on 1 January 1571 the Queen granted him a seven-year licence to export 1,000 tods of wool yearly, stating that 'through the late tempestuous weather he has suffered great loss in his sheep and cattle, which are the chief part of his livelihood'.[13] In 1572 Lee received another licence, this time for ten years, to buy in England and export 500,000 woolfells.[14] Granting export licences was a typical way of rewarding the Queen's favourites: for example, major wool grants were made to the Earl of Leicester in 1560, Sir Francis Walsingham in 1575 and Simon Bowyer, Gentleman Usher to the Queen, in 1576.[15]

Invariably, such licences were sublet to agents or sold to alien merchants, with the licensee taking a cut from the profits. As the export market for English wool was in decline by the 1570s, such licences were not as profitable as they had once been, and, as his flocks recovered, Lee would probably have sold his own wool on the domestic market. The licence he obtained in 1576 to buy and export 200,000 calfskins over the next twelve years may well have been more profitable.[16] A more singular source of income was the three patents granted to Lee in 1575 and 1576 to seek out and manumit bondmen and bondwomen

---

[12]   Thomas Knell, *The declaration of such tempestuous and outrageous fluddes as hath been in divers places of England 1570* (London, 1571), *RSTC* 15032. See also Raphael Holinshed, *Holinsheds Chronicles of England, Scotland and Ireland* (hereafter Holinshed, *Chronicles*) (London, 1577), IV, p. 257. *RSTC* 1358.

[13]   *CPR*, 13 Eliz. I, Part VI, p. 253 (1 January 1571). A tod is a unit of weight for wool, equivalent to about 28 lbs.

[14]   *CPR*, 14 Eliz. I, Part XII, p. 487 (undated).

[15]   Bowyer's patent, for example, licensed him to buy and sell 500 sarplers within the next ten years (1,092 lbs of wool or 19 tods).

[16]   *CPR*, 18 Eliz. I, Part VII, p. 86 (10 July 1576).

from the Queen's estates, discussed below in more detail.[17] As with many of the Queen's favours to courtiers, this involved Lee in considerable hard work and expense before he saw any financial reward, and potential income was liable to be spread over several years in the future.

In addition to grants and patents, Lee also received some fees and perquisites for his various roles in the Queen's service. Although his wife and daughter continued to live at Quarrendon, after 1570 Lee's own attention turned to the Queen's manor at Woodstock, Oxfordshire, where he lived at High Lodge. Lee had initially purchased the patent for stewardship from Edward Dyer around 1571 but subsequently received an annual Exchequer fee of 100s.[18] From 1572 he received 3d a day as Keeper of the Great Park, 3d a day as Keeper of other parks within the manor and, after 1574, 4d a day for the office of the Wardrobe and Beds at Woodstock. From 1579 he was granted 3½d a day as Keeper of the garden and meadows. He was allowed to keep seventy cattle and forty horses on the demesne, and to cut 108 loads of firewood and eighteen loads of hay and brushwood annually to the value of £7. When Lee became Master of the Armoury at the Tower of London in 1580, he received an annual Exchequer fee of £31 18s 9d, additional payments for keeping armour in the Great Gallery at Greenwich of £66 13s 4d and various rents for tenements adjacent to the Tower.[19]

Regardless of the honours that accrued from royal favour, there is evidence that by the later 1570s Lee was increasingly falling into financial difficulties. A review in 15 March 1580 of recent loans made by the Queen indicated that Sir Henry Lee had received a loan of £3,000 in 1576 repayable at £300 a year, the first repayment to be made by midsummer 1577. By 1580 he had only repaid £600.[20] Lee's position was not unusual for a courtier, as the Earl of Leicester, Lord Stafford, Sir John Smythe and Edward Dyer were also named as having received loans from the Queen. Dyer, who was of similar rank and position to Lee, received a royal loan of £3,000 in 1579 – a sum he never managed to repay.[21] Royal servants could expect some remuneration for their labours, but payment was usually in arrears and the sums involved did not compare with the income

---

[17]   For a discussion of Lee's manumission patents, see pp. 134–9 below.

[18]   The patents for the stewardship had originally been granted to Edward Dyer on 23 June 1570, but Dyer, perennially short of money, had assigned them to his deputy Thomas Peniston, Lee's cousin. The patents had passed rapidly to Sir Gerard Croker and hence to Lee by purchase, until the death, forfeiture or surrender of Edward Dyer. Lee's reversionary lease of 1573 meant that the patents would eventually pass to Lee in his own right. Dyer lost his offices at Woodstock in 1603 at the accession of James I, but, despite royal attempts to assign them elsewhere, Lee retained the patents until his death.

[19]   BL, Harleian MS 7457.

[20]   *CSPD*, 1547–1580, p. 646; TNA, PRO, SP 12/136/135.

[21]   Early in 1582 a Spanish agent at Court described Dyer as 'that bankrupt poltroon': *CSP Foreign*, 1581–82, p. 472.

of gentry like Lee's Buckinghamshire neighbours, the Dormers, who remained at home, husbanding their profits from wool. None of Lee's royal licences or patents was such as to afford him an immediate financial windfall, and there is no evidence that as Master of the Armoury he supplemented his income in the manner practised by his colleagues in the Ordnance Office.

Much of Lee's income from Woodstock would have been spent on maintaining his position when the Court visited on progress. Entertaining the Queen and Court was costly, and Lee's friends – Edward Dyer, Philip Sidney and Fulke Greville – were notorious for their impecunious lifestyle and rising debts. The Court tournaments, for which Lee was increasingly responsible, could be ruinous, and here Lee was competing with some of the most profligate spenders among the aristocracy.

Philip Howard, before he succeeded to his grandfather's dignities as Earl of Arundel in 1581, spent lavishly on tournaments and in 1580, £14,000 in debt, had been forced to leave the Court in disgrace and sell some of his properties.[22] Edward de Vere, Earl of Oxford, who appeared as the Knight of the Tree of the Sun before Elizabeth in February 1581 was still being pursued by his tailor in 1584 for payment for apparel and livery for his servants to wear at 'tiltings'.[23] Lee had a position to maintain as Queen's Champion and by 1586 was in possession of three highly expensive suits of Greenwich armour and a stable of appropriate horses.[24] Self-appointed, Lee received no financial payment from the Queen, who increasingly used the Accession Day tournaments to entertain visiting foreign dignitaries at no cost to herself.

Lee was usually able to find the money for purchases he regarded as important because he still owned sizeable estates. Indeed in 1583, notwithstanding his debt to the Queen or perhaps because the loan had made capital available to him, Lee acquired his second territorial estate containing the three Oxfordshire townships of Spelsbury, Charlbury and Stonesfield and centred on Ditchley near Woodstock. For several years Lee's immediate interest in his family estates at Quarrendon seems to have been dwindling. Regular manorial courts were still held there, but the predominant part of Quarrendon's demesne land, the

---

[22]   H.G. Fitzalan-Howard, *The Lives of Philip Howard Earl of Arundel and Anne Dacre, his Wife* (London, 1857), p. 7.

[23]   Alan Nelson, *Monstrous Adversary: The Life of Edward de Vere, 17th Earl of Oxford* (Liverpool, 2003), p. 184.

[24]   Thom Richardson, Keeper of Armour and Oriental Arms and Armour at the Royal Armouries, Leeds, suggests unofficially that Lee, as Master of the Armoury in charge of the Greenwich workshops, might have had some financial discount on his second and third armours. Certainly, these were as lavishly decorated as any nobleman's armour included in the Almain *Album*.

Berryfield, had been leased out for some time, and Lee sold 160 acres of land in Fleetmarston in 1580 to release capital.[25]

By contrast, as early as May 1570, Lee had bought a reversionary lease of the Oxfordshire manors of Spelsbury and Shipton on the deaths of Anne, Duchess of Somerset and Anne, Countess of Warwick.[26] In January 1571 he obtained a grant of all 'tymbre trees of oke' and all other woods in woods and demesne lands belonging to the manors of Spelsbury and Shipton. He failed to acquire the manor of Spelsbury outright in 1575, but bought the house and estate at Ditchley in 1583 for £1,000. He later added land at Charlbury and additional freehold parcels of land at Stonesfield, Spelsbury and Taston, as well as realizing his reversionary lease of Spelsbury in 1587, on the death of Anne Somerset.

Lee's purchases raise the obvious question of why he sought to create this second separate estate. His Buckinghamshire neighbours, the Dormers, had bought estates in Oxfordshire to extend their sheep-grazing activities, but John Chamberlain's survey of Ditchley, commissioned by Lee in May 1581 prior to purchase, indicated that the land was very poor.[27] The house and forty-seven acres of arable land adjacent to it were burdened with annuities to William Gibbons and his family, which Lee had to buy out. The 900 acres which comprised the principal part of the estate had been 'so turned ... as it is neither good arable or pasture'. The arable land

> ... groweth so small a quantitie ... that some yeares it is skant worth the gathering ... there is no hay nor help for cattle ... and the barronesse of the ground worne out to the uttermost.

The sheep commons were overstocked, and the 326 acres of woods 'so cropped with cattell as will not yeald of long time any present peece of money'. Chamberlain had warned Lee that, given the state of the land, 'no man will over bidd you & therefore be not over hasty to purchase a hard bargain'.

It was not, however, the farming potential of Ditchley that probably appealed to Lee but its proximity to the Queen's manor of Woodstock. As Steward at Woodstock, Lee had the use of four lodges on that estate, but his hold on them was dependent on Court favour, and by then his decisions had been overruled by Burghley and he had been harassed by Comptroller George Whitton. Lee relished his roles in the service of the Queen, but by 1581 his experience of ten years as a royal servant contrasted poorly with the benefits from his previous

---

[25]   Courts Leet and Courts Baron were held regularly at Quarrendon: see ORO, DIL X/a/14; DIL X/a/15; DIL X/a/16. The Berryfield, some 330 acres out of 350 acres of demesne land, were leased to a George Duncombe by 1581. ORO, DIL X/h/1.

[26]   *CPR 12 Eliz.I part m.19 p. 5 (26 May 1570); CPR*, 13 Eliz. I, X, p. 303 (1 January 1571).

[27]   ORO, LEE 1/3a (9 May 1581).

three decades as an independent landowner. Ditchley was Lee's own solution to the classical controversy of corrupt Court versus the purer pastoral idyll so often referred to in Court entertainments: he would establish his own independent estate at the gates of Woodstock while continuing to run the Queen's manor.

From 1583 Ditchley became Lee's home, and he created his own hunting domain within the forest of Wychwood. He had made financial provision for his wife Anne at Quarrendon in December 1581 by arranging that, in the event of his death, she should enjoy the profit from the lease of the Berryfield.[28] There is no indication that she ever came to Ditchley. The Quarrendon lands were entailed, but both Lee's sons had died young, leaving only a daughter, Mary, to inherit. On the death of Mary around 1583, Lee effected a recovery on his estates, transforming his holdings from fee entail to fee simple, which enabled him legally to leave his lands to whom he wished.[29]

The poor state of Lee's finances continued throughout the 1580s and was frequently mentioned in his letters. When sending a present to Sir Francis Walsingham's daughter, Frances, on her marriage to Philip Sidney in 1583, he apologized for the smallness of the gift stating 'he cannot send much that hath but little'.[30] In particular, his debt to the Queen was turning out to be a major embarrassment and, given the extortionate interest rates of the time, usually 10 per cent or more, it was proving impossible to pay. In a letter to Walsingham in February 1587 from his brother's house in Thorne, Yorkshire, Lee wrote that he was eager to 'satisfy her majesty and the worlde to whom I am in dette'.[31] By August 1589, after he had incurred expenses as Master of the Horse in the north of England during the Armada crisis, Lee still owed the Queen £900 and had to obtain a ruling from Burghley that no process would be made against him over his debt to the Queen if he repaid £300 yearly.[32] In another letter to Walsingham in October 1589 on the state of the armour in the Tower, Lee stated plainly that he lacked the finance to come to London as 'I am this week ... to send up such little plate I have to answer [the] debt to her Majesty [and] this year past I sold a farm I might evil spare'.[33] He also requested that the Lords might delay questioning him about the Armoury until his annual engagement in London on 17 November, when he might 'stop two gaps with one brush'.

---

28 ORO, DIL X/h/1.

29 A recovery is a collusive action – a fake legal procedure in the Court of Chancery whereby estates are converted from holding in fee entail to fee simple. Lee's recovery was registered in Recovery Rolls, 25 Elizabeth Easter, m. 93. Ditchley was conveyed to feoffees for the purposes of Lee's will in 1593.

30 *CSPD*, 1581–90, p. 95 (10 February1583).

31 BL, Harleian MS 286, f. 100.

32 TNA, PRO, SP46/37/41, Burghley's letter to Fanshawe (16 August 1589).

33 *CSPD*, 1581–90, p. 623 (3 October 1589).

Lee was also borrowing from other sources. He had been promised a loan of £500 from George Talbot, sixth Earl of Shrewsbury and had received £200 in September, prior to the earl's death on 18 November 1590. On 7 December 1590 he wrote to the seventh earl, Gilbert Talbot to say that he had hoped to receive the outstanding £300 at Christmas 1590, as 'the hope of that munny whyche I so much bylte on, made me take some groundes in to my hands whyche is now lyke to turn to my hurte'.[34] Gilbert Talbot, with enough financial problems of his own, was lending money to no-one.

Like many other courtiers, Lee could plead poverty and yet spend lavishly when the occasion demanded. He had just renewed a lease for the manor of Charlbury from St John's College Oxford and had purchased the residue of a lease of Abbots Wood at Charlbury. He spent heavily on the entertainment at his retirement tilt on 17 November 1590, but this was the last tournament for which he would lay out considerable sums. It was fortunate that on 5 July 1593 Burghley again ruled that no action should be taken against Lee in the matter of his debt to the Queen and, later that year, a quittance of a debt of Sir Henry Lee was officially recorded, with a proviso that the £100 that still remained should be paid.[35]

Despite Lee's letter in 1600 to Sir Robert Cecil, pleading poverty as a reason for not entertaining the Queen on her progress, his overall expenditure increased considerably in the years between 1596 and 1608. In 1597 Lee could afford to ride from Charing Cross to Windsor for his investiture as a Knight of the Garter with a train of some 200 retainers, all dressed in blue. He also engaged in a rash of construction work that was typical of Elizabethan gentry at this time and his *Memorium Sacrae* records that he built 'four goodly houses', as well as an almshouse and family tombs in St Peter's church at Quarrendon.

The new-found wealth needed to finance this came, in Lee's case and in the case of many other Buckinghamshire graziers, from the substantial rise in the price of wool in the latter years of the 1590s – a rise that peaked in 1603 before a substantial decline by 1610.[36] Lee was well positioned to benefit from this. Gervase Markham noted that Buckinghamshire produced 'large-boned sheep of the best shape and deepest staple', and Camden, writing at the end of the sixteenth century, recorded the 'infinite numbers of fleecie sheepe' at Quarrendon and Eythorp, where Sir Robert Dormer farmed.[37] Lee was raising his own sheep and

[34]   Lambeth Palace Library (hereafter LPL), Talbot Papers, MS 3199, f. 211 (7 December 1590).

[35]   TNA, PRO, SP46/38/344, Burghley to Fanshawe (5 July 1593); BL, Add. MS 75718, charters after 5 December 1593.

[36]   For a very detailed discussion of this complex topic, see Bowden, *Wool Trade*. Bowden also includes a table of wool prices at pp. 219–20.

[37]   Gervase Markham, *Cheap and Good Husbandry* (London, 1676), Wing M681; W. Camden, *Britannia* (London, 1610), *RSTC* 4527. The latter was a first translation into English

in July 1594 he sent 'six sheep of his own breeding' from Quarrendon to the Earl of Shrewsbury at Sheffield.[38] In 1598 Lee sold 4,905 fleeces at an average weight of 4.1 lb each, some from Ditchley but most from Quarrendon.[39]

Lee undertook building work at Ditchley itself, updating the old house before the Queen's visit in 1592, and he later built a lodge four miles from Ditchley known as Lee's Rest or Little Rest for his mistress Anne Vavasour at a cost of £5,000, in keeping with the late Elizabethan fashion for building private lodges in the grounds of an estate.[40] Although there is little evidence that Lee enclosed any land on his Oxfordshire estates at this time, he was perceived to be guilty of enclosing. Benjamin Steer, the putative leader of the 'Oxfordshire rising' against enclosures in November 1596 named Lee as one of the six Oxfordshire landowners to be attacked.[41] It is possible that Lee's enlargement of the Queen's hunting domain at Woodstock two decades earlier accounted for his inclusion on the list. In the event, the rising failed to materialize.

Lee's principal building works were in and around Quarrendon, and it is interesting to speculate why, having settled with his mistress in Ditchley, he should have chosen to develop his Buckinghamshire property at this point. The scale and design of Lee's building work was very much in keeping with the enthusiasm for building current among the Elizabethan gentry in the last decade of the century, and Lee, despite still having no legitimate heir but with intimations of mortality growing apace, presumably sought to leave some mark upon his ancestral family home before his death. Possibly, he simply chose to develop the gardens at Quarrendon because Ditchley, on much poorer soil and heavily wooded, was totally devoted to hunting. Although no part of the Elizabethan estate now exists above ground level, with the exception of a few stones of St Peter's Church, the RCHME/English Heritage archaeological survey in 1989 reveals a precise picture of Lee's home that is absent from contemporary documents[42] (see Ills 14 and 15).[43]

---

by Philemon Holland of the original text in Latin published in 1586, which by 1607 was in its seventh edition.

[38]   LPL, Shrewsbury Papers 701, f. 145 (Lee to Shrewsbury, 15 July 1594).

[39]   ORO, DIL III/b/2; *VCH Bucks*, IV, 101. This was 700 tods of wool.

[40]   Burghley had a lodge at Theobalds, and Sir Thomas Tresham built the triangular lodge at Rushton in 1596.

[41]   John Walter, 'A Rising of the People? The Oxfordshire Rising of 1596', *Past and Present*, CVII (May 1985), pp. 90–143. The date set for the rising was very close to 17 November, when several of the named potential victims, such as Lee, would have been in London. It is probable that the aim was to damage property or seize arms, rather than to perpetrate violence on landowners.

[42]   RCHME survey 1989–1990, taken for English Heritage. The whole complex is designated as a scheduled ancient monument: National Monument No.12004. Such was the extent of the earthworks of the formal gardens that they had earlier been misinterpreted as military earthworks from the civil wars and are so named on some Ordnance Survey maps.

[43]   Ill. 15 is reproduced from Everson, *Peasants*, p. 6.

This survey gives us an added perspective on Lee's lifestyle and interests since, with the virtual abandonment of Quarrendon by his heirs, the Elizabethan garden layout was not remodelled by later generations.

The estate, as it was left to Lee in 1548, comprised a moated manor house and courtyard with nearby orchards (see Ill. 14a). By 1600 the manor house had been enlarged and boasted major garden developments. To the west of the house there was a moated water garden (Ill. 14b) – a complex of ponds and islands, surrounded by raised banks and walkways from which to view the islands. The estate continued west to St Peter's church (Ill. 14c), which was damaged in the floods of 1570. At some point after 1597 Lee restored St Peter's church, erecting family tombs and church armorial glass bearing his coat of arms with the Order of the Garter. The church itself is now reduced to a few stones above ground, but is by far the best documented part of the estate, being the last structure to be demolished.[44] Lee's tomb inscription also claimed that he had 'reised the foundation of the adjoininge Hospitall' or almshouses. These are undocumented, and although Chambers and Dillon denied their existence, the archaeological survey reveals a possible site for the almshouses near the church (Ill. 14d).

The major part of the Quarrendon gardens lay to the south of the church and included features typical of late Elizabethan gardens (Ill. 14e).[45] These were bounded by prominent earthworks, and within them were sizeable raised islands surrounded by canals and ponds and accessible by ornamental bridges. In the garden were viewing platforms, garden buildings and possibly an ornamental mill. The most prominent feature of the garden appeared to be a broad inner canal running from west to east and acting as a bypass system from the garden's many water features (Ill. 14f). The garden was heavily reliant on a complex system of water management (see Ill. 15), and the archaeological survey and a recent aerial photograph (Ill. 16) reveal that certain drainage features still survive as functioning drains and dyked hedgerows.

Everson suggests that these drains and dykes would have converted a large area of the floodplain north of the site formerly vulnerable to floods, as in 1570, into rich grazing meadows.[46] This would argue for the creation of such a garden scheme after the floods of 1570: had it existed before, the losses Lee experienced and the flood damage to St Peter's church might have been averted. The size of the undertaking suggests that a considerable sum of money was spent on the expertise and manpower needed to execute the design. Many other features are

[44] BL, Lansdowne MS 874, ff. 35, 50b, epitaphs and arms from many of the churches in England, gathered by the College of Arms, including a contemporary description of Lee's tomb. Engravings exist from 1815 and 1828, and photographs from 1908 show sixteenth-century alterations to the church roof and nave.

[45] See P. Henderson, *The Tudor House and Garden* (New Haven, CT, and London, 2005).

[46] Everson, 'Peasants', p. 31.

revealed by the archaeological survey, including a sizeable managed Tudor coney warren, placed very prominently to the east of the great house, with a typical complex of pillow mounds, ditches and possibly a warrener's cottage.[47] Everson notes that 'the formal garden, earthworks and the warren are notable for their scale, detail and completeness.'[48]

Is the survey of Sir Henry Lee's gardens significant in understanding his actions and aspirations at this stage in his life? Of itself, it is little more than an interesting recovery of a lost Elizabethan garden, proving that Lee was well in the forefront of the contemporary fashion for house and garden development. Taken together with the intricate symbolism of the 1592 Ditchley portrait and other portraits commissioned by Lee, and his known talent for producing tournament *imprese*, the complicated layout of the gardens on such a large scale would suggest that Lee had a mind far deeper and more complex than has been hitherto suspected.

Everson goes as far as to suggest that the somewhat eccentric triangular layout of Lee's formal gardens at Quarrendon shows a 'concern in this garden's creation for didactic ratios and scientific geometry very much beyond the organization and rectangularity characteristic of early post-medieval formal gardens in England.'[49] Whether this is true or not remains a matter for speculation. In all probability Lee did not plan every feature of the gardens himself, any more than he planned every aspect of the Ditchley portrait. He did, however, commission and pay for them and would have had a major say in their formulation.

One of the major difficulties with using the 1989 archaeological survey of Quarrendon is that there is virtually no contemporary written evidence on Lee's garden development. We only know that land including the 'upper warren' was leased to an Aylesbury butcher in 1607.[50] It is therefore difficult to date Lee's development of his estate at Quarrendon and any attempt must be conjectural, based on the evidence of his other actions. While the principal developments at Quarrendon appear to have taken place in the second half of the sixteenth century, they need not necessarily have been effected at the same time. Such a large-scale development of Quarrendon itself would have necessitated three things from Lee – time, inclination and, most importantly, money.

The formal courtyards around the moated great house existed in Sir Anthony Lee's day, but the house itself appears to have been enlarged by Sir Henry Lee. The visit of the Earl of Leicester in 1566 would perhaps have necessitated some enlargement, but house extension tended to be a continuous project in

---

[47]   Pillow mounds were pillow-shaped, flat-topped rectangular mounds often surrounded by a shallow ditch, used to farm rabbits from Norman times.

[48]   Everson, 'Peasants', p. 1.

[49]   Ibid., p. 40.

[50]   ORO, DIL X/g/1.

late Elizabethan England. After 1570, although Lee had neither the time nor money to devote to Quarrendon, his wife was nominally living there with their daughter Mary, and the creation of the coney warren could have been her work. The melancholic and deserted Lady Lee was, however, spending an increasing amount of time with her mother at the Paget family home at West Drayton, Middlesex, and died in 1590. From 1595 Lee had both the money and the freedom to indulge his new passion for building, and the style of the gardens themselves is typical of others developed elsewhere in the 1590s and 1600s. Before his death, Lee had also built two more manor houses near Quarrendon – one at Burston and another called Laelius at Weedon.[51]

The late Elizabethan fashion for house-building also brought a rash of borrowing for, as Lee remarked in 1607, 'builders seldome swymme in money'.[52] The demand for short-term loans saw the rise of a new type of moneylender, and Michael Hickes, secretary to Lord Burghley and friend of Sir Robert Cecil typified the careful professional man who was prepared to advance money to friends under certain conditions. Borrowing by landowners did not necessarily indicate poor finance. Rather, it was a product of the fact that rents from leases on land tended to be paid only twice a year and income from wool annually. Many landowners, finding themselves in temporary difficulties or seeing an opportunity to buy land adjacent to their own, preferred to take out a short-term loan rather than sell assets.

Most of Lee's loans either took the form of a bond or were secured by statute, and in both cases the creditor could sue for repayment. Raising money by mortgage was a more risky procedure which could result in the forfeiture of the land, and Lee only resorted to this once in 1598, when he briefly mortgaged some coppices in Charlbury and ten acres in Blackgrove to his nephew Lee Symonds. Lee borrowed frequently from Hickes – he borrowed £2,000 secured by statute in April 1598 and another £500 in June 1599, for example – and he continued to do so until 1608 while remaining on the friendliest of terms with his creditor.[53]

In 1601 Lee received, as a compliment from the Queen, 'in consideration of good and faithful service done by Sir Henry Lee', a confirmation of his former patent 'of the Manor of Quarrendon & all the tythes marshes woodes etc. and all the courts whatsoever and all the fairs markets toles ... and all rent & annual

---

51   The house now standing on the site of Laelius is called Lilies, with little apparent appreciation of the significance of the original name.

52   BL, Lansdowne MS 90, no. 36, f. 72 (Lee to Sir Michael Hickes, 1607); L. Stone, *An Open Elite? England 1540–1880* (Oxford, 1984), p. 247.

53   TNA, PRO, LC4/195/73 (1598) and LC4/194/165 (1599). The penalty for non-payment was £4,000. See also A.G.R. Smith, *Servant to the Cecils: The Life of Sir Michael Hickes, 1543–1612* (London, 1977), pp. 108–11.

profit ... by fealty only'.[54] This new patent was highly complimentary, but its wording necessitated a second recovery on Lee's hereditary estates.[55]

Lee's Position as a Typical Elizabethan Landowner and Grazier

It is interesting to compare Lee's financial position with other gentlemen of the same status. His closest neighbours, the Dormers at Wing, four miles from Quarrendon were, like the Lees, a gentry family whose great wealth was built on sheep-farming. They had land in Oxfordshire as well as Buckinghamshire, and Sir Robert Dormer (1485–1552), like Sir Robert Lee, had built up the family fortunes. Both families appreciated their responsibilities as local gentry. Sir William Dormer (1512–1575) served in Parliament with Sir Henry Lee as knight of the shire for Buckinghamshire on at least three occasions. Lee served on eight occasions between 1558 and 1584, and sat on four parliamentary committees in 1581. Members of both the Lee and Dormer families served as local magistrates and as muster-masters for Buckinghamshire.[56] Whereas Lee's main preoccupation was his service to the Queen and much of his Quarrendon land was leased out, the Dormers preferred to remain at home, developing and extending their manors and flocks.

The principal difference between the two families was the fact that the Dormers were Catholic. The leading men of the family were prepared to conform publicly to the established religion, which enabled them to play a part in county administration and avoid recusancy fines, but overall it was deemed politic and infinitely more profitable to eschew a Court career.[57] The younger Sir Robert Dormer (1550/51–1616) occasionally came to Court with Lee in the 1590s, but he followed his father and grandfather's tradition of concentrating on his lands. Before his death, he had more than twenty-six sheep-rearing manors and had become Baron Dormer of Wing through the purchase of a title that eluded Lee.[58]

The experience of the Dormers contrasted with another great sheep-rearing gentry family, the Treshams of Northamptonshire. Sir Thomas Tresham (1544–1605), an erstwhile participant in Lee's tournaments, had sought a Court career,

---

[54]   BL, *Rotulorum Patentium* (Rot. Pat.) 44 Eliz., Part IV, M22 (Lee's renewed patent for Quarrendon).

[55]   *Trinity Term in the first year of James I's Reign* (1 Jac. I Trinity), M 21 (1603).

[56]   See, for example, HMC *Salis*. V, p. 523 (1595).

[57]   Jane Dormer (1538–1612), a gentlewoman to Queen Mary, married the Duke of Feria in December 1558, the only important marriage between the servants of Philip II and those of Mary. As Duchess of Feria, Jane's house became a centre for English Catholic exiles in Spain.

[58]   It was said that he paid £10,000 for the title of Baron Dormer in 1615, in the first of the substantial sales of peerages at the Jacobean Court.

but his open Catholicism brought him a term of imprisonment and ruinous recusancy fines. Sir Henry Lee, although he had a Catholic wife, avoided such financial pitfalls by his firm adherence to the established church. The experience of Lee and the Dormer family as gentlemen graziers can also be compared to that of the Spencer family of Althorp, Northamptonshire. Whereas Lee had chosen a Court career and the Dormers had extended their land in Oxfordshire and Buckinghamshire, the Spencers had a long tradition of eschewing attendance at Court, concentrating on building up flocks and developing breeds of sheep. This exercise, over several generations, had rendered them one of the wealthiest gentry families in England. Unlike Lee, Sir John Spencer had a large family to provide for, including six daughters, but money and judicious marriages ensured that the family rapidly entered the peerage under James I.

It is also interesting to compare Lee's building activities with those of his contemporaries. Quarrendon was what Paul Everson calls 'a country house within a manipulated setting',[59] a wealthy gentry estate typical of the late sixteenth and early seventeenth centuries and incorporating many features found in the properties of Lee's friends. The Dormer family's original house at Wing had been moated like Quarrendon, but in 1606 Sir Robert Dormer commissioned Ascott House, a pleasant half-timbered dwelling, not unlike contemporary descriptions of Lee's house at Ditchley. Dormer, like Lee, also borrowed money from Sir Michael Hickes to finance his building work.[60] Lee's almshouses at Quarrendon were typical of other charities of the time. Robert Dudley, Earl of Leicester, had already founded Lord Leicester's Hospital at Warwick in 1571, and Sir Robert Dormer's mother, Dame Dorothy Dormer, founded almshouses known as Dormer's Hospital in 1596 for eight men and women. Sir Baptist Hickes, a good friend of Lee, endowed twelve almshouses in Chipping Campden in 1612, near his newly built Campden House.

The garden earthworks and water gardens at Quarrendon would have closely paralleled those at Lyveden New Bield in Northamptonshire, where the Catholic Sir Thomas Tresham developed a formidable system of water gardens with raised terraces and moatside walks from 1593.[61] Coney warrens, such as Lee's, were a common feature of medieval and post-medieval gardens. At least twelve pillow mounds still exist at Woodstock; the Dormers' estate at Wing incorporated a rabbit warren within an elaborate garden; Petworth House in Sussex boasted

---

[59] Paul Everson, 'Peasants, Peers and Graziers: The Landscape of Quarrendon, Buckinhamshire, Interpreted', *Records of Buckinghamshire*, XXXI (2001), pp. 1–45.

[60] TNA, PRO, LC4/193/69.

[61] Henderson, *The Tudor House and Garden*. Unlike Quarrendon, Sir Thomas Tresham's work at Lyveden is well documented: BL, Add. MS 39832, 39833 and 39836, f. 164. The building accounts from 1593–97 and 1599–1600 were used in M.E. Finch, *The Wealth of Five Northants Families, 1540–1640* (Oxford, 1956), pp. 66–94 and pp. 182–4.

Conigar Lodge; and Sir Thomas Tresham built his heavily symbolic, triangular Warrener's Lodge at Rushton, Northamptonshire.

Although it was not part of his personal estates, Lee was prepared to use his experience and influence as a member of the leading county gentry to benefit New Woodstock, Oxfordshire. The township, which was chiefly dependent on its proximity to the Queen's manor at Woodstock had 'fallen into great poverty' but was allowed to set itself up as a wool staple in 1576, in the hope that this would attract trade and industry to the borough.[62] Lee was responsible for New Woodstock being granted its own parliamentary seat, usually filled by Lee family nominees. Despite his *contretemps* with the tenants of Woodstock in 1576, he was appointed High Steward of the borough of Woodstock in 1580, a 'ceremonial position providing the political patronage regarded as vital for the town', and held this position until 1611.[63]

Lee's Singularity: The Manumission of Bondmen on The Royal Estates

If the majority of Sir Henry Lee's financial affairs were reasonably typical of Elizabethan gentlemen of his standing, the patents to manumit or free some 300 bondmen and bondwomen on the royal estates granted to Sir Henry Lee by the Queen in 1575 and 1576 were unique. A study of these illustrates the last days of the archaic system of villeinage that was all but dead in most parts of England. One way in which the Queen could reward favourites at no expense to herself personally was to grant permission for them to seek out certain of her subjects who could be forced to forfeit their goods or money for various reasons. In Lee's case, the subjects to be sought out were bondmen or villeins on royal manors, and his task was to manumit them, or grant them their freedom, for a fee. If the bondmen themselves refused manumission, Lee was entitled to claim up to a third of the bondman's 'goods, chattels, leases, lands, tenements and hereditiments'.

Villeinage en gros, though mentioned in Lee's commission, had virtually died out, but the state of villein regardant to a particular manor still existed, especially on Crown lands.[64] The term was still used in manorial records, but by the reign of Elizabeth, the granting of manumissions to such bondmen who still existed had degenerated into a fund-raising exercise for the Signet office or for a favoured courtier. Sir Henry Lee was the last major beneficiary of patents of

---

[62]   BL, Statutes of the Realm 18, Elizabeth I, C 21. Complaints were made in 1577 that the new wool staple at New Woodstock in Oxfordshire had led to much local English wool being engrossed into a few rich men's hands – TNA, PRO, SP12/114/39.

[63]   *Woodstock Chamberlain's Accounts 1609–1650*, ed. M. Maslen (Stroud, 1993), Vol. 58, p. 3.

[64]   Villeins en gros were attached to an individual lord, and the practice had all but disappeared. Villeins regardant were attached to a specific manor.

manumission, and although the patents were a sign of substantial royal favour, they would not make his fortune overnight.

The survival of villeinage into late Elizabethan England was something of an anachronism. Some contemporary Elizabethan authors, such as Sir Thomas Smith, denied its existence, and it is not a subject that has much exercised present-day historians. It was discussed in 1903 by Alexander Savine in what was then a ground-breaking article, and revisited by Diarmaid MacCulloch in 1988.[65] Apart from these publications, the demise of Elizabethan villeinage has tended to be relegated to the researches of local historians.[66] While a study of manumission under Lee adds little to the overall work of Sabine and MacCulloch, it does add to our knowledge of Lee himself. In the absence of detailed financial accounts for his landholdings in Quarrendon and Ditchley, it gives an interesting insight into the one specific aspect of Lee's finances that remains well documented.

What Diarmiad MacCulloch calls 'the last great manumission campaign' began on 3 April 1574 with a charter for Burghley and Sir Walter Mildmay.[67] The preamble informs us that the Queen's

> ... poore faithfull and loyal Subjects, being borne in Blode and regardant to ... manors [had] made humble Suyte unto Us to be Manumysed Enfranchised and made free with theire Children ... [to become] more apte and fitte members ... of our Common Wealthe.

Whether or not they had made suit, the fact remained that they had to 'compound ... for Suche resonable Somes of Money ... for Manumission', in this case, the sum of 12s 8d.

A letter from Burghley to Thomas Fanshawe on 11 July 1574 makes it clear that the benefit of this particular commission had originally been intended for Sir Henry Lee, and that her Majesty now desired that Lee should have a full grant in his own name to manumit a number of bondmen.[68] On 7 January 1575 Lee, as

---

[65]   A. Savine, 'Bondmen under the Tudors', *TRHS*, 2nd series, XVII (1903), pp. 235–89; D. MacCulloch, 'Bondmen under the Tudors', in C. Cross, D. Loades and J.J. Scarisbrick (eds), *Law and Government under the Tudors: Essays Presented to Sir Geoffrey Elton* (Cambridge, 1988), pp. 91–109; Thomas Smith, *De Republica Anglorum*, III, pp. 107–14, quoted in Savine 'Bondmen', p. 239.

[66]   F.G. Davenport's *The Economic Development of a Norfolk Manor, 1086–1565* (Cambridge, 1906; reprinted London, 1967) is typical of such studies, and fortunately extends its survey to include Lee's manumissions on the manor of Forncett in 1575.

[67]   T. Rymer, *Foedera*, 20 vols (London,1704–35), XV, pp. 731–3.

[68]   TNA, PRO, SP46/30/49.

...[the Queen's] wellbeloved and faithfull subject and servant ... for the speciall trust & confidence ... in your ... wisdome & fidelitie' [was to] appoint accept admitt & cause to be manumysed infranchised & made free such two hundreth of o[u]r bondmen & bondwomen in bludd ... either bondmen ... in gros or els ... regardant to all or any of o[u]r mann[o]rs.[69]

The procedure was laid down in the commission. The holder was to seek out some 200 bondmen and bondwomen, with 'their children and sequells', and compound with them for their freedom. In Lee's case, a fee of 26s 8d was mentioned in his patent of 17 January 1575.[70] A warrant was to be drawn up, signed by Lee and presented to the Chancellor of the Duchy of Lancaster.[71] Lee's first warrant is dated 1 February 1575, and the whole business was of sufficient contemporary importance for Lee's patents and warrants to be copied out chronologically some time shortly after 1591.[72]

The case of Long Bennington in Lincolnshire illustrates how Lee's commission was implemented. By his first patent, he was entitled to manumit some 200 bondmen with their children: Lee took care to choose only the bondmen who could afford to pay. Various manorial surveys had been undertaken earlier in the reign, probably with the purpose of manumission in mind, and Lee was fortunate that one existed for the royal manor of Long Bennington. The survey had been conducted by some eighteen local men and women, and depositions sworn on 18 April 1570, recording the ages of all bondmen and women with their families, goods and chattels, and inventories of recently deceased bondmen. Clearly, many bondmen had prospered. For example, the late Robert Gilbarte, a villein regardant unto Long Bennington was worth £195 3s 6d on the day of his death.[73]

The Long Bennington roll also illustrates how candidates for manumission were selected. The original 1570 roll was meticulously annotated by Lee's agent Thomas Grey in 1575, and little was secret. Thomas Huys, deceased, 'died riche by marrying of a wydoo sister to Isake of London', and the children of the late Robert Gilbarte were to pay 'out of their porcion for ther manumising'. When manumission was granted to bondmen with their children, no mention was made of the bondman's wife, as she had no monetary value to the manor. When

69   TNA, PRO, DL 42/102 (Duchy of Lancaster Miscellania). Lee's original patent was sold as part of 'property of a gentleman' at Sotheby's on 20 November 1973 and was purchased privately. Lee's second patent, dated 20 June 1575, is now on display at Ditchley Park, Oxfordshire.

70   'Sequells', the term used in the document, derives from the Latin *sequella* – progeny or brood. *CPR*, 17 Eliz. I, Part VIII, p. 511 (17 January 1575).

71   TNA, PRO, DL 41/553 – Lee's actual warrants and draft deeds of manumission are retained among the Duchy's papers in a large unwieldy bundle. See also E178/1550.

72   TNA, PRO, DL 42/102 – chronological copies. The last recorded is 12 May 41 Eliz.

73   TNA, PRO, DL 41/553, ff. 1–8.

the wife was a freewoman, a note was made. Against widows' names are details of their property. In the case of the widow Margaret Isake, who had £6 18s 4d, the note reads 'this woman will pay nothing'. The pauper status of the cottars Humfrey Huys and Robert Baynbrigg was recorded, and it is unlikely that Lee would have regarded them as worth manumitting.

Lee therefore had access to an evaluation of the holdings of each bondman and bondwoman regardant to the manor of Long Bennington in both 1570 and 1575. Armed with this information and other similar rolls, Lee could choose who the most profitable subjects for manumission were. Savine suggests that the annotations to the Long Bennington roll were made by Lee, but it seems highly unlikely that he actually did the work himself, given his other activities in the service of the Queen.[74] The vigorous and muscular writing used on the roll, not dissimilar from Lee's, is the hand of his agent Thomas Grey, who signed and delivered each manumission warrant to Lee.[75] Savine quite rightly calls the seeking out of bondmen 'mean work' and, although Lee was nominally in charge, the close inquiry needed to implement this was more the work of a land steward.

By the time of Lee's second commission in June 1575 it was obvious that he was meeting some opposition, possibly from prosperous bondmen such as the large Gilbarte family of Long Bennington.[76] On 30 June Lee received a second grant to enfranchise an additional 100 bondmen and bondwomen. This time the commission had teeth – not only could Lee seize the lands and chattels of any such who refused reasonably to compound with Lee for their manumission, but he could cause inquiry to be made of all lands alienated by bondmen and bondwomen. Lee received a third commission on 17 December 1576, granting him further powers to seize for himself any land that had been recently alienated by bondmen and bondwomen. To aid him in his enquiries, he already had a 1570 list of landholdings in Long Bennington and in other manors with similar surveys.[77]

The records illustrate that not all the bondmen still surviving into Elizabethan times were content to remain as mere labourers on their manor. Many chose to live some distance from the manor and paid the fine of *chevage* for the privilege. For example, William Wanklen, a villein regardant to the manor of 'Leompster', Herefordshire, was found to be living as a harmaker in Saint Katheryns, London. Some had become educated. William Baynbrigg from Long Bennington was a curate in Norwich as was his brother Thomas, and on 12 May 1576 Lee

---

[74]   Savine, 'Bondmen', p. 18.

[75]   TNA, PRO, DL 41/553.

[76]   *CPR*, 17 Eliz. I, Part XIV, p. 564 (20 June 1575).

[77]   *CPR*, 18 Eliz. I, Part VIII, p. 330 (17 December 1576). Davenport, *Norfolk Manor*, reprints part of the survey taken there in 1565. Alienated land was manorial land sold off by bondmen.

presented for manumission William Dunne, fellow of Exeter College, Oxford, and Daniel Dunne, fellow of All Souls College, Oxford, both villeins regardant to the honour of Eye.[78]

Some wealthy bondmen who had risen in the world welcomed manumission as a chance to improve the standing of their family at a bargain price: a frequent complaint in the past had been the difficulty villeins experienced in making advantageous marriages. Many villeins preferred not to advertise their servile status and to deny their villeinage. In Forncett in Norfolk, a manor escheated to the Crown after the execution of Thomas Howard, Duke of Norfolk in 1572, Robert Bolytout and Thomas Lound refused to pay for manumission, denied villein status and took Lee to court.[79] This was not an isolated case and others must be hidden in the hundreds of manor rolls still extant. Local magistrates were not above aiding villeins who were not prepared to pay for manumission. In Norfolk, for example, magistrates of six parishes obligingly found there to be no villeins regardant within their purlieu.[80]

What do Lee's actions in this matter tell us about Lee himself? The manumission patents reveal him as a man who was meticulous in their implementation, signing each warrant and continuing the process up to 1599. Despite having been a substantial landowner in Buckinghamshire for two decades, Lee's experience of dealing with recalcitrant tenants by 1575 would have been scant and his experience of villeinage even smaller. MacCulloch points out that villeinage survived into Elizabethan England on older traditionally conservative manors lying mostly in wetland levels or in rich river bottoms mostly devoted to agrarian farming. This was precisely where sheep farming would not have flourished.

Quarrendon itself had been enclosed and depopulated long since. In 1563 it was only supporting four families, and Fleetmarston had only five cottages for shepherds. Lee did not purchase Ditchley until 1583, and that manor was sparsely tenanted. Obviously, dealing with tenants could be very different with differing forms of farming. If Lee's experience with recalcitrant tenants was coloured by his experiences when manumitting bondmen, it throws a new light on his impatience when dealing with difficult tenants at Woodstock between 1576 and 1580.

How much money Lee made out of his manumission warrants is not known. Dillon was of the opinion that Lee only got 'a nice clutch of lawsuits', but by

---

[78]   TNA, PRO, DL 41/553, ff.1–8. See also BL, Lansdowne MS 23, no. 74, (a letter from Daniel Dunne in Latin to Lord Burghley thanking him for dealing for him with Sir Henry Lee, 19 May 1576).

[79]   Davenport, *Norfolk Manor,* Appendix XIV, pp. xcii–xciii.

[80]   TNA, PRO, E178/1550, inquisitions as to bondmen of blood regardant to the Queen's manors in the parishes of Martham, West Walton, Walpole, Terrington, East Dereham and Wymondham.

1581 Lee's patents were being cited as a reason for the decay of the Profit of the Signet and Privy Seal.[81] The activity appeared to have been sufficiently profitable for more than 200 warrants to have been presented to the Duchy of Lancaster, mostly between 1575 and 1581, with the last being presented in 1599. In total, Lee manumitted some 495 named individuals in 137 villein families from Lincolnshire, Suffolk, Norfolk, Somerset, Cornwall, Berkshire, Hereford and the Isle of Wight. As Lee was entitled to manumit 300 bondmen and their named offspring, in many cases numbering four or five other individuals, this would suggest that Lee fell short of his 300 'bondmen of bloud'. He must have realized quite quickly that, however potentially lucrative the manumissions might prove in the long run, they were not going to solve his short-term financial problems. If Lee's handling of his manumission patents do not reveal him as a man of great financial acumen, it might also indicate that there was not necessarily a great deal of money to be made out of the Queen's favours, however flattering they might be, and however hard a courtier worked to implement them.

Sir Henry Lee and the Cyclical Rise and Fall of the Finances of Elizabethan Gentleman Graziers

In private life, Sir Henry Lee's economic fortunes followed a pattern typical of landowning gentleman graziers. Financial returns rose and fell with the vagaries of the wool trade, and the extent to which one profited depended on one's own personal aspirations and family circumstances. Ideally, a gentleman's path to prosperity was to remain at home, husbanding and developing one's estates, with one healthy male heir prepared to continue this tradition. It was preferable to avoid the necessity for copious dowries for daughters, to stay firmly Protestant, and be prepared to wait for the next monarch to prove generous with titles. Little of this was either attractive or available to Sir Henry Lee. Clearly, taking the example of the Dormers, Lee would have found it more profitable to remain at home in Quarrendon, extending his family lands and wool business in contented domesticity, but it was not in Lee's nature to find this sufficient. He failed to profit financially from his marriage, and family life proved disappointing and fruitless. Service to the Crown brought excitement, challenge and a wide range of friends.

The Queen's various favours in the 1570s were never very lucrative. Lee was frequently in debt, like many other courtier gentlemen, and only after his retirement from Court did he find himself sufficiently wealthy to indulge in the contemporary enthusiasm for house-building. On the death of his wife he

---

[81]   E.K. Chambers, *Sir Henry Lee: An Elizabethan Portrait* (Oxford, 1936), p. 46; *CSPD*, 1581–90, p. 40.

could have sought a profitable second marriage to some wealthy widow, and it is a testimony to the closeness of his relationship with Anne Vavasour that this was never mooted. Lee did not die a wealthy man, but at least he avoided the crippling financial ruin that was the lot of many of his contemporaries at Court.

Chapter 6
Sir Henry Lee's Family, Mistress, Friends and Art Collection

In the chivalric culture in which Sir Henry Lee was raised, links of kinship and friendship in private life and loyalty and service to the monarch were regarded as equally important. From the day he achieved his majority in 1554, Lee was the head of a large family grouping. He took his responsibilities seriously. If he himself relied on the patronage of others at Court, his family and his subordinates relied on him for advancement and employment. Lee's immediate family relationships proved to be weak. He became estranged from his wife, Anne Paget, and distanced himself from his Paget relations, whose Catholic activities became increasingly damaging in the last twenty years of Elizabeth's reign.

Yet, unusually for a courtier in the Queen's favour, from 1590 Lee lived openly with his mistress Anne Vavasour, and achieved the domestic contentment missing from his marriage. He also developed a wide circle of friends at Court during his long career, and his interests after retirement reflected his equal devotion to Queen, friends and family. A study of this aspect of Sir Harry Lee's private life provides an opportunity to not only see a more rounded view of the man in his own context, but also to glimpse domestic interests, responsibilities, priorities and concerns typical of many Elizabethan courtier gentlemen.

Lee and his Immediate Family

Sir Henry Lee's wife was Anne, second daughter of William, Lord Paget. As Paget's ward, Lee had little choice over who he married, and the couple were wed by July 1551. His personal life did not flourish. His two young sons John and Henry died in infancy and, after twenty years of marriage, Lee's only heir was his daughter Mary. There is little evidence that Lee spent much time with his wife after his appointment at Woodstock. Lady Lee's letters to her brother, Thomas, Lord Paget, make it clear that as early as 1572 she was spending much of her time with her widowed mother, Lady Anne Paget, at the Paget family home at West Drayton, and was also administering her mother's household.[1]

---

[1] SRO, D603/K/1/4/6; D603/K/1/10/21–23.

Lee was recalled to his paternal duties in February 1578 when the lords of the Privy Council were informed that:

> ... one Worsley had stolen away the daughter of Sir Henry Lee knight and marryed her, contrary to the lawes of the Realme and all good order, theire lordships require ... Sir Henry Lee to repaire unto them and call before them all sutche as he shall chardge to have delt in this matter.[2]

By March 1578 George Monoux of Walthamstow, together with the vicar and the parish clerk of that parish, had been imprisoned for complicity in the matter, although they were later released.[3] No more was heard of Lee's only surviving child until her death around 1583.

Lee did not entirely ignore his wife as he continued to send her game regularly from his many visits to the Earl of Leicester at Kenilworth, and there is evidence that he shared his copy of Sidney's *Old Arcadia* with her.[4] In 1581, when contemplating the purchase of Ditchley in Oxfordshire and as recorded earlier, he made financial provision for Lady Lee in the event of his death.[5]

By 1583 any links he had with the Catholic Paget family were becoming an embarrassment to Lee, and he took care to distance himself from them. Anne Lee came from a large family with four sisters and two brothers still alive in 1583, and Sir Henry Lee was one of the few within the extended family who did not profess Catholic sympathies.[6] The position of English Catholics was becoming increasingly difficult politically, and the Pagets, with much justification, were viewed with suspicion. Lady Lee's younger brother Charles Paget had long been active as a Catholic agent in France and the head of the family, Lord Thomas Paget, fled to Paris in December 1583 following the Resolutions of the Council for 'the execution of the laws against evil affected subjects and Jesuits'.[7] Lord Paget left the ordering of his affairs, discharge of his servants and sale of his

---

[2]   Dasent, *APC*, XI, pp. 56–7 (February 1578).

[3]   Dasent, *APC*, XI, p. 79 (March 1578). George Monoux was the heir of the very wealthy merchant and Mayor of London George Monoux (1465–1544), later of Walthamstow.

[4]   CKS, U1475 (Penshurst Papers) E93, ff. 5r, 7r,16v. Gifts of venison to Lady Lee are recorded in 1574, 1575 and 1578. Presumably, as Lee was responsible for the Queen's game at Woodstock, it was inappropriate to send his wife venison from there. In *Sir Philip Sidney and the Circulation of Manuscripts 1588–1640* (Oxford, 1996), pp. 264–66, H.R. Woudhuysen suggests that *Henry Stanford's Anthology,* containing eleven of Sidney's poems, owes much to Lee's own copy of the *Old Arcadia*. Stanford was tutor from 1581 to the young William Paget at his grandmother's home in West Drayton, where Anne Lee also lived.

[5]   ORO, DIL X/h/1.

[6]   The scant evidence of Lee's own religious beliefs is discussed below in Chapter 7.

[7]   L. Hicks, *An Elizabethan Problem: Some Aspects of the Careers of Two Exile-Adventurers, Thomas Morgan and Charles Paget* (London, 1964).

horses in the hands of his sister Lady Lee, and his mother was entrusted with the care of his young son William.[8]

In January 1584 Anne Lee wrote from West Drayton to her brother Charles in Paris:

> ... you knowe my malyngcholy nature wellinough, and beinge dayly oppressed with greifes and troubles and wantynge the good and comfortable company of them whiche I was wont to have ... for now we live alone and almost ther is none that dareth come to us ... my lady [their mother] is in helth and I thank god hathe passed over thes trowbles a greate deale better then I loked for. My nephew William with all the rest here are in helth.[9]

This and a similar letter to their brother from her sister Griselda Waldegrave née Paget were both intercepted by Walsingham's agents. Thereafter the fortunes of the Paget family did not improve. In August 1584 Lord Paget's goods and chattels were confiscated by the Crown, reserving just enough for his son and his mother. Anne Lee received another letter from Lord Paget on 14 October 1584, containing a missive to be forwarded to the Council pleading his case.[10]

In September 1585 Ightham Mote in Kent, the home of another Catholic Paget sister Ethelreda, wife of Sir Christopher Allen, was searched for 'knowledge of an unknown person come from beyond the sea'.[11] It was found that 'Sir Christopher Allen ... kept a vile and papistical house' and had received a messenger from the Paget brothers in Paris.[12] Lord Thomas Paget was formally attainted for treason in 1586, and the barony and family estates were forfeited in 1587. After the death of the dowager Lady Anne Paget in February that year, the wardship of young William Paget was given to the Queen's kinsman Sir George Carey.[13]

---

[8]   TNA, PRO, SP12/164/7. Paget's estranged wife Nazareth Newton had already died in April 1583.

[9]   TNA, PRO, SP12/167/13 (29 January 1584); SP12/167/98 (Griselda Waldegrave née Paget to Charles Paget). The dowager Lady Paget's houses in Staffordshire and in Fleet Street, London, had been searched in December 1583 as was that of Griselda Waldegrave: *CSPD, 1581–90*, p. 138.

[10]   *CSPD, Addenda 1580–1625, Eliz. I*, p. 128.

[11]   *CSPD, 1581–90*, p. 266.

[12]   *CSPD, 1581–90*, p. 267.

[13]   Dasent, *APC* (1586–87), p. 352. Young William Paget appeared to be more like his grandfather than his father and had rented back the family lands by 1597. He was restored in blood and honours by James I in 1604. His will in 1629 required his children to be brought up in the Church of England 'and in no way otherwise'. See Michael A.R. Graves, 'Paget, William, Fifth Baron Paget (1572–1629), Politician', *Oxford Dictionary of National Biography*, September 2004; online edn, January 2008 at: http://www.oxforddnb.com/view/article/21122.

Lady Lee's letters to her brothers suggest that she was an intelligent and capable woman, but after twenty years of marriage that had produced only one living daughter, she had little to attract her husband. Any fiction of a union was over by 1585, when her mother, Lady Anne Paget, made her will. Lady Lee was the only member of the Paget family to be left property directly, 'during such time as Sir Henry Lee husband to the said Ladie Lee my daughter and she[,] shall live separate and asunder one from the other'.[14]

The fact that Lady Lee received the use of all her mother's household goods suggests that she brought little away from her marital home at Quarrendon. She was the chief mourner at her mother's funeral in February 1587, and her husband was conspicuous by his absence.[15] After that date Lady Lee may have resided in the house her mother had left her in Fleet Street, London, but more probably she moved in with her sister Griselda Waldegrave.[16] The date of Anne Lee's death is not known: Chambers states that she was buried in Aylesbury church on 31 December 1590 but can only base this on evidence from a secondary source.[17]

Lady Anne Lee's lavish alabaster tomb in St Mary's Church, Aylesbury, bears the date 1584, which is clearly wrong. There is a curious entry in the church register of 1586 [1587] which records that 'the corpes of Mistress Mary Lee daughter to Sir Henry Lee Knight was layd in the vaute in the church wher hir mothers tombe now standeth on xij of ffebruary'.[18] It is probable that Mary had died in 1583, accounting not only for Lee's recovery of his lands in that year, but also for the 'greifes and troubles' referred to by Lady Lee. Possibly, Anne Lee consoled herself by constructing an elaborate tomb, and Mary's coffin was moved as soon as it was ready.[19] Whenever Lady Lee died, her tomb inscription records that she

> ... bare thre impes which had to name
> Ihon Henry Mary slayne by fortvnes spight
> First two bei'g yong which cavsd ther pare[n]ts mo[an]e
> The third in flower a[n]d prime of all her yeares
> All thre do rest within this marble stone.

---

[14]   TNA, PRO, PROB/11/72 – will of Lady Anne Paget.

[15]   SRO, D603/K/1/4/57–63.

[16]   The codicil in Lady Paget's will had entrusted the upbringing of the young William Paget to Lady Lee, and Sir William and Lady Griselda Walgrave. This was not implemented.

[17]   E.K. Chambers, *Sir Henry Lee: An Elizabethan Portrait* (Oxford. 1936).

[18]   Ibid., p. 261. The interment was within days of the funeral of her grandmother, Lady Anne Paget.

[19]   Henry Stanford, tutor to William Paget at Drayton, probably composed the verses inscribed on Lady Lee's tomb in Aylesbury church. Texts of the poem in Stanford's hand are preserved in his private manuscript anthology, now in Cambridge University Library (MS Dd.5.75) and another at Berkeley Castle.

By a trick of fortune, Anne Lee's tomb has long outlasted that of her more famous husband, and the good people of Aylesbury still observe the last supplication of this unhappy lady:

> Good fre[n]d sticke not to strew with crimso[n] flowers,
> This marble stone wherein her cindres rest.

Sir Henry Lee, although mentioned on his wife's tomb, continued to prioritize his position as a loyal servant of the Queen and to maintain his distance from the remaining Pagets. When, in December 1602, he received a letter from his brother-in-law Charles Paget in Paris, he swiftly forwarded it to Sir Robert Cecil as a missive from 'an evil deserver to the state and her Majesty'.[20]

Lee and Anne Vavasour

Lee's waning affections for his sad and melancholic wife may well have been influenced by his growing interest in Anne Vavasour, his 'dearest deare' who became his long-term mistress and the mother of his bastard son Thomas.[21] This colourful lady is typical of several Elizabethan women in and around the Court, who occasioned both scandal and genuine affection, and were survivors of the penalties imposed by the double moral standard that existed for men and women. Anne Vavasour was the daughter of Henry Vavasour and Margaret Knyvet of Copmanthorpe, Yorkshire, and through her mother's good Court connections she became a gentlewoman of the bedchamber to the Queen in 1579 or 1580.[22] The young Anne was rapidly seduced by Edward de Vere, Earl of Oxford, and was pregnant by him in February 1580. There is evidence that Oxford offered marriage despite the existence of his wife, Burghley's daughter, but the first pregnancy ended in miscarriage.[23] It is highly unlikely that Anne attempted an abortion, as she was pregnant again by Oxford in July 1580. On 23 March 1581 Anne gave birth to his son in the maids' chamber, adjacent to that

---

[20]   Cecil MS 97.144 (HMC *Salis*. XII, p. 532) (Paget to Lee); Cecil MS 91.92 (HMC *Salis*. XII, p. 532) (Lee to Cecil). Paget's letter from France to Lee is dated 10 February 1603, reflecting the differing calendars used at the time.

[21]   This is John Aubrey's phrase. See J. Aubrey, *Brief Lives*, ed. Oliver Lawson Dick (London, 1992), II, p. 31.

[22]   TNA, PRO, SP40/1/86. Anne's aunt, Catherine Knyvet, had been a gentlewoman of the bedchamber.

[23]   TNA, PRO, SP12/151/118–119. Lord Henry Howard charged Oxford with having evolved a scheme 'to cary away Nan Vaviser ... a 12 monthe [ago] when he thought hir first to haue bene with child'.

of the Queen at Whitehall, and the delivery in so public a place caused a furore. Sir Francis Walsingham reported to the Earl of Huntingdon that:

> ... on Tuesday at night Anne Vavysor was brought to bed of a son in the maidens' chamber. The E. of Oxeford is avowed to be the father, who hath withdrawn himself with intent ... to pass the seas. The ports are laid for him [and] ... it is not likely that he will escape. The gentlewoman the selfsame night she was delivered was conveyed out of the house and the next day committed to the Tower ... Her Majesty is greatly grieved with the accident.[24]

Oxford, having failed to flee abroad, was briefly incarcerated in the Tower in somewhat more luxurious accommodation than that provided for Anne. Following pressure on the Queen by his father-in-law and Walsingham, he was released on 8 June, confined to his house until July and barred from Court for two years. However, through Burghley's good offices, he was back in the Queen's favour by the end of July 1581.

Although she was of a good gentry family, Anne Vavasour had no such influence at Court, and the pillorying to which she was subjected reflects not only the double moral standard of the time, but also the Queen's attitude to her ladies. If the illicit marriages entered into by her maids and gentlewomen could arouse the ire of the Queen and banishment from Court, an illegitimate child would place the woman beyond any royal forgiveness.[25] Anne's baby was placed under the care of Sir Francis Vere, Oxford's cousin, and we do not know how long Anne remained in the Tower.

It is unclear how much of this Sir Henry Lee would have known. Gossip travelled fast, even to Woodstock, and little was secret at Court. Lee had tilted with Oxford, and as a gentleman at Court with business at the Tower, he had probably met Anne in one of these locations.[26] The Oxford–Vavasour affair was one of the most public scandals of the decade, with the story circulating abroad and becoming a potential source of embarrassment to Elizabeth.[27] The scandal broke within weeks of Henry Hawkins' widely reported statement that 'Lord Robert hath had fyve children by the Quene and she never goethe in progresse but to be delivered', and the behaviour of her ladies reflected badly upon her.[28]

---

[24]   HMC Hastings, MS II p. 29.

[25]   See P. Hammer's 'Sex and the Virgin Queen: Aristocratic Concupiscence and the Court of Elizabeth I', *Sixteenth Century Journal*, XXXI (Spring 2000) pp. 77–97 for a copious listing of the misalliances of Elizabeth's women servants.

[26]   There was a distant connection between Lee and Anne Vavasour, as her aunt, Catherine Knyvet, was the widow of Henry Paget, Lee's former brother-in-law.

[27]   *Fugger Newsletters*, 2nd series (1568–1605), ed. Victor von Klarwill, trans. L.S.R. Byrne (London, 1926), p. 55.

[28]   TNA, PRO, SP12/148/157; *CSP Spanish,* I p.362; 2 p.491; *CSPD*,1581–90, p. 12.

In accepting an affair with the Earl of Oxford, Anne Vavasour had been playing with fire – or at least with one of the most profligate and volatile nobles at Elizabeth's Court. A member of the old aristocracy, Oxford had achieved considerable notoriety through murder, mayhem and sodomy and had attempted to repudiate his wife and bastardize their child. Anne's liaison with Oxford had been an open secret at Court – Oxford had earlier threatened to kill Anne's uncle Sir Henry Knyvet 'for spekeing evell of him to his ni[e]ce'.[29] The following anonymous poem, later attributed to Sir Walter Raleigh, was subscribed 'written to Mistress A.V.' in two manuscript versions and circulated at Court:

> ... many desire, but few or none deserve
> To pluck the flowers and let the leaves to fall;
> Therefore take heed, let fancy never swerve
> But unto him that will take leaves and all.
> For this be sure, the flower once pluckt away
> Farewell the rest, thy happy days decay.[30]

More importantly, Anne was implicated in the brief flirtation Oxford had with a group of leading Catholic intriguers at Court: Lord Henry Howard, Charles Arundel and Francis Southwell. In December 1580 Oxford betrayed his fellow plotters to the Queen to clear his own name, but in the ensuing treason and sedition case, Anne was named as the go-between for Oxford and Charles Arundel.[31] Elizabeth demanded a very high standard of behaviour among her gentlewomen, and if Anne's sexual incontinence was not enough to condemn her in the eyes of the Queen, her implication in a political intrigue would have damned her permanently.

The scandal was not allowed to die a natural death because Anne's Knyvet cousins, seeking revenge, would not let the matter rest. Throughout 1582 a bitter feud was waged on the backstreets of London, where 'my lord of oxford fought with master Knyvet about the quarrel of Bessie Bavisar'.[32] Oxford was wounded by Thomas Knyvet, and the quarrel resulted in several lethal affrays before tempers cooled. As late as 1585 Anne's own brother, Thomas Vavasour, was prepared to revive the feud and challenged Oxford, stating that 'if thy

---

[29]   TNA, PRO, SP12/151/103–04.

[30]   Bodl. MS Rawlinson, Poetry 85, f. 116; also BL, Add. MS 22601, f. 71; W. Ralegh, *The Poems of Sir Walter Ralegh*, ed. A. Latham (London, 1929), p. 66.

[31]   *CSPD, Addenda 1580–1625*, pp. 48–49. In his declaration, Charles Arundel refers to 'my cousin Vavisor who was the means of our meeting'.

[32]   BL, Cotton MS, App. 47; *Calendar of State Papers Colonial Series, East Indies, China and Japan, 1513–1616* (hereafter *CSP Colonial*) (London, 1864), II, pp. 85–86 (diary of Rev. Richard Madox, 3 March 1582).

body had been as deformed as thy mind dishonourable, my house had been yet unspotted and thyself remained with thy cowardice known'.[33]

The majority of the Queen's ladies who fell from grace did so because of an ill-conceived marriage without royal permission. Doubtless other unmarried girls had left the Court pregnant, but none ever made such a public display of their condition as Anne Vavasour. On release from the Tower, her options would have been few. For a Yorkshire girl of seventeen, the complete loss of child, lover, marriage prospects and good name, along with any royal favour and protection, must have been intolerable. She did not return home, but her Knyvet relations appeared to be keener on pursuing their vendetta against Oxford than on protecting her from the continuing slander.

Burghley, writing to Hatton in 1583, complained bitterly that Oxford was being punished twice 'first by her majesty and then by the drab's friend'.[34] In 1584 the anonymous *A Copie of a Letter*, later known as *Leicester's Commonwealth* named Anne as one of the many Court ladies complicit in Leicester's seductions, 'she being but the leavings of another man' and he being 'nothing squemish ... to gather up the crummes when he is hungry in the very laundry itself or other places of baser quality'.[35]

In no position to support or protect herself, at some point after her release from the Tower Anne Vavasour married a John Finch of London. Chambers, with his fascination for genealogy, speculates that he was the John Finch who traded in Russia from 1584 until sent home in disgrace in 1591. He was subsequently imprisoned in 1597 for perjury.[36] If Chambers is correct, it would at least explain why Anne, with proven fecundity, had no children by Finch and was free to pursue another affair. It says much for Anne Vavasour's strength of character that she not only survived the years between 1581 and 1585, but also emerged to create a more lasting alliance under the protection of the Queen's Champion, Sir Henry Lee. It also says much for Lee's affection for 'his dearest deare' and his ability to find a way through the jungle that was the Elizabethan

---

[33]   BL, Lansdowne MS 99, no. 93: 'An impudent scurrilous challenge of Thomas Vavasor sent to the Earl of Oxford, to fight him, 1584.'

[34]   H. Nicolas, *Memoirs of the Life and Times of Sir Christopher Hatton, K.G.* (London, 1847), pp. 256, 321.

[35]   *Leicester's Commonwealth: The Copy of a Letter Written by a Master of Art at Cambridge (1584) and Related Documents*, ed. D.C. Peck (Athens, OH, 1985), pp. 88–9.

[36]   Chambers, *Sir Henry Lee*, p. 163. It is not known whether Finch was paid to marry Anne, possibly by the Knyvetts, and whether trading privileges were obtained for him. In Russia, animosity developed between Finch and Sir Jerome Horsey, a well-known English figure at the Russian Court. Horsey caused Finch to be sent home in disgrace from Moscow in 1591, and in 1595, on the encouragement of the English ambassador to Russia, Sir Jerome Bowes, Finch accused Horsey of high treason. When the case came before Privy Council in April 1597, Finch was proved to be a liar.

Court that he could not only envisage a liaison with the scarlet woman of the decade, but live happily with her for at least twenty-one years. Given his financial situation when his wife eventually died, marriage to some wealthy widow would have been infinitely quieter and more profitable.

One reason why Anne Vavasour has retained the fascination and speculation of historians and literary editors is the existence of two more poems subscribed 'Vavasor' in some manuscripts – poems that unite generations of readers with Anne's contemporaries in seeking clues as to her thoughts and motives.[37] The hauntingly enigmatic echo poem 'Sitting alone upon my thought' is entitled 'verses made by the Earle of Oxforde and Mrs Ann Vauesor' in one text, although Chambers convincingly argues that this identifies them as the principals in the work rather than as its authors.[38] At the beginning of the poem, the male author is 'sitting alone' near the sea caves when a fair young lady comes to bewail her sad fate with sighs and tears. As she questions her predicament aloud,

> ... the Echo answered her to every word she spake.

> *An Vavesors eccho*
> O heauens, quothe she, who was ye fyrst that bredd in me this feauere? Vere.
> Whoe was the first yt gaue ye wounde whose scarre I ware for euere? Vere.
> What tyrant, Cupid! To mye harme vsurpes thy goulden quiuere? Vere.
> What wighte first caughte this hart and can from bondage it deliuere? Vere.

> Yet who doth most adore this wighte, oh hollow caues tell trewe? You.
> What nymph deserues his lykinge best, yet doth in sorrowe rewe? You.
> What makes him not rewarde good will with some remorse or reuthe? Youth.
> What makes him show besydes his birrthe suche pryde and suche untrvth? Youth.
> May I his fauor matche wth louue if he my loue will trye? I.
> Maye I requite his birthe wth faythe than faythfull will I dy? I.

> And I that knew this ladye well
> Sayde Lord howe great a mirakle,
> To he[a]r howe eccho toulde the truthe
> As trewe as Pheobus' orakle.

Steven May includes the poem in his section on Oxford's work but admits that both its tone and point of view are inappropriate for it to have been written

---

[37]   Folger MS, V.a.89, f. 9. 'Sitting along' is subscribed 'vavasor'. Ruth Hughey, *The Arundel–Harington Manuscript of Tudor Poetry* (Columbus, OH, 1960) records it as subscribed 'Ffinis qd E Vere count d'Oxford' in Harington's hand.
[38]   Bodl. MS Rawlinson, Poetry 85, f.11; Chambers, *Sir Henry Lee*, p. 152.

by either Oxford or Vavasour.[39] Ilona Bell, fastening on the male sentiments voiced by one who ' knew this lady well', seeks to identify the poem with Lee in the early days of his courtship of Anne and turns the last two lines of the echo into an avowal of Lee's love for her.[40] The sentiments would, however, fit a pregnant Anne Vavasour better than the rejected 'drab', and it is unlikely that Lee would have fallen headlong in love by 1580 with an Anne Vavasour who had only recently come to Court. More improbably, Bell credits Lee with the poem's authorship. If one compares it to verses known to have been Lee's such as 'My golden locks are to silver turned', his poetic talents must have regressed markedly between 1581 and 1590 for this to be correct.

A second poem, 'Though I seem strange, sweet friend, be thou not so', is also subscribed 'Vavaser' in one manuscript, and here Ilona Bell's attempt to identify it with the Lee–Vavasour relationship is more credible.[41] Even Chambers, who prints the poem in full, concedes that the author is a woman and that it would fit Anne's position well enough in 1580.[42] Bell attributes it to Anne's position in 1590 and finds many parallels both with Anne's situation and the words in the 1592 Ditchley entertainment. An analysis of the text, alongside a close study of Lee's and Vavasour's careers would, however, suggest that the poem best fits the context around 1585, just before their liaison became semi-public.

> Thoughe I seeme straunge sweete freende be thou not so
> Do not accoy thy selfe with sullen will
> Myne harte hathe voude althoughe my tongue saye noe
> To be thyne owne in freendly liking styll.
>
> Thou seeste me liue amongst the Lynxes eyes
> That pryes into the priuy thoughte of mynde
> Thou knowest ryghte well what sorrowes maye aryse
> If once they chaunce my setled lookes to fynde.
>
> Contente thyself that once I made an othe
> To sheylde my self in shrowde of honest shame

---

[39]   S.W. May, 'The Poems of Edward de Vere, Seventeenth Earl of Oxford, and of Robert Devereux, Second Earl of Essex', *Studies in Philology*, 77 (1980), pp. 1–32; S. May, *The English Courtier Poets: The Poems and their Contexts*, 2nd edn (Columbia, MI, 1999).

[40]   I. Bell, *Elizabethan Women and the Poetry of Courtship* (Cambridge, 1998), pp. 75–99.

[41]   The poem in Folger MS V.a.89, pp. 8–9, is subscribed 'Vavaser'; BL, Harleian MS 6910, ff. 145r–v is subscribed 'La. B. to N' and BL, Harleian MS 7392(2), f. 40 (a partial text) was at first assigned to 'H W'; the initials were later crossed out in favour of 'Ball', possibly an abbreviation for 'ballad' in this anthology.

[42]   Chambers, *Sir Henry Lee*, p. 153.

And when thou lyste make tryall of my trouthe
So that thou save the honoure of my name

And let me seme althoughe I be not coye
To cloak my sadd conceyts with smylinge cheere
Let not my iestures showe wherein I ioye
Nor by my lookes lett not my loue apeere.

We seely dames that falles suspecte, do feare
And liue within the moughte [mouth] of enuyes lake
Muste in oure heartes a secrete meaning beare
Far from the reste which outwardlye we make

So were I lyke, I lyste not vaunte my loue
Where I desyre there most I fayne debate
One hathe my hande an other hathe my gloue
But he my harte whome I seeme most to hate

Thus farwell freende I will continue straunge
Thou shalte not heere by worde or writing oughte
Let it suffice my vowe shall never chaunge
As for the rest I leave yt to thy thoughte.[43]

This is not the poem of a young girl: the sentiments voiced are those of a mature woman who has few illusions. The poem is so personal in its address that it 'seems straunge' that it ever found its way into an anthology. The author has learned how to protect herself from 'the Lynxes eyes', the gossip and slander of Court often referred to in the Ditchley manuscript. The lady has learned how to dissemble, as Anne Vavasour must have done, but she fears that a new liaison might destroy the frail edifice of self-respect she has created to protect herself. Ilona Bell makes much of the references to 'rest' as referring to the lodge at Ditchley, Lee's Rest, but this was not built for Anne until the mid-1590s.

Of much more interest is the third verse which contains exact parallels to Anne's situation. The lady has made an oath, and in this case it is clearly differentiated from the vow that she mentions twice. An oath is usually a legal undertaking, externally administered before witnesses: a vow is a private promise. The oath was taken in order to shield her in what seems like a 'shrowde of honest shame'. Was this an oath in a marriage of convenience, hastily arranged by embarrassed male relatives? The lady has no other option, but feels shamed, having to give her body to a man she neither knows nor likes in exchange for the

---

[43]   Bodl. MS Rawlinson, Poetry 85, f. 17.

appearance of honesty and respectability. To a young woman with her life before her, this would feel like a shroud.

In the last two lines of the third verse, she warns her would-be lover that, if they go any further, he must at least protect the only thing she has got out of this unpleasant arrangement: a respectable name. The writer's predicament must have been replicated by thousands of unfortunate women, yet seldom is it so clearly expressed. Matters had moved on since her disgrace. Even though Oxford might still have her heart, a husband has her hand, leaving only a glove for a would-be champion. What she offers here is 'to be thyne owne in freendly liking'. Friendship is mentioned three times while love, possibly still reserved for Oxford, does not enter the equation. Above all there is caution and a desire not to be hurt again.

It is not known at what point Anne began her relationship with Sir Henry Lee. For all his shining armour, at over fifty years of age he was not exactly a young girl's dream of romance. Perhaps by 1585 Anne Vavasour had become sufficiently worldly-wise to appreciate the safety of an older man's devotion compared to the volatile excitement that had been offered by Oxford.

Lee's personal life had been far from fulfilling, but his name had not been linked with any lady at Court, despite his somewhat oblique reference in the Woodstock entertainment to 'a new mistress that lived every day in [the Queen's] eye'.[44] Lee enjoyed the company of men in the hunting field and at tournaments, but his interest in the rising young stars of the tilt – Philip Sidney, Robert Devereux, and even Prince Henry at a later date – appears similar to his paternal or avuncular interest in the young men who passed through his care at Ditchley, such as his godson Robert Dudley, Edward Vere, his own illegitimate son Thomas Vavasour and his nephew Owen Cooke. His devotion to the Queen's service seems to have been sufficient until he met Anne Vavasour.

Although Anne Vavasour was not mentioned until 1590 in the Ditchley Steward's Book, it is probable that the relationship began earlier, and there is a temptation to equate Lee's purchase of his private estate at Ditchley in 1583 with possible expectations of changed circumstances. Certainly, the Queen's disgraced gentlewoman would not have been welcome at the royal manor at Woodstock.[45] The will of Lee's mother-in-law in December 1585 states openly that Lee and his wife were living 'separate and asunder'.

One clue to the dating of Lee's commitment to Anne Vavasour is an 'AV' monogram, which appears twice as an integral part of the decoration on Lee's third suit of armour. In the *Almain Armourer's Album*, the sketch for this armour

---

[44]   In 1575 Lee hunted at Kenilworth with Lady Susan Bourchier, one of the Queen's ladies and niece of Sir Walter Mildmay. He borrowed money from her in 1578, which he repaid in his will, but there was little indication of a romance between them.

[45]   ORO, DIL XXI/4.

is bound with others commissioned around 1585–86. It is a field armour that Lee used as Master of the Horse in the north of England and was not for tournament use within sight of the Queen. There is no evidence that the 'AV' monogram was added at a later date, which would suggest that Lee was sufficiently sure of Anne to commission her initials as a motif on an expensive suit of armour by that date.

Lee would have had major problems in publicly declaring his love for Anne and giving her the protection she needed. He was, after all, the Queen's own champion. While Elizabeth might, and did, give her glove to other men at tournaments, Lee could wear no other favours but the Queen's. Elizabeth had been swift to forgive Oxford his misdemeanours, welcoming him back to Court and even giving him an annuity of £1,000, but there was no royal forgiveness for Anne Vavasour. In addition, the Oxford–Vavasour affair had sorely wronged Burghley's favourite daughter, and Lee was a long-time friend of Burghley and to some extent dependent on him for alleviation of the debt he owed the Queen.

The affair between Lee and Anne naturally occasioned numerous comments, few of them complimentary. Sir Edward Stafford later claimed that Ambrose Dudley, Earl of Warwick, had entrusted young Robert Dudley's affairs to him in February 1590, as 'Sir Henry Lea loved the countreye and his pleasure so much as that he could hardlie attend the poore Boys estate'.[46] In November 1590 Sir John Stanhope, writing to Gilbert Talbot, mentioned Anne as 'the subject of much mirth and scandal among the courtiers, on account of her attachment to the old gallant Sir Henry Lee',[47] but there is little evidence that Lee was ever in real disgrace with the Queen over his affair with Anne Vavasour.

After 1590 Lee retained his royal appointments, followed the royal progress in summer 1591 and welcomed the Queen back to Woodstock in 1592. Elizabeth's visit to Lee's own home at Ditchley in the course of that visit does not suggest royal disfavour. In the two-day entertainment he provided for her, Lee was sufficiently sure of his position with the Queen to make the heart of the performance indulgently autobiographical, even making reference to his new love, who was probably not present. Echoes of 'Though I seem straunge' returned as Lee confessed his faults to the Queen:

> but loe unhappie I was ouertaken
> by fortune forced a straunger ladies thrall
> whom when I saw all former care forsaken
> to fynd her out I lost my self & all.[48]

---

[46]   CKS, U1475 (Penshurst Papers) L2/4, ff. 80–81. Ambrose Dudley and Lee were both godfathers to Leicester's illegitimate son, Robert, in August 1574.

[47]   Edmund Lodge, *Illustrations of British History*, 3 vols (London, 1791), III, p. 16.

[48]   Chambers, *Sir Henry Lee*; and Jean Wilson, *Entertainments for Elizabeth I* (Woodbridge, 1980).

Lee and Anne were both fortunate in their relationship, which lasted until Lee's death in 1611. Anne gave Lee a son, the illegitimate Thomas Vavasour, and the companionship and care which became necessary as his health declined.[49] He gave her the protection she needed and a standard of living commensurate with her birth. It would have been unusual for a wife, let alone a mistress, to have accompanied Lee to London, but Lee built 'Lee's Rest', a lodge in the grounds of Ditchley, for Anne and commissioned a handsome portrait of her, probably by John de Critz.[50]

Lee and his Extended Family

Although Sir Henry Lee had no children of his own who outlived him, he was the head of an extended family of five brothers (three legitimate) and numerous sisters (two illegitimate) (see Appendix 2). Two of his brothers died in early manhood, and although the other three married wealthy widows, none left legitimate offspring to become Lee's heir. None of his brothers appears to have been particularly pleasant or successful individuals, yet Lee, like many other gentlemen in his position, exercised a patriarchal care not only over them but also over various nephews and cousins for whom he found positions in government service. Some of the latter, such as Captain Thomas Lee, caused Sir Henry nothing but grief.

The oldest of Sir Henry's brothers was Robert Lee. In 1570 he had become Keeper of the Game at the royal hunting grounds of Hatfield Chase in Yorkshire, which boasted the largest collection of red deer in the country. Hunting was a common bond of interest between Lee's brothers, and when Robert Lee leased the parsonage at Hatfield in 1562, Sir Henry used it as a base when visiting the north of England.[51] Robert did not endear himself to many. His wife complained to the Queen in 1585 'both of his hard usage of her whilst she lived with him and of her miserable estate since she left him, being destitute of all things'.[52] The Archbishop of York reported in 1587 that Robert was not fit to be a justice of the peace as 'he is a notable open adulterer. One that giveth great offence and

---

[49]   Lee never gave his bastard son his name, but secured a position as Yeoman of the Armoury for him in 1608. This would suggest Thomas Vavasour was born around 1592 – another good reason for Anne Vavasour to absent herself during the royal visit of that year.

[50]   The portrait, c.1605, is now in the possession of the Worshipful Company of Armourers and Brasiers, London.

[51]   TNA, PRO, *Calendar of Patent Rolls* (hereafter *CPR*), 660, 23 Eliz. I, Part XI, 660 mm. 25–6 (1594). Robert Lee was confirmed as Master of the Hunt of Game within the lordships of Hatfield and Thorne, Yorkshire, for life on 11 August 1581, with an annuity of £100.

[52]   P.W. Hasler, *The History of Parliament: The House of Commons, 1558–1603* (London, 1982), II, p. 450.

will not be reformed. He useth his authority ... to work private displeasure ... a very bad man and one that doeth no good.'[53] Nevertheless, Robert Lee became a magistrate in 1588, served under his brother by leading horsemen from the county of Yorkshire in the summer of 1588 and received a personal letter of thanks from the Queen.[54] He also sat as MP for Huntingdon but made only one appearance in that role. He surrendered his position at Hatfield in 1594 and died near London in 1598, leaving Sir Henry Lee what little money he had.

Lee's second brother, Cromwell Lee, was the scholar of the family, existing on rents from various advowsons and leases secured for him by his brother. He was a Fellow of St John's Oxford, spent some years travelling in Italy and, upon settling in Oxford, composed the first Italian–English dictionary. According to Chambers, more than one Oxford epigram records Cromwell's morals 'in the grossest terms'.[55] He died in 1601 and, like his brothers, left no legitimate heirs.

Sir Henry Lee had most in common with his half-brother Sir Richard Lee, some twelve years younger and the illegitimate son of Sir Anthony Lee and Anne Hassell. Sir Richard successively married two wealthy widows and became an MP for Canterbury, but spent most of his time either at Woodstock or in Lee's rooms at the Savoy in London. Both brothers had a lively interest in contemporary politics, as shown by the long political letters exchanged between them in June 1592, discussing the state of the war with Spain and the safety of the Earl of Essex.[56] Richard Lee's chief moment of glory came in 1599 when the merchants of the Muscovy Company chose him to represent them as an ambassador to Russia and contributed £2,000 towards the enterprise. He wrote to Sir Robert Cecil asking for his aid in persuading the Queen to confirm his appointment:

> The merchants have resolved of myself by general consent ... my brother Sir Henry Lee ... has provided a present of better than two hundred marks. I hope her majesty ... will not suffer me to be disgraced but will be pleased with the merchants' free choice.[57]

Richard Lee was knighted on 1 June 1600, set sail in mid-June and spent some ten months in Russia. The embassy was not a success; Sir Richard failed to gain an extension of merchants' trading rights through Russia to Persia or to promote a marriage alliance between an unnamed Englishman and the Tsar's daughter.

---

[53]   John Strype, *Annals of the Reformation and Establishment of Religion during Elizabeth I's Reign*, 8 vols (London, 1824), III (2), p. 463.

[54]   *CSP Border*, I, p. 324 (no. 608); p. 331 (no. 630); p. 332 (no. 631) (23 August 1588).

[55]   Chambers, *Sir Henry Lee*, p. 223. Cromwell Lee's dictionary is still in the archives of St John's College, Oxford.

[56]   Cecil MS 21.22 (HMC *Salis*. IV, pp. 206–7) (5 June 1592).

[57]   Cecil MS 69.10 (HMC *Salis*. X, p. 76) (20 March 1600).

Consequently, on his return to England, the Muscovy Company refused to pay his expenses and the Queen refused to recompense him, leaving him with grave financial problems. Sir Henry attempted to help, passing on the constableship of Harlech Castle which he held, but Sir Richard's debts continued to haunt him until his death in 1608.

Sir Henry Lee's sense of obligation as head of his family also extended to the sons of his sisters and to his cousins. Whereas this display of patronage was expected of a courtier gentleman in Lee's position, it also behoved him to have a network of dependants that he could trust, especially in the fraught world of the Armoury and the Office of the Ordnance at the Tower. Lee's deputy at the Tower was his cousin John Lee. John, much the same age as Sir Henry, had had a somewhat dubious career in the Low Countries in the 1570s, reporting to Burghley on the activities of English exiles in Antwerp until his own imprisonment there in 1572. On that occasion he begged Sir Henry to importune his influential friends to obtain his release, which Lee did by June 1573. It was probably due to his cousin's influence that John Lee became MP for New Woodstock in 1589, 1593 and 1597. Although Sir Henry failed to obtain the clerkship of the Armoury for him in 1589, he worked as Sir Henry's deputy from 1590. He became a yeoman of the Armoury at Greenwich in 1594 and lived in the armoury house there. When, for financial reasons, John Lee took up the additional position of Keeper of the Great Store in the Ordnance Office, he was forced to put up a bond for £3,500 to guarantee his good behaviour in office, and Sir Henry Lee cajoled some thirty of his friends to put up £100 each in bond as surety for his cousin.[58] On John Lee's death in 1603, his role as Sir Henry's deputy passed to Lee Symonds, son of Sir Henry's sister Katherine. Lee Symonds also acted as his uncle's amanuensis and agent until his own death in 1607.[59] Sir Henry's own illegitimate son, Thomas Vavasour, was appointed Yeoman of the Armoury in 1608, thus sustaining the family interest in this post.

Sir Henry also obtained lucrative export contracts for his relatives. In October 1590 he requested a licence from Burghley for his brother-in-law Mr Symonds of Clay in Norfolk to transport 3,000 quarters of wheat to France, 'corn being in that shire in great plenty and good cheap'.[60] Lee frequently employed his Symonds nephews as messengers and postmen. The white vellum folder containing the tournament texts of the Ditchley manuscript is inscribed 'delivered to the Earl of Cumberland by William Symonds'.[61] Lee promoted the marriage between his niece Elizabeth Symonds and Lawrence Tanfield, and later received from

---

[58] TNA, PRO, SP39/9/105.

[59] BL, Lansdowne MS 90, no. 36, f. 72.

[60] *CSPD*, 1581–90, p. 690 (3 October 1590).

[61] BL, Add. MS 41498. This white vellum binder now contains Lee's copy of Sidney's *Old Arcadia*.

their young daughter Elizabeth a handwritten translation of Ortelius' *Mirror of the Worlde, translated out of French into Englishe* with an effusive dedication to Sir Henry Lee.[62] The precociously intelligent Elizabeth Tanfield later became Elizabeth Cary, author of *The Tragedy of Miriam* and other works.

Lee also exercised the same care over his nephew Owen Cooke, who he described to Walsingham as 'a nevew of myne who I have browght uppe and muche love, and is better able to serve her [the Queen], then ... my sellfe'.[63] When Lee purchased the constableship of Harlech Castle in 1587, he requested that Burghley might 'juyne him in patent with me, that my sisters sonne may supply my place when god shall call me awaye. His name is Owen Couke, very honest and one I love much'.[64] The constableship carried with it a fee of £50 a year; most of this went to Cooke and later to Sir Richard Lee. Sir Henry saw little of the money, although he travelled to the castle in 1592 and continued to concern himself with the position until 1611.

Nowhere is Sir Henry's sense of responsibility for his family's good name and well-being more clearly illustrated than in the case of Thomas Lee, son of his father's half-brother. A study of this most troublesome cousin reveals not only how useful Sir Henry Lee could be to his relatives, but also how far Sir Henry would go in furthering their prospects, even at considerable risk to his own integrity and purse. Thomas Lee, born around 1551, was seldom out of trouble, and Sir Henry was his most consistent advocate over some twenty years, more from family duty than from conviction. In July 1577 Sir Henry obtained a pardon for him for 'all robberies, felonies and burglaries' he had committed in England before that year, but Thomas was again before the Privy Council in May 1580 for highway robbery in Oxfordshire.[65] Thomas Lee was principally a soldier and adventurer in Ireland and typical of many impecunious younger sons of English gentry who saw the fraught world of Irish conflict as a means of making their fortunes.

Having been recommended to Walsingham for service in Ireland by Sir Geoffrey Fenton, Principal Secretary to successive Lords Deputy of Ireland from 1580, from his early twenties, Thomas acted as a mercenary captain with twenty-four horse and fifty foot soldiers in the service of various Lords Deputy of Ireland, including Walter Devereux, Earl of Essex, Lord Grey of Wilton, Sir John Perrot and, disastrously, Sir William Fitzwilliam. As a military leader, Thomas was a somewhat loose cannon as, while successfully pursuing valiant and murderous service for the Crown and accruing property for himself,

---

[62]   Folger Library, Film Acc. 700.6. Ortelius' work seems not to have been printed in English until 1601.

[63]   BL, Harleian MS 286, f. 100 (from Thorne, 24 February 1587).

[64]   *CSPD*, 1581–90, p. 577 (5 February 1589).

[65]   *CPR*, 19 Eliz. I, Part VIII, p. 331 (29 July 1577).

he often trespassed into territory held by Irish nobles such as the Butlers, Earls of Ormond.

For twenty years Thomas was seen as a useful, if erratic, tool of the English Crown, although his freelance activities meant he was frequently in debt, and his enemies secured his imprisonment on several occasions. He was always released, and James Myers suggests that 'someone other than Sir Henry – possibly the Cecils or the Queen or even all three' protected him from his enemies in Dublin Castle.[66] From 1590, possibly encouraged by Sir Henry, Thomas began to pin his hopes on Robert Devereux, Earl of Essex. Thomas Lee was typical of the coterie of men that began to form around the Earl, and in a letter to his brother Richard in June 1592, Sir Henry discussed how Essex might do Thomas Lee some good, or at least protect him against his enemies:

> ... his troubles spring of malice ... by the Butlers ... his enemies will adventure much to have their will ... [but] none will adventure his life more willingly to requite ... my lord's favour and goodness.[67]

It was the unrest in Ulster and Thomas Lee's earlier friendship with Hugh O'Neill, Earl of Tyrone, that encouraged him to believe he could adopt a more pivotal role in Irish politics. He saw himself as an intermediary between Tyrone and the Crown and in 1594 he came to the English Court to voice Tyrone's grievances against the 'corrupt administration' of Elizabeth's deputy Sir William Fitzwilliam. Thomas Lee also wrote two political tracts, *Informacion given to Queen Elizabeth against Sir William Fitzwilliams* and *A brief declaration of the government of Ireland*, which can be seen either as the ramblings of a man who had spent too long in Ireland or idiosyncratic solutions to an intransigent problem. The famous portrait of a bare-legged Thomas Lee in Irish costume was painted at this time by Sir Henry's favourite artist, Marcus Gheeraerts the Younger.[68]

In June 1595 Tyrone was declared a rebel, but Thomas Lee, on returning to Ireland, was employed as mediator between Tyrone, who saw him as a willing dupe, and the English authorities in Ireland who were suspicious of his motives. His dubious position and debts made him vulnerable to his Butler enemies who secured his imprisonment in Dublin Castle in 1598, but his military abilities

---

[66]   J.P. Myers, 'Murdering Heart ... Murdering Hand: Captain Thomas Lee of Ireland, Elizabethan Assassin', *Sixteenth Century Journal*, XXII (Spring 1991), p. 49.

[67]   Cecil MS 21.44 (HMC *Salis*. IV, p. 207) (5 June 1592).

[68]   This portrait, acquired by the Tate Britain in 1980, portrays Thomas Lee in a masque costume of an Irish soldier with bare legs. As the gallery caption states, nudity equates with truthfulness in Renaissance symbolism. The Latin inscription on the tree in the portrait refers to Mucius Scaevola, who remained true to Rome even when among enemies. The implication is that Thomas Lee is faithful to the Crown, despite the accusations of his enemies in Dublin.

ensured his release. Thomas's attempts, in April 1599, to mediate between Tyrone and the Earl of Essex, the new military commander in Ireland, failed and led to suspicions of his being a double agent. When Essex deserted his army in Ireland and returned precipitously to Court in September 1599, Thomas Lee accompanied him and, like Essex, was placed under house arrest.

Sir Henry Lee now became more deeply involved in his cousin's affairs than he might have wished, as house arrest for Thomas Lee meant residence either at Ditchley or in Sir Henry's apartment at the Savoy in London. Thomas Lee remained in disgrace for the remainder of his life and became increasingly divorced from reality. During his enforced inactivity, he completed his blueprint for solving the Irish problem *The discoverye and recoverye of Ireland* and importuned Sir Robert Cecil to present it to the Council.[69] The treatise, much wilder than his earlier work, contained offers to assassinate Tyrone as a way of solving the Ulster crisis, and letters flowed from Thomas to various captains in Ireland attempting to organize such a scheme.

Sir Henry's letters to Sir Robert Cecil throughout 1600 were dominated by his cousin's position. Whether his attempts to obtain a pardon for Thomas and permission for him to return to Ireland were a product of a genuine belief in his innocence or exasperation with an unwelcome guest who had outstayed his welcome is unknown. Sir Henry risked a great deal by giving Cecil his personal assurances of Thomas's good faith and offered himself in bond for his cousin's behaviour.[70] There was, wrote Sir Henry, no villainous intent in Thomas towards her Majesty or his country, except that he would 'prefer Ireland with all the beggars before his natural country'.[71] Thomas became increasingly depressed, and in June 1600 Sir Henry wrote to Cecil of 'my unfortunate couysin, whose case grows worse and worse'.

By September 1600 Sir Henry was describing the desperate state in which he found Thomas at the Savoy where he was in 'such great extremity … all looked for his last farewell'. In December Sir Henry reported to Cecil that 'my coosin is now … trodden down underfoote … being not worthy of life, not deserving better himself'.[72] Despite his age and infirmity, Sir Henry then wrote to the Council on his cousin's behalf and even personally importuned the Queen, to no avail. The matter of Thomas Lee seems to have dominated Sir Henry's life in 1600, and it is difficult to see what else he could have done to help his undeserving and unwelcome guest. By January 1601, however, Cecil had, at Sir Henry's request,

[69]   Cecil MS 67.113 (HMC *Salis*. X, pp. 12–13) (22 January 1600); Cecil MS 69.16 (HMC *Salis*. X, p. 77) (22 March 1600).

[70]   Cecil MS 78.10 (HMC *Salis*. X, p. 85) (29 March 1600); Cecil MS 80.24 (HMC *Salis*. X, p. 24) (13 June 1600); Cecil MS 81.36 (HMC *Salis*. X, p. 278) (14 August 1600).

[71]   Cecil MS 251.38 (HMC *Salis*. X, p. 306) (7 September 1600).

[72]   Cecil MS 82.80 (HMC *Salis*. X, p. 427) (22 December 1600).

obtained some money for Thomas Lee along with a commission to return to Ireland with a small troop of men.[73]

In the event, Sir Henry's faith in his cousin was not rewarded. The Earl of Essex had not included this loose cannon in his rising on 8 February 1601, and Thomas, eager to establish his innocence, sent a list of the conspirators to Sir Henry four days later.[74] But the mental instability that had been increasingly obvious to Sir Henry manifested itself on the evening of 12 February when Thomas Lee was apprehended loitering at the door of the Queen's privy chamber, 'his color pale and his face ... [with] great drops of sweat standing upon it'.[75] He stated that he only wished to 'step unto the Queen and kneel before her and never rise till she had signed a warrant' pardoning the Earls of Essex and Southampton.

This claim, which was probably a truthful reflection of Thomas's disturbed mind, was regarded as far-fetched; he was subsequently found guilty of high treason and hanged, drawn and quartered on 14 February 1601. Sir Henry Lee was horrified and personally alarmed, not only at Essex's conduct but because his own cousin's treason would reflect badly on him. By 16 February he was describing Thomas to Cecil in very different terms: 'of all creatures most hated to me ... in the course of his life, the wretch has spent me much; I pay interest [on] no small sum and have since his coming over increased it'.[76]

Sir Henry was not the only one to turn rapidly against Thomas. John Lee, Sir Henry's deputy at the Tower, complained that 'that bloody murderer' still owed him £100, and the Irish Secretary, Sir Geoffrey Fenton, originally a sponsor, described Thomas Lee to Cecil as having 'a murdering heart and a murdering hand'.[77] Sir Henry Lee himself was briefly placed under house arrest, but, despite this, both he and his brother Sir Richard Lee worked to secure some sort of inheritance for Thomas's children. They wrote to Cecil in December 1602 hoping to confirm that Thomas Lee's lands at Roscommon and Castlereban, County Kildare, would be passed to 'some poor innocents, the children of an unhappy father'.[78]

Sir Henry Lee's sense of obligation extended beyond his own blood relations. In 1574 he had, with Ambrose Dudley, stood as godfather to Leicester's

---

[73]   Cecil MS 76.1 (HMC *Salis.* XI, pp. 9–10) (14 January 1601). Cecil MS 180.2. (HMC *Salis.* XI.

[74]   Cecil MS 76.56 (HMC *Salis.* XI, p. 44) (12 February 1601).

[75]   *CSPD, Addenda 1580–1625*, p. 409, testimony given by William Poynes at Thomas Lee's trial. Poynes had apprehended Lee outside the Queen's chamber. See also Myers, 'Murdering Heart', p. 48.

[76]   Cecil MS 76.79 (HMC *Salis.* XI, p. 48).

[77]   Cecil MS 180.32 (HMC *Salis.* XI, p. 90) (1 February 1601); BL, *CSP Irish*, X, p. 203 (26 February 1601).

[78]   Cecil MS 96.104 (HMC *Salis.* XII) (10 December 1602).

illegitimate son Robert by Douglas Lady Sheffield, and had accommodated the young man from time to time at Woodstock. It is possible that the 'son in chivalry' whom he introduced to the tilting fraternity at some undated Accession Day tournament after 1590 was Robert Dudley, who made his tournament debut in 1593.[79] Lee also encouraged Sir Edward Vere, Anne Vavasour's son by the Earl of Oxford, in his military career in the Netherlands and promoted the renewed relationship between mother and son.

Lee and his Friends

It is obvious from the sources that Sir Henry Lee was a good friend to many, but the quality of Lee's friendship takes on a whole new meaning when one recalls that Philip Sidney in his *New Arcadia* refers to Lee as 'Lelius' (see Appendix 5). Sidney, classically educated and conversant with Cicero, would have used the name advisedly, revealing new depths of meaning as to how he saw his friendship with Lee and possibly how Lee himself defined friendship. Gaius Laelius, Roman general and statesman, was described by Silius Italicus as an eloquent orator, a brave soldier and a poet. More importantly, Laelius is the chief discussant in Cicero's *On friendship, Laelius de Amicitia*, the principal text and practical guide to perfect friendship during the Renaissance, similar to the conduct books for courtiers and gentlemen. Friendship, in Cicero's work, was the key to happiness and more valuable than worldly goods: it did not depend on closeness of age but on a mutual love of virtue. Sidney would have known that Petrarch, too, had his 'Laelius', who was described as a man with wide literary interests and the friend of leading statesmen.

Lee and Philip Sidney met first in 1575 during the Queen's visit to Kenilworth, the home of Sidney's uncle, the Earl of Leicester. Sidney and his sister Mary were also present during the Queen's later visit to Woodstock. The Ditchley manuscript contains an anonymous sonnet '"To Layius" for 3 kallender of October 1575'.[80] When, in 1577, twenty-two year-old Sidney was sent with his young friends Edward Dyer and Fulke Greville on a diplomatic mission to Prague, to offer the Queen's condolences to the Emperor Rudolf II on the death of his father Maximilian II, Burghley had added two older men to the party. These were Jerome Bowes, a somewhat volatile diplomat, and Sir Henry Lee, at forty-four, the oldest and most experienced member of the group. Friendships

---

[79]   BL, Add. MS 41499A, ff. 1 and 1v. Chambers suggests that this 'son in chivalry' was Cary Reynolds, but offers no substantiation. Strong suggests that it was Sir John Lee. Although Cromwell Lee had an illegitimate son, John, he was in holy orders and never knighted. Sir Robert Dudley, as Lee's godson, appears to be a simpler and more obvious candidate.

[80]   BL, Add. MS 41499A, f. 8.

developed on that journey, and, despite the age difference, Lee was not a little influenced by the charismatic young Sidney. Unlike on his earlier travels, there is no evidence that Lee wrote privately to Burghley during the journey.[81]

Edward Berry makes the interesting suggestion that when he first came into close contact with Lee in 1577, Sidney was finding the friendship of his earlier mentor and tutor, the philosopher Hubert Languet, both controlling and threatening.[82] Lee, as instructor of Sidney's new tournament skills, would have offered a less intimidating friendship. The two collaborated in devising tournament entertainments; they tilted together; Sidney gave Lee a manuscript copy of his *Old Arcadia*; and they shared lodgings at Theobalds in 1583. When Sidney introduced Lee into his *New Arcadia* as Laelius in the Iberian tilt, it was a major compliment. Cicero's Laelius was 'at once a wise man ... and eminent for his famous friendship'. But Cicero's Laelius had also spoken on bereavement, and his words were prescient: 'the loving remembrance and the regret of friends which follows us to the grave, whilst they take the sting out of death, they add a glory to the life of the survivors.' On 17 November 1586 it was Lee who organized the first public tribute after Sidney's death at the Battle of Zutphen; at the start of the Accession Day parade, Dyer and Greville led Sidney's riderless horse around the tournament ground in full mourning.[83]

As is to be expected in a 'complete courtier' who lived to be seventy-seven, Lee had many other friendships. His oldest and most profitable was with Burghley and his son Sir Robert Cecil, Lee being related, through the Cookes, to Burghley's wife Mildred. Wallace McCaffrey has observed that Burghley, unlike Leicester, 'used his position to establish friendly relations with a broad range of courtiers, nobles and gentry who came to owe him thanks for favours done', and Lee's long relationship with Burghley substantiates this opinion.[84] Similarly, Lee's early friendship with his brother-in-law, Henry Lord Paget, led to a long relationship with Paget's close friend, Lord Robert Dudley, Earl of Leicester. Both Lee and Leicester shared a passionate interest and prowess in the tilt and in hunting; Lee entertained Leicester at Quarrendon in 1566, and Leicester reciprocated with hospitability at Warwick and Kenilworth.[85] Lee

---

[81]   It is possible that Lee concealed things from Burghley. Languet, Sidney's mentor and former tutor suggested that Sidney was attempting to marry the sister of John Casimir of the Palatinate and 'Monsieur Ley was privy to the scheme'. Sidney's marriage into a foreign ruling house would have outraged Elizabeth.

[82]   E. Berry, *The Making of Sir Philip Sidney* (Toronto, 1998), pp. 38–48.

[83]   BL, Add. MS 41499A, f. 7b.

[84]   W.T. MacCaffrey, 'Cecil, William, First Baron Burghley (1520/21–1598)', *Oxford Dictionary of National Biography*, September 2004; online edn, January 2008 at: http://www.oxforddnb.com/view/article/4983.

[85]   See Thomas Kemp (ed.), *The Black Book of Warwick* (Warwick, 1898), f. 33; J.C. Nichols, *The Progresses, Public Processions etc. of Queen Elizabeth*, 3 vols (London, 1823; New York, 1967),

visited Warwick in September 1571 and in August 1574 stood as godfather with Ambrose Dudley, Earl of Warwick, to Leicester's illegitimate son Robert by Douglas, Lady Sheffield.

When Robert's later attempt to claim legitimacy was tried before the Star Chamber in 1604, Lee was described as one of the 'fower of the privatest frends of the Earle of Leyster'.[86] The Kenilworth Game Book shows that Lee hunted there in 1571, in 1574, during the Queen's visit in 1575, in 1576 and in 1577.[87] The easy friendship continued throughout Leicester's life, and his household accounts record sums lost at dice or expended on entertainment in Lee's company at High Lodge, Woodstock.[88]

Lee was occasionally asked to act as an intermediary between disputing parties in Elizabethan society, bearing testimony both to his diplomatic abilities and the esteem in which he was held. In 1587 Gilbert Lord Talbot asked Lee to mediate between him and his father George Talbot, sixth Earl of Shrewsbury. The relationship between Gilbert Talbot and his father, former custodian of Mary Stuart and fourth husband of the forceful Bess of Hardwick, was fraught with estrangements, family feuds and financial problems. Several well-meaning courtiers, such as Gilbert's uncle Roger Manners had previously attempted to effect reconciliation between father and son, but Gilbert Talbot's financial difficulties ensured that no settlement lasted for long. As a friend to both parties, Lee visited the Earl on at least four occasions between July and October in 1587, bearing letters from the Earl's son and eloquently arguing his case.

In a series of long letters to Gilbert Talbot, Lee narrated the conversations he had had with the Earl and the arguments he had put forward – arguments that reveal much of Lee's tact and insight in the world of family relationships.[89] The Earl, he told Gilbert, 'is owlde and unwyldy, and dysceyved by shuche he trustethe, and you shunne to assyst hem'. On the other hand, he warned the Earl that Gilbert Talbot's financial desperation could drive him abroad in 'thys dowtfull tyme', and 'if he shulde ... be taken from you and not be recovered, ... your grefe wolde accompne your whyte haires to your end with a grave full of cares'.[90]

Lee obviously had a great deal of sympathy and understanding for the much-afflicted older man, even though he had been recruited by Gilbert Talbot to put his case. In July 1587, reporting on the conversation he had with the Earl of

I, p. 291.

[86]   CKS, U1475 (Penshurst Papers), L2/4, f. 72.

[87]   CKS, U1475 (Penshurst Papers) E93.

[88]   *Household Accounts and Disbursement books of Robert Dudley, Earl of Leicester*, ed. S. Adams, Camden Society 5th Series, VI (Cambridge, 1996), pp. 186, 213–15, 237, 292–4, 299 (1558–1561, 1584–1586).

[89]   LPL, Talbot Papers MSS 3198, 3199.

[90]   LPL, Talbot Papers MS 3198, ff. 362–4 (13 August 1587).

Shrewsbury, Lee told Gilbert Talbot to remember 'that you deale with a kynde man'.[91] The friendship between Lee and the Earl of Shrewsbury appeared to be mutual, as Shrewsbury wrote privately to Lee, regretting that he could not accommodate his son but welcoming Lee's visits. Shrewsbury seems to have been very lonely, and, despite family accusations against her, Lee empathized with Shrewsbury's relationship with his mistress Eleanor Britton, who at least gave the old man some company.

When peace was temporarily restored between father and son in 1587, Shrewsbury was complimentary to Lee, assuring him that 'the most eloquent orator in England can do no more with me than you have'.[92] It seems unlikely that Lee's considerable efforts at intervention were for any motive other than friendship as he received little for his pains except the warm approval of the old and harassed sixth Earl. The only practical benefit Lee appeared to receive was a later promise of a £500 loan from the old man in summer 1590 – the promise that Gilbert Talbot reneged upon when his father died in November 1590. In June 1591 Lee was even prepared to speak up for Eleanor Britton, who was promised some 'harde meanes' by the new earl, not a move for a gentleman wishing to endear himself to the new seventh earl of Shrewsbury. Lee's friendships were not confined to nobles, and several lesser men, both in Court and out, such as the Zinzan alias Alexander family who trained the royal horses and rode professionally in the tournaments, benefited from Lee's interest. In September 1597 Lee wrote to Cecil requesting a pension for his friend, Robert Alexander, and this type of action was not an isolated occurrence.[93]

Two interesting testimonies bear witness to the number of friends Sir Henry Lee amassed during his long lifetime. After the spectacular entertainment staged by Lee after his retirement tournament in 1590, he presented the Queen with a cloak, set with gold buttons, each embroidered with a nobleman's device. Segar notes here that Lee had said: 'I would that all my friends might have bene remembered in these buttons, but there is not roome enough to contain them.'[94]

Similarly, in 1597 Lee received a near-unanimous vote from the members of the *Comes* to the Order of the Garter, and the roll-call of the nine peers who endorsed Lee's election can be read not only as a testimony to the high personal esteem in which he was held, but also as a list of those whom he had helped during his lifetime.[95] Lee's affiliations with Lord Burghley, his proposer, went back to the 1560s, and his affection and support for the Earl of Essex dated from the Earl's first appearance on the tournament ground in 1586. Charles, Lord

---

[91]   LPL, Talbot Papers MS 3198, ff. 359–60 (15 July 1587).
[92]   LPL, Talbot Papers MS 3198, f. 365 (6 September 1587).
[93]   Cecil MS 55.77 (HMC *Salis*. VII, p. 402).
[94]   Nichols, *The Progresses ... of Queen Elizabeth*, III, p. 49, quoting from Sir William Segar, *Honor Military and Civill* (London, 1602).
[95]   BL, Add. MS 36768 (*Regulations of the Order of the Garter*).

Howard of Effingham, was Lee's old tilting partner from the 1570s, and Lord Sheffield was the legitimate half-brother of Lee's godson, Sir Robert Dudley. Lord Gilbert Talbot, now the seventh Earl of Shrewsbury, still maintained a lively correspondence with Lee and endorsed his candidature. The Earl of Cumberland had tilted with Lee for many years and had succeeded him as the Queen's personal champion in 1590. Lord Buckhurst was a long-time friend of Lee's at Court. Lee also received votes from Lord Burgh, possibly a boyhood tilting partner from Lullingstone in Kent, soon to be appointed briefly as Lord Deputy of Ireland, and the Earl of Ormond.[96] Only the Earl of Northumberland withheld his vote.[97] The Queen might have been unwilling to appoint Lee, a mere gentleman, but the overwhelming support for him from peers of the realm ensured his election.

Not all of Sir Henry Lee's friendships were as harmonious as they might first appear, and it would have been unusual if they had been. In one of the very few surviving letters addressed to Lee, dated November 1587, Sir Christopher Hatton's secretary, Samuel Cox, upbraided Lee for a harsh reaction to Cox's tardy repayment of a loan,[98] although the circumstances are only obliquely referred to. The friendship between Cox and Lee was longstanding. Cox writes that he had specifically 'made choice to live near you' at Fulbrook, Oxfordshire, and Lee had stayed with him there in September 1587. Cox had severely overstretched his resources by his purchase of the manor and may have been relying on Lee to help him financially. Cox voiced surprise 'that so small a matter could draw you so quickly to forsake your friend', but in November 1587 Lee was facing his own grave financial embarrassments.

Lee's disappointment at his failure to secure the vice-chamberlainship after 1595 also brought him some temporary disillusionment with his friends and might have occasioned the portrait of Lee with his large mastiff, executed by Gheeraerts around that date (see Ill. 17).[99] The 'Bevis' portrait, supposedly commemorating the occasion when Lee was saved from burglars at Ditchley by the barking of his dog, bears the sonnet:

> Reason in Man cannot effect such love
> As nature doth in them that reason wante

---

[96]   Lord Burgh's son was being raised in the house of Lee's friend Essex. One assumes that Ormond's vote was by proxy as Ormond, brother-in-law to Lord Sheffield, was in Ireland at the time.

[97]   It is unclear whether this was through enmity with Essex or resentment over Lee's links with the Tower, where Northumberland's father had mysteriously died in 1585.

[98]   Letter Book of Sir Christopher Hatton, BL Add. MS 15891, transcribed in Nicolas, *Memoirs of ... Sir Christopher Hatton*, p. xxxviii.

[99]   The 'Bevis' portrait was said to have inspired Sir Walter Scott to write his novel *Woodstock*, and the name for the faithful hound 'Bevis' arises from this.

Ulisses true and kinde his dog did prove
When faith in better frendes was very scante.

My travailes for my frendes have been as true
Though not so farre as fortune did him beare
No frendes my love and faith devided knewe
Though neyther this nor that once equalde were.

Only my Dog whereof I made no store
I finde more love then them I trusted more.

There are similarities between this portrait and that of Lord Robert Dudley, Earl of Leicester, attributed to Steven Van der Meulen (c.1564), now at Waddesdon Manor, Buckinghamshire (Ill. 18), and Lee may have been quoting, and even parodying, it.[100] Leicester, in white or silver doublet, trunk hose and cannions, is proudly wearing the Order of the Garter around his neck, and the motif is echoed in the Garter crests behind him. At his right hand, his faithful dog gazes up in admiration. Lee, similarly dressed in white or silver, also has his faithful dog, but he has neither a chain of office nor Order of the Garter around his neck – only a cord holding no decoration. In place of the Garter crests, he has his sonnet of disillusionment and the *impresa* 'More faithfull than favoured'. It is noteworthy that in 1596 Lee not only failed to secure the vice-chamberlainship, but also received only one vote for his election to the Order of the Garter. This, the most endearing portrait of Lee's collection, still hangs in Ditchley.

Lee's Collection of Symbolic Portraits and Coins

Lee was neither a vain man nor one for self-glorification, but like most prosperous landowning gentry, he knew his status in the social order of his day and was well aware of his own worth in the public and private spheres. It is also clear that he regarded friendship as central to his life. It is therefore apposite that, in retirement, one of his principal interests was his collection of portraits of himself, his family and his friends. Much has been written on the politics and inner meaning of Tudor portraiture. While Lee would have agreed with Sir John Harington in seeing an art collection as being 'the pleasing ornaments

---

[100] I am grateful to Tracey Wedge at the University of Southampton Textile Conservation Centre, Winchester (now closed) for pointing out the similarity between the two pictures.

of a house and good remembrance of our friends', he also chose to celebrate the occasions when his social status was enhanced by having his portrait painted.[101]

There had been a tradition of family portraits in Lee's family. His maternal grandfather Sir Henry Wyatt had commissioned portraits of himself, his son Sir Thomas Wyatt and Lee's mother Margaret from Hans Holbein. Sir Henry Lee himself had sat for Antonis Mor during his Antwerp journey in 1568, and Lee's lifelong fascination with symbolism extended back to this first portrait (see Ill. 1). The armillary spheres on his shirt have already been discussed, but the symbolism of his malformed left thumb looped by a ring hung by red cord around his neck has baffled many commentators. James Hall suggests that the prominent display of the wounded left thumb, imprisoned in a ring and supported by the red cord, adheres to the Petrarchean symbolism of the left side being wounded for love, as seen in Moroni's portrait of *A Knight with his Jousting Helmet*.[102] He argues that Lee, with his bold display of true-love knots, rings and the erotic position of his wounded left thumb, is conveying the message that he has been wounded for love, possibly by the Queen herself. Hall's thesis is somewhat undermined, however, by the fact that in the companion portrait of Lord Edward Windsor, it is Windsor's right finger that is suspended through a ring. Also, the idea that this was of contemporary significance is undermined by Lee's portrait remaining at Ditchley until 1932. As a result, few of Lee's contemporaries can have viewed the work.

When Lee began to build his portrait collection in earnest after 1590, he turned to Marcus Gheeraerts the Younger. Gheeraerts was born around 1561 in Bruges and fled to London in 1568 with his father Marcus Gheeraerts the Elder. Father and son joined the Dutch Protestant Stranger Church in London, which numbered several artists among its congregation, and this enabled Marcus Gheeraerts the Elder to obtain several prestigious Court commissions. Although he enrolled in the painters' guild in Antwerp in 1577, it is possible both he and his son continued to reside in London thereafter.[103] Lee had probably already made the acquaintance of several of the Dutch artists at Court or at Kenilworth in 1575, and Lee's Woodstock entertainment of that year had featured 'enchanted pictures', although the name of the artist involved remains unknown.[104] Gheeraerts the Elder died around 1587, but his son sought

---

[101]   J. Peacock, 'The Politics of Portraiture', in K. Sharpe and P. Lake (eds), *Culture and Politics in Early Stuart England* (Basingstoke, 1994), pp. 195–228. Harington's comment is from his 1591 translation of Ariosto's *Orlando Furioso*, quoted by Peacock.

[102]   J. Hall, *Sinister Developments: A Lost Key to Western Art* (Oxford, forthcoming).

[103]   E. Tahon, 'Marcus Gheeraerts de Oude Brugge ca. 1521–1587 Londen?' in M.P.J. Martens (ed.), *Brugge en de Renaissance: Van Memling tot Pourbus* (Bruges, 1998), p. 231.

[104]   Marcus Gheeraerts the Elder is attributed with a panel now in private hands, 'Queen Elizabeth and her Court at Kenilworth, 1575'. See A.C. Sewter, 'Queen Elizabeth at Kenilworth', *Burlington Magazine*, LXXVI (March 1940), pp. 70–76.

commissions from a range of courtiers, including Sir Henry Lee. In 1592, when the Queen returned on progress to Woodstock, Lee commissioned a very large portrait of her as an integral part of the dramatic presentation he staged in her honour at his home at nearby Ditchley. This iconographic portrait of Elizabeth became the cornerstone of Lee's collection (see Ill. 12). Gheeraerts the Younger produced other portraits for Lee, and many of his early commissions came from Lee's circle of friends.

At a time when great aristocrats such as Leicester and John, Lord Lumley, were building up art collections that presaged those of the Stuart Court, mere gentleman such as Lee tended to have less ambitious aims, limiting his commissions to portraits demonstrating loyalty to the monarch and commemorating his family and friends. He also followed the contemporary convention of building a long gallery at Ditchley to house his collection. In addition to the Antonis Mor portrait (1568) and the Ditchley portrait of Elizabeth I (1592), Lee's collection included Gheeraerts' full-length study of Sir Henry's cousin Captain Thomas Lee (1594), the 'Bevis' portrait of himself with his dog (c.1596), and five matching portraits of Sir Henry and his four brothers, Robert, Cromwell, Thomas and Richard (1600). In 1602 Gheeraerts completed a full-length study of Lee in his Garter robes (see Ill. 13), and Lee later acquired a Gheeraerts' portrait of Henry, Prince of Wales, possibly given him by James I. The collection also included portraits of Sir Henry's numerous friends, such as Sir Christopher Hatton by Cornelius Ketel, Philip Sidney and the Earl of Essex. In 1605 he commissioned a full-length portrait of Anne Vavasour from Gheeraerts' brother-in-law John de Critz.[105]

Whereas Lee's choice of subject was conventional, what he required in a portrait was far from ordinary. Several of the portraits associated with Lee are unusual in a collection by a country gentleman, and suggest that Lee insisted on the inclusion of some specific elements. In at least two portraits Gheeraerts placed the sitter in front of a landscape, a feature only found in his portrait of Essex at this time. Three portraits contain rich allegorical symbols and references with which Lee would have been familiar through his long experience of tournament *imprese*. The pattern was set by the Ditchley portrait which placed Elizabeth on a map of England with sunshine and storms behind her. This was filled with allegorical references and *imprese* mottos and included a sonnet. The use of a natural setting for a portrait was used again in the portrait of Captain Thomas Lee in 1594, together with allegorical references to Scaevola and his

---

[105] H.A. Dillon, *Catalogue of Paintings in the Possession of Viscount Dillon at Ditchley, Spelsbury, Oxfordshire* (Oxford,1908); R. Strong, 'Marcus Gheeraerts the Younger', *Burlington Magazine*, CV (April 1963), pp. 149–57; O. Millar, 'Marcus Gheeraerts the Younger: A Sequel through Inscriptions', *Burlington Magazine*, CV (December 1963), pp. 533–41. Dillon quotes George Vertue as having seen two full-length portraits of Mary and Anne Fitton, dated 1601, in the collection, but the connection with Lee is unclear.

faithfulness to his country in the face of adversity. The portrait of Sir Henry Lee with his dog also included a sonnet, playing on Lee's family motto and stressing the animal's fidelity and constancy.

The similarity of the symbolism, sonnets and calligraphy found in portraits connected with Sir Henry Lee has led Roy Strong to argue forcefully for Lee's hand in the creation of the mysterious and enigmatic *Unknown Lady in a Fancy Dress* portrait by Marcus Gheeraerts, painted around 1600 (see Ill. 19).[106] This portrait, rich in symbolism, is of a pregnant lady in 'strange fantastick habit', possibly Persian, her headdress and costume scattered with pansies, set against a woodland background with her hand resting on a white stag. Like the Ditchley portrait, there are three enigmatic mottos in Latin, one being *Iniusti Justa querela* –'a just complaint for injustice' – and a sonnet framed in a cartouche, obliquely referring to the lady's grief and the weeping stag. What is important in the context of Lee's habit of specifying aspects of a portrait is the purpose he intended it should be used for.

The subject, Strong argues, is the pregnant Frances Walsingham, wife of the Earl of Essex. In March 1599 Essex had departed for Ireland with the greatest army ever to leave England in Tudor times, only to return unexpectedly on 24 September 1599 to defend himself from domestic enemies. His precipitous entry into the Queen's apartments at Nonsuch Palace caught the Queen in a state of undress, and by lunchtime that day Essex had been exiled from Court and the Queen's presence. Elizabeth, if anyone, would have understood the classical reference in the painting to Actaeon, who was turned into a stag for disturbing the goddess Diana and her nymphs while bathing. For Essex, caught between house arrest, mental and physical degeneration and increasing financial embarrassment, it was imperative both to regain access to the Queen and renew his licence on sweet wines, due to expire on 30 October 1600. By November 1600 he had exhausted his own repertoire of appeals, and Strong argues that the creation of the portrait of the suppliant and pregnant Countess of Essex was Lee's attempt to break the impasse between Essex and the Queen. The portrait was probably intended to be presented to the Queen, and Strong noted that 'Lee knew more than anyone what pleased [the Queen], and in the Persian lady we should be looking at his work'.

Certainly, the scenario of the portrait was typical of the tactful approach to the Queen that Lee had always used, which contrasted markedly from that of Essex. Lee was no great earl but he was a gentleman who in both 1575 and 1592 had made bold requests to Elizabeth, using 'enchanted portraits' and entertainments to intrigue her, flatter her knowledge of allegory and classical illusion, and seek forgiveness. In the summer of 1598 when Essex was originally barred from the

---

[106] R. Strong, 'My Weeping Stag I Crowne' in Michael Bath, John Manning and Alan Young (eds), *The Art of the Emblem: Essays in Honour of Karl Josef Holtgen* (New York,1993), pp. 103–41.

Queen's presence, Lee had advised him to swallow his pride and to appeal to Elizabeth as a woman as well as a monarch. Now the message of the faithful wife in the portrait and in the sonnet repeated the same tactful approach. Lee was not alone in suggesting ways of reconciling Essex and Elizabeth. In November 1600 the Countess of Warwick, as a lady of the bedchamber, had also advised the earl to surprise the Queen when she was in a good mood and cast himself at her feet, begging her forgiveness.

If this was the purpose of the portrait, the attempt failed. For some reason the portrait was never presented to the Queen, and perhaps the appeal was futile from the outset. Elizabeth might have been prepared to forgive her old knight who had timed his indiscretions with Anne Vavasour to coincide with his retirement, but she was not prepared to forgive a leading nobleman who had deserted his post as military commander and had become an embarrassment she no longer needed. But if Strong's suggestion that Sir Henry Lee had a major input in the creation of this particular portrait is correct, it reinforces the image of a highly creative and innovative mind that was the guiding force behind the Quarrendon garden and the Ditchley portrait.

Lee was not above using personal portraits to get a message across. In 1595 he appears to have responded to his failure to gain not only membership of the Order of the Garter but also the vice-chamberlainship by commissioning the famous 'Bevis' portrait, later to inspire Sir Walter Scott's novel 'Woodstock'. When, in 1596, Lee was elected to the Order of the Garter, a most unusual honour for a commoner, he commissioned the portrait of himself in full Garter robes from Marcus Gheeraerts, and he would later do the same for the Prince Henry Frederick, in a vain attempt to introduce his favourite artist to the young Prince of Wales.

Lee's love of symbolism can first be seen in the portrait of himself executed by Antonis Mor in 1568. The blackwork embroidery on the sleeves depicts an armillary sphere. This image was loved by the Court and became the motif of the tournament. Like planets round the sun, young knights at Court revolved around their Virgin Queen as they vied with each other to impress her. In the famous 'Ditchley' portrait of 1592, Elizabeth wears an armillary sphere as an earring. An interesting thought is that, by tradition, the blackwork on men's shirts was embroidered by their wives. Perhaps when Henry Lee set out on his travels to the Continent in 1559, his long-suffering wife Anne Paget, who had embroidered his shirts, already realized that his commitment to her was already being replaced by his devotion to the Queen.

Lee also drew up a book of possible *imprese* for use in tournaments and left a range of *imprese* mottos which were later found among his papers.[107] Several

---

[107] 'Sir Henry Lee's Devices' BL, Add. MS 41499A, f. 6, (three suggestions for mottos). See also BL, Add. MS 41499B (Viscount Dillon's Victorian transcription of the Tudor original).

of the portraits he commissioned from Marcus Gheeraerts included *imprese* mottos, and he quoted the *impresa*, '*Coelumque, solumque, beavit*', in the Ditchley entertainment of 1592. The extent to which a London crowd would have understood the carefully worded Latin allegories on these shields is debatable. Few knights based them on their own family mottos. Instead, the *impresa* motto was a thinly veiled message for the Court or even the Queen herself, and referred to a courier's hopes and aspirations, or the entertainments they were about to stage for the Queen, who delighted in the enigmatic classical witticisms of her courtiers.

Examples of these *imprese* mottos were '*Te stante virebo*' ('You standing, I flourish') and '*Dum splendes floreo*' ('While you shine I flourish') used by the Earl of Leicester, the Queen's favourite for many years. Elizabeth herself often used '*Semper eadem*' ('Always the same'), and frequent mention of this was made in entertainments for her. The Earl of Leicester's nephew and heir, Sir Philip Sidney, famously used '*Spero*' ('I hope'), and when his uncle's second wife fell pregnant '*Speravi*' ('I have hoped'). In an entertainment for 1577 Sir Philip Sidney used '*Nec habent occulta sepulchra*' ('Graves have no secrets').[108]

After the defeat of the Spanish Armada, the Queen gave the 'Dangers averted' gold medallion (see Ill. 20) to certain leading courtiers. Since Lee had been Master of the armoury in 1588 he would certainly have received one. This gold medal by Nicholas Hillyard showed Elizabeth not in the traditional full profile aspect but in a three-quarter view. The loops at the bottom were probably intended for the hanging of drop pearls, and it is possible that this piece was originally devised as a costly gift from Elizabeth to a favoured courtier or overseas head of state.

The obverse of the coin shows her crowned, with a ruff above an jewelled open gown and a large rose, and carries the inscription '*Ditor in toto non alter circulus*' ('No circle in the whole world more rich'). The accompanying laurel tree is labelled Elizabeth Regina and its legend translates as 'Not even danger affects', while the bay tree standing on an island with ships in the background has the accompanying inscription '*Nen ipsa pericultangunt*' ('Not even dangers affect it'). According to legend, the laurel was immune from lightning, and the inscriptions refer to Elizabeth's resistance to the dual threat of Catholicism at home and Philip II of Spain abroad.[109] When the Queen visited Ditchley in 1592, Lee's portrait of her, showing Elizabeth standing on the Island of Britain defeating the storms was an integral part of the entertainment. This could be interpreted as Lee returning the compliment for receiving her medal.

---

[108]   Peter Beal, "Poems by Sir Philip Sidney: The Ottley Manuscript", *Library*, Fifth Series, 33 (1978), pp. 284–95 as quoted in Woodhuysen, *Sir Philip Sydney*, pp. 413–15.

[109]   I am grateful to Peter Barber of the British Library for this suggestion.

The narrative of the 1592 entertainment suggests that the origin of its pictures was the 1575 entertainment, with some having subsequently been preserved and magically transported to Ditchley. Little is known about the 1575 pictures, but Elizabeth's portrait by Marcus Gheeraerts the Younger (Ill. 12) appears to have been commissioned by Lee around 1592, and its enigmatic nature suggests that it played a major role in the first day's entertainment. The nature of the other pictures that were used is unknown, and any indication of the association they may have had with Ditchley has long disappeared.

Lee's dramatic presentation required a very large portrait as an integral part of the entertainment to be visible to all the onlookers and to contain the amount of symbolism needed. The 'Ditchley portrait', the largest ever painted of Elizabeth, is in oil on canvas. This was a relatively new medium for England in 1592, and the decision to use it was possibly influenced by the huge canvases prepared for pageants by the Flemish Chambers of Rhetoric. Gheeraerts, trained by his father Marcus Gheeraerts the Elder and the Flemish artist Lucas de Heere, had been a member of the chamber of St Luke in Antwerp. On Lee's instructions, Gheeraerts placed riddles and puzzles in the portrait and, as the text related to them suggests, these were not easy to construe:

> Many there were that could no more but vewe them,
> Many that ouer curious nearer pried
> Manie would conster needes that neuer knewe them
> Some lookt, some lyked, some questioned, some aymed
> One asked them too who should not be denied.

Only the Queen, as 'Ladye or Goddesse', had sufficient power to interpret her own portrait and rescue her enchanted courtiers.

The puzzles in the portrait were many and were echoed in the text. Elizabeth, in a dress similar to the one she wore to the Thanksgiving celebrations after the defeat of the Armada in 1588, descends upon a map of southern England, her feet alighting at Woodstock and Ditchley.[110] This was possibly a depiction of one of the new Sheldon tapestry maps, again showing Lee's innovative imagination. With gloves in one hand against the cold, and fan in the other against the heat, the Queen dispels the 'darksom bandes' of stormy night and 'flying cloudes of vaine conceites' shown behind her, and '*Coelumque, solumque, beauit*' – 'she blesses both heaven and sun' as the sunshine breaks through.[111] Here Lee was

---

[110]   The sketch of the Thanksgiving celebrations by an unknown artist is now in the Royal Library, Windsor Castle and is similar to an engraving by William Rogers in the British Museum. The dress subsequently appeared in several portraits of the Queen, notably in *Elizabeth in procession to Blackfriars* in 1600 in the style of Peake.

[111]   Camden records that Lee had earlier used '*coelumque, solumque, beauit*' as a tournament *impresa*: William Camden, *Remaines Concerning Britain* (London, 1605), *RSTC* 4521.

making a direct reference to the contemporary identification of Elizabeth with the 'Woman Clothed by the Sun' in the Book of Revelations.[112] Helen Hackett has accurately noted the similarity to a ballad of 1587 which declared:

> As Shyning Sunne recleeres the darkned Skye
> And foorth recalles eche thing, from shiv'ring Shrowds,
> So hath our Second Sunne, both farre and nye
> by brightening Beames, outcleered erronious Clouds.

The image was repeated in Spenser's *Faerie Queene* of 1590:

> In widest Ocean she her Throne does rear
> That over all the Earth it may be seen
> At morning Sun her Beams dispredden clear.

Elizabeth wears a red rose, often the sign of the Virgin Mary. Her dress is adorned with pearls, sapphires and especially garnets, the symbol of her own constancy. Unlike the knights and ladies whom she is to rescue, Elizabeth was true to her own motto, '*Semper eadam*' ('Always the same'). Elizabeth also wears one earring, fashioned as an armillary sphere, recalling the motif Lee portrayed on his sleeve in his portrait of 1568.

If the Queen found riddles in the portrait itself, there were more in the sonnet and in the *imprese* inscribed on it. The portrait itself was substantially cut down by subsequent owners, and the sonnet, designed to be enigmatic, is doubly so because many of its lines are truncated. What can be read continues the image of the sun overcoming the thunder, and the fruitfulness of 'this ile [set in a] 'boundless ocean'. The Latin *imprese*, though damaged, are usually construed as 'She gives and does not expect', 'In giving back she increases' and particularly 'She can but does not take revenge'.

The Human Side of Sir Henry Lee: Playing to the Rules of the Elizabethan Game

In many ways, Sir Henry Lee's private life typified the standards, concerns, responsibilities and enthusiasms of his contemporaries among the landowning gentry. Sir Henry Lee felt his family responsibilities keenly, and his actions reflected the whole patronage system that existed in late Elizabethan society.

---

[112] The Book of Revelations 12, v. 1–2; Maurice Kyffin, 'The Blessedness of Brytaine', quoted in Helen Hackett, *Virgin Mother, Maiden Queen*, 2nd edn (Basingstoke, 1996), p. 133; Edmund Spenser, *Faerie Queene*, Book II, canto 2, 40 (London, 1590).

Great men at Court could show their power and influence by obtaining positions for their suppliants, ensuring the placement of men who they could trust, and obligations on which they could call when the occasion arose. In similar manner, gentlemen such as Lee could demonstrate their influence on such leading lights of the Court when obtaining positions for their own family. Occasionally, cream rose to the top, but the Tudor method of allocating government positions, both great and small, did not necessarily depend on talent or fitness for purpose. In the tangled web of obligation and patronage, Sir Henry Lee, as head of his family, clearly knew the rules and played his part deftly. His long experience in Court circles and his genial nature made him a good friend to have – a fact appreciated by those both in and out of favour with the Queen.

Chapter 7
Sir Henry Lee in the Reign of James I, 1603–1611

The months following the death of Queen Elizabeth on 24 March 1603 were busy for anyone in royal service. Sir Henry Lee travelled from Woodstock to attend the lavish funeral of his royal mistress on 28 April in his formal capacity as Master of the Armoury. He was among the knights who rode out to Stamford Hill to welcome James I to London on 7 May. He was attended by sixty mounted men, thirty of them on 'great horses' and all wearing yellow scarves embroidered with Lee's motto '*Fide et constantia*'. It was recorded that 'to this old Knight his majestie spake very lovingly, and so paced through his Troupes very well pleased'.[1] It was a pleasant gesture that cost the new king little and was typical of James's actions as he progressed through the kingdom to his capital.

As a Knight of the Garter, Lee had already attended the St George's Day ceremonies on 23 April at Whitehall when nine year-old Prince Henry was chosen to join their number, and was again present at the Prince's investiture at Windsor on 2 July. It is not known whether Lee was present at James's coronation on 25 July 1603, and of necessity the numbers were kept to a minimum as a virulent plague was raging in London that eventually claimed more than a quarter of the city's population.[2] As Master of the Armoury, Lee took part in the long-postponed state entry of King James and Queen Anne into the city of London on 15 March 1604 and acted as judge in the Accession Day tournament held on the new date of 24 March at Whitehall.[3] In addition, Lee played host when the King, Queen and Court visited Woodstock in September 1603 and again in the summer of 1604. For a man in his seventh decade, it was a busy schedule.

How was an old knight, the quintessential Elizabethan courtier, going to adapt to the new reign? Inevitably, Sir Henry Lee was increasingly going to play the part of bystander, which he had often claimed in the past. At seventy, he was largely freed from the need to importune for office or play much of a part at Court, and retirement absolved him from the rush for honours or positions

---

[1]   J. Nichols, *The Progresses, Processions and Magnificent Festivities of King James the First*, 4 vols (London, 1824; New York, 1969), I, p. 113.

[2]   The Earl of Worcester's letter to the Earl of Shrewsbury of 19 June 1603 outlined the discussion among the Garter knights whether 'we should make ayny shewe at all'. See E. Lodge, *Illustrations of British History*, 3 vols (London, 1791), III, pp. 166–7.

[3]   BL, Stowe MS 574, f. 46.

that accompanied the accession of the new king. Lee's age militated against any chance of elevation to the peerage. He had already failed to secure any lucrative prominent household position in the latter days of Elizabeth's reign, and the few courtiers who had been promoted suffered from the Queen's reluctance to grant them titles.[4]

When James became King in 1603, honours went to younger men. Sir William Knollys, the treasurer of the household, was elevated to the peerage in 1603; Lord Henry Howard, who had worked with Cecil for James's smooth accession, was created Earl of Northampton in May 1604; and Cecil himself became the Earl of Salisbury in 1605. Sir John Stanhope, erstwhile Vice-Chamberlain of Elizabeth's household and closer to Lee in rank became Baron Stanhope in the same year. Had Lee been ten years younger, the story might have been different. As it was, he merely received an annuity of some £200 from the Crown.[5]

In truth, Lee had little to gain from attendance at Court, although he was brought out of retirement for the staging of the first Accession Day tournament of James's reign on 24 March 1604, when 'old Sir Henry Lee' had a place of honour as one of the judges.[6] The appearances he did make at Court thereafter were on a few well-chosen occasions, and his letters after 1606 reflect more his own concerns and interests as a country gentleman. This 'antient and redoubted Champion ... this remarkable old Warrior and accomplished Courtier' could afford to observe the new reign at some leisure from his home at Ditchley or from Woodstock.[7]

Lee, Woodstock and the Royal Family

If Lee did not go to Court, the Court clearly came to him on numerous occasions. Woodstock, with some of the best hunting in England, had been a favourite venue for Elizabeth in the late summer months, and the Stuart royal family followed her example. With plague rife in London in the summer of 1603, the Court escaped to the country, although as Sir Thomas Edmonds reported to the Earl of Shrewsbury:

---

[4]   Charles Howard, three years younger than Lee and of noble birth, was a rare exception. He was created Earl of Nottingham in 1597.

[5]   *CSPD*, 1603–10, p. 58 (10 December 1603).

[6]   Quoted in R. Strong, *The Cult of Elizabeth* (London, 1977), p.133.

[7]   Lodge, *Illustrations*, III, pp. 171–3. Lodge's opinion of Lee, of course, was from the eighteenth century.

... the Court has been so contynnuallie haunted with the sicknes by reason of the disorderlie companie that doe followe us ... and doe infect all places where we come.[8]

Lee received the King and the whole Court from 11 to 15 September 1603. There had been no royal visit to Woodstock since 1592, and it was no small undertaking for Lee to accommodate everyone.

Sir Robert Cecil was scathing in his opinion of Woodstock, writing that:

> ... this place is unholsom all the house standing uppon springe ... only the K & Q w[i]th the privy cham[ber] ladyes and 3 or 4 of the Scottish counsaile are lodged in the house and neyther Chamberlain nor English counsailor have a room ... once a week one or other [person] dyes in our tents.[9]

The King, however, was delighted with Woodstock as all thought of business was abandoned and he gave himself wholeheartedly to his passion for hunting. On 15 September James and his Queen, Anne of Denmark, dined privately with Lee at Lee's Rest, Ditchley, and Arbella Stuart, who was at Court, reported to the Earl of Shrewsbury, that they

> ... weare accompanied by the French imbassador and a Dutch Duke ... I will not say we weare merry at the Dutchkin, least you complaine of me for telling tales out of the Queene's coche.[10]

For King James, Woodstock provided exactly what he wanted: his own lodge and deer park with close proximity to the well-stocked forest of Wychwood. He came to hunt privately in December 1603, and the Court returned on its summer progress in August 1604.

New monarchs brought changes, and, despite Lee's thirty-three years in charge of the royal hunting and of the palace at Woodstock, James was preparing to replace him there. Lee had been ill after the 1603 royal visit, and in 1604 the King granted the reversion of the lieutenancy at Woodstock to two young favourites, James, Lord Hay, and Sir Philip Herbert. It was suggested that Lee should offer his resignation, with a promise to 'dyscharge [his] dette consyderyng the great rents this xxxiii years [he had] payed'.[11] However, Lee knew how to muster heavyweight opposition. He wrote to the Earl of Northampton, Baron

---

8   Nichols, *The Progresses ... of King James*, III, p. 258; Lodge, *Illustrations*, III, p. 186.

9   Cecil to Shrewsbury, 17 September 1603 from Lodge, *Illustrations*, III, p. 187.

10   LPL, Talbot Papers MS 3201; Lodge, *Illustrations*, II, p. 25 (Arbella Stuart to Shrewsbury, 16 September 1603). Arbella Stuart, the somewhat unbalanced granddaughter of Bess of Hardwick, was of royal blood, and James preferred to keep her close to the Court.

11   *CSPD*, 1603–10, p. 152 (25 September 1604); TNA, PRO, SP14/9/152.

Home of Berwick, the new Chancellor of the Exchequer and Sir Robert Cecil, now Viscount Cranbourne, requesting help in retaining his office. If the King remained adamant, he confessed he would 'quench the overmuch affection I carry for this place ... and so drawe my selfe to a pryvate tyme of lyfe to pray for his Ma[jes]tie'.[12] It is not clear if there had been accusations of maladministration at Woodstock, but Lee, an old hand at Court politics, was quick to assert that 'tyme the tryar of truthe wyll dyscover howe ... my innocence was clouded to cowller the imperfections of others'. The result was that Lee retained his office.

The royal progress to Woodstock became a regular feature of the late summer Court calendar, with Lee complaining in 1606 that 'the kinges oft beinge heere has number of deere killed, many carryed a waye to the newe parke at Richmond'.[13] It is probable that Lee relinquished oversight of the palace at Woodstock to others while retaining supervision of the deer park.[14] After 1606 his letters were being sent from Ditchley and not from Woodstock itself, and, ever conscious of his own reputation, Lee was clearly working with an eye to the future. In 1607 he asked the Council for assistance in safeguarding

> ... [my] priviledges belonginge to woodstocke ... [to] keepe thynge here aboutes in better order that I may leve this place in such sorte as shall become me, both to the satisfyeing of his Ma[jes]tie and my selfe.[15]

In the light of Lee's infrequent Court attendance, it was fortunate that he shared quite discrete interests with the three leading members of the royal family. With King James he shared an obvious passion for hunting. If Lee could not actively participate in the hard riding favoured by James during his many visits, he could appreciate the royal achievement of the kill. There still remain at Ditchley six sets of stags' heads, testimony to royal kills in August 1605 and August 1610. Such was the honour conferred on Lee by the gifts that not only were these stags' heads mounted and accompanied by verses inscribed in brass to 'Great Britain's King', but Lee's successors had them transferred to the new house at Ditchley Park in 1722.

To Queen Anne, Lee was the quintessential Elizabethan courtier, well practised at charming great ladies. The Queen dined with Lee in 1603 and shared his love of portraiture. She became an active patron of Lee's favourite

---

[12]   Cecil MS 107.124 (HMC *Salis*. XVI, p. 355). (Lee to Cecil, now Viscount Cranbourne, 14 November 1604).

[13]   BL, Lansdowne MS 89, no. 98, f. 191. Summer progresses were made to Woodstock in 1603, 1604, 1605, 1608, 1610 and, after Lee's death, in 1612, 1614, 1616, 1617, 1619, 1621 and 1624.

[14]   *CSPD*, 1603–10, p. 40. (4 February 1608 – warrant to pay Sir Henry Lee £40 for hay for feeding the King's deer at Woodstock).

[15]   Cecil MS 123.65 (HMC *Salis*. XIX, p. 347) (Lee to the Council, 30 November 1607).

artist, Marcus Gheeraerts, helping him become the leading Court painter, and Lee was given a full-length portrait of Henry Prince of Wales in his Garter robes. In September 1608, with a fine disregard for convention, Anne dined with Lee and Anne Vavasour at their home at Lee's Rest and indulged in a long feminine heart-to-heart with Lee's mistress, the only record of Anne Vavasour ever receiving any feminine sympathy. It was reported that:

> The Queen ... dined with Sir Henry Lee ... and gave great countenance and had long discourse with Mrs Vavasour; and within a day or two after, sent a very fair jewell valued at above £100; which favour had put such new life into the old man, to see his sweet-heart so graced.[16]

As Lee had composed at least two poems for Queen Elizabeth, it behoved him to write one for Queen Anne on this occasion. Like all Lee's poems, it was self-referential and benefited much from being set to music by John Dowland.[17] Lee might still have the spirit to flatter a Queen but, at seventy-five, the flesh was weak:

> Far from triumphing Court and wonted glory
> He dwelt in shady unfrequented places,
> Time's prisoner now, he made his pastime story;
> Gladly forgets Court's erst-afforded graces.
> That goddess whom he served to heaven is gone,
> And he on earth in darkness left to moan.
> But lo, a glorious light from his dark rest
> Shone from the place where erst this goddess dwelt;
> A light whose beams the world with fruit hath blest;
> Blest was the knight while he that light beheld.
> Since then a star fixed on his head hath shined,
> And a saint's image in his heart is shrined.
>
> Ravished with joy, so graced by such a saint,
> He quite forgat his cell and self denaid;
> He thought it shame in thankfulness to faint,
> Debts due to princes must be duly paid;
> Nothing so hateful to a noble mind
> As finding kindness for to prove unkind.

---

[16]　John Chamberlain to Dudley Carleton, *CSPD*, 1603–10, p. 40; Nichols, *The Progresses ... of King James*, II, p. 208.

[17]　Published in Robert Dowland's anthology of lute songs, *A Musicall Banquet* (London, 1610), *RSTC* 7099.

> But ah! poor knight, though thus in dream he ranged,
> Hoping to serve this saint in sort most meet,
> Time with his golden locks to silver changed
> Hath with age-fetters bound him hands and feet.
> Ay me! he cries, goddess, my limbs grow faint,
> Though I Time's prisoner be, be you my saint.

The 'fruit' that had so blest the world to which Lee refers were the royal children born to Queen Anne, especially Prince Henry, for whom Lee had a special regard. Although there is no written evidence that this regard was ever reciprocated, Lee and the Prince shared many interests, such as the practice of arms and a love of the tournament, and it seems highly unlikely that Prince Henry would have come to Woodstock and not met Lee personally. Contemporary descriptions of the young Prince show that he took the utmost pleasure in practising his tournament skills every day, and his earliest public appearance was running at the ring at the age of twelve during the visit of his uncle, Christian IV of Denmark, in August 1606. Prince Henry, who died before his nineteenth birthday, never became old enough to participate in a full tournament, but always included chivalric elements, such as barriers, in his entertainments. Roy Strong claims that the Prince, had he lived, would have been the leader of a pan-European Protestant crusade against Catholicism and the future creator of a Court that would surpass that of Gloriana.[18]

Sir Henry Lee himself believed that the young Prince would at least revive the glories of the Accession Day tournaments and the practical chivalric values they represented. Lee had long emulated the practice advocated by Ramon Lull of encouraging young men in knightly practice and virtues, and had been the tournament mentor of many of his 'sons in chivalry'. Now in old age, in an undated letter to the young Prince Henry, he wrote that his wish was

> ... to bestow the remnant of my tyme all I may to please you. Your Highnes aptnenes to horsemanship, and matters of armes is such, that a meane director may make you most perfect in that exercise, on whom my duty shall never fayle, when it shall please so greate, so devine and so mightie a Prince to comaund me.[19]

What practical use the old man might have been to the young Prince is not clear, but in 1608 Lee presented Prince Henry with armour worth £200, made at the Greenwich workshop. The armour embodied Lee's hopes for the young Prince,

---

[18]   R. Strong, *Henry, Prince of Wales, and England's Lost Renaissance* (London, 1986). See also Timothy Wilks, 'The Court Culture of Prince Henry and his Circle 1603–1613', D.Phil. thesis (University of Oxford, 1987).

[19]   BL, Harleian MS 7008, f. 279.

despite John Chamberlain's derisive letter to Dudley Carleton that it 'within a year or two will serve ... neither in jest or earnest'.[20] Lee's gift was one of several suits of armour given to the heir to the throne, and, as Prince Henry grew, it became obvious that the tournament was as much a passion with him as hunting was to his father.

Prince Henry also continued the ideas developed by Lee of seeing the tournament as something more than an unscripted passage of arms for the entertainment of the Court. Lee's *Tale of Hemetes the Hermit* in 1575 had been one of the first entertainments to incorporate a tournament into the script, and it is possible to see a direct line of development from this through Sidney's 1581 'Fortress of Perfect Beauty' and Essex's ill-advised 1595 *Erophilus* to the entertainments of Prince Henry that revolved around the tournament theme. In particular, this is true of Ben Jonson and Inigo Jones's masque *Barriers*, which inaugurated the Prince's public career in January 1610. Lee would not have been in Whitehall to see the chivalric triumph of the Accession Day tournament in March 1610, staged by the Prince's followers to impress the visiting Duke of Württemberg and Prince of Brunswick, but, in the eyes of many, what had been started by Sir Henry Lee now appeared to be in good hands.

As he developed his own Court, Prince Henry shared many other tastes with Lee. Both collected paintings, although Prince Henry preferred the work of Robert Peake to that of Gheeraerts.[21] Lee sent gifts of venison to the Prince, and Woodstock itself was being refurnished for his use – a somewhat strange choice as Prince Henry was known to despise his father's addiction to the chase and shared little enthusiasm for it.[22] Woodstock under Prince Henry would have been a very different place. Before his death he was actively planning a water-garden there similar to that in his palace at Richmond, and, again, he and Lee would have shared a common interest. At Prince Henry's last visit to Woodstock, which took place after Lee's death between 28 August and 2 September 1612 and just before his own in November 1612, the Prince staged a chivalric entertainment for his family, just as Lee had staged one for his Queen thirty-seven years earlier.

---

[20]   *CSPD*, 1603–10, p. 40; Nichols, *The Progresses ... of King James*, II, p. 208.

[21]   In 'Time Stands Still', *Early Music*, 34, 3 (2006), p. 13, Anthony Rooley suggests, somewhat improbably, that the figure of Time in Peake's portrait of Prince Henry Frederick, Prince of Wales at the tilt barrier, c.1610, now at Parham House, is modelled on Lee himself. The image of a generic old man would fit any number of men of that age.

[22]   41 Pat. James I 1610–11 (grant to Henry Prince of Wales of the manor house and Manor of Woodstock).

Lee as a Public Servant in Retirement

Despite his preference for a country life, Lee still had official responsibilities in retirement. He retained his position as Master of the Armoury until 1611, but the practical work was usually delegated to his deputy and the clerk. Regardless of who was actually doing the work, all warrants dormant to pay the wages of the Greenwich armourers or the staff at the various armouries across the country continued to be paid in the name of Sir Henry Lee.[23] Clearly, the Exchequer held Lee personally responsible for the Armoury from 'the accompte beganne the ffyrste day of January 1601 [1602] and ended the laste day of December 1610'. This, delivered to Lee's heir and executor in 1611, listed monies paid biannually into 'Sir Henry Lee's handes' totalling £5,593 17s 8d.[24] When the very substantial costs for 'repayring and keepinge clene the armors within the Tower of London, Grenewich and Wollwich', the wages of named individuals employed there, the charges for provision and carriage of swords for Ireland, the costs of a coronation tournament for James I in 1603 and a 'triumph' for the visit of the Danish King in 1606 were subtracted, a bill of £389 3s 7d was presented, payable from Lee's personal estate.[25] Lee continued to sign all the Armoury accounts until his death, and while not greatly improving the administrative situation there, managed to keep himself free of the corruption at the Tower that would engulf his successor at the Armoury, Sir Thomas Monson, in 1616.

Another position Sir Henry Lee still held was the constableship of Harlech Castle, originally purchased in 1587 and held jointly with his nephew Owen Cooke.[26] It was clear from the outset that local elites resented the appointment of 'a stranger among them', and a quarrel had rapidly developed between Lee and the local MP, William Maurice. As Constable and Mayor of Harlech, Lee owned land in Harlech Marsh, which Maurice forcibly enclosed in 1592.[27] Lee visited Harlech in that year and wrote to Cecil on behalf of the townspeople, requesting that the quarter sessions and assizes of Merioneth be regularly held in the castle.

---

[23]   See *CSPD*, 1603–10, p. 434 (28 May 1608), warrant dormant to pay Sir Henry Lee Master of the Armoury to the Clerk of the Armoury at Greenwich the wages of the twenty-one armourers; *CSPD*, 1603–10, p. 445 (4 July 1608), warrant dormant to pay Sir Henry Lee £400 a year for the service of the armouries at the Tower, Hampton Court, Westminster, Windsor, Greenwich and Portsmouth and Woolwich; *CPSD*, 1603–10, p. 524 (3 July 1609), warrant to pay Sir Henry Lee £600.

[24]   Surrey History Centre (hereafter SHC), Loseley MS LM/64.

[25]   The very detailed provision of tilt staves, long pikes and parting staves for barriers, swords, vamplates and coronels in June 1603 would suggest that a coronation tournament had been planned for James I, and cancelled because of the plague.

[26]   Cecil MS 38.23 (HMC *Salis*. XIII, p. 467).

[27]   National Library of Wales (hereafter NLA), Brogyntyn archives, Clenennau Letters and Papers 58. Sir William Maurice was MP for Harlech from 1592 to 1614.

The townspeople had, he reported, given £100 to 'some who rule in those parts', to no avail. Although Cecil raised the matter in Parliament, Harlech failed to get the assizes on a regular basis, but William Maurice continued to take monetary gifts from the town. Sir Henry Lee outlived his young nephew but, despite the undivided constableship reverting back to him in 1603, he spent little time in Harlech. It is clear that Maurice coveted Lee's position, frequently claiming that, unlike Lee, his ancestors had been constables who had dwelled in the castle and kept it in good repair. By 1608 Maurice had enlisted the services of Ralph, Lord Eure, Lord President of the Marches of Wales, to press his case against Lee. Eure complained to Salisbury that Harlech

> ... a castle of strength ... [is] not fit to be in strangers' hands who neither remain nor come at any time into that country but make benefit off the fee of £50 paid without respect to the King's service.[28]

Maurice wrote to the Privy Council in 1609, accusing Lee of letting the castle fall into decay and also wrote to Lee in 1610, raising the matter. Lee's last existing letter from Ditchley in February 1610 shows that, even at seventy-seven, he was in fully possession of his faculties. He may have been an absentee constable, he admitted, but he noted that the last repair he effected on the castle had been funded in full, a rare occurrence, and he intimated that if Maurice had 'bene better with me touching the land I have in the marshe', he might have been more successful in purchasing Lee's constableship.[29]

The incident illustrates much about the interests of local gentry at this time. Undoubtedly Lee had bought the position at Harlech for his nephew, and after 1603 it became little more than a profitable sinecure. The ambitious William Maurice, busily acquiring substantial estates in North Wales and Shropshire through marriage and enclosure, became MP for Merioneth from 1594, was sheriff of Caernarvonshire and Beaumaris, was knighted in 1603, and was bailiff of Harlech. Profitable local perquisites were not numerous, and typically Maurice resented the constableship remaining in the inactive hands of an aged courtier from the previous reign. He might, however, have had more success in purchasing the position from Lee had he not enclosed Lee's lands in 1592. In matters of property, Sir Henry Lee was not one to forget an affront.

In his latter years, Lee made the journey to London for specific reasons and seldom for pleasure. In 1604 he appeared as a deponent in the Star Chamber case between his godson Sir Robert Dudley and the Countess of Leicester, who was contesting Dudley's claim to legitimacy. Lee's deposition has not survived,

---

[28] Cecil MS 126.108 (HMC *Salis.* XX, p. 295).

[29] NLW, Clenennau Letters and Papers 253 (Lee to Maurice, 8 February 1609/10).

and it seems that he could have provided little aid to his godson.[30] In December 1604 Lee and Anne Vavasour travelled up to London to stand as godparents to Marcus Gheeraerts' fifth child, Henry, at the Dutch church, but by March 1605 Lee was writing to Sir Michael Hickes that 'our coming to London is like to be seldome'. Later that year Lee Symonds, Lee's agent, noted that various items, such as the ornate saddles used on Lee's great horses, were being moved from London to Ditchley.[31]

Lee's appearance at the Garter feasts and processions at Windsor ceased after 1605, although he appeared at the Accession Day tournament in 1606 in an honorary capacity. Lee made his last journey to London in the summer of 1608 to present Prince Henry with the suit of armour noted earlier, and that year he gave up the very substantial lodgings he had held at the Savoy since 1563.[32] Even at seventy-five, Lee remained interested in the affairs of the Court and after Queen Anne's visit to Ditchley in September 1608 he claimed that he wanted 'one fling more at the Court before he die, though he thought he had taken his leave this summer'.[33]

Lee also exercised local responsibilities. He was mayor of New Woodstock and was entitled to receive a 'sugar loffe 9s 6d and a cake 9s' each Christmas.[34] He was involved in setting up a grammar school at Woodstock, endowed in 1585 by Richard Cornwall, a London skinner and Lee himself gave two messuages of land for a grammar school in Aylesbury. The old practice of leaving charitable works for posterity in one's last years was deeply ingrained, although Aylesbury fared better than Woodstock. Lee was still holding £55 of the Woodstock legacy money himself on loan on his death, and the debt was paid from his estate.

In retirement at Ditchley, Lee was not forgotten by his friends, even among the great. In 1607 Sir Thomas Lake forwarded a letter to Salisbury for the King from the Prince of Nassau that contained a 'letter of the Prince's to Sir Henry Lee' which has not survived.[35] One of the best indications as to how Sir Henry Lee passed his last few years, however, comes from the eight lively letters he wrote to Sir Michael Hickes from 1603 to 1608. Lee had been borrowing steadily from Hickes since 1598, mostly short-term loans to finance his substantial building works at Ditchley and Quarrendon, and these letters, written very much in a

[30]   CKS, U1475 (Penshurst Papers) L2/4, item 3, r.81 (Sir Edward Stafford's deposition in the case of Sir Robert Dudley). Stafford had married Sir Robert Dudley's mother, Douglas, Lady Sheffield.

[31]   BL, Lansdowne MS 89, no. 82, f. 160 (3 March 1605).

[32]   See F.G. Lee, 'The Palace of the Savoy', *Walford's Antiquarian*, ed. E. Walford, VIII (July–December 1885), pp.119–24 for an inventory of Lee's Savoy apartment.

[33]   *CSPD*, 1603–10, p. 459; Nichols, *The Progresses ... of King James*, II, p. 208.

[34]   *Woodstock Chamberlain's Accounts 1609–1650*, ed. M. Maslen (Stroud, 1993), LVIII, p. 3.

[35]   Cecil MS 128.42 (HMC *Salis*. XIX, p. 334).

spirit of friendship between the two men, reveal many aspects of Lee's private life. By 1604 Lee finally admitted the illegibility of his own handwriting and employed his nephew Lee Symonds as amanuensis and bookkeeper. Ostensibly, the purpose of the letters was financial, dealing with Lee's loans. In 1606 Lee still owed Hickes £300 which he was repaying at a £100 a year plus 10 per cent interest, payable biannually. In March he wrote to Hickes to say that Symonds had sent £10 and £110 would be paid shortly, with 'the rest' being provided in November. Lee asked Hickes' forbearance for 'one of the two hundred pounds three months longer'.[36] In April 1607 Lee refers to the 'remaynt of the three hundred pounds', as £130 had been paid to Hickes 'a yere past' via Lee's clothier Harry Russell of 'Cyssitter' – an interesting insight into the circulation of money at that time. The sum of £120 was promised for 1607 with the £110 remaining to be paid in 1608.

Lee was now grappling again with his own accounts, which had been thrown into disarray in 1607 by 'the deathe of Lee Symonds who kept these reckonninges, whose notes I fynd not'.[37] With the appearance of the first indications that wool prices, which had been buoyant for a decade, were beginning to fall, Lee added that he would prefer to repay Hickes in July 1608 when 'my woole monney should come', but it was possible that he would withhold his clip as 'I shall not sell it [to] my further losse'.[38] On 4 July 1608 Lee wrote from Ditchley asking for a year's indulgence. He was, he said, 'ou £1200 rent ... which will not come in until midsummer next ... when, if God will, I shall be able to do much more than I can now'.[39] Despite what Lee called his 'bad fortune and former unthriftiness', borrowing was not necessarily a sign of impecunity; it was more a reflection of the cash-flow problems that could face even prosperous wool graziers, dependent, as they were, on a biannual income from the shear and from rents.

Lee's need for Hickes' money to finance his passion for building continued long into his retirement. His work on his 'four goodly manors', begun around 1595, continued with the imparking of Ditchley in 1605, but his chief concern was his ancestral lands in Buckinghamshire.[40] In 1607 Lee had building work in hand at Quarrendon on the church and possibly the almshouse, and invited Hickes to 'come this way ... [to] see my further preparations for this tyme and the tyme to come'.[41] In July 1608 Lee apologized to Hickes that since he had 'sondry fron[d]s in the fyre and [was] mending my house at Burstone in Buckingham

---

36   BL, Lansdowne MS 89, no. 82, f. 160.
37   BL, Lansdowne MS 90, no. 36, f. 72 (from Ditchley, 20 April 1607, 'Cyssitter' is Cirencester).
38   BL, Lansdowne MS 90, no. 36, f. 72.
39   BL, Lansdowne MS 90, no. 98, f. 196.
40   ORO, DIL XXI/17.
41   BL, Lansdowne MS 90, no. 36, f. 72.(20 April 1607).

shyre ... the payinge of your mony at your tyme appoynted' was in doubt.[42] Lee was not spending his retirement in idleness.

What is remarkable about Lee's letters to Hickes is that, for all the financial dealings between them, Hickes retained a genuine affection for, and friendship with, Lee. Hickes and his wife received numerous invitations to visit. In August 1606 Lee wrote that:

> ... the kinge of Denmark ... is upon his departure, all the shewe at Tibbalts finished, your care lighted and the tyme of the yeare more fitt for pleasure and visitynge of freinds. It is but sixteen myles further to come to this homely manner and I think I heare my lady say she will accompany you.[43]

In May 1607 Lee urged Hickes:

> ... if you will make a sommer voyage ... I will meete you and my lady at my house nearest to London not above 27 or 28 myles of[f] ... from hence would I guyde you from one house to another with the help of an Alehouse untill you come to Woodstocke from hence to Ditchley [and] so to Lee's Rest.[44]

In one of his last letters to Hickes, in November 1607, Lee paid his friend the following compliment:

> ... more kyndnes more truthe and playne meaning I never found than in Sir Michael Hickes ... my debts by bond ... may have an end but my love for your kynd courtesy must end when I leave the world.[45]

Sir Michael Hickes, apart from being an excellent friend, was Lee's social equal, having risen to be a 'country gentleman and man of affairs' through his work as patronage secretary to Burghley and as an intimate of Sir Robert Cecil, now Earl of Salisbury.[46] Lee clearly felt that he could mention his mistress Anne Vavasour to Hickes in a way he could never do in his correspondence with Salisbury or the Earl of Shrewsbury, and the letters give an insight into the domestic felicity that existed for some twenty-one years between Lee and his mistress.

Anne Vavasour is mentioned in all eight letters to Hickes, and Lee never neglected to send their joint love to Lady Hickes in the manner of an established married couple. Lee's Rest, which Lee had built for Anne at Ditchley in the

---

42   BL, Lansdowne MS 90, no. 98, f. 196.

43   BL, Lansdowne MS 89, no. 98, f. 191 (8 August 1606).

44   BL, Lansdowne MS 90, no. 37, f. 74 (4 May 1607).

45   BL, Lansdowne MS 90, no. 48, f. 95 (23 November 1607).

46   A.G.R Smith, *Servant to the Cecils: The Life of Sir Michael Hickes, 1543–1612* (London, 1977), p. 109.

mid-1590s, became their home, and all invitations were issued jointly. There had never been any question of Anne returning to Court, but she received the King and Queen at Lee's Rest in 1603 and 1608. Lee, unable to give Anne his name, did his best to shield her from scandal and harassment. Her husband, John Finch, must have reappeared in 1605, as Lee gave him an annuity for £20 which he subsequently sold. If Anne was fortunate that she found both love and protection from a courtier who was untroubled by her past, it is clear that Lee's longevity was, to some extent, the result of her care. In 1606 he sent Hickes 'well wishes from Mrs Vauasor ... through whose louinge care & diligence I doe throughe gods goodness continewe the longer'.[47] He described Lee's Rest as 'my corner of resolution ... where by good loue I will leve the world and end my last days'.[48] Evidence of such domestic contentment was rare in the correspondence of other courtiers.

Lee's Health, Funeral, Will and Tomb

For the greater part of his life, Sir Henry Lee enjoyed remarkably good health. The fact that he tilted until his fifty-seventh year is notable in itself, and the score cheque for 1590 confirms that Lee's participation was far from merely ceremonial. The alterations made to his third suit of armour would suggest that he wore field armour well into his sixties – probably in 1596 when he visited the Earl of Essex at Plymouth prior to the Cadiz expedition. He certainly hunted well into his seventh decade. Lee outlived not only his immediate contemporaries, such as the Queen and the Earl of Leicester, but also his five younger brothers. Like many of his contemporaries, he suffered from gout, which in his letters to Burghley he described as 'their joint enemy', and, given his physically active life, he probably had arthritis.[49] When necessary, Lee consulted the leading physicians of the day. In June 1575 he obtained permission to seek 'councell in physicke' from the Catholic Dr Atslowe, then imprisoned at the Tower of London for his support of Mary Stuart.[50]

Lee's health appeared robust until early in 1587 when, on a visit to his brother at Hatfield, Yorkshire, he 'fell sycke of a contynuall fever which held me xxii dayes ... excedynge wecke'.[51] This probably accounted for Lee's uncharacteristic

---

[47]   BL, Lansdowne MS 89, no. 82, f. 160 (3 March 1606).

[48]   BL, Lansdowne MS 90, no. 37, f. 74 (4 May 1607).

[49]   On several occasions Lee described his limbs as 'fast bound'. He appeared at some date at the tournament as 'the inchaunted knight whose armes be locked for a tyme' and who sends the damsel of the Queen of the Fairies with a cupid jewel brooch to present to the Queen. See BL, Add. MS 41499A, ff. 1–16.

[50]   Dasent, *APC*, VIII, p. 396 (10 June 1575).

[51]   BL, Harleian MS 286, f. 100 (Lee to Walsingham, February 1587).

absence from the funeral of his friend Sir Philip Sidney in February 1587. Atslowe attended Lee on this occasion, and Lee wrote to Walsingham in February 1587, requesting that the doctor visit him again so he might be 'clered of the drages of my dyssease'.[52] Lee could recover rapidly when necessary and later that year was covering many miles on horseback to mediate between Gilbert Talbot, sixth Earl of Shrewsbury, living in London and George Talbot his son, the future seventh Earl of Shrewsbury, living in Sheffield. Lee was eager to serve his Queen when invasion from Spain threatened in 1588 and wrote to Walsingham that 'my body, (God be thanked) never better in younger years never lustier nore my mind never warmer to prove myself'.[53]

Lee's retirement from the tilt in 1590 was timely. In September 1591 he confessed to Heneage that he could no longer follow the Queen's summer progress as:

> I am owld ... the payne and fluxe I fele in my eye doth rather increase than dymynyshe. I fynd myselfe evill provyded for of all thynges necessesary for me ... the inconvenyences of progresses [make me] more fytte to pray for her Ma[jes]tie than ... to wrestell wth the umors of cowrt.[54]

Despite this, Lee travelled to Harlech in February 1592 and received the Queen on progress at Woodstock and Ditchley in September. From 1595 until 1597, he was prepared to entertain the possibility of becoming either Vice-Chamberlain or Comptroller of the Household, both demanding Court positions. In June 1596, in his capacity of Master of the Armoury, he accompanied Fulke Greville to inspect the fleet at Plymouth.[55] His health affected his most triumphant moment at Windsor in 1597 as his formidable cousin Elizabeth, Dowager Lady Russell, related to Sir Robert Cecil that Lee's 'payne' had forced him to leave his Garter investiture early, but had thanked Cecil for 'sending George [the Order of the Garter medal] from his own neck'.[56] Lee recovered to attend the annual Garter feasts and processions on a fairly regular basis.

From 1598 few of Lee's letters fail to mention his physical condition, especially the lameness associated with gout.[57] When Orsini, Duke of Bracciano, visited Woodstock to hunt in December 1600 during his visit to England, Lee

---

[52] Atslowe was also attending the son of the Earl of Northumberland, who died in 1587, probably in the north of England.

[53] TNA, PRO, SP12/213/95; *CSPD*, 1581–90, p. 515 (28 June 1588).

[54] Cecil MS 20.26 (HMC *Salis*. IV, p. 136) (Lee to Heneage from the Vyne, 18 September 1591).

[55] Cecil MS 14.46 (HMC *Salis*. VI, p. 208) (Gorges to Cecil, 3 June 1596).

[56] Cecil MS 58.53 (HMC *Salis*. VII, p. 536) (Lady Russell to Sir Robert Cecil, April 1597).

[57] See, for example, Cecil MS 177.123 (HMC *Salis*. VIII, p. 403) (Lee to Essex 1598); Cecil MS 70.87 (HMC *Salis*. IX, p. 196) (Lee to Cecil 1599).

received him from his bed at Woodstock Lodge 'much against my wil'.[58] The ten weeks during which Lee was 'forsed to keep his bedde' provided him with a good excuse not to ride to London when news reached him of the Essex rebellion and the arrest and execution of his cousin Thomas Lee on 8 February 1601.[59] To amend his 'newe passyon of the gowte', Lee wrote to Cecil in March 1601 that he intended 'to see Bathe' and then to 'pylgrymage ... to the welles in Cheshire'.[60] Lee was in vogue. The therapeutic well at Utkinton, Cheshire, had only been made public in August 1600 and by 1601 it was attracting more than 2,000 visitors a day.[61]

In May 1601 Lee was reporting to Cecil that, having reached Bath, 'the death of Mr Done, the governer of [the] Cheshire welles and some other of my friends who sought health and found death in that place' had halted his journey until 'time shall make trial' whether the Cheshire wells were efficacious or not.[62] The news of the death of Mr Done, Forester Royal of Utkinton Hall was somewhat premature, but Lee refrained from travelling north. His correspondence with Sir Robert Cecil about his health was typical of the time. Both Cecil and his father, Burghley, were preoccupied with their own health and kept meticulous notes on the medications they took. Healing waters and 'physick' were not the only remedies: Lee wrote to Cecil that 'exercyce is as necessary for your healthe as chaynge of ayer'.[63]

Despite his earlier incapacity, in 1603 Lee threw himself into six hectic months' service for King James I. Such effort took its toll on a septuagenarian: in December 1603 he wrote to Hickes that 'it is now nine weeks synce I came owt of my chamber', possibly accounting for the King's attempt to replace him at Woodstock.[64] Lee, although not suffering from any major illness, increasingly fell prey to the crippling effects of gout, which seriously affected his general mobility. In August 1606 he complained to Hickes that 'the gowte had too longe possesion of my ioyntes, therefore my retourne to London very unlikely'.[65] In 1607 he was treated by the eminent Sir William Paddy, former physician to Lord Burghley and personal physician to James I. Like many of

---

[58]   Cecil MS 82.80, (HMC *Salis*. X, p. 427) (Lee to Cecil, 22 December 1600).

[59]   Cecil MS 76.70 (HMC *Salis*. XI, p. 52) (Lee to Cecil 14 February 1601); Cecil MS 76.79 (HMC *Salis*. XI, p. 58) (Lee to Cecil, 16 February 1601).

[60]   Cecil MS 77.33 (HMC *Salis*. XI, pp. 110–11) (6 March 1601).

[61]   G.W., *Newes out of Cheshire of the New Found Well* (London, 1600), *RSTC* 24904.

[62]   Cecil MS 98.139 (HMC *Salis*. XIV, p. 178) (27 May 1601).

[63]   Cecil MS 81.74 (HMC *Salis*. X, p. 307). Lee was not alone in this. In 1573 Leicester had advised Elizabeth that 'so good a medycyne I have alway found exersise with the open good ayre ... my best remedye ageynst those dellycate deceases gotten about yor deynty cytty of London': TNA, PRO, SP15/17/205.

[64]   BL, Lansdowne MS 88, no. 94, f. 185.

[65]   BL, Lansdowne MS 89, no. 98, f. 191.

his contemporaries, Lee suffered acutely from constipation and haemorrhoids, and Paddy's notebook gives graphic details of results from his prescriptions for 'a purging physike and a puke'.[66] By July 1608, despite journeying to London and travelling between his various estates, Lee was writing to Hickes that 'my hand cannott nowe aid me to wryte muche nor my legges to cary my body one pace. My strength [is] dyminished as my yeares increaseth.'[67] He used an amanuensis reluctantly, signed all his later letters and appears to have stayed mentally alert to the end. At his death, he was being attended by Oxford physician John Cheynell.

Lee was certainly well in possession of his faculties when his will was drawn up on 6 October 1609.[68] As a result of various legal devices, Lee was free to leave his properties as he wished. With a consciousness of what was due to his family name and in the same spirit with which he developed the Lee hereditary holdings at Quarrendon, he dug deep into his own family tree to secure an heir. Lee outlived not only his own generation, but also the majority of his nephews, few of whom were legitimate. He seems to have wanted an heir of his own name and eventually identified the grandson of his grandfather's brother, 'a one-eied young man' Henry Lee, later first baronet.[69] The inquisition taken after Lee's death shows that the settlement of Lee's multiple land interests and leases was complicated and already encumbered with a considerable jointure of £700 a year settled on Anne Vavasour for sixty years or the term of her life.

Lee had foreseen that his own demise would leave his mistress and their bastard son vulnerable and he tried his utmost to deal with the situation. Anne was still technically married to John Finch and, as her husband, he would have had rights over her property. Lee left to his executors, Sir Thomas Vavasour, Anne's brother, and John Walter Lee the houses and furnishings of Lee's Rest at Ditchley and Laelius in Buckinghamshire, together with half his furniture and plate, for such uses as he appointed in writing. These were clearly for the use of Anne with the reversion going to Lee's heir, and she was required to submit an inventory of all furnishings. Among the usual small legacies was an annuity of £40 to Lee's natural, but illegitimate, son Thomas Vavasour.

Awareness of imminent death was not unusual in Tudor correspondence. As early as 1587 Lee was making reference to 'when god shall call me awaye', and this was a refrain he repeated regularly as he grew older.[70] Lee made no statement whatsoever as to his religious views, and there is little to suggest that he was anything other than conventionally religious, not particularly devout and without extreme opinions. His letters reveal nothing more than the customary

---

[66] Bodl., Rawlinson MS A369, f. 74 (6 March 1607).

[67] BL, Lansdowne MS 90, no. 98, f. 196 (4 June 1608).

[68] TNA, PRO, PROB 11/117.

[69] John Aubrey's description in *Brief Lives*, ed. Oliver Lawson Dick (London, 1992), II, p. 30. Until 1932 all owners of Ditchley had 'Henry Lee' somewhere in their names.

[70] BL, Harleian MS 286, f. 100.

'god be thanked' – for example, when referring to an improvement in his health. As a major local landowner, Lee held the advowson of St Mary's, Aylesbury, and presented at least three incumbents as the lessee tenant under the prebendary.[71] None of these – John Hitchcock in 1572, John Price in 1597 and Robert Bell in 1598 – were notable for holding anything other than conventional beliefs. The same is true of Lee's other presentments; he appeared more intent on helping friends or fellows of his own New College Oxford and his brother's St John's College than furthering any specific religious tenet. In 1567 Lee presented Robert Challoner, his own household steward, to the living at Fleetmarston and in 1594 tried unsuccessfully to obtain the wardenship of Winchester College for William Swaddon, a fellow of New College. Cromwell Lee's illegitimate son, John Lee of St John's College Oxford became rector of Fleetmarston and Wootton in 1601, and was followed by two other St John's men: Thomas Jones in 1609 and Theophilus Tuer in 1610.

By the standards of the day, the virtual absence of any religious statement in a very long life is interesting, although Lee's contemporary, John Selden, in his *Table-Talk*, noted that 'gentlemen have ever been Temperate in their Religion'.[72] It is possible that Lee deliberately kept his religious beliefs above suspicion. His wife, Anne Paget, had been a member of the large recusant Paget family, and whereas her father, Sir William Paget, had been at best a *politique* in religion, Lady Lee, her five sisters and their husbands, as well as her two brothers Thomas and Charles Paget, maintained dangerous and potentially treasonable Catholic affiliations throughout Elizabeth's reign. Lee took pains to separate himself from the whole Paget clan.

Frances Yates and others have taken Lee's poems, especially 'Time's eldest son' and the better-known 'My golden locks time hath to silver turned', as proof of the Elizabethans' substitution of the Virgin Mary by the Virgin Queen.[73] By extension, it has been presumed that Lee must have shared these sentiments and be conversant with the words of the Catholic liturgy which sprang easily to his lips:[74]

---

[71]   Aylesbury, in the diocese of Lincoln, retained its prebendary, and the Prebendary of Aylesbury occasionally occupied the living himself. More usually, Lee was allowed to present the next incumbent.

[72]   John Selden, *Table-Talk; being the Discourses of John Selden, Esq.* (London, 1689), p. 64, Wing S2437.

[73]   See E.C. Wilson, *England's Eliza* (Cambridge, MA, 1939; repr. 1966), p. 206; F. Yates, 'Elizabethan Chivalry: The Romance of the Accession Day Tilts', *Journal of the Warburg and Courtauld Institutes*, XX (1957), p. 74; R.H. Wells, *Spenser's Faerie Queen and the Cult of Elizabeth* (London, 1983), p. 46.

[74]   John Dowland, *Second Book of Songs*, ed. E.H. Fellowes (London, 1600), nos. VI–VIII, p. 469; S. May, *The English Courtier Poets: The Poems and their Contexts*, 2nd edn (Columbia, MI, 1999), pp. 356–7.

Time's eldest son, old age, the heyre of ease,
Strengths foe, loves woe, and foster to devotion,
Bids gallant youthes in martial prowes please'
As for himselfe hee hath no earthly motion,
But thinkes sighes, teares, vowes, praiers and sacrifice
As good as shewes, maskes, justes or tilt devises.

Then sit thee downe and say thy *Nunc dimittis,*
With *De profundis, Credo* and *Te Deum,*
Chant *Miserere,* for what now so fit is
As that, or this, *Paratum est cor meum?*
O that thy Saint would take in worth thy hart,
Thou canst not please hir with a better part.

When others sing *Venite exultemus*
Stand by, and turne to *Noli aemulari;*
For *quare fremuerunt* use *Oremus,*
Vivat Eliza for an *Ave Maria;*
And teach those swains that lives [*sic*] about thy cell
To say *Amen* when thou dost pray so well.[75]

Helen Hackett makes the telling point that the Latin phrases quoted were not necessarily a sign of Catholicism but were still in continual use by the Elizabethan church in the Book of Common Prayer.[76] She also points out that Lee, like the Queen and the Earl of Leicester, were of a generation that would have known the Catholic liturgy from childhood, regardless of what their own adult views might have been. In some ways there may have been some truth in Frances Yates' assertions. Lee made no reference whatsoever to his own religious beliefs. All his actions and writings reveal his devotion to his sovereign and the tenets of chivalry. Possibly there was little room for anything else.

With an old man's zeal, Lee devoted much time to the preparation of his lavish tomb in St Peter's Church at Quarrendon and that of Anne Vavasour, when she should need it.[77] These two tombs with their inscriptions were finished by 1609, and tombs for Lee's mother and father were also erected. Money was left in Lee's will for tombs for his brothers, his sister Joyce and even for his uncle Sir Thomas

---

[75]   This poem by Lee is recorded in John Dowland's *Second Book of Songs.*

[76]   H. Hackett, *Virgin Mother, Maiden Queen,* 2nd edn (Basingstoke, 1996), pp. 144–50.

[77]   Chambers gives a detailed description of the Quarrendon tombs in Sir Henry Lee: An Elizabethan Portrait (Oxford, 1936), pp. 301–8. His descriptions are reconstructed from BL, Lansdowne MS 874, f. 35 and f. 50b (Nicholas Charles' Inscriptions, 1611); Browne Willis (12 April 1704); Bodl. Willis MS, 13 f.111v and George Lipscomb in *Gentleman's Magazine,* LXXXVII (1817), I, p. 504 and II, p. 105; LXXXVIII (1818), I, p. 116.

Wyatt, but these do not appear to have been constructed. Lee's monument was described as an altar tomb of white and red veined marble, bearing the painted and gilded alabaster figure of a recumbent mailed knight with sword in hand and the accoutrements of the Order of the Garter. The inscriptions, under Lee's motto of '*Fide et constantia*', were more a statement of Lee's knightly virtues than a testimony of any devout beliefs. Above Lee's tomb was his *Memoriae Sacrum*, composed by his kinsman William Scott.[78]

The adjacent empty tomb of Anne Vavasour was said to have had an effigy of a kneeling lady. The inscription on it was simple, and in an era when virtue, piety and fecundity were paramount in women, Lee's testimony to their love is very moving.[79]

> Vnder this stone intombed lies a faire & worthy Dame
> Daughter of Henry Vauasor Ann Vauasour her name
> Shee liuing with Sir Henry Lee for loue long tyme did dwell
> Death Could not part them but that here they rest within one cell.

Sir Henry Lee died on 12 February 1611.[80] With his accustomed thoroughness, the preparations for his funeral had long been complete, and Lee received a spectacular funeral as behoved an Elizabethan Knight of the Garter on 4 April 1611 at Quarrendon.[81] His heir, soon to be promoted to baronet, and distant members of his family attended, as did his executors and servants, his great horses, Garter King of Arms and Lancaster and Chester Heralds, representatives of the King and Oxford University, members of leading Buckinghamshire and Oxfordshire families, and some eighty poor men to represent the years of Lee's life. Somewhere among the lower ranks of mourners marched his bastard son, his only descendant. William Swaddon, who Lee had tried to help in 1594, was now Prebendary of Aylesbury and preached at the funeral. Such great funerals, similar to that of Philip Sidney or Sir Henry Unton, were not uncommon among gentleman at this time. They were more a testimony to worldly achievement than a statement of devout faith.

Lee's monuments were never completed and did not last long. Anne Vavasour's monument lasted only a short time: within a year it was the subject

---

[78]   See Appendix 7 for the full inscription.

[79]   BL, Add. MS 14417, p. 22v (Proceedings at the funeral of Sir Henry Lee at Quarrendon on April 4 1611). See also D. Lyson and S. Lyson, *Magna Britannia: being a Concise Topographical Account of the Several Counties of Great Britain* (London, 1806), I, p. 624.

[80]   From Lee's *Memoriae Sacrum*.

[81]   BL, Add. MS 14417, f. 22b (Nicholas Charles' papers, 'Proceedings at the funerals of … Sir Henry Lee KG').

of crude graffiti and demolished by order of the bishop.[82] Anne herself was hounded for her possessions by Lee's heir and after a salacious epigram by Sir John Harington to 'Lelia' was published in 1615, she again found herself the subject of ribald slander. When she remarried in 1618, Sir Henry Lee (Bart.) was swift to pounce. He discovered that John Finch was still alive, and the new Sir Henry had a charge of bigamy brought against her, potentially a capital offence. When the case came before the High Commission in 1621, Anne, at nearly sixty years of age, was condemned to pay a fine of £2,000 but with 'dispensation from public penitence or other bodily penalty'.[83] With the abandonment of Quarrendon by the Lees, Sir Henry Lee's tomb fell into disrepair and was subsequently demolished. *Sic transit gloria.*

Some Reflections on Lee's Final Years

For many at Court, by 1611 Lee was more a curiosity of a bygone age than a figure of any significance. Despite the lavishness of the funeral, there were few statements of regret or surprise at his passing. It became merely another item of interest in letters sent from the Court that the old man had finally died.[84] Lee's coveted official offices at Woodstock, at the Armoury and at Harlech Castle were rapidly occupied by others and his stall at Windsor filled by a new Knight of the Garter.[85] But if Sir Henry Lee was not particularly missed he, the great Elizabethan, avoided seeing the changes of the years to come.

Living only until 1611 and at some remove from the Court, Lee could partake in the hopes and expectations of the new Jacobean age without experiencing its

---

[82]   The graffito was much repeated and read:

Here lies the good old knight Sir Harry,
Who loved well but would not marry;
While he lived and had his feeling,
She did lie and he was kneeling.
Now he's dead and cannot feel,
He doth lie and she doth kneel.

[83]   Pat. Roll, 2272, *CSPD*, 1619–23, p. 239.
[84]   See BL, *CSP Buccleuch* MS, I, p. 97 (19 February 1611, George Blundell to Sir Ralph Winwood); NLW, Clenennau Letters and Papers 484 (19 February 1611, Sir William Maurice to Ralph Lord Eure); Thomas Birch, *The Court of James I*, 2 vols (London, 1600), I, p. 108 (6 March 1611, John Sanford to Sir Thomas Edmondes); BL, *CSP Downshire* MS, III, p. 28.
[85]   During the twentieth century it was the stall occupied by Sir Edmund Hillary. This seems to have been more than appropriate.

later concomitant disappointments. On 29 March 1611 Samuel Calvert wrote to William Trumbull, the ambassador in Brussels that:

> Viscount Bindon and Sir Henry Lea are dead, and two Garters void ... when you are returned, you may find a change at Court, not the houses or mansions, but the men and manners, both growing from worse to stark naught.[86]

It was a change that Sir Henry Lee was not called upon to witness.

---

[86] BL, *CSP Downshire* MS, II, p. 42.

Chapter 8

An Evaluation of 'The Most Accomplished Cavaliero I Have Ever Seen'

Few men are unique, but many have singular talents which set them apart from their contemporaries. Sir Henry Lee was one such man and is worth studying in his own right. In 1575 Monsieur de Champenaye, ambassador in England from the Low Countries assessed his unique qualities in the following terms: 'a man of arms, excellently mounted, richly armed, and indeed the most accomplished cavaliero I have ever seen'.[1] Lee was a member of the elite gentry, of long-established wealth and only one degree below the peerage. He lived a very long and sociable life, and to study him is to become acquainted with a wide range of his contemporaries and social equals. Such a study can therefore give insights into the lives of other courtier gentlemen and show something of their typical concerns, values, expectations and frustrations.

It is possible to discern three distinct, but not necessarily exclusive, groups of people that fall within the category of 'elite gentry'. A gentleman could be a member of all three groups, and over time Lee demonstrated an affinity to each one. The majority of 'elite gentry' belonged to the predominant category, the county gentry. These were wealthy landowners whose principal interests lay in sheep-breeding and the acquisition and management of their estates. By visiting the Court in their youth to pay homage and service to their monarch, they would briefly have been 'courtier gentlemen'. They would then return home to become the backbone of the Elizabethan commonweal, serving as local magistrates, MPs and muster-masters. The government's dependence on these gentlemen to provide stability in the provinces is illustrated in the Lord Keeper's speech in November 1599 as he exhorted MPs to return to their estates:

> ... there to maynteyne hospitalitie, and relieve their poure neighboures, and to see good order kept, whereby natural Love will growe, and be continued between Landlordes and their Tenants and the gentlemen and those of the poorer and meaner sorte ... for the goode and quiet of the Common Weale.[2]

---

[1]   Frederic Perrenot, Sieur de Champagney, Segar *Honor Military and Civill*, Book IV, (RSTC 22164), p. 200.

[2]   TNA, PRO, SP12/273/35.

The county gentlemen might entertain the Queen when on progress and at their own cost, and might erect a royal coat-of-arms or portrait in their houses as mute and lasting testimony to the event.[3] They would pay their taxes, but their priorities lay with their lands and the promotion of their families through advantageous marriages. Some, like the Spencers and the Dormers, would concentrate all their time on developing their family wealth and estates. Others, like the Treshams, would be forced reluctantly into a provincial role by their adherence to the Catholic faith. Many would build new fashionable houses and, with the accession of James I, purchase a title for themselves and their heirs. Lee, as a substantial landowner, played the 'elite gentry' role expected of him as magistrate and MP for his county. But, despite telling the Earl of Shrewsbury that he was 'a mere contry man, no cowrtyar', the comfortable role of county gentleman was clearly insufficiently stimulating for Sir Henry Lee.[4]

A second group were the courtier gentlemen who sought profitable service at Court, sometimes of a bureaucratic nature, sometimes as a Gentleman Pensioner or in the royal household. For some, like Cecil, Buckhurst, Hatton, Heneage, Walsingham and Stanhope, this involved following a well-defined route from university through the Inns of Court to royal service. The rewards could be great, even occasionally rising to a peerage. For many others, like Edward Dyer, constant attendance at Court in the faint hope of gaining some lucrative positions was a frustrating path to financial ruin. Lee clearly cherished his Crown appointments and the status they gave him, as well as the opportunity to serve his Queen, although they also brought him many frustrations and, overall, little financial reward. His role as Steward and Lieutenant at Woodstock gave him some freedom of action, but his decisions could be overruled by others, such as Burghley. His position as Master of the Armoury required attendance in London, the financial rewards were few, and it proved impossible to accomplish the task of combating the corruption in the system. Some of the frustration he felt during his uncharacteristic pursuit of the vice-chamberlainship emerges in the decision to commission a portrait of himself with his dog.

There remained a third group: the courtier gentlemen who preferred to serve the Queen away from the Court, in roles that offered them both greater freedom of action and the possibility of great rewards. Several, like Sir Francis Drake, speculated with foreign trade and exploration in the New World, while others, like Sir Jerome Horsey and Sir Jerome Bowes, travelled to Russia and acted as ambassadors to Moscow and agents of the Muscovy Company. Yet others, like Sir Thomas Shirley of Wiston House, Sussex, sought to further English trade with Persia and the Levant. Many served themselves before they served their Queen, but there was a wealth of potential talent in this group of gentlemen. Each is

---

[3]   See M.H. Cole, *The Portable Queen: Elizabeth I and the Politics of Ceremony* (Amherst, MA, 1999), pp. 181–202 for a list of Elizabeth's hosts when on progress.

[4]   LPL, Shrewsbury Papers, 701, f. 145 (15 July 1594).

worthy of a study, and it was unfortunate that Burghley and Walsingham could channel only some of their potential talents into activities that would benefit the commonweal. Sir Henry Lee fits in well with this group. He was more devoted to the commonweal than most – unique in the specific service he brought his Queen but typical of a group of men who all had singular talents. An important factor in the success of these men was the extent to which they enjoyed freedom of action and freedom of choice – something that Lee was fortunate to possess.

Why Did Sir Henry Lee Enjoy Greater Freedom of Action than Other Courtier Gentlemen?

What gave Sir Henry Lee his freedom of action? It is, perhaps, what Lee was not which gave him the freedom to choose what he would become. First, Lee was neither a peer of the realm nor a scion of a noble house; he was, and remained, a gentleman. In the late Tudor Court, the distinction between the aristocracy and the gentry was clear, even though the boundaries could be porous. If we are to believe Fulke Greville, Queen Elizabeth herself, when intervening in the quarrel between Philip Sidney and the Earl of Oxford in 1581, stressed 'the difference in degree between earls and gentlemen, the respect inferiors ought to show their superiors, and the necessity in Princes to maintain their own creations'.[5] Sidney, reminded by his father of 'the noble blood yow are descended of' and the need to 'be an Ornament to that illustre Famylie', was acutely conscious of the gap between his lineage and talents, and his status at Court.[6]

Philip Sidney had a position to maintain, which was expensive. Lacking his own fortune, and with a father financially ruined in royal service, he was heir to both his uncles, the Earls of Leicester and Warwick, but his hopes and expectations could be dashed by the birth of a legitimate heir to either of them. Neither Sidney nor Robert Devereux, Earl of Essex, had the freedom of action Lee possessed to pursue what alternative career they chose, be it military action or travel.

Lee, on the other hand, had the advantage in being secure and content with his pedigree: the Lees had been armigerous for several generations. Unlike more aspiring gentlemen such as Sir Henry Sidney, Lee saw no need to resort to the popular tactic of procuring a pedigree from the College of Arms proving his descent from some fictitious twelfth-century ancestor.[7] Unlike Sir Roger

---

[5]   F. Greville, *The Prose Works of Fulke Greville, Lord Brooke*, ed. J. Gouws (Oxford, 1986), p. 41; L. Stone, *The Crisis of the Aristocracy, 1540–1880* (Oxford, 1986), p. 747.

[6]   A. Collins, *Letters and Memorials of State ... [of the Sidney family]*, 2 vols (London, 1746), I, p. 294.

[7]   CKS, U1475(Penshurst Papers) T4/1–25; U1475 F15 (pedigree prepared by Robert Cooke, Chester Herald, proving Sidney's descent from the fictitious Sir William de Sidenie c.1151–1208).

Manners, third son of the Earl of Rutland, Lee had no great family interests to uphold at Court, and, with the exception of the unfortunate Thomas Lee, no nephews or cousins to rescue from their follies.

In addition, Lee was not a poor man and nor had he experienced a long wait to inherit his estates. In this he was reasonably unusual. The gap between coming to maturity and inheriting land from a dominant father often forced young gentlemen to importune for some lowly office at Court, pursue unwelcome legal training, seek military service abroad or, if all else failed, pursue some wealthy widow. Lee needed to employ none of these financial expedients, and this again gave him considerable freedom of action. Although his finances fluctuated throughout his life and his attendance at Court proved costly, he had both the security of considerable lands and the optimistic assurance of a man who had never known the need to struggle financially. Moreover, by choice he did not have a large family of hopeful children, which was often the ruination of prosperous county gentlemen.

Nor did Lee appear to have any great ambitions for political office, if one interprets his pursuit of the vice-chamberlainship from 1596 to 1597 as solely a response to Burghley's and Cecil's flattering suggestions that he should do so. This was not because of lack of interest. Lee's many letters – to his brother Sir Richard Lee, to Burghley and to Cecil – reveal that he followed foreign and military affairs closely. He had political views, but seldom gave advice and displayed no aspirations to a seat on the Privy Council.

Gentlemen wishing to pursue a political career needed an influential patron, an informed concern for interest groups at Court, an eye on the next political opportunity and continuous expensive attendance in London. It was possible for ambitious sons of merchants, such as Sir Thomas Lake, Sir Thomas Smith and Sir Michael Hickes, to become gentlemen with political influence, having beaten a lucrative path from local grammar school to university and then employment with a great noble. Lee, on the other hand, was largely apolitical and appeared to place little value on political office. This gave him the freedom to make friendships where he chose and to absent himself from Court for long periods of time if it suited him to do so.

Lee was also no religious zealot. He kept his own religious beliefs private and demonstrated only conventional conformity to the established church. He chose to keep his distance from the Catholic recusant gentry, especially those in his wife's family. He had no leanings towards extreme Protestantism and embarked on no crusade that would detract from the service of his Queen. Lastly, Sir Henry Lee was no callow youth when he came into royal favour. He was thirty-five, somewhat divorced from youth's ambitions, whims, enthusiasms and expediencies. He had had time to decide what his priorities were and, unlike many of his contemporaries, had the freedom and the money to realize them.

What Made Sir Henry Lee so Singular?

Apart from some over-effusive book dedications, little was written directly about Sir Henry Lee during his lifetime until Sir William Segar published his *Booke of honor and armes* in 1590 and *Honor Military and Civill* in 1602. Although Segar's principal motive for engaging in these tasks may have been to enhance the reputation of the College of Arms by association with the most famous proponent of the tournament extant, the primary sources do show that Sir William's identification of Lee as a chivalric hero was apposite. Many gentlemen of Sir Henry Lee's status and the majority of nobles claimed adherence to chivalric values as the accepted code of conduct among men of honour. Whereas Lee would have had to be a saint to live up to Segar's descriptions of his chivalric virtues, he was better placed than many to live up to this code. Other men were often forced to compromise their principles by political ambitions, family circumstances, religion or financial problems. Lee, by contrast, left himself sufficient freedom of action to attempt to follow the tenets of chivalry. As 'the Queen's knight', it was fortunate that he did.

The Elizabethan tournaments may now be seen to be anachronistic, but in the popular imagination of the time they represented something tangible: a code of knightly conduct and an order of chivalry. The public spectacle of the Virgin Queen, surrounded by her knights doing battle in her honour, was a powerful symbol. The tenets of chivalric conduct might have been difficult to define precisely, and even more difficult to find at Court, but it behoved knights who set themselves up to protect the Queen's honour to attempt to demonstrate their commitment to these standards. Nobles, like Oxford, could behave in a manner less than chivalrous and still maintain the Queen's favour. But a mere gentleman, who boldly claimed the unique position of Queen's Champion in the tournaments, had a far greater duty to show that the chivalric virtues were not merely hypothetical. Annually for twenty years, Lee led out the troops in the Queen's name before a crowd of up to 12,000 spectators. Any scandal or slander attached to his name would reflect badly on his monarch.

What Were the Tenets of Chivalry that Lee Demonstrated?

Few treatises surpass the thirteenth-century *Booke of the Ordre of Chyualry* by Ramon Lull as a standard against which a man's chivalric virtues can be measured.[8]

---

8   Ramon Lull, *The Booke of the Ordre of Chyualry*, trans. and printed by William Caxton, 1484, ed. A. Byles (London, 1926). Immediately after Lee's death in 1611, a copy of the book came into the possession of St John's College Oxford, a college closely associated with both Sir Henry and Cromwell Lee.

Whether Lee personally possessed a copy is unknown, but his writings and his actions demonstrate that chivalry, as defined by Lull, was a principal motivator of his life. It is a moot point whether Lee consciously set out to follow Lull's ideals. If that was the case, it would have been a major undertaking and commitment. Lee was as realistic as the next man but had been raised in an environment where adherence to a natural code of gentlemanly behaviour was expected. Whereas the nobility could voraciously claim to have rediscovered a code of chivalry in later Tudor England that served to assuage their aristocratic pride, many of the older gentry were quietly following the example of their fathers and grandfathers, and behaving in a manner many succeeding generations would recognize as 'conduct becoming a gentlemen'. Lee was fortunate in that he had the upbringing, inclination and circumstances to come much closer than most to Lull's ideal of the chivalric knight.

Paramount among chivalric virtues was loyalty and service to one's monarch: a knight's duty to 'maintain and defend his worldly lord'. Lee's *Memoriae Sacrum* states that he 'served five succeedinge princes'. John Aubrey later claimed that Lee was the 'supposed brother of queen Elizabeth'. Although dates make this highly unlikely and there is no evidence that Lee was even aware of the rumour, he could not have had greater care for his Queen if it had been true.[9] Lee demonstrated loyalty to the Queen's interests regardless of personal cost and, by extension, loyalty to the state. Few courtier gentlemen rivalled Lee in the immense gift he bestowed on his Queen: an annual occasion that brought her the public adulation of thousands. The Accession Day tournaments, Lee's own creation, were a massive display of public diplomacy in the Queen's honour, unprecedented in Europe.

What we do not know is anything about Elizabeth's attitude to Lee. One hears everything from Lee's side through his writings, letters and actions, but nothing from the Queen's. Lee clearly spoke to her on numerous occasions, hunted with her and played cards with her in old age, but we only know this from the pens of Court gossips. He rode south to personally present his reports on the state of affairs in the North in both 1573 and 1588, and her honour and her interests were the focus of his life. There is no doubt that the Queen's wishes were paramount at Court, and everyone knew them, although they could change radically. Her opinions must have been conveyed orally as there is little evidence as to how courtiers, including Lee, knew what would please the Queen. Lee expressed his loyalty to her in every letter he sent to Burghley and Cecil, but the few references Elizabeth made to him in letters to others are restricted to the early 1570s when he first came into favour. After that, lacking evidence to the contrary, we can merely assume that what he did was acceptable.

---

[9]   John Aubrey, *Brief Lives*, ed. O. Lawson Dick, 2 vols (London, 1949), II, p. 32.

Whereas monarchs took members of the aristocracy for granted at their peril, it was their prerogative to regard the service of their courtier gentlemen as a given, especially one as undemanding as Lee. In Sir Henry's case, this assumption was correct: it was not until 1600 that he voiced any dissent, and this was when the Queen 'threatened a progress'. As Elizabeth had never stayed at Lee's home in Ditchley, one assumes the progress would have been to Woodstock. What right Lee had to object to the Queen's visit to her own property is unclear, but his letter to Cecil does confirm that the Queen's visits to Woodstock came at Lee's personal cost. Elizabeth frequently treated even her most loyal gentlemen servants parsimoniously: both Sir Christopher Hatton and Sir Thomas Heneage were deeply in debt to the Queen when they died. In comparison, Lee escaped quite lightly.

A second major tenet of the code of chivalry was a knight's personal honour and integrity. Lee wrote to Sir Michael Hickes in November 1607, towards the end of his life, claiming, with some truth, that 'I have bene ever carefull to deale kyndly with such as deale kyndly with me'.[10] There is little evidence that Lee ever had to compromise his personal integrity, but there also were few occasions when he was called upon to do so. After his appointment at Woodstock he did, to all practical purposes, desert his wife, but it was not unusual for the Queen's courtiers to see little of their spouses. By 1571 Lee had lived with his wife for some twenty years, and it was not until the 1580s that an actual rift was confirmed. Anne Lee, on the other hand, was spending increasing amounts of time with her mother after 1572. It appears obvious that, regardless of marriage vows taken as minors, there was little to keep Lee and his wife together.

Lee found it easier to demonstrate his personal integrity in the two positions as a royal servant which he chose to exercise himself. At Woodstock, he changed his entire lifestyle to accommodate it to his royal duties and prosecuted the Queen's interests with some zeal against those who would encroach on her demesne. At the Tower, he kept himself above the sordid intrigues of the Office of the Ordnance, even though he failed to remedy entrenched corruption. By the standards of the day, his prosecution of the patents of manumission were what was expected of a patentee, and there is no record of Lee hounding villeins to prison.

The code of chivalry also involved shared ideals of fellowship and comradeship. In a profoundly hierarchical world, Lee's prowess at the tournament not only enabled him to approach all ranks of men as equals, but also made him a welcome guest at many courts. In the absence of genuine warfare, participation in the tournament, like very few other contemporary sports, was seen as an affirmation of masculinity – a feeling of men testing themselves against each other and, when the test was over, a feeling of comradeship. Whether this was all the more

---

[10]   BL, Lansdowne MS 90, no. 48, f. 95.

necessary in a Court dominated by a Queen is a subject for a whole new debate. Lee's personal friends were drawn from the ranks of the nobility as much as from the gentry, and his eventual election to the Order of the Garter reflected the esteem in which his comradeship was held.

A knight was expected to show prowess in the battlefield, which was not an easy thing to do in an England that studiously eschewed warfare between 1563 and 1584. Gentlemen eager to prove themselves had three options: to be content with the tournaments; to seek service abroad; or to seize the few occasions for military action that presented themselves. Gentlemen and nobles who merely fought at tournaments were often accused of vain posturing. This was a source of great frustration to the likes of Philip Sidney and Essex, who longed to see genuine action. Others, like John Smythe and Sir Thomas Shirley, sought mercenary service abroad, fighting the Turks or serving with rebel armies. Sir Henry Lee belonged to the third category. He had already seen military action against the Scots in 1558 and served again in the North in 1569, in 1573 and in 1588, with some distinction. Until 1584 there were few tilters, other than those who had been mercenaries, who could claim such a record.

Lull's *Ordre of Chyualry* also exhorted knights to perfect their excellence in arms by jousts and tourneys – an instruction that Lee followed to the letter. He also complied with the exhortation to encourage and instruct younger men in the art. Over his twenty-year period as Queen's Champion he provided opportunities for several generations of aspiring tilters to further their aspirations. His 'sons in chivalry' were many.

Lastly, Lull stressed that the office of knight was to maintain and defend the weak, who were defined as women, widows and orphans, men diseased and those who were neither powerful nor strong. It is only by putting together all the sources on Sir Henry Lee that it becomes clear that throughout his life he provided sympathy and practical help for unfortunates, usually those rendered so by their own misdeeds. If Lee had been seeking to make powerful friends or even gain financial reward, he would seem to have been sadly misguided in his choice of whom to assist. There were too many of them for this to have been a minor aberration on his part.

Lee was present at the burning of the heretics Latimer and Ridley in Oxford in 1555; his was the arm that steadied the traitorous Duke of Norfolk on the scaffold in 1572; and he was the recipient of Norfolk's last whispered words. He stood as godfather to Leicester's illegitimate son by Douglas, Lady Sheffield, in 1574 – not a move guaranteed to endear him to the Queen. He openly supported Philip Sidney's actions, which were frowned upon by Elizabeth, and twice attempted to get Robert Devereux, Earl of Essex, back into royal favour. His treatment of his wife has already been discussed, but his championship of the scarlet woman of the decade, Anne Vavasour, which in practice brought him lasting happiness, was not an act that endeared him to the Elizabethan Court.

Lee also spoke up for the notorious Eleanor Britton, the mistress of George Talbot, sixteenth Earl of Shrewsbury. He stood by his wayward cousin Thomas Lee until Thomas was arrested for treason, and even then attempted to help his cousin's unfortunate children. His quiet concerns extended to more mundane and obscure cases. He served on the parliamentary commission to investigate accusations of libellous publication, brought against Arthur Hall in 1581, and even attempted to help the fraudulent Edward Fisher in 1593.[11] There was little praise or reward for Lee's actions in this context, but he was clearly a good friend to have, and one whose good name and reputation were not tarnished by association with miscreants.

Did Lee Have Other Attributes Other Than Chivalric Virtues?

Lee shared many of the fashionable interests of his day; yet, here again, his actions were bound up with the chivalric values that defined him. Works that Lee commissioned, such as his portraits, were distinguished with wit and ingenuity, but their implications went further than similar commissions by other 'elite gentry'.

One example is the use Lee made of the newly fashionable interest in maps – something he shared with others, such as Leicester and Burghley. Burghley used his map collection largely for administrative purposes. The 1588 Armada portrait used a globe for propaganda by showing the victorious Queen pointing to the New World, denoting a desire for overseas empire. In 1592 Lee chose to unite Saxton's map of England with the Low Countries' expertise of Marcus Gheeraerts, not for English propaganda but in a way that would glorify Elizabeth personally. The Ditchley portrait shows the Queen not merely standing on Oxfordshire, but as an autochthonous being, both at one with the land she ruled and a goddess descending to her people. This portrait of Elizabeth was full of enigmatic references, not all entirely explained even today, and the full implications of the symbolism in Lee's portrait collection remains the subject for speculation among art historians. The young Elizabeth Tanfield showed appreciation of Lee's interest in maps in her gift of Ortelius' *Mirror of the Worlde*. The symbolism contained in Lee's garden has barely been investigated. With a thorough and modern review of Lee's whole life and career now available, many specialist topics within it can be identified for further research.

---

[11] See BL, Lansdowne MS 75, no. 65. Edward Fisher had sold a house to Sir John Puckering, Speaker of the House of Commons, in 1582, but the fraudulent nature of the transaction had necessitated an Act of Parliament confirming Puckering's title. In 1593 Sir Henry Goodere wrote to Burghley, stating that he and Sir Henry Lee were attempting to 'help Mr Edward Fisher in his distress'.

Was Sir Henry Lee Successful in his Long Service to the Queen?

Had Sir Henry Lee put material interests above personal values he would have been a disappointed man. Early in his long career as a royal servant he received some rewards, but overall his service to his Queen probably cost him more financially than he received. Honours from both Elizabeth I and James I passed him by, with the sole exception of the proud accolade of the Order of the Garter. Moreover, Elizabeth opposed his receiving it, and it came as a result of votes from his friends. Indeed, he wore the Garter more as a testimony to his character and values than as a reward for long service.

His personal values were those of chivalry – a code which appeared to come naturally to him and which he took pride in following. Posterity may have soon forgotten him, but the picture of the man that emerges from this study is an engaging one. As such, he is worthy of this new biography.

One unpublished item in the Ditchley manuscript is an 'Epistle in praise of country life for the 3rd Kallendar Oct 1575'.[12] The author is unknown, but given the company Lee was keeping in 1575, it could have been Edward Dyer or even Philip Sidney. It is addressed to 'Layius' or Lee, who

> ... ever constant in a settled place,
> Doth scorne the toyes of all the common route
> Who void of care when phebus shewes his face
> Doth sleep secure, when he is falne about.
> And if I might according to my will.
> Devise a lyfe that wold content me best
> No mare for pompe nor riches seed of ill
> Wold I desire, nor be triumphant drest;
>
> to Layius heare my frende I gladlie wold
> Die well to god, a great man & old.

If Sir Henry Lee did not die 'a great man', he certainly enjoyed a long life, and died more content and fulfilled than many others who chose the career of an Elizabethan courtier gentleman.

---

[12]   BL, Add. MS 41499A, f. 8.

Appendices

Appendix 1
The Wyatt Family Tree

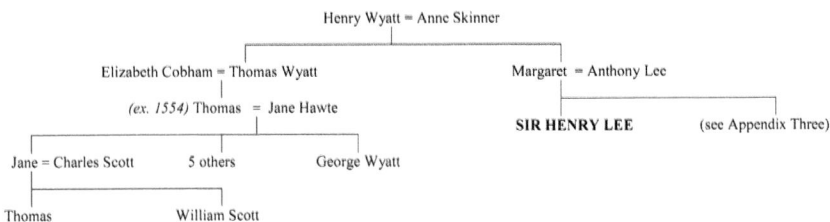

Appendix 2
The Lee Family Tree

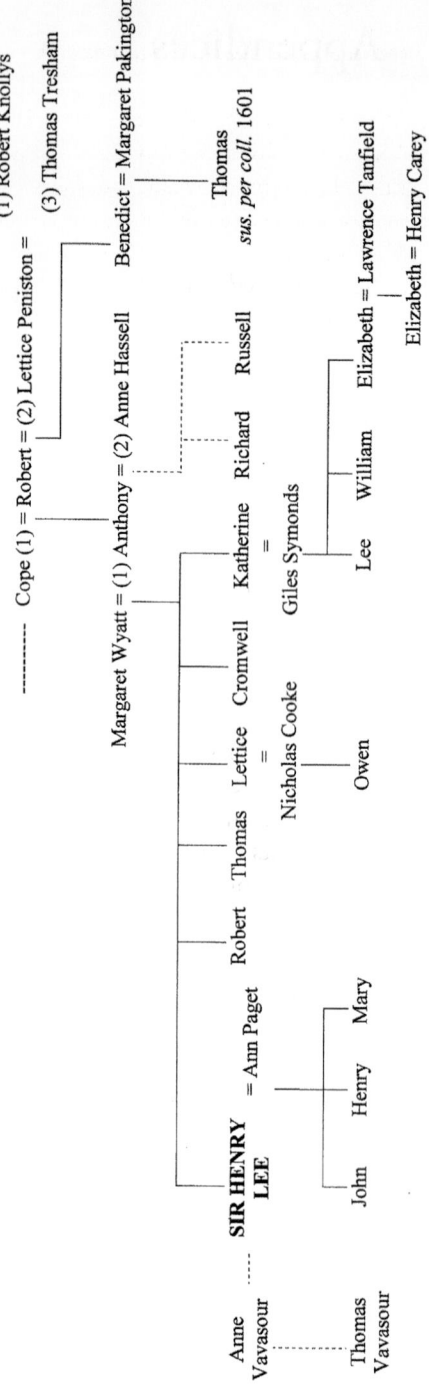

Appendix 3
A Foreign Visitor's Account of an Elizabethan Tournament

Now approached the day, when on November 17 the tournament was to be held, as I mentioned before, St. Elizabeth's day being November 19th. About twelve o'clock the queen and her ladies placed themselves at the windows in a long room at Weithol [Whitehall] palace, near Westminster, opposite the barrier where the tournament was to be held. From this room, a broad staircase led downwards, and round the barrier stands were arranged by boards above the ground, so that everybody by paying 12d. could get a stand and see the play ... many thousand spectators, men, women and girls, got places, not to speak of those who were within the barrier and paid nothing.

During the whole time of the tournament all those who wished to fight entered the list by pairs, the trumpets being blown at the time and other musical instruments. The combatants had their servants clad in different colours, they, however, did not enter the barrier, but arranged themselves on both sides. Some of the servants were disguised like savages, or like Irishmen, with the hair hanging down to the girdle like women, others had horses manes over their heads, some came driving in a carriage, the horses being equipped like elephants, some carriages were drawn by men, others appeared to move by themselves; altogether the carriages were very odd in appearance. Some gentlemen had their horses with them and mounted in full armour directly from the carriage. There were some who showed very good horsemanship and were also in fine attire. The manner of the combat each had settled before entering the lists. The costs amounted to several thousand pounds each.

When a gentleman with his servants approached the barrier, on horseback or in a carriage, he stopped at the foot of the staircase leading to the queen's room, while one of his servants in pompous attire of a special pattern mounted the steps and addressed the queen in well-composed verses or with a ludicrous speech, making her and her ladies laugh. When the speech was ended he in the name of his lord offered to the queen a costly present, which was accepted and permission given to take part in the tournament. In fact, they make sure of the permission given before preparing for combat. Now always two by two rode against each other, breaking lances across the beam. On this day not only many fine horses were seen, but also beautiful ladies, not only in the royal suite, but likewise in the companie of gentlemen of nobility and citizens.

The fête lasted until five o'clock in the afternoon, when millurt [milard] Lester [Leicester], the royal Master of the Horse, gave the sign to stop. The queen handed the first prize to the Counts of Ocsenfortt (Oxford) and of Arundel, the latter being the eldest son of the Duke of Nortfech [Norfolk}, whom the Queen had ordered to be beheaded. The son for a long time also [had] been in disgrace on account of his father, but he was pardoned and given permission to take part in the tournament. The others got prizes according to their performance, and thus the tournament ended'.

From 'A Journey Made through England and Scotland Made by Lupold von Wedel between the Years 1584 and 1585', *TRHS,* New Series IX (1895), pp. 258–9.

Appendix 4
Sir Philip Sidney Reflecting on the Nature of the Tilt

Astrophil and Stella
41
Having this day my horse, my hand, my launce
Guided so well, that I obtain'd the prize,
Both by the judgement of the English eyes,
And of some sent from that sweet enemie *Fraunce;*
Horsemen my skill in horsemanship advaunce;
Towne-folkes my strength; a daintier judge applies
His praise to sleight, which from good use doth rise;
Some luckie wits impute it but to chaunce;
Others, because of both sides I do take
My bloud from them, who did excell in this,
Thinke nature me a man of armes did make.
How farre they shoote awrie! the true cause is'
Stella lookt on, and from her heavenly face
Sent forth the beames, which made so faire my race.
49
I on my horse, and *Love* on my doth trie
Our horsemanships, while by strange worke I prove
A horsman to my horse, a horse to Love;
And now man's wrongs in me, poore beast, descrie.
The raines wherewith my Rider doth me tie,
Are humbled thoughts, which bit of Reverence move,
Curb'd in with feare, but with guilt bosse above
Of Hope, which makes it seeme faire to the eye.
The Wand is Will, thou Fancie Saddle art,
Girt fast by memorie, and while I spurre
My horse, he spurres with sharpe desire my hart:
He sits me fast, how ever I do sturre:
And now hath made me to his hand so right,
That in the Manage myself takes delight.

51

In Martiall sports I had my cunning tride,
And yet to breake more staves did me addresse:
While with the people's shouts I must confesse,
Youth, lucke, and praise, even fild my veines with pride.
When *Cupid*, having me his slave descried
In *Marse's* liverie, prauncing in the presse:
'What now sir foole', said he, 'I would no lesse,
Looke here, I say'. I look's, and *Stella* spide,
Who hard by made a window send forth light.
My heart then quak'd, then dazled were mine eyes,
One hand forgott to rule, th'other to fight.
Nor trumpets' sound I heard, not friendly cries;
My Foe came on, and beat the aire for me,
Till that her blush taught me my shame to see.

From *The Poems of Sir Philip Sidney*, ed. William A. Ringler (Oxford, 1962), pp. 185–91.

Appendix 5
Sir Philip Sidney on the Queen, Laelius and the Tilt

The Countess of Pembroke's Arcadia, Book Two, Chapter 12

The time of the marrying that queen was, every year, by the extreme love of her husband and the serviceable love of the courtiers, made notable by some public honours which did as it were proclaim to the world how dear she was to that people: among other, none was either more grateful to the beholders, or more noble in itself, than justs both with sword and lance, maintained for a seven night together; wherein that nation doth so excel both for comeliness and ableness that from neighbour countries they ordinarily come, some to strive, some to learn and some to behold.

... we came into the field, where, I remember, the manner was that the forenoon they should run at tilt one after another, the afternoon in a broad field in manner of a battle, till either the stranger, or that country knights won the field.

The first that ran was a brave knight whose device was to come in all chained, with a nymph leading him. Against him came forth an Iberian, whose manner of entering was with bagpipes ... and by him a dozen apparelled like shepherds ... his impresa was a sheep marked with pitch, with this word, 'Spotted to be known' ... before the ladies departed from the windows – among whom ... that was the Star whereby his course was only directed – the shepherds attending upon Philisides went among them and sang a eclogue ... I only remember six verses.

... when he began to run against Laelius, it had near grown (though great love had ever been betwixt them) to a quarrel. For Philisides breaking his staves with great commendation, Laelius, who was known to be second to none in the perfection of that art, ran ever over his head but so finely, to the skilful eyes, that one might well see he showed more knowledge in missing than others did in hitting, for with so gallant a grace his staff came swimming close over the crest of the helmet, as if he would represent the kiss and not the stroke of Mars. But Philisides was much moved with it while he thought Laelius would show a contempt for his youth; till Laelius (who therefore would satisfy him because he was his friend) made him know that to such bondage he was for so many many courses tied by her, whose disgraces to him were graced by her excellency, and whose injuries he could never othrwise return than honours.

But so by Laelius' willing missing was the odds of the Iberian side, and continued so in the next by the excellent running of a knight ...'.

From *The Countess of Pembroke's Arcadia*, ed. M. Evans (Harmondsworth, 1977), II, 21, pp. 351–5.

Appendix 6
Sir Henry Lee's Letter to the Earl of Essex, August 1598

By my occasion of being at courte, i did observe that w[hi]ch I was sorrye and glad to see a Court to naked without you, and yet not without a longing desire to have you there again. Mr Secretarie hath made report of your lordships good service in counsel, how well her Ma[jes]tie lyked of it, protesting that you wold doe better for othrs than for yorselfe. With Mr Secretarie both his opinion that all might and would be well, and his disposition to doethe best offices that laie in him not withstanding your L[or]dships hard conceit of him for some things, w[hi]ch whereof if nothing satisfie your L[or]dship he did not doubt but time should clear up. Her Ma[jes]tie veued upon me with great grace, but yet so that I might plainlie see her commendation of my kindness and care to please her, to be a secret complaintive that she could not find the like where she most desired it. I know how unfit I am to advise one wiser than myself in this case, where your honour is mor deare unto you than yor life. But yet may it please y[ou]r L[or]dship to consider these circumstances, she is your sovereigne, with whom you may not treate uppon equall conditions. She denies the ground of your difference, with [out?] a kinde of satisfaction, by all lyklyhood she would be glad to meete you half waie, if that w[hi]ch doth nowe not a little trouble her should further distemper her upon whose life and health you know howe many do depend. I am sure it would be a greater greife unto you than the loss of her favour, one the other side. That w[hi]ch you seeke, as ... your friends in Courte doe wiselie forsee, can be noe benefit to you. For admit you draw her to forgett her powers, and yeild in her affection to that w[hi]ch she is unwilling to doe, your peace cannot be without a matter of newe difference, in always as she will hardlie forgett to what unequal conditions you brought her, whereas if you present in kindness, and yeilde to her, to whome there is no disparagement to yeild to her will, all circumstances considered you shall do nothing unworthie yor selfe, you shall make a sure peace and come with more ease to it, w[hi]ch I take to be your owne end. I grant your wrongs to be greater than so noble a harte may well desgest, but consider, my good Lord, how great she is with whome you deal, how willing, with how little yielding to be conquered; what advantage by yielding when you are wronged, what disadvantage by facinge her, whome though you deserve never somuch, you must rely upon for favour, how strong you make your enemies, how weake your friends, how provoked patience turning into furie and delaid anger into hatred, what opportunities her late loss, and the State's present necessity maye give you to benefit you and yours, and what offence the world may take if, to right yourself /and lastlie what offence the worlde that honoreth your virtue may take ... to right yourself,/ you neglect her.

But this at all in my loue I refer to your better judgement and only advise, that whatsoever peace you make you use no means but yourself, w[hi]ch will be more honorable for you and more acceptable to her'.

From BL, Add. MS 48126, f. 97.

Appendix 7
Memoriae Sacrum of Sir Henry Lee, 1611

Sir Henry Lee, Knight of the most noble Order of the Garter, sonne of Sir Anthony Lee & Dame Margaret his wife, daughter to Sir Henry Wiat, that faithfull and Constant Servaunt & Counselour of the two Kings of famous Memory, Henries the 7th and eight. Hee owed his birth and Cildhood to Kent and his highly Honourable Uncle Sir Thomas Wiat at Alington castle, his Youthe to the Courte and Kinge Henry the eight, to whose service he was sworne at 14. Yeares olde, His prime of Manhood (after the calme of that blest Prince Edward the sixth) to the Warrs of Scotland in Queen Maries Daies, till called home by her whose soddeine Death gave beginninge to the Glorious Reigne of Queene Elizabeth he gave himself to Voiage and Travaile into the florishinge States of France Ittaly & Germany, wher soone puttinge on all those Abbillities that become the backe of Honour, Especially Skill and Proofe in Armes, He lived in

Grace and Gracinge the Courtes of the most renowmed princes of that Warlike Age, Returned home charged with the Reputation of a well formed Travailour & adorned with those flowers of Knighthood, Courtesie Bounty Valour, which quickly gave forth their Fruicte, as well in the ffeilde to the Advantages (at once) of ye two divided parts of this happely united State and to both their Princes his Soveraignes Successively in that Expedition into Scotland the Yeare 1573, when in goodly Equipage he Repayred to the Siege at Edinburgh, their quarteringe before the castle and commanding one of the Batteries he shared largely in the Honour of Ravishinge that Maiden Forte, as also in Court wher he shone in all those fayre partes became his profession & Vowes, honouringe his highlye gracious Mris with Reysinge thgose later Olimpiads of her Coronation Justs and Tournaments (Therby Tryinge & Treininge the Courtier in those Exercises of Armes that keepe the Person bright & steeled to Hardiness, That by Soft Ease Rusts & Weares) wherin still himselfe lead and Triumphed, caryinge away the Spoyles of Grace from his Soveraigne & Renowne from the Worlde for the fairest Man at Armes & most complete Courtier of his Times, till singled out by the choyce hand of his Sovereigne Mrs for med of his Worth (after the Lieutenancy of the Royal Manour of Woodstock & the Office of the Royal Armory) He was called up an Assessour on the Bench of Honour Emonge Princes & Peeres Receivinge at her Majesties hands the Noblest Order of the Garter, whilst the Worme of time knowinge the Root of this plant, yeildinge to the Burden Age and the Industrie of an Active Youth imposed on him, full of the Glorye of the Court, He abated of his Sence to pay his better parte, resigned his Dignity & honour of her Majtes Knight to the Adventurous Compt George Earle of Cumberland, Changinge pleasure for ease, for Tranquility honour, makinge Rest his Sollace & contemplation his Employment, so as absent from the Worle present with himselfe he chose to loose the fruit of publique Use & Action for that of Devotion & piety, in which time (besides the building of 4. goodly Mannors) he renued the Ruines of this Chappell, added these Manuments to honour his blood and Frends, Reised the foundation of the adjoininge Hospitall, & lastly as full of Yeares as of Honour, Havinge served five succeedinge princes and kept himself Reight & Steady in many dangerous Shokes & 3. utter Turnes of State, with a body bent to Earth & a mind erected to Heaven, Aged 80. Knighted 60. yeers, he mett his longe attended ende & now rests with his Redeemer leaving much Patrimony with his Name, honour with the Worlde, & plentifull Teares with his Freinds. Of wich Sacrifice he offers his part that beinge a sharer in his blood as well as in many his honourable Favours and an honourer of his vertues thus narrowly Registreth his spread worth to ensuinge Times.
William Scott

Written by William Scott, grandson of Sir Reginald Scott of Scott Hall, Kent. (His mother was Jane, daughter of Sir Thomas Wyatt the younger.)

Glossary

Almain rivet   form of armour created in Germany around the end of the fifteenth and early sixteenth centuries.

burgonette   burgonet helmet.

caliver   a light kind of musket or harquebus; lightest portable firearm, except the pistol.

coronel   the head of a tilting lance, ending in three short spreading points to prevent the lance penetrating armour.

corselett   a comparatively light cuirass, usually a breastplate.

cuirass   complete body-armour, including both the breast and the back plates.

impresa (**plural:** *imprese*)   emblematic device consisting of a motto and symbolic picture relevant to the bearer. Painted onto pasteboard *impresa* shields.

jack of plate   type of armour comprising small iron plates sewn between layers of felt and canvas.

messuage   a dwelling with its outbuildings and the surrounding land that is used by the dwelling's occupants.

morrions   headpieces.

rebated   blunt, as in lance tips.

running at the ring   catching a series of suspended rings on the point of a lance while riding along a line. More suitable for children.

socage   a form of land tenure in which the tenant lived on the land in return for an agricultural service or payment of money rent. On the death of the tenant, the land went to the tenant's heir after a payment to the landowner of a sum of money known as a relief.

tassets plate armour designed to protect the upper legs.

trunk hose and cannions short padded hose. Very short trunk hose were worn over **cannions**, fitted hose that ended above the knee.

vamplate a plate fixed on a lance to serve as a guard for the hand in tilting.

Many others terms are explained in the relevant footnotes.

Bibliography

Primary Sources

Bodleian Library, Oxford (Bodl.)

Ashmole 48; 845; Rawlinson A369; Rawlinson Poetry 85.

British Library, London (BL)

Calendar of State Papers, Border.
Calendar of letters and State Papers relating to English affairs principally in the archives of Simancas Spanish.
Calendar of State Papers, Downshire.
MS II, p. 42.
Calendar of State Papers, Buccleuch.
MS I, p. 97
Calendar of State Papers, Irish.
HMC de Lisle and Dudley I (stable accounts of Sir Henry Sidney); II.
HMC Hastings (manuscripts of the Hastings family).
Statutes of the Realm 18, Eliz.1, C21; *Rotulorum Patentium*, 44 Eliz., Part IV, M22.

Additional Manuscripts
62135 (Wyatt Papers); 41499A and 41499B (Ditchley MS); 41498 (Sidney's *Old Arcadia*); 36768; (Register of the Order of the Garter); 36768 (*Regulations of the Order of the Garter*); 39832–3; 39836; 15891(Sir Christopher Hatton's letter book); 14417; 22601; 8159; 4827; 48126; 9772; 75718; 33735.

Cott. Caligula
CIV, ff. 60–67 and 91–2 (letters referring to the siege of Edinburgh Castle 1573); Cotton MS App. 47; Cotton Titus MS C10.

Egerton MS
3052.

Harleian MS
135; 282; 286/62; 6064; 6910; 7008; 7392; 7457.

Lansdowne MS
5, 26, 63 (letters referring to the Armoury); 25, 27, 104 (letters referring to Woodstock); 75, 88, 89, 90, 99, 874 (letters to Michael Hickes); MS 23, no. 74 (manumission of Lee's bondmen).
Royal MS 18A, XLVIII, ff.1–37.
Sloane MS 1519, pp.144, 209, 216.
Stowe MS 574, f. 76.
Cecil Papers – consulted on microfilm.

Centre for Buckinghamshire Studies, Aylesbury (CBS)

D-LE/1; D-LE/2; D-LE/5.

Centre for Kentish Studies, Maidstone (CKS)

U1475 E93; L 2/4 (Penshurst Papers).

College of Arms, London (CA)

M4 bis; Portfolio of Tournament cheques; M6.

Deutsches Historisches Museum, Berlin (DHM)

Monatsbild Januar-Februar-Marz, Jörg Bren, 1531 (DHM 1990/185.1).

Folger Shakespeare Library, Washington DC

Folger MS.
Film Acc. 700.6 (Also Bodleian Library, Oxford Shelfmark Dep. D. 817).
MS – *Mirror of the Worlde, translated out of French into Englishe by Elizabeth Tanfield*, with dedication to her great-uncle Sir Henry Lee); Cecil Papers (consulted on microfilm).

Guildhall Library, London (GL)

Guildhall Library MSS 12,079/1; 12,071/2; 12,065/2.

Inner Temple Library, London

Pat. James 1 1610–11.
Petyt MS, 538, XXXIII, ff. 299–300.

Lambeth Palace Library, London (LPL)

Shrewsbury Papers, MSS 698, 701; Talbot Papers, MSS 3198, 3199, 3201 (consulted on microfilm).

Metropolitan Museum, New York (MMNY)

32.130.6 (Duke of Cumberland's armour); 11.128.1 (Scudmore armour)

National Archives, Public Record Office, London (TNA, PRO)

AO1/2483/300; E133/10; E351/3363; E101/64; E101/670; E101/671; E351/541 (Thomas Heneage's accounts); E351/542 (Woodstock).
AO1/2299/3, AO1/2299/4, E351/2963 (Armoury).
C1/847/7; C1/1024/17–18 (court case between Sir Anthony Lee and Lettice Lee); C66/1076; C66/1093.
E351/3204; E351/3215; E351/3229; E351/542; PRO 31/3/27; PRO 31/3/28 (preparation of the tiltyard and Accession Day tournaments).
SC6/Eliz. 1/1825, (Special Collections: Ministers' and Receivers' Accounts and General accounts of crown lands).
SP14/9; SP15/17; SP40/1; SP46/38; SP46/30; SP46/37; SP46/125; SP39/9; DL 41/553; DL 42/102; DL 44/258; E178/1550 (manumissions).
LC9/193/370; LC4/193/69; LC4/194/165; LC4/195/73 (loans from Michael Hickes).
SP12 (State Papers Domestic Elizabeth I); SP70 (State Papers Foreign Elizabeth I) – these have usually been consulted on microfilm; SP46; SP52.
Wills – PROB/11/27 (Sir Robert Lee); PROB/11/33 (Sir Anthony Lee); PROB/11/117 (Sir Henry Lee); PROB/11/26 (Sir Henry Wyatt); PROB/11/72 (Lady Anne Paget); PROB/11/46 (Sir William Paget).
Calendar of Patent Rolls, Elizabeth I.

National Library of Wales, Aberystwyth (NLW)

Clenennau Letters and Papers.

Oxfordshire Record Office, Oxford (ORO)

DIL III/b/2; DIL XXI/3–20; DIL X/b/2–3; DIL X/f/1–2; DIL X/g/1; DIL X/h/1; DIL X/a/1–16; LEE 1/3a; DIL V/a/2–6; LEE II/1; LEE II/7.

Princeton University, New Jersey, USA

Taylor Medieval and Renaissance Manuscripts.

Royal Armouries Library, Tower of London (RATL)

RAR 0–244; 0–23; 0–296; 0–100; 0–99; and other documents in uncatalogued file.

Staffordshire Record Office, Stoke-On-Trent (SRO)

D603/K/1/4; D603/K/1/5; D603/K/4; D603/1/10 (letters to Lord Thomas Paget; details of the funeral of Lady Anne Paget); Paget MS X/12 (12 May 1574).

Surrey History Centre, Woking (SHC)

LM/64 (Loseley Papers – Armoury accounts, January 1602–December 1610).

Victoria and Albert Museum, London (V & A)

DA586 & 586A (1894) – DA664 and DA664A (1894) (*An Almain Armourer's Album*); National Art Library MSL/1984/75 (a copy of the Statutes of the Order of the Garter made for Sir Henry Lee with a letter from 'Somerset' (probably Sir William Segar) to Lee, 1597); National Art Library 86.ZZ.202 (original will of Sir Henry Lee).

Worshipful Company of Armourers and Brasiers, London

Miscellaneous uncatalogued items, queries and letters on Sir Henry Lee, all twentieth century.

Printed Sources

Acts of the Privy Council of England, ed. John Roche Dasent, New Series, 46 vols (London, 1890–1964).

Alfield, Thomas, *A true reporte of the death & martyrdome of M. Campion Iestuite* (London, 1582), *RSTC* 4537.

Astley, John, *The Art of Riding* (London, 1584), *RSTC* 884.

Bacon, Francis, *The Works of Francis Bacon*, 10 vols (London, 1819).

Beer, Barrett L. and Sybil M Jacks (eds), 'Letters of William, Lord Paget of Beaudesert', *Camden Miscellany*, XXV, Camden Society, 4th Series XIII (Cambridge: Cambridge University Press, 1974).

Birch, Thomas, *Memoirs of the Reign of Queen Elizabeth, From the Year 1581 till her Death*, 2 vols (London, 1754).

Birch, Thomas, *The Court of James 1*, 2 vols (London, 1600).

Calendar of Letters and State Papers Relating to English Affairs: preserved principally in the Archives of Simancas, 4 vols (London: Longmans, 1894).

Calendar of State Papers, Colonial Series, East Indies, China and Japan, 1513–1616 (London: Longmans, 1864).

Calendar of State Papers, Domestic Series, of the Reigns of Edward VI, Mary, Elizabeth (London: Longmans, 1856–72).

Calendar of State Papers, Domestic Series, of the Reign of Elizabeth, 1581–1603, 7 vols (London: Longmans, 1865).

Calendar of State Papers, Domestic Series, of the Reigns of Elizabeth and James I, with Addenda 1580–1625 (London: Longmans, 1872).

Calendar of State Papers, Foreign Series, of the Reign of Elizabeth, 1561–62, ed. J. Stevenson, 23 vols (London: Longmans, 1863–1912).

Calendar of State Papers Relating to English Affairs in the Archives of Venice (London: Longman, 1864–1947).

Calendar of State Papers Scotland, ed. William K. Boyd (London: Longmans, 1905).

Calendar of State Papers, Spanish, 13 vols in 20 (London: Longmans, 1862–1954).

Calendar of the manuscripts of the Most Honourable the Marquess of Salisbury, K.G., ... : preserved at Hatfield House, Hertfordshire (London: HMSO, 1883–1976).

Camden, William, *Remaines Concerning Britain* (London, 1605), *RSTC* 4521; R.D. Dunn, edited critical edition (Toronto: University of Toronto Press, 1984).

Camden, William, *Britannia*, first edition of seven in Latin (London, 1586); first English edition with maps (London, 1610), *RSTC* 4527.

Camden, William, *The history of the most renowned and victorious Elizabeth, late Queen of England* (London, 1615), Wing C362.

Carey, Robert, *The Memoirs of Robert Carey*, ed. F.H. Mares (Oxford: Clarendon Press, 1972).

Castiglione, Baldasarre, *The Courtier, done into English by Thomas Hobby* (London, 1588), *RSTC* 4781.

Castiglione, Baldassare, *The Courtier*, trans. and ed. George Bull (London: Penguin, 1967).

Cecil, William, *The copie of a letter sent out of England to Don Bernardin Mendoza, ambassadour in France for the King of Spaine* (London, 1588), *RSTC* 15412.

Collins, Arthur, *Letters and Memorials of State ... [of the Sydney family]*, 2 vols (London, 1746).

Corte, Claudio, *The Art of Riding* (London, 1584), *RSTC* 5797.

Davison, Francis, *A Poetical Rhapsody* (London, 1602), *RSTC* 6373.

de Maisse, *A journal of all that was accomplished by M. de Maisse, Ambassador in England from King Henry IV to Queen Elizabeth Anno Domini 1597*, trans. G.B. Harrison and R.A. Jones (London: Nonesuch Press, 1931).

Dillon, Harold Arthur Lee, *Catalogue of Paintings in the Possession of Viscount Dillon at Ditchley, Spelsbury, Oxfordshire* (Oxford: Oxford University Press, 1908).

The Domesday of Inclosures, 1517–1518, ed. I.S. Leadam, 2 vols (London: Royal Historical Society, 1897).

Dowland, John, *Second Book of Songs*, ed. E.H. Fellows (London 1600), revised by Thurston Dart.

Dowland, John, *A Musical Banquet* (London, 1610), *RSTC* 7099.

Exhibition of Armour made in the Royal Workshops at Greenwich, held at the Tower of London, 22 May–29 Sept. 1951, ed. James Mann (London: HMSO, 1951).

Fénelon, Bertrand de Salignac, Seigneur de la Mothe, *Correspondance Diplomatique de Bertrand de Salignac de La Mothe Fénelon, Ambassadeur de France en Angleterre de 1568 à 1575*, ed. J. Teulet, 7 vols (Paris and London: Charles Purton Cooper, 1838–70).

Feuillerat, Albert (ed.), *Documents relating to the Office of the Revels in the time of Queen Elizabeth* (London: David Nutt, 1902).

Ffoulkes, Charles J., *Inventory and Survey of the Armouries of the Tower of London*, 2 vols (London: HMSO, 1916).

Fitzalan-Howard, H.G., *The Lives of Philip Howard Earl of Arundel and of Anne Dacre, his Wife* (London, 1857).

Foxe, John, *Acts and Monuments* (London, 1563), *RSTC* 11222.

Foxe, John, *Acts and Monuments*, ed. S.R. Cattley (London: John Day, 1838).

Fugger Newsletters, 2nd series (1568–1605), ed. Victor von Klarwill, trans. L.S.R. Byrne (London, 1926).

Gawdy, Philip, *Letters of Philip Gawdy 1579–1616*, ed. Issac Jeayes (London: Roxburghe Club, 1906).

Goldwell, Henry, *A brief declaration of the shews, devices, speeches and inventions performed before the Queen's majestie & the French ambassadors* (London, 1581), *RSTC* 11990.

Greville, Fulke, *The Prose Works of Fulke Greville, Lord Brooke*, ed. J. Gouws (Oxford: Oxford University Press, 1986).

Guevara, Anthony, *Epistoles*, translated out of the Spanish tongue by Edmund Hellowes, Groom of the Leash (London, 1574), *RSTC* 12432.

G.W., *News out of Cheshire of the New Found Well* (London 1600), *RSTC* 24904.

Harrington, John, *Nugae Antiquae*, ed. Thomas Park (London, 1804: facsimile New York: Ams Press, Inc., 1966).

Holinshed, Raphael, *The firste volume of the chronicles of England, Scotlande, and Irelande* (London, 1577), *RSTC* 1358.

Holinshed, Raphael, *Holinsheds Chronicles of England, Scotland and Ireland* (London, 1577), *RSTC* 1358.

Household Accounts and Disbursement books of Robert Dudley, Earl of Leicester, ed. Simon Adams, Camden Society 5th Series, VI (Cambridge: Royal Historical Society, 1996).

Kemp, Thomas (ed.), *The Black Book of Warwick* (Warwick: H.T. Cooke, 1898).

Kirby, T.F., *Winchester Scholars* (London and Winchester, 1888).

Knell, Thomas, *The declaration of such tempestuous and outrageous fluddes as hath been in divers places of England 1570* (London, 1571), *RSTC* 15032.

Lee, Frederick G., 'The Palace of the Savoy', *Walford's Antiquarian*, ed. E. Walford, VIII, (July–December 1885), pp. 119–24.

Leicester's Commonwealth: The Copy of a Letter Written by a Master of Art of Cambridge (1584) and Related Documents, ed. D.C. Peck (Athens, University of Ohio Press, 1985).

Leland, John, *The Itinerary of John Leland the Antiquary*, ed. Thomas Hearne, 9 vols (Oxford, 1710–12).

Letters and Papers, Foreign and Domestic of the Reign of Henry VIII, ed. J.S. Brewer, R.H. Brodie and J. Gairdner, 23 vols (London, 1864).

Lodge, Edmund, *Illustrations of British History*, 3 vols (London, 1791).

Lull, Ramon, *The Booke of the Ordre of Chyualry*, trans. and printed by William Caxton, 1484, ed. Alfred Byles (London: Early English Text Society, 1926). Lyson, D. and Lyson, S., *Magna Britannia: being a Concise Topographical Account of the Several Counties of Great Britain* (London, 1806).

Machyn, Henry, *The Diary of Henry Machyn – Citizen and Merchant-Taylor of London (1550–1563)*, ed. J.G. Nichols, Camden Society Old Series XXXXII (London: Royal Historical Society, 1848).

Markham, Gervase, *Cheap and Good Husbandry* (London, 1676), Wing M681.

Nicolas, H., *Memoirs of the Life and Times of Sir Christopher Hatton, K.G.* (London: Richard Bentley, 1847).

Nichols, John C., *The Progresses, Public Processions etc. of Queen Elizabeth*, 3 vols (London, 1823; New York: Burt Franklin, 1967).

Nichols, John C., *The Progresses, Processions and Magnificent Festivities of King James the First*, 4 vols (London, 1828, New York, 1969).

Parker, Matthew, *Correspondence of Matthew Parker DD, Archbishop of Canterbury*, ed. John Bruce and Thomas Perowne for the Parker Society (Cambridge: Cambridge University Press, 1853).

Peele, George, *Polyhymnia, describing the honourable Triumph at Tylt* (London, 1590), *RSTC* 260.

Platter, Thomas and Horatio Busino, *The Journals of Two Travellers in Elizabethan and Early Stuart England*, ed. Peter Razzell (London: Caliban Books, 1995).

Ralegh, Walter, *The Poems of Sir Walter Ralegh*, ed. A. Latham (London, 1929).

Rymer, T., *Foedera*, 20 vols (London, 1704–35).

Segar, Sir William, *The booke of honor and armes* (London, 1590), *RSTC* 22163.

Segar, Sir William, *Honor Military and Civill* (London, 1602), *RSTC* 22164.

Selden, John, *Titles of Honour* (London, 1614).

Selden, John, *Table-Talk; being the Discourses of John Selden, Esq.* (London, 1689), Wing S2437.

Sidney, Philip, *Poems of Sir Philip Sidney*, ed. W.A. Ringler (Oxford: Clarendon Press, 1962).

Sidney, Philip, *The Countess of Pembroke's Arcadia*, ed. Maurice Evans (Harmondsworth: Penguin, 1977).

Smith, Thomas, 'Of Bondage and Bondmen', *De Republica Anglorum* (London, 1583).

Smythe, John, *Certen instructions, observations and orders militarie* (London, 1594), *RSTC* 22884.

Sotheby's catalogue, 24 May 1933 (catalogue of the sale of Ditchley Park and its remaining contents).

Spenser, Edmund, *Faerie Queene* (London, 1590).

Strutt, Joseph, *The Sports and Pastimes of the People of England* (London, 1841).

Strype, John, *Life and Acts of Matthew Parker*, 4 vols (London: John Wyat, 1711).

Strype, John, *Annals of the Reformation and Establishment of Religion during Elizabeth I's Reign*, 8 vols (London, 1824).

Sylvester, Joshua, *Bartas, his Devine Weekes and Workes* (London, 1605).

The Elizabethan Garden at Kenilworth (English Heritage, 2014).

The Queen's Majesty's Entertainment at Woodstock, 1575, ed. A.W. Pollard (Oxford: Daniel and Hart, 1910).

The Victoria County History of Buckinghamshire.

The Victoria County History of Oxfordshire.

Trinity Term in the first year of James I's Reign (1603).

Vergil, Polydore, *Anglica Historia of Polydore Vergil*, ed. and trans. D. Hay, Camden Series LXXIV (London: Royal Historical Society, 1950).

Whitney, Geoffrey, *A Choice of Emblemes* (London, 1586), *RSTC* 25438.

Woodstock Chamberlain's Accounts 1609–1650, ed. M. Maslen (Stroud: Oxfordshire Record Society, 1993).

Wyatt, Thomas, *Life and Letters of Sir Thomas Wyatt*, ed. Kenneth Muir (Liverpool: Liverpool University Press, 1963).Wyatt, George, *Papers*, ed. D.M. Loades Camden Society, 4th Series V (Cambridge: Cambridge University Press, 1968).

Secondary Sources

Adams, Simon, *Leicester and the Court* (Manchester: Manchester University Press, 2002).

Adamson, J. (ed.), *The Princely Courts of Europe* (London, 1999).

Alford, Stephen, *Burghley: William Cecil at the Court of Elizabeth I* (London: Yale University Press, 2008).Anglo, Sydney, *Spectacle, Pageantry and Early Tudor Policy* (Oxford: Clarendon Press, 1969).

Anglo, Sydney, *Chivalry in the Renaissance* (Woodbridge: Boydell Press, 1990).

Anglo, Sydney, *Images of Tudor Kingship* (London: Seaby, 1992).

Archer, Ian (ed.), *Religion, Politics and Society in Sixteenth Century England*, Camden Society 5th Series XXII (Cambridge: Cambridge University Press, 2003).

Asch, Ronald G. and Adolf M. Birke (eds), *Princes, Patronage and the Nobility: The Court at the Beginning of the Modern Age c. 1450–1650* (London: Oxford University Press, 1991).

Aubrey, John, *Brief Lives*, ed. Oliver Lawson Dick (London: Mandarin, 1992).

Axton, Marie, *The Queen's Two Bodies* (London: RHS, 1977).

Barber, Richard and Barker, Juliet, *Tournaments: Jousts, Chivalry and Pageants in the Middle Ages* (Woodbridge: Boydell & Brewer Inc., 1989).

Barbour, Richard, *The Knight and Chivalry*, 2nd edn (Woodbridge: Boydell Press, 1995).

Bell, Ilona, *Elizabethan Women and the Poetry of Courtship* (Cambridge: Cambridge University Press, 1998).

Bergeron, David M., *English Civic Pageantry 1558–1642* (London: Edward Arnold, 1971).

Bernard, G.W., *Power and Politics in Tudor England* (Aldershot: Ashgate, 2000).

Berry, Edward, *The Making of Sir Philip Sidney* (Toronto: University of Toronto Press, 1998).

Berry, Philippa, *Of Chastity and Power: Elizabethan Literature and the Unmarried Queen* (London: Routledge, 1989).

Bowden, Peter J., *The Wool Trade in Tudor and Stuart England* (London: Cass, 1962).

Bray, Alan, *Homosexuality in Renaissance England*, 2nd edn (London: Gay Men's Press, 1988).

Bryson, Anna, *From Courtesy to Civility* (Oxford: Clarendon Press, 1998).

Burke, Peter, *The Fortunes of the Courtier: The European Reception of Castiglione's Cortegiano* (Cambridge: Polity Press, 1995).

Bushby, Lady Frances, *Three Men of the Tudor Time* (London: David Nutt, 1911).

Byron, William, *Cervantes: A Biography* (London: Cassell, 1979).

Campbell, Louise and Francis Steer, *A Catalogue of Manuscripts in the College of Arms: vol. 1* (London: College of Arms, 1988).

Chambers, E.K., *The Elizabethan Stage* (Oxford: Clarendon Press, 1924).

Chambers, E.K., *Sir Henry Lee: An Elizabethan Portrait* (Oxford: Clarendon Press, 1936).

Cicero, *Cicero: On Old Age, On Friendship, On Divination*, trans. W.A. Falconer, Loeb Classical Library (Cambridge, MA: Harvard University Press, 1923).

Cole, Mary Hill, *The Portable Queen: Elizabeth I and the Politics of Ceremony* (Amherst: University of Massachusetts Press, 1999).

Colvin, H.M. (ed.), *The History of the King's Works*, 6 vols (London: HMSO, 1982).

Conway, Agnes, *Henry VII's Relations with Scotland and Ireland* (Cambridge: Cambridge University Press, 1932).

Corbett, Elsie Cameron, *A History of Spelsbury including Dean, Taston, Fulwell and Ditchley* (Long Compton: The King's Stone Press, 1931).

Cressy, David, *Bonfires and Bells: National Memory and the Protestant Calendar in Elizabethan and Stuart England* (London: Weidenfeld and Nicolson,1989).

Cruickshank, C.G., *Elizabeth's Army* (Oxford: Clarendon Press, 1966).

Davenport, F.G., *The Economic Development of a Norfolk Manor, 1086–1565* (Cambridge: Cambridge University Press, 1906; reprinted London: Cass, 1967).

Davis, Alex, *Chivalry and Romance in the English Renaissance* (Cambridge: D.S. Brewer, 2003).

Dickens, A.G. (ed.), *The Courts of Europe – Politics, Patronage and Royalty 1400–1800* (London: Thames and Hudson, 1977).

Dillon, Harold Arthur Lee, *An Illustrated Guide to the Armoury at the Tower of London* (London, 1910).

Dillon, Harold Arthur Lee, *Armour* (repr. London: Arms and Armour Press, 1968).

Dop, Jan Albert, *Eliza's Knights – Soldiers, Poets and Puritans in the Netherlands, 1572–1586* (Alblasserdam: Remak, 1981).

Doran, Susan, *Monarchy and Matrimony: The Courtships of Elizabeth I* (London: Routledge, 1996).

Duncan-Jones, Katherine, *Sir Philip Sidney, Courtier Poet* (London: Hamish Hamilton, 1991).

Eaton, Peter, *A History of Lilies* (Weedon: Peter Eaton, 1982).

Finch, Mary E., *The Wealth of Five Northamptonshire Families 1540–1640* (Oxford: Northamptonshire Record Society, 1956).

Frye, Susan, *Elizabeth I: The Competition for Representation* (Oxford: Oxford University Press, 1993).

Gammon, S.R., *Statesman, and Schemer: William, First Lord Paget, Tudor Minister* (Newton Abbot: David & Charles, 1973).

Guy, John (ed.), *The Reign of Elizabeth I* (Cambridge: Cambridge University Press, 1995).

Guy, John (ed.), *The Tudor Monarchy* (London: Arnold, 1997).

Hackett, Helen, *Virgin Mother, Maiden Queen*, 2nd edn (Basingstoke: Macmillan, 1996).

Hall, J., *Sinister Developments: A Lost Key to Western Art* (Oxford, forthcoming).

Hammer, Paul E.J., *Elizabeth's Wars* (Basingstoke: Macmillan, 2003).

Hasler, P.W., *The History of Parliament: The House of Commons, 1558–1603*, 3 vols (London: Secker and Warburg, 1982).

Hassell Smith, A., *County and Court: Government and Politics in Norfolk, 1558–1603* (Oxford: Clarendon Press, 1974).

Heal, Felicity and Richard Holmes, *The Gentry in England and Wales 1500–1700* (Basingstoke: Macmillan, 1994).

Hearn, Karen, *Marcus Gheeraerts II, Elizabethan Artist* (London: Tate Publishing, 2002).

Henderson, Paula, *The Tudor House and Garden* (New Haven, CT and London: Yale University Press, 2005).

Hicks, L., *An Elizabethan Problem: Some Aspects of the Careers of Two Exile-Adventurers* (London: Burns and Oates, 1964).

Holt, Mack P., *The Duke of Anjou and the Politique Struggle during the Wars of Religion* (Cambridge: Cambridge University Press, 1986).

Hughey, Ruth, *The Arundel–Harington Manuscript of Tudor Poetry* (Columbus, OH, 1960).

Hurstfield, J., *The Queen's Wards: Wardship and Marriage under Elizabeth I* (London: Longmans, Green & Co, 1958).

Ives, E.W., *Anne Boleyn* (Oxford: Blackwell, 1986).

James, Mervyn, *Society, Politics and Culture: Studies in Early Modern England* (Cambridge: Cambridge University Press, 1986).

Keen, Maurice, *Chivalry* (New Haven, CT, and London: Yale University Press, 1984).

Kilgour, R.L., *The Decline of Chivalry* (Cambridge, MA: Harvard University Press, 1937).

Kipling, G., *The Triumph of Honour: Burgundian Origins of the Elizabethan Renaissance* (The Hague: Leiden University Press, 1977).

Levin, Carole, Jo Eldridge Carney and Debra Barrett-Graves (eds), *Elizabeth I: Always her Own Free Woman* (Aldershot: Ashgate, 2003).

McCoy, Richard C., *Sir Philip Sidney: Rebellion in Arcadia* (Brighton: Harvester Press, 1979).

McCoy, Richard C., *The Rites of Knighthood: The Literature and Politics of Elizabethan Chivalry* (Berkeley: University of California Press, 1989).

Mann, James (ed.), *Exhibition of Armour Made in the Royal Workshops at Greenwich, Held at the Tower of London, 22 May–29 Sept. 1951* (London: HMSO, 1951).

Marsh, Christopher W., *The Family of Love in English Society 1550–1630* (Cambridge: Cambridge University Press, 1994).

Marshall, Edward, *The Early History of Woodstock Manor and its Environs* (Oxford and London: J. Parker, 1873).

May, Steven, *The English Courtier Poets: The Poems and their Contexts*, 2nd edn (Columbia: University of Missouri Press, 1999).

Miller, Amos C., *Sir Henry Killigrew: Elizabethan Soldier and Diplomat* (Leicester: Leicester University Press, 1963).

Mingay, G.E., *The Gentry: The Rise and Fall of a Ruling Class* (London: Longmans, 1978).

Mulryne, J.R., Helen Watanabe-O'Kelly and Margaret Shewring (eds), *Europa triumphans: Court and Civic Festivals in Early Modern Europe* (Aldershot: Ashgate, 2004).

Murray, John Joseph, *Flanders and England – A Cultural Bridge: The Influence of the Low Countries on Tudor–Stuart England* (Antwerp: Fonds Mercator, 1985).

Nelson, Alan H., *Monstrous Adversary: The Life of Edward de Vere, 17th Earl of Oxford* (Liverpool: Liverpool University Press, 2003).

Osborn, James M., *Young Philip Sidney 1572–1577* (New Haven, CT: Yale University Press, 1972).

Parker, Geoffrey, *The Army of Flanders and the Spanish Road 1567–1659* (Cambridge: Cambridge University Press, 1972).

Prestage, Edgar (ed.), *Chivalry* (London: Kegan Paul, 1928).

Simpson, A., *A Wealth of Gentry 1540–1660* (Cambridge: Cambridge University Press, 1963).

Simpson, Richard, *Edmund Campion: A Biography* (London: Williams and Norgate, 1867).

Smith, Alan G.R., *Servant to the Cecils: The Life of Sir Michael Hickes, 1543–1612* (London: Jonathan Cape, 1977).

Steward, Alan, *Philip Sidney: A Double Life* (London: Chatto & Windus, 2000).

Stewart, R.W., *The English Ordnance Office, 1585–1625: A Case Study in Bureaucracy* (Woodbridge: Boydell, 1996).Stone, Lawrence, *An Elizabethan: Sir Horatio Palavicino* (Oxford: Clarendon Press, 1956).

Stone, Lawrence, *The Crisis of the Aristocracy 1558–1641* (Oxford: Clarendon Press, 1965).

Stone, Lawrence, *An Open Elite? England 1540–1880* (Oxford: Oxford University Press, 1984).

Strong, Roy, *Splendour at Court: Renaissance Spectacle and Illusion* (London: Weidenfeld and Nicolson, 1973).

Strong, Roy, *The Cult of Elizabeth* (London: Thames and Hudson, 1977).

Strong, Roy, *Art and Power: Renaissance Festivals 1450–1650* (Woodbridge: Boydell Press 1984).

Strong, Roy, *Henry, Prince of Wales, and England's Lost Renaissance* (London: Thames and Hudson, 1986).

Strong, R.C. and J.A. van Dorsten, *Leicester's Triumph* (Leiden and Oxford: Leiden University Press, 1994).

Thomson, Patricia, *Sir Thomas Wyatt and his Background* (London: Routledge and Kegan Paul, 1964).

Vale, Malcolm, *War and Chivalry* (London, 1989).

Watanabe-O'Kelly, Helen, *Triumphall Shews: Tournaments at German-speaking Courts in their European Context 1560–1730* (Berlin: Mann, 1992). Williams, Alan, *The Knight and the Blast Furnace* (Leiden and Boston, MA: Brill, 2003).

Williams, Alan and Anthony de Reuck, *The Royal Armoury at Greenwich, 1515–1649* (London: Trustees of the Royal Armouries, 1995).

Williams, Penry, *The Later Tudors: England 1547–1603* (Oxford: Oxford University Press, 1995).

Wilson, E.C., *England's Eliza* (Cambridge, MA: Harvard University Press, 1939; repr. 1966).

Wilson, Jean, *Entertainments for Elizabeth I* (Woodbridge: Brewer, 1980).

Woodall, Joanna, *Anthonis Mor: Art and Authority* (Zwolle: Waanders Publishers, 2007).

Worden, Blair, *The Sound of Virtue: Philip Sidney's Arcadia and Elizabethan Politics* (New Haven, CT, and London: Yale University Press, 1996).

Woudhuysen, H.R., *Sir Philip Sidney and the Circulation of Manuscripts 1558–1640* (Oxford: Clarendon Press, 1996).

Yates, Frances, *The Valois Tapestries* (London: Warbourg Institute, 1959).

Yates, Frances, *The Rosicrucian Enlightenment* (London: Routledge and Kegan Paul, 1972).

Yates, Frances, *Astraea, the Imperial Theme in the Sixteenth Century* (London: Routledge and Kegan Paul, 1975).

Young, Alan R., *Tudor and Jacobean Tournaments* (London: George Philip, 1987).

Young, Alan R., *The English Tournament Imprese* (New York: AMS Press, 1988).

Articles

Adams, Simon, 'Eliza Enthroned', in. C.A. Haigh (ed.), *The Reign of Elizabeth I* (Basingstoke: Macmillan, 1984).

Alsop, J.D., 'Government, Finance and the Community of the Exchequer', in C. Haigh (ed.), *The Reign of Elizabeth I* (Basingstoke: Macmillan, 1984), pp. 101–25.

Anglo, Sydney, 'Archives of the English Tournament: Score Cheques and Lists', *Journal of the Society of Archivists*, II, 4 (1961), pp. 153–62.

Anglo, Sydney, 'Financial and Heraldic Records of the English Tournament', *Journal of the Society of Archivists*, III, 1 (1962), pp. 183–95.

Anglo, Sydney, 'Reception of Katherine of Aragon', *Journal of the Warburg and Courtauld Institute*, XXVI (1963), pp. 53–89.

Anglo, Sydney, 'Anglo-Burgundian Feats of Arms: Smithfield June 1467', *Guildhall Miscellany*, II, 7 (1965), pp. 271–83.

Archer, Ian W., 'The London Lobbies in the Later Sixteenth Century', *HJ*, 31, 1 (1988), pp. 17–44.

Ashley, R., 'Getting and Spending: Corruption in the Elizabethan Ordnance', *History Today*, XL (November 1990), pp. 47–55.

Ashley, R., 'War in the Ordnance Office: The Essex Connection and Sir John Davis', *BIHR*, LXVII, 164 (October 1994), pp. 337–45.

Axton, Marie, 'Robert Dudley and the Inner Temple Revels', *HJ*, XIII (1970), pp. 371–2.

Barter-Bailey, Sarah, 'Lord Dillon', *Royal Armouries Yearbook*, VII (2002) pp. 108–29.

Baskervill, C.R., 'The Genesis of Spenser's Queen of Faerie', *Modern Philology*, XVIII, 1 (May 1920), pp. 49–54.

Beal, Peter, 'Poems by Sir Philip Sidney: The Ottley Manuscript', *Library*, 5th Series, 33 (1978), pp. 284–95.

Blair, Claude, 'The Armourers' Bill of 1581: The Making of Arms and Armour in 16th Century London', *Journal of the Arms and Armour Society*, XII (1986), pp. 20–53.

Blakeley, E., 'Tournament Garniture of Robert Dudley, Earl of Leicester', *Royal Armouries Yearbook*, 2 (1997), pp. 55–63.

Bruce, John, 'Unpublished Anecdotes of Sir Thomas Wyatt, the Poet, and of Other Members of that Family', *Gentleman's Magazine*, XXXIV, 2 (1850), pp. 235–41.

Clayton, Thomas, 'Sir Henry Lee's Farewell to the Court: The Texts and Authorship of his "Golden Locks Time Hath to Silver Turned"', *English Literary Renaissance*, 4, 2 (1974), pp. 268–75.

Coss, P.R., 'The Formation of the English Gentry', *Past and Present*, CXLVII (May 1995), pp. 38–64.

Cunliffe, J.W. (ed.), 'The Queenes Majesties Entertainment at Woodstocke', *Proceedings of the Modern Language Association*, XXVI (1911), pp. 92–141.

Dillon, Harold Arthur Lee, 'A Letter of Sir Henry Lee, 1590, on a Trial for Armour', *Archaeologia*, LI, 1 (1885), pp. 167–72.

Dillon, Harold Arthur Lee, 'An Elizabethan Armourer's Album', *Archaeological Journal*, LII, Second Series, II (1895), pp. 113–28.

Dillon, Harold Arthur Lee, 'Tilting in Tudor Times', *Archaeological Journal*, LV, Second Series, V (1898), pp. 296–321.

Dillon, Harold Arthur Lee, 'Armour Notes', *Archaeological Journal*, LX, Second Series, X (1903), pp. 96–136.

Doran, Susan, 'Juno versus Diana: The Treatment of Elizabeth I's Marriage in Plays and Entertainments, 1561–1581', *HJ*, XXXVIII (June 1995), pp. 257–74.

Doran, Susan, 'Virginity, Divinity and Power: The Portraits of Elizabeth I', in S. Doran and T. Freeman (eds), *The Myth of Elizabeth* (Basingstoke: Macmillan, 2003), pp. 171–200.

Duncan-Jones, Katherine, 'Christs Teares, Nashes's "Forsaken Extremities"', *Review of English Studies*, New Series, 49, 194 (May 1998), pp. 167–80.

Eaves, Ian, 'The Greenwich Armour and Locking Gauntlet of Sir Henry Lee in the Collection of the Worshipful Company of Armourers and Brasiers', *Journal of the Society of Arms and Armour*, XVI, 3 (1999), pp. 133–64.

Elton, G., 'The Elizabethan Exchequer: War in the Receipt', in S.T. Bindoff, J. Hurstfield and C.H. Williams (eds), *Elizabethan Government and Society: Essays Presented to Sir John Neale* (London: Athlone Press, 1961), pp. 213–49.

Everson, Paul, 'Peasants, Peers and Graziers: The Landscape of Quarrendon, Buckinghamshire, Interpreted', *Records of Buckinghamshire*, XXXI (2001), pp. 1–45.

Ffoulkes, C., 'The Armourers' Company of London and the Greenwich School of Armourers', *Archaeologia*, LXXVI (1927), pp. 41–58.

Goldring, Elizabeth, 'Portraits of Queen Elizabeth I and the Earl of Leicester for Kenilworth Castle', *Burlington Magazine*, CXLVII, 1231 (October 2005), pp. 654–60.

Guy, J., 'The 1590s: The Second Reign of Elizabeth I?', in J. Guy (ed.), *The Reign of Elizabeth: Court and Culture in the Last Decade* (Cambridge: Cambridge University Press, 1995).

Hammer, Paul E., 'Upstaging the Queen: The Earl of Essex, Francis Bacon and the Accession Day Celebrations of 1595', in David Bevington and

Peter Holbrook (eds), *The Politics of the Stuart Court Masque* (Cambridge: Cambridge University Press, 1998), pp. 42–66.

Hammer, Paul E., 'Sex and the Virgin Queen: Aristocratic Concupiscence and the Court of Elizabeth I', *Sixteenth Century Journal*, XXXI (Spring 2000), pp. 77–97.

Hanford, James and Sara Watson, 'Personal Allegories in the Arcadia: Philisides and Laelius', *Modern Philology*, XXXII (August 1934), pp. 1–10.

Heaton, G. 'The Queen and the Hermit: The Tale of Hemetes, 1575', in P. Beal and G. Ioppolo (eds), *Elizabeth I and the Culture of Writing* (London: British Library Publishing, 2007), pp. 87–115.

Jones, Rica, 'Portrait of Captain Thomas Lee 1594', in S. Hackney, R. Jones and J. Townshend (eds), *Paint and Purpose* (London: Tate Gallery, 1999), pp. 26–33.

McCoy, Richard C. 'From the Tower to the Tiltyard: Robert Dudley's Return to Glory', *HJ*, XXVII (1984) pp. 425–35.

MacCulloch, Diarmaid, 'Bondmen under the Tudors', in Claire Cross, David Loades and J.J. Scarisbrick (eds), *Law and Government under the Tudors: Essays Presented to Sir Geoffrey Elton on his Retirement* (Cambridge: Cambridge University Press, 1988), pp. 91–109.

Mann, James, 'The Exhibition of Greenwich Armour at the Tower of London', *The Burlington Magazine*, LXXXXIII (December 1951), pp. 378–83.

May, S.W., 'The Poems of Edward de Vere, Seventeenth Earl of Oxford, and of Robert Devereux, Second Earl of Essex', *Studies in Philology*, 77 (1980), pp. 1–32.

Millar, Oliver, 'Marcus Gheeraerts the Younger: A Sequel through Inscriptions', *Burlington Magazine*, CV (December 1963), pp. 533–41.

Myers, James P., 'Murdering Heart ... Murdering Hand: Captain Thomas Lee of Ireland, Elizabethan Assassin', *Sixteenth Century Journal*, XXII (Spring 1991), pp. 47–60.

Peacock, J., 'The Politics of Portraiture', in K. Sharpe and P. Lake (eds), *Culture and Politics in Early Stuart England* (Basingstoke: Macmillan, 1994), pp. 195–228.

Piper, David, 'Some Portraits by Marcus Gheeraerts and John de Critz Reconsidered', *Proceedings of the Huguenot Society*, XX (1960), pp. 210–29.

Read, Conyers, 'Queen Elizabeth's Seizure of the Duke of Alva's Pay-Ships', *The Journal of Modern History*, V (December 1933), pp. 443–64.

Roe, F. Gordon, 'The Last of Sir Henry Lee', *Connoisseur*, CX (1942), pp. 3–12.

Rooley, Anthony, 'Time Stands Still: Devices and Designs, Allegory and Alliteration, Poetry and Music and a New Identification in an Old Portrait', *Early Music*, 34, 3 (2006), pp. 443–64.

Starkey, David, 'The Court: Castiglione's Ideal and Tudor Reality, Being a Discussion of Sir Thomas Wyatt's Satire Addressed to Sir Francis Bryan', *Journal of the Warburg and Courtauld Institutes*, VL (1982), pp. 239–57.

Savine, Alexander, 'Bondmen under the Tudors', *TRHS*, 2nd series, XVII (1903), pp. 235–89.

Sewter, A.C., 'Queen Elizabeth at Kenilworth', *Burlington Magazine*, LXXVI (March 1940), pp. 70–76.

Strong, Roy, 'Marcus Gheeraerts the Younger', *Burlington Magazine*, CV (April 1963), pp. 149–57.

Strong, Roy, 'My Weeping Stag I Crowne', in Michael Bath, John Manning and Alan Young (eds), *The Art of the Emblem: Essays in Honour of Karl Josef Holtgen* (New York: AMS Press, 1993), pp. 103–41.

Tahon, E. 'Marcus Gheeraerts de Oude Brugge ca. 1521–1587 Londen?', in M.P.J. Martens (ed.), *Brugge en de Renaissance: Van Memling tot Pourbus* (Bruges: Memling in Sint-Jan-Hospitaalmuseum, 1998).

Taylor, Andrew, 'The Sounds of Chivalry: Lute Song and Harp Song for Sir Henry Lee', *Journal of the Lute Society of America*, XXV (1992), pp. 1–23.

von Wedel, Lupold, 'Journey Made through England and Scotland in the Years 1584 and 1585', *TRHS*, New Series, IX (1895), pp. 223–70.

Walter, John, 'A Rising of the People? The Oxfordshire Rising of 1596', *Past and Present*, CVII (May 1985), pp. 90–143.

Watanabe-O'Kelly, Helen, 'Tournaments and their Relevance for Warfare in the Early Modern Period', *European History Quarterly*, XX (1990), pp. 451–63.

Williams, Penry, 'Court and Polity under Elizabeth I', in John Guy (ed.), *The Tudor Monarchy* (London: Arnold, 1997), pp. 372–75.

Woodcock, Matthew, 'The Fairy Queen in Elizabethan Entertainments', in C. Levin, J. Eldridge Carney and D. Barrett-Graves (eds), *Elizabeth I: Always Her Own Free Woman* (Aldershot: Ashgate, 2003), pp. 97–119.

Yates, F., 'Elizabethan Chivalry: The Romance of the Accession Day Tilts', *Journal of the Warburg and Courtauld Institutes*, XX (1957), pp. 4–25.

Doctoral Theses and Unpublished Papers

Gapper, Claire, 'Plasters and Plasterwork in City, Court and Country 1530–1640' (University of London, 1998).

Heaton, G., 'Images of a Champion: The Tiltyard Personae of Sir Henry Lee', unpublished paper presented at Courts, Courtiers and Courtliness in the Tudor Age Conference, Kingston University, 9 September 2004.

Mears, Natalie, 'The Personal Rule of Elizabeth I: Marriage, Succession and Catholic Conspiracy, 1578–1587' (University of St Andrews, 1999).

Merton, Charlotte, 'The Women Who Served Queen Mary and Queen Elizabeth: Ladies, Gentlewomen and Maids of the Privy Chamber, 1553–1603' (University of Cambridge, 1991).

Tighe, W.J., 'The Gentlemen Pensioners in Elizabethan Politics and Government' (University of Cambridge, 1983).

Wilks, Timothy Victor, 'The Court Culture of Prince Henry and his Circle 1603–1613' (University of Oxford, 1987).

Woodall, Joanna, 'The Portraiture of Antonis Mor' (Courtauld Institute, 1989).

Web Sources

Graves, R., 'Paget, William, Fifth Baron Paget (1572–1629), Politician', *Oxford Dictionary of National Biography* (2004), online edn, January 2008 at: http://www.oxforddnb.com/view/article/21122.

MacCaffrey, W.T., 'Cecil, William, First Baron Burghley (1520/21–1598)', *Oxford Dictionary of National Biography* (2004) at: http://www.oxforddnb.com/view/article/4983.

Index

Illustrations are referenced in **bold**.

Sir Henry Lee is referred to as 'Lee' throughout the index, except for his own main entry where he is entered as Lee, Henry, Sir.

For Product Safety Concerns and Information please contact our
EU representative GPSR@taylorandfrancis.com Taylor & Francis
Verlag GmbH, Kaufingerstraße 24, 80331 München, Germany